"From the time of Irenaeus to that of Jonathan Edwards, motor automatisms have long puzzled—and indeed scandalized—the church. Greene succeeds in situating these manifestations common to Pentecostal and Charismatic spirituality within the context of the prophetic tradition of Scripture. His tour de force survey of the Old and New Testaments will leave readers with the profound reminder that the Spirit blows where he wills."

—MATTHEW C. MCGUIRE
Author of *A Magical World: How the Bible Makes Sense of the Supernatural*

"Merrill G. Greene's *Drunk in the Spirit* is a bold and enlightening exploration of the supernatural love of God and discerning the truth from the counterfeit. His scholarly yet accessible approach challenges readers to reconsider what's possible through the Holy Spirit. As one of his friends, I've seen firsthand Merrill's passion for truth and his genuine heart for the church. This book is a must-read!"

—BRANDON SPAIN
Host, *Unrefined Podcast*

"Greene provides a detailed study of the many places in the Bible where God chooses to work through 'ecstatic' experiences. Scholars, pastors, and students alike will benefit from the thorough exegesis and diligent engagement with the historical context of Scripture throughout. Christians of all denominational backgrounds will find this to be a valuable resource for carefully considering the outworkings and purposes of the ministry of the Holy Spirit in both ancient and modern contexts."

—DAVID J. FULLER
Director of Library Services, Canadian Baptist Theological Seminary and College

"From the alliterative chapter titles to the meticulous footnotes, Dr. Greene provides an accessible yet thought-provoking treatment of 'altered states of consciousness' found throughout the Hebrew Bible and New Testament. He successfully brings attention to texts that are often glossed over, and he raises fresh questions which have practical and theological ramifications for laypeople and scholars alike. While I may not align with every conclusion, I appreciate the valuable insight and dialogue this book fosters."

—MICHAEL GABIZON
Associate Professor of Jewish Studies, Moody Bible Institute

"This book by Dr. Greene is a profound and helpful resource for anyone looking to know more about how altered states of consciousness fit into Christian beliefs. *Drunk in the Spirit* is a well-researched examination of the Biblical texts, some church history, and current phenomena within some current church circles. Even if you do not find yourself agreeing with all his conclusions, this is an essential read on the topic."

—ANDY ARDERN
Lead Pastor, Wayfarers' Church, Nova Scotia, Canada

Drunk in the Spirit

Drunk in the Spirit

What the Bible Says About Trance, Ecstasy, and God's Supernatural Love

Merrill G. Greene

Foreword by Dustin G. Burlet

WIPF & STOCK · Eugene, Oregon

DRUNK IN THE SPIRIT
What the Bible Says About Trance, Ecstasy, and God's Supernatural Love

Copyright © 2025 Merrill G. Greene. All rights reserved. Except for brief quotations in critical publications or reviews, no part of this book may be reproduced in any manner without prior written permission from the publisher. Write: Permissions, Wipf and Stock Publishers, 199 W. 8th Ave., Suite 3, Eugene, OR 97401.

Wipf & Stock
An Imprint of Wipf and Stock Publishers
199 W. 8th Ave., Suite 3
Eugene, OR 97401

www.wipfandstock.com

PAPERBACK ISBN: 979-8-3852-4383-9
HARDCOVER ISBN: 979-8-3852-4384-6
EBOOK ISBN: 979-8-3852-4385-3

VERSION NUMBER 082525

For Benjamin

πλησμονὴ σοφίας φοβεῖσθαι τὸν κύριον
καὶ μεθύσκει αὐτοὺς ἀπὸ τῶν καρπῶν αὐτῆς

To fear the Lord is the fullness of wisdom,
and she makes them drunk from her fruit.

—Sirach 1:16 (NRSV)

Contents

Permissions | xi
Foreword by Dustin G. Burlet | xiii
Preface | xvii
Acknowledgments | xxiii
Abbreviations | xxv
Introduction | xxxiii
    Setting the Stage | xxxiv
    Why This Book? | xl

1 Trance, Ecstasy, and Other Scary Words | 1
    Ecstasy | 3
    What Did Ecstasy Look Like? | 5
    Trance | 9
    Altered State of Consciousness | 11
    Automatism | 17
    Spirit Possession | 21
    The Septuagint | 27
    Conclusion | 28

2 Getting Tipsy with the Torah | 30
    Trance and Ecstasy in the Ancient Near East | 32
    Patriarchs of Trance | 35
    The Cup of Intoxication | 45
    Miriam and Music | 52
    High on God? | 56
    Ecstatic Elders | 60
    Balaam's Assessment | 65
    Conclusion | 67

3 Getting Plastered with the Prophets | 69
Deborah and Divination | 70
Is Hannah Hammered? | 76
Saul Among the Prophets | 80
Going Berserk | 85
Eccentric Ecstatics | 95

4 Getting Wasted with the Writings | 102
Chronicling Verbal Automatisms | 102
Music in Chronicles | 105
David's Automatisms? | 106
David the Ecstatic? | 110
Conclusion | 112

5 Gin and Gospels | 114
En Pneumati | 115
Temple Trances | 124
Birthing the Miraculous | 129
Fear and Falling | 131
Jesus's Journeys | 138
Conclusion | 150

6 Alcoholics in the Acts of the Apostles | 152
Morning Drinks | 153
Open Heavens | 160
Stoned in the Spirit | 163
Magicians and Manifestations | 164
Conclusion | 166

7 Pinot Noir with Paul | 167
Paul's Travels | 167
Crazy and/or Corinthian? | 172
Ephesian Ethanol | 179
Conclusion | 183

8 Counterfeit Cocktails | 184
Drugs and Magic | 185
Self-Mutilation | 186
Spirits | 187
Occultic Objects | 190
Other Means | 190
Scriptural Allegations | 191
Conclusion | 193

9 **Eliminating and Illuminating Ecstasy in the Church** | 198
　Examples of ASCs in Church History | 202
　Conclusion | 208

Conclusion: The Supernatural Love of God | 209
　These Manifestations Are "Too Weird" to Be Beneficial | 217

Bibliography | 219

Permissions

Unless otherwise marked, Scripture quotations are from the ESV® Bible (The Holy Bible, English Standard Version®), © 2001 by Crossway, a publishing ministry of Good News Publishers. Used by permission. All rights reserved.

Scripture quotations marked (CEB) have been taken from the Common English Bible. Copyright © 2011 Common English Bible. All rights reserved. Used by permission. (www.CommonEnglishBible.com).

Scripture quotations marked (CEV) are from the Contemporary English Version. Copyright © 1995 by American Bible Society. Used by permission.

Scripture quotations marked (CSB) have been taken from the Christian Standard Bible®, copyright © 2017 by Holman Bible Publishers. Used by permission.

Scripture quotations marked (DRA) are from the Douay-Rheims 1899 American Edition Bible and are in the public domain.

Scripture quotations marked (GNT) are from the Good News Translation in Today's English Version—Second Edition. Copyright © 1992 by American Bible Society. Used by permission.

Scripture quotations marked (KJV) are from the King James Version and are in the public domain.

Scripture quotations marked (NAB) are from the New American Bible © 1970 Confraternity of Christian Doctrine, Washington, DC, and are used by permission of the copyright owner. All rights reserved. No part of the New American Bible may be reproduced in any form without permission in writing from the copyright owner.

Scripture quotations marked (NASB) are taken from the (NASB®) New American Standard Bible®, copyright © 2020 by The Lockman Foundation. Used by permission. All rights reserved. lockman.org.

Scripture quotations marked (NET) are from the NET Bible® copyright © 2019 by Biblical Studies Press, LLC https://netbible.com. All rights reserved.

Scripture quotations marked (NIV) are taken from the Holy Bible, New International Version®, NIV®. Copyright © 2011 by Biblica, Inc.™ Used by permission of Zondervan. All rights reserved worldwide. www.zondervan.com.

Scripture quotations marked (NLT) are taken from the Holy Bible, New Living Translation, copyright © 2015 by Tyndale House Foundation. Used by permission of Tyndale House Publishers, Carol Stream, Illinois, 60188. All rights reserved.

Scripture quotations marked (NRSV) are from New Revised Standard Version Bible, copyright © 1989 by the National Council of the Churches of Christ in the United States of America. Used by permission. All rights reserved worldwide.

Scripture quotations marked (RSV) are from the Revised Standard Version of the Bible, copyright © 1971 by the National Council of the Churches of Christ in the United States of America. Used by permission. All rights reserved worldwide.

Scripture quotations marked (WEB) are from the World English Bible and are in the public domain.

Scripture from Brenton's English Septuagint is in the public domain.

Scripture quotations marked (LES) are from the Lexham English Septuagint. Copyright 2012 Logos Bible Software.

Scripture quotations marked (NETS) are from A New English Translation of the Septuagint, © 2007 by the International Organization for Septuagint and Cognate Studies, Inc. Used by permission of Oxford University Press. All rights reserved.

Scripture quotations marked (NJPS) are taken from the NJPS (Tanakh). Copyright 1985 by the Jewish Publication Society. First edition. All rights reserved.

The Orthodox Jewish Bible copyright @ 2023 by AFI International. All rights reserved.

Foreword

ANYONE COMMITTED TO HELPING others grow in conformity to the image of Christ (Col 1:28-29; 1 John 5:1-4) must wrestle with what it means to cultivate and nurture an increased familiarity with Jesus's Holy Spirit (John 14:16, 26; 15:26; 16:7, 13-15; cf. Gal 4:6-7; 5:22; 1 John 2:1).

While the truth of the gospel message is resoundingly clear (see John 3), the Bible is a complex, multifaceted book. As such, different Christian denominations, institutions, and individuals will often interpret its teachings in various ways—even, sometimes, within the same organization.

For example, Christians usually have different theological perspectives on the Holy Spirit. While some may emphasize specific manifestations of the Spirit, such as speaking in tongues and/or the gift of prophecy, for example, other Christians may downplay these experiences (1 Cor 12-14).

Navigating these theological differences can often be challenging, particularly when seeking validation for personal encounters with the Spirit. Many people, as such, continually experience confusion about the authenticity of somewhat "odd" spiritual experience(s) such as revelations, dreams, visions, and the like that may seem to contradict or perhaps even challenge certain biblical teachings and doctrines that trusted members of their faith community taught them.

Discerning whether these experiences are genuinely from the Lord's Holy Spirit or a product of oneself can be a delicate process often fraught with turmoil and uncertainty (cf. 1 Cor 14:33).

The Bible warns believers to "test the spirits" (1 John 4:1; cf. 1 Cor 14:27-33) and to discern whether they are from God. This requires mature, careful, spiritual reflection and discernment alongside a deep, intimate, familiar knowledge of Scripture in all its facets. It is not always easy to distinguish between genuine spiritual experiences and deceptive or misleading influences.

Speaking plainly, there is a legitimate and genuine apprehension among many followers of Christ of being led astray by false spirits and teachings. This can often result in an acute reluctance or extreme hesitation to embrace otherwise good, healthy, beneficial experiences with the Holy Spirit.

This fear can be a significant barrier to fully exploring and understanding spiritual encounters.

Sharing "unusual" spiritual experiences (and, of course, many other matters) in a church/religious community is usually (but not always!) met with varying degrees of acceptance or skepticism.

Fear of rejection or judgment from one's faith community can also often hinder open and honest discussions about many personal experiences thereby inhibiting and stunting growth in God.

Navigating these challenges requires a balance between personal faith and scriptural grounding.

Seeking guidance from trusted spiritual mentors, engaging in thoughtful theological reflection, and maintaining humility in the face of personal experiences (see 2 Cor 12) are crucial steps in addressing these things while remaining grounded in one's faith and understanding of the Bible.

Enter *Drunk in the Spirit: What the Bible Says About Trance, Ecstasy, and God's Supernatural Love*.

Merrill Gary Greene brings impressive scholastic rigor and unique pedagogical sensitivity to a complex set of topics. The meticulous (but not overdone) research and profound insights have resulted in a book that is not only intellectually stimulating but also spiritually enlightening.

One of the standout qualities of Greene's book is his ability to bridge the gap between the lay person in the pew and the professor in their study without compromise. Greene deftly navigates the oft misunderstood terrain of biblical prophecy, visions, and ecstasies, providing readers with a comprehensive understanding that is accessible (and informative!) to both scholars and lay people alike. Whether you are a seasoned theologian or someone with a casual interest in the Bible, you will find this book to be a valuable resource (so long, of course, as you keep reading!)

In conclusion, I wholeheartedly endorse Merrill G. Greene's *Drunk in the Spirit: What the Bible Says About Trance, Ecstasy, and God's Supernatural Love* as a groundbreaking, transformative work that will enrich the lives of its readers, providing them with a deeper understanding of Scripture, God's Holy Spirit, and general phenomena involved with respect to the supernatural.

Drunk in the Spirit is a testament to Greene's expertise, passion, and commitment to advancing the church's understanding of the experiences recorded in Scripture and contemporary society.

This book will surely leave a lasting impact on both the scholarly and spiritual communities.

Soli Deo gloria.

Dustin G. Burlet, PhD (McMaster Divinity College)
Millar College of the Bible, Winnipeg, MB, Canada

Preface

The one who states his case first seems right, until the other comes and examines him.

—Proverbs 18:17

I HAVE ALWAYS BEEN interested in theology. When I was young, I enjoyed listening to my father and cousin discuss their faith and theology at the kitchen table, even if I understood little of what they were saying. I have also always been interested in the bizarre. As a teenager, I became intrigued by the supernatural. My avenues to explore such things were admittedly limited. The church I grew up in was, for all intents and purposes, functionally cessationist.[1] I had no exposure to any form of the Pentecostal-charismatic movement other than what people told me in passing and strange clips I found on the internet criticizing the movement. Thus, my introduction to the supernatural, besides my upbringing with the stories of Scripture, was

---

1. Christians can be divided into three main categories in terms of their beliefs about the supernatural work of God in present times. The first group are known as cessationists. Cessationists are those Christians who believe that some of the gifts of the Holy Spirit (usually prophecy, the gift(s) of healing, and speaking in tongues) ceased sometime in the apostolic age or early church period when the Bible was completed or the apostles died. Most cessationists believe that God does still do miracles today, but that specific miracles were only used to authenticate the message of the apostles or first Christians. Thus, when the Bible was completed or when the apostles died, the need for such authenticating signs was eliminated. The second group of Christians are called continuationists. Continuationists believe the opposite of cessationists—that all of the gifts of the Holy Spirit are still for today. Continuationists may or may not pursue such spiritual gifts, but they do not deny their existence. The third group of Christians are called charismatics. Charismatics can be differentiated from continuationists insofar as a charismatic is a practitioner of those spiritual gifts that cessationists view as having ceased in earlier times. Thus, all charismatics are continuationists, but not all continuationists are charismatics.

confined to media representations on TV, movies, and obscure internet forums. I spent countless hours watching the Harry Potter franchise (my favorite character was Luna Lovegood) and was drawn toward horror movies, especially those dealing with possession, haunted houses, and other spiritual phenomena. Such an oversaturation of Hollywood material surely distorted my perception of the spiritual realm, demons, and the Holy Spirit (though at such a young age, it was hard to realize). I rarely saw positive religious experiences portrayed in media. I had never seen anyone speak in tongues, be healed, or anything overtly charismatic. As a result, anything that looked odd to me was automatically sifted into the category of the demonic.

After high school, I spent two years at a conservative Bible school in Atlantic Canada. This was a period in my life when asking questions and exploring theological alternatives was frowned upon. Indeed, I vividly recall being yelled at for asking otherwise benign questions to the teachers and given poor marks for daring to use sources outside of those prescribed by the school. Naturally, I internalized much of this and came to think I was the problem. Thus, I was prone to adopt the theological proclivities of the faculty. Upon leaving the Bible school, I was an ardent cessationist, general antisupernaturalist, and a theological buzzkill. Little tolerance was given for apparent foolishness or what I thought of as "Pentecostal nonsense" in my life. I had been taught that the so-called sign gifts of the Spirit had ceased and that anyone who spoke in tongues probably had a demon or was faking. In fact, I actively tried to debunk people's stories of miraculous healing, despite any evidence given to me to the contrary. I elevated empty intellectualism to a point of ultimate virtue and anybody that did not share my presuppositions about the Bible were not to be entertained. Suffice it to say, I was a lost cause when it came to having a civil conversation during this time.

In 2011, I transferred to Crandall University in Moncton, New Brunswick, where I now teach from time to time as an adjunct professor. Once there, I experienced a renaissance of theological introspection and maturity. I was invited by my friend Joel to attend a young adults group with the pastor of a local charismatic church. Joel and I had not seen eye to eye on much up to this point, but I was interested in at least hearing a different perspective. Suddenly I found myself regularly attending a charismatic church where people claimed to be speaking in tongues, seeing angels, experiencing visions, falling on the ground, and (most strange to me at the time) pretending to be drinking from large barrels of invisible beer! A shift had begun to take place in my life where the pride I had in thinking I had everything figured out was slowly stripped away. God was truly using what I considered foolish to shame me (1 Cor 1:27). That year, I came to the realization that my faith in Jesus had not been genuine, but merely an intellectual exercise, and I eventually gave my life to the Lord. In point of fact, it was the man drinking the imperceptible keg of alcohol that led me to faith when God spoke to him about various abuses I had suffered in my spiritual life that no one had known about. God certainly has a sense of humor. After this initial conversion experience, I soon saw God move in ways I never thought possible.

The blessing of that charismatic congregation was also paralleled by a blessing of my biblical studies professors at the university. Dr. Stephen Dempster and Dr. Keith Bodner taught me Old Testament and were exceptionally kind and gentle in helping me process through the fundamentalism I had grown accustomed to. They cherishingly provided me with books and other resources to feed my insatiable appetite for the academic study of Scripture. Their nonjudgmental guidance made a world of difference. During my time at that charismatic church, I also discovered that one of the other biblical studies professors was attending there. Dr. Barry D. Smith taught New Testament and philosophy and he eventually became my thesis supervisor (for those interested, my topic was death and the afterlife in the Jewish text First Enoch). The idea of someone having a PhD from a reputable university attending these services caught my immediate interest. I assumed he was simply doing some kind of anthropological study by observing the weekly services. To be honest, part of me was a little embarrassed to be seen at the church as I thought he might think I was a little off kilter.

I later found out that Barry was a charismatic Christian who, among other things, regularly spoke in tongues and had been involved in an exorcism of a student with another professor at that church. Barry's presence at the church confirmed my sneaking suspicion that intellectualism and discernment were not the same thing. Having all the right book learning did not give me the special ability to know what was truly from the Spirit, nor did it allow me to be objective when reading the Scriptures. Instead, it forced me to turn down certain interpretations of the biblical text because they made me uncomfortable and gave me a lack of control. This led me to a slight existential crisis. Had I wasted my life up to that point? Had I been wrong about my approach to the Bible and my perception of God's character? I was happy to accept many of the things I was witnessing in the charismatic movement based on the fruit alone, but I still wanted to "chapter and verse" everything. Additionally, I wanted to know more about the historical and cultural context of the Scriptures to have a biblical defense of some manifestations and practices that outsiders viewed with disdain or skepticism.

After completing my bachelor's degree at Crandall, I went on to do a master's degree and eventually a doctorate in Second Temple Judaism with

McMaster University's religious studies department in Hamilton, Ontario. Because I was not at a seminary, there was less pressure to dogmatically accept every point of doctrine without question. While many of the faculty and students in my classes were themselves Christians, many were not, and it was refreshing to ask "why?" without immediate dismissal or chastisement. I am still theologically conservative and have a high view of Scripture to this day, but I realized that, as others have aptly pointed out, the Bible was written *for* us but not *to* us.[2] Thus, my Western eyes were quick to conform Scripture to my presuppositions about how the world and God operated. Obviously, not everyone needs to go to university for a decade to discover this, even if I did.

While studying and developing research skills was exciting, I found my spiritual walk with God becoming stagnant. This happens more often than is probably acceptable in academic contexts and part of my departure from seeking the things of the Spirit likely had to do with developing a subconscious desire to seem respectable to my colleagues. In 2019, I moved back to Atlantic Canada and was finishing my doctoral studies long distance. My friend Joel, in good providential fashion, invited me to a small gathering of charismatic believers at a campground in Nova Scotia. I happily accepted. I remember, however, a lot of pride welling up in me while attending. Although I was being edified by the speakers, I had feelings of superiority because of what I considered anti-intellectualism on the part of those in attendance. The judgmentalism was tangible. In an evening service, one speaker said that God's presence had suddenly entered the room in a specific location and that there was a heaviness in the atmosphere. *What am I doing here?* I asked myself. *Are these people delusional?* Again, God has a sense of humor. I stood up and went to the front of the room where God's supposed presence was. After being prayed over, I found myself on the floor in what I can only describe as an ecstasy. I was on the floor for what I estimate to be half an hour (and I was awkwardly laying in the middle of where a talent show was about to take place!). During that ecstatic experience, God convicted me of my arrogance and I found myself in the deep throngs of repentance. Ironically, my first thought when I hit the floor was, *If anybody from the university were to see me right now, they would take away my degree.* I was no longer thinking that!

After that experience, I realized I wanted to use my skills and talents to benefit the church. I was made aware that many in the body of Christ were quick to dismiss moves of God based on their presuppositions of how God

---

2. A phrase most attributed to the biblical scholar John H. Walton and often quoted by the late Michael S. Heiser.

should act. Many were simply listening to the same three discernment ministries and concluding their study on a given topic there. There is nothing wrong per se with looking to others for discernment on difficult subjects, of course. It became clear, however, that many were resting in the opinions of humans in echo chambers that did not expand their ability to interpret Scripture themselves. Indeed, many times, such discernment ministries gave a critical spirit to those who drank in their words all too willingly.

When I looked at the landscape of the Pentecostal-charismatic movement, I saw many who were giving articulate and reasonable defenses of various practices and supernatural phenomena. Academics like Craig Keener, Michael Brown, and Sam Storms, as well as podcasts like *The Remnant Radio*, were a breath of fresh air and seemed to care deeply for integrity within the movement and regularly demonstrated what discernment should look like. While some certainly had the scholarly credentials to bolster their claims, other channels were less than helpful. While many important topics were and are being covered by qualified Pentecostal-charismatic podcasts and programs, there are many topics that either slip through the cracks or simply do not receive adequate coverage so as to convince the critic or skeptic.

Thus, this book is the product of a labor of love to talk about a topic that many in conservative protestant circles are quick to ridicule and which has not received satisfactory investigation by the Pentecostal-charismatic community. Even if you do not reach the same conclusions I have, I pray that this exercise of setting the Scriptures within their appropriate context will be fruitful and edifying. I make no apologies about being a charismatic myself. I have experienced trances, ecstasies, visions, and other supernatural events. I do not want to pretend that I do not have a bias in writing. Throughout this book, however, I do not talk about personal experiences as a means of interpreting Scripture. Rather, I discuss stories from the past and today in order to highlight Scripture's impact on those who experience these things. Above all else, I want Jesus to be glorified in this exploration. I have attempted to write in a neutral academic way, evaluating the materials based on their own merits and the findings of modern biblical scholarship. I am under no delusion that whatever my findings, there will be people on either side of the theological spectrum who disagree with my conclusions. Yet, joy and wisdom seldom come from choosing the easy path.

Merrill G. Greene

Acknowledgments

GOOD FRIENDS ARE HARD to come by, yet I have had the pleasure of not only having some, but many from various fields of research and at various levels of academic training who have made this book much more readable as a result. Giving them a simple "thank you" seems a poor repayment for their kindness and intellectual engagement with this topic, but I still wish to honor them here. Thanks to Dustin Burlet who was a perpetual encouragement during the writing process and who always was willing to hold me to a higher standard. Thanks to Mark Hanson who read through the manuscript and offered a number of insightful changes to the writing style. A huge thanks to Matthew McGuire who, among other things, sifted through and (lovingly) pointed out any egregious errors and/or typos so that I would not look as foolish as I often am. Thanks to Mari who went through the painstaking process of editing the bibliography and footnotes of the first draft of this book when my brain was completely at capacity (an effort which the aforementioned Dr. Hanson also partook in). Thanks to Ben Bedecki and Darren Howse for their interest in the bizarre which often left me asking more questions than I could find answers for. Thanks to my colleagues Marc Jolicoeur and Jake Hron who read through various parts of the book and gave pushback and insights that, as a result, made the arguments in this book much stronger. Thanks to Christopher McCready who helped me not lose my mind when dealing with technology. Thanks to Cody Guitard for sharing personal testimonies that helped inform some aspects of this book. Finally, a special thanks to my mother and father who, among the many things that parents typically do, inspire me to think about the reason I am writing, which is to equip the church and to show generosity and compassion wherever possible.

Abbreviations

AASF	Annales Academiae Scientiarum Fennicae
ABRL	Anchor Bible Reference Library
AGJU	Arbeiten zur Geschichte des antiken Judentums und des Urchristentums
ANE	Ancient Near Eastern
ANET	*Ancient Near Eastern Texts Relating to the Old Testament*. Edited by James B. Pritchard. 3rd ed. Princeton: Princeton University Press, 1969
ANF	*Ante-Nicene Fathers*
ApOTC	Apollos Old Testament Commentary
ASC	Altered state of consciousness
ASOR	American Schools of Oriental Research
AYBC	Anchor Yale Bible Commentaries
AYBRL	Anchor Yale Bible Reference Library
BAR	*Biblical Archaeology Review*
BASOR	*Bulletin of the American Schools of Oriental Research*
BBR	*Bulletin for Biblical Research*
BCOTWP	Baker Commentary on the Old Testament Wisdom and Psalms
BDAG	Danker, Frederick W., Walter Bauer, William F. Arndt, and F. Wilbur Gingrich. *Greek-English Lexicon of the New Testament and Other Early Christian Literature*. 3rd ed. Chicago: University of Chicago Press, 2000
BDB	Brown, Francis, S. R. Driver, and Charles A. Briggs. *A Hebrew and English Lexicon of the Old Testament*

BECNT	Baker Exegetical Commentary on the New Testament
Bib	*Biblica*
BibInt	*Biblical Interpretation*
BibSem	The Biblical Seminar
BRev	*Bible Review*
BSac	*Bibliotheca Sacra*
BTB	*Biblical Theology Bulletin*
BZAW	Beihefte zur Zeitschrift für die alttestamentliche Wissenschaft
CahRB	Cahiers de la Revue biblique
CBC	Cambridge Bible Commentary
CBQ	*Catholic Biblical Quarterly*
CHANE	Culture and History of the Ancient Near East
COS	*The Context of Scripture*. Edited by William W. Hallo and K. Lawson Younger. 4 vols. Leiden: Brill, 1997–2016
DCH	*Dictionary of Classical Hebrew*. Edited by David J. A. Clines. 9 vols. Sheffield: Sheffield Phoenix Press, 1993–2014
DDD	*Dictionary of Deities and Demons in the Bible*. Edited by Karel van der Toorn, Bob Becking, and Pieter W. van der Horst. 2nd rev. ed. Grand Rapids: Eerdmans, 1999
DSD	*Dead Sea Discoveries*
Dtn	Deuteronomic (History; writer)
Dtr	Deuteronomistic (History; writer); Deuteronomist
EBR	*Encyclopedia of the Bible and Its Reception*. Edited by Constance M. Furey et al. Berlin: De Gruyter, 2009–
EC	*Encyclopedia of Christianity*. Edited by Erwin Fahlbusch and Geoffrey William Bromiley. Grand Rapids: Eerdmans, 1999–2003
ECL	Early Christianity and Its Literature
EDNT	*Exegetical Dictionary of the New Testament*. Edited by Horst Balz and Gerhard Schneider. ET. 3 vols. Grand Rapids: Eerdmans, 1990–1993
ER	*Encyclopedia of Religion*. Edited by Lindsay Jones. 2nd ed. 15 vols. Detroit: Macmillan Reference USA, 2005

ExpTim	*Expository Times*
FC	Fathers of the Church
FRLANT	Forschungen zur Religion und Literatur des Alten und Neuen Testaments
GELS	*A Greek-English Lexicon of the Septuagint*. Takamitsu Muraoka. Leuven: Peeters, 2009
GKC	*Gesenius' Hebrew Grammar*. Edited by Emil Kautzsch. Translated by Arthur E. Cowley. 2nd ed. Oxford: Clarendon, 1910
HALOT	*The Hebrew and Aramaic Lexicon of the Old Testament*. Ludwig Koehler, Walter Baumgartner, and Johann J. Stamm. Translated and edited under the supervision of Mervyn E. J. Richardson. 4 vols. Leiden: Brill, 1994–1999
HCOT	Historical Commentary on the Old Testament
HTR	*Harvard Theological Review*
HTS	Harvard Theological Studies
HUCA	*Hebrew Union College Annual*
ICC	International Critical Commentary
ISBE	*International Standard Bible Encyclopedia*. Edited by Geoffrey W. Bromiley. 4 vols. Grand Rapids: Eerdmans, 1979–1988
JBL	*Journal of Biblical Literature*
JBQ	*Jewish Bible Quarterly*
JSOTSup	Journal for the Study of the Old Testament Supplement Series
JSNT	*Journal for the Study of the New Testament*
JSNTSup	Journal for the Study of the New Testament Supplement Series
JSJ	*Journal for the Study of Judaism in the Persian, Hellenistic, and Roman Periods*
JTS	*Journal of Theological Studies*
K&D	Keil, Carl Friedrich, and Franz Delitzsch. Biblical Commentary on the Old Testament. Translated by James Martin et al. 25 vols. Edinburgh, 1857–1878. Repr., 10 vols., Peabody, MA: Hendrickson, 1996
KAT	Kommentar zum Alten Testament

KEK	Kritisch-exegetischer Kommentar über das Neue Testament (Meyer-Kommentar)
KTU	*Die keilalphabetischen Texte aus Ugarit*. Edited by Manfried Dietrich, Oswald Loretz, and Joaquín Sanmartín. Münster: Ugarit-Verlag, 2013
L&N	Louw, Johannes P., and Eugene A. Nida, eds. *Greek-English Lexicon of the New Testament: Based on Semantic Domains*. 2nd ed. New York: United Bible Societies, 1989
LCL	Loeb Classical Library
LEH	Lust, Johan, Erik Eynikel, and Katrin Hauspie, eds. *Greek-English Lexicon of the Septuagint*. Rev. ed. Stuttgart: Deutsche Bibelgesellschaft, 2003
LHBOTS	The Library of Hebrew Bible/Old Testament Studies
LNTS	The Library of New Testament Studies
LSJ	Liddell, Henry George, Robert Scott, Henry Stuart Jones. *A Greek-English Lexicon*. 9th ed. with revised supplement. Oxford: Clarendon, 1996
LXX	Septuagint (the Greek OT)
MRS	Mission de Ras Shamra
MT	Masoretic Text (of the Hebrew Bible)
NAC	New American Commentary
NCB	New Century Bible
Neot	*Neotestamentica*
NICNT	New International Commentary on the New Testament
NICOT	New International Commentary on the Old Testament
NIDNTTE	*New International Dictionary of New Testament Theology and Exegesis*. Edited by Moisés Silva. Grand Rapids: Zondervan, 2014
NIDOTTE	*New International Dictionary of Old Testament Theology and Exegesis*. Edited by Willem A. VanGemeren. 5 vols. Grand Rapids: Zondervan, 1997
NIGTC	New International Greek Testament Commentary
NovTSup	Supplements to Novum Testamentum
NPNF[1]	*Nicene and Post-Nicene Fathers*, Series 1

NTL	New Testament Library	
NTS	*New Testament Studies*	
ODCC	*The Oxford Dictionary of the Christian Church*. Edited by F. L. Cross and E. A. Livingstone. 3rd ed. rev. Oxford: Oxford University Press, 2005	
OECS	Oxford Early Christian Studies	
OTL	Old Testament Library	
OtSt	Oudtestamentische Studiën	
PEQ	*Palestine Exploration Quarterly*	
PDM	*Papyri Demoticae Magicae*. Demotic texts in PGM corpus as collated in Hans Dieter Betz, ed. *The Greek Magical Papyri in Translation, including the Demotic Spells*. Chicago: University of Chicago Press, 1996	
PGM	*Papyri Graecae Magicae: Die griechischen Zauberpapyri*. Edited by Karl Preisendanz. 2nd ed. Stuttgart: Teubner, 1973–1974	
R&T	*Religion and Theology*	
RAC	*Reallexikon für Antike und Christentum*. Edited by Theodor Klauser et al. Stuttgart: Hiersemann, 1950–	
SBLDS	Society of Biblical Literature Dissertation Series	
SHBC	Smyth & Helwys Bible Commentary	
SNTSMS	Society for New Testament Studies Monograph Series	
StPatr	Studia Patristica	
TA	*Tel Aviv*	
TDNT	*Theological Dictionary of the New Testament*. Edited by Gerhard Kittel and Gerhard Friedrich. Translated by Geoffrey W. Bromiley. 10 vols. Grand Rapids: Eerdmans, 1964–1976	
TENTS	Texts and Editions for New Testament Study	
THKNT	Theologischer Handkommentar zum Neuen Testament	
TJ	*Trinity Journal*	
TOTC	Tyndale Old Testament Commentaries	
TS	*Theological Studies*	

TWOT	*Theological Wordbook of the Old Testament*. Edited by R. Laird Harris, Gleason L. Archer Jr., and Bruce K. Waltke. 2 vols. Chicago: Moody, 1980
TZ	*Theologische Zeitschrift*
UBS	United Bible Society
UNT	Untersuchungen zum Neuen Testament
VT	*Vetus Testamentum*
VTSup	Supplements to Vetus Testamentum
WBC	Word Biblical Commentary
WC	Westminster Commentaries
WO	*Die Welt des Orients*
WUNT	Wissenschaftliche Untersuchungen zum Neuen Testament
ZAW	*Zeitschrift für die alttestamentliche Wissenschaft*

Abbreviations and Note for Primary Sources

Unless otherwise noted, translations of apocryphal/deuterocanonical works are taken from the New Revised Standard Version. Translations of the pseudepigrapha are taken from James H. Charlesworth, ed., Old Testament Pseudepigrapha, 2 vols. (New York: Doubleday, 1983, 1985). Translations of the Dead Sea Scrolls are taken from Florentino García Martínez and Eibert J. C. Tigchelaar, eds., *The Dead Sea Scrolls Study Edition*, 2 vols. (Leiden: Brill, 1997–1998). Translations of Philo are taken from C. D. Yonge, trans., *The Works of Philo: Complete and Unabridged* (Peabody, MA: Hendrickson, 1995). Translations of Josephus are taken from William Whiston, trans., *The Works of Josephus: Complete and Unabridged* (Peabody, MA: Hendrickson, 1987). Translations of rabbinic texts come from Jacob Neusner, trans., *The Mishnah: A New Translation* (New Haven: Yale University Press, 1988); Jacob Neusner, trans., *The Tosefta: Translated from the Hebrew with a New Introduction*, 2 vols. (Peabody, MA: Hendrickson, 2002); Jacob Neusner, trans., *The Babylonian Talmud: A Translation and Commentary* (Peabody, MA: Hendrickson, 2011); and Sefaria (sefaria.org). Translations of the apostolic fathers and other early Christian works come from J. B. Lightfoot and J. R. Harmer, *The Apostolic Fathers* (London: Macmillan, 1891); Alexander Roberts and James Donaldson, eds., *ANF*, 10 vols. (1885–1896. Repr., Peabody, MA: Hendrickson, 1994); and Philip Schaff and Henry Wace, eds.,

*NPNF*¹, 14 vols. (1886–1889. Repr., Peabody, MA: Hendrickson, 1994). Translations of classical works are taken from the Perseus Digital Library (perseus.tufts.edu/hopper/).

Apocrypha

2 Esd	2 Esdras
1 Macc	1 Maccabees
2 Macc	2 Maccabees
3 Macc	3 Maccabees
4 Macc	4 Maccabees
Sir	Sirach
Sus	Susanna
Tob	Tobit
Wis	Wisdom of Solomon

Apostolic Fathers

1 Clem.	1 Clement
Barn.	Barnabas
Did.	Didache
Herm. Mand.	Shepherd of Hermas, Mandate(s)
Herm. Vis.	Shepherd of Hermas, Vision(s)
Ign. *Eph.*	Ignatius, *To the Ephesians*
Mart. Pol.	Martyrdom of Polycarp

Apuleius

Apol.	*Apology*

Aristides

Or.	*Oratio*

Aristotle

Parv. Nat.	*Parva Naturalia*

Athanasius

C. Gent.	*Against the Pagans*

Athenaeus
Deipn.   *Deipnosophistae*

Athenagoras
Leg.   *Legatio pro Christianis*

Augustine
Civ.   *The City of God*
Enarrat. Ps.   *Enarrations on the Psalms*
Serm.   *Sermones*
Tract. Ev. Jo.   *Tractates on the Gospel of John*

Clement of Alexandria
Strom.   *Stromateis*

Cornutus Philosophus
Nat. d.   *De natura deorum*

Cyprian of Carthage
Epist.   *Epistulae*

Dead Sea Scrolls
1QH^a Hodayot^a or Thanksgiving Hymns^a
1QpHab   Pesher Habakkuk
1QS   Serek Hayahad or Rule of the Community
4Q51   Sam^a
4Q166   Pesher Hosea^a
4Q242   Prayer of Nabonidus
4Q292   Work Containing Prayers B
4Q381   Non-Canonical Psalms B
4Q410   Vision and Interpretation
4Q416   Instruction^b
4Q425   Sapiential-Didactic Work B
4Q427   4QH^a
4Q546   Visions of Amram^d ar

4Q458	Narrative A
11Q5	11QPsalms[a]
CD	Cairo Genizah copy of the Damascus Document

Didymus

In Gen.   *On Genesis*

Epiphanius

Pan.   *Refutation of All Heresies*

Euripides

Bacch.   *Bacchae*

Gregory of Nyssa

C. Eun.   *Against Eunomius*

Herodotus

Hist.   *Histories*

Hippocrates

Morb. sacr.   *The Sacred Disease*

Hippolytus

Haer.   *Refutation of All Heresies*

Iamblichus

De Mysteriis   *On the Mysteries of Egypt*

Jerome

Epist.   *Epistulae*
Hom. Matth.   *Homilia in Evangelium secundum Matthaeum*

John Chrysostom

Anna   *De Anna*
Hom. Act.   *Homiliae in Acta apostolorum*
Hom. Gen.   *Homiliae in Genesim*
Hom. Matt. 26:39   *In illud: Pater, si possibile est, transeat*

Josephus

Ag. Ap.	*Against Apion*
Ant.	*Jewish Antiquities*
J.W.	*Jewish War*

Justin Martyr

1 Apol.	*First Apology*
Dial.	*Dialogue with Trypho*

Lucian of Samosata

Alex.	*Alexander the False Prophet*
Bacch.	*Bacchus*
Men.	*Menippus, or Descent into Hades*
Nigr.	*Nigrinus*

Methodius of Olympus

Symp.	*Symposium*

New Testament Apocrypha and Pseudepigrapha

Acts Pil.	Acts of Pilate
Acts Thom.	Acts of Thomas
Prot. Jas.	Protevangelium of James
Ps.-Clem.	Pseudo-Clementines
Ps.-Mt.	Gospel of Pseudo-Matthew

Origen

Cels.	*Against Celsus*
Princ.	*First Principles*

Other

Corp. herm.	*Corpus hermeticum*

Philo

Abraham	*On the Life of Abraham*
Alleg. Interp.	*Allegorical Interpretation*
Contempl. Life	*On the Contemplative Life*

Dreams	On Dreams
Drunkenness	On Drunkenness
Heir	Who Is the Heir?
Her.	Quis rerum divinarum heres sit
Moses	On the Life of Moses
Spec. Laws	On the Special Laws
Worse	That the Worse Attacks the Better

Philostratus

Vit. soph.	Vitae sophistarum

Plato

Leg.	Laws
Phaedr.	Phaedrus
Resp.	Republic
Tim.	Timaeus

Pliny the Elder

Nat.	Natural History

Plutarch

Amat.	Amatorius
Def. orac.	De defectu oraculorum
Luc.	Lucullus
Mor.	Moralia
Quaest. rom.	Quaestiones romanae et graecae
Sept. sap. conv.	Septem sapientium convivium

Pollux

Onom.	Onomasticon

Porphyry

Aneb.	Epistula ad Anebonem

Pseudepigrapha

2 Bar.	2 Baruch

3 Bar.	3 Baruch
1 En.	1 Enoch
2 En.	2 Enoch
Apoc. Ab.	Apocalypse of Abraham
As. Mos.	Assumption of Moses
Hist. Rech.	History of the Rechabites
Jos. Asen.	Joseph and Aseneth
Jub.	Jubilees
LAB	Liber antiquitatum biblicarum
LAE	Life of Adam and Eve
Liv. Pro.	Lives of the Prophets
Mart. Ascen. Isa.	Martyrdom and Ascension of Isaiah
Pss. Sol.	Psalms of Solomon
Sib. Or.	Sibylline Oracles
T. Ab.	Testament of Abraham
T. Ash.	Testament of Asher
T. Benj.	Testament of Benjamin
T. Dan	Testament of Dan
T. Job	Testament of Job
T. Jos.	Testament of Joseph
T. Jud.	Testament of Judah
T. Levi	Testament of Levi
T. Naph.	Testament of Naphtali
T. Reu.	Testament of Reuben
T. Sim.	Testament of Simeon
T. Sol.	Testament of Solomon

Rabbinic Texts

ʾAbot R. Nat.	ʾAbot de Rabbi Nathan
b.	Babylonian Talmud
Ber.	Berakot

Gen. Rab.	Genesis Rabbah
Lev. Rab.	Leviticus Rabbah
m.	Mishnah
Mek.	Mekilta
Meg.	Megillah
Midr.	Midrash
Midr. Ps.	Midrash on the Psalms
Naz.	Nazir
Pesah.	Pesachim
Pirqe R. El.	Pirqe Rabbi Eliezer
Qoh. Rab.	Qoheleth Rabbah
Sanh.	Sanhedrin
Shir Rab.	Shir Hashirim Rabbah
t.	Tosefta

Rufinus

Clem. Recogn.   *Recognitions of Clement*

Seneca (the Younger)

Dial.   *Dialogi*

Strabo

Geogr.   *Geography*

Tertullian

1 Apol.   *First Apology*
An.   *The Soul*
Marc.   *Against Marcion*
Mart.   *To the Martyrs*

Xenophon

Hell.   *Hellenica*
Mem.   *Memorabilia*
Symp.   *Symposium*

Introduction

Eat, friends, drink, and be drunk with love!
—Song of Solomon 5:1

THIS IS A BOOK about altered states of consciousness (ASCs) in the Bible. We will get into the nitty-gritty specifics of what an ASC is in the following chapter but generally, as the phrase implies, an ASC is a temporary psychological change from one's everyday waking experience to something else. Sleep, for example, can generically be classified as an ASC, but so can hypnosis, intoxication, daydreaming, and many other common states people experience every day. You yourself have likely experienced multiple ASCs today. Yet, these more common ASCs are not the primary focus of this book. Instead, our investigation is aimed at trances, ecstasies, and related concepts in the Bible.

This is also a book concerning how to think about contemporary Christian experiences. When someone in a Christian gathering suddenly falls to the ground, shakes, acts drunk, spontaneously begins singing or offering praise to God, frantically runs around the sanctuary or conference center, or otherwise behaves (from our perspective) utterly weird, what are we to make of it? Can the Bible provide us with the information we need to sift through these odd, but universal, experiences? I believe the answer is a resounding yes! Despite the temptation by some to swiftly categorize those involved in such Christian circles as ignorant of the Bible or silly for engaging in such bizarre behaviors, one must recognize that this is (often) an emotional response, not (always) an exegetical one.

Exegesis is the process of interpreting the Bible based on various factors such as historical and cultural context, linguistics, genre, and other important considerations. It can be easy to dismiss an idea when it's your first time hearing it and haven't investigated it yourself. But study is key. We cannot rely on external observations to form our opinions about what Christians should or should not be doing, nor can we just blindly accept a broad consensus—evidently, many Christians have historically had deeply rooted misguided beliefs on a number of topics. This book, therefore, is meant to be exegetical in nature. It is a study of relevant material from the Bible having to do with ASCs.

Contrary to what one might expect, ASCs can be found throughout the biblical text, and there are more than a few people in the Hebrew Bible and New Testament that act in ways we might consider unhinged. Some of these accounts are obvious upon a surface reading of the text. When Saul "prophesied before Samuel and lay naked all that day and all that night" (1 Sam 19:24) it makes sense to view him as an ecstatic, lost in an ASC imposed by God. Yet, other passages are not so clear and require teasing out some of these features through careful analysis. You are thus invited on a journey to explore some difficult (and at times humorous) stories in which God does the most amazing and, quite frankly, peculiar things.

Setting the Stage

Discernment is a process. As much as we might like the idea that we can just know something is right or wrong through intuition or an impulse by the Holy Spirit, more often than not real discernment requires study. In some cases, study requires knowledge of a series of complicated and interrelated fields and subjects. In biblical studies, for example, one needs to be aware of archaeology, history, philology (the study of language), and geography, among many other disciplines such as textual criticism (comparing manuscripts of the Bible) and methodologies such as rhetoric (persuasion) and literary criticism (the study of narrative structures). As much as we desire that someone can just pick up the Bible and understand all its contents fully and unhindered by their biases, this is not reality. Sometimes we need to put in the hard and often uncomfortable (and sometimes boring) work to understand what the Bible is actually saying.

In an attempt to remedy the low biblical literacy of the church, some have taken to creating discernment ministries with the hope of educating and challenging the church during a time of moral and intellectual relativism. Popular discernment ministries today appear on YouTube, Instagram, and TikTok, often responding to claims made in video clips that espouse questionable beliefs. A number of these ministries are unapologetically cessationist, which obviously informs how they discern ideas and practices that don't fall in line with their belief system. On the one hand, their consistency is appreciated. On the other hand, however, there is a presupposition baked into their discernment process that can overshadow their exegetical processes. If a cessationist assumes, for example, that all instances of people falling down in church are caused by unfettered emotionalism, manipulation, or demons, it will be difficult for them to be given any evidence to the contrary. Similarly, if a charismatic Christian is given evidence that something they believe is in error, they may default to ignoring the evidence and turn to authority figures within their movement and experience for justification. In both cases, an emotional response or logical fallacy is used to suspend the need for fine-tuning one's belief system to accommodate the evidence. But this is not just an issue for the average Christian sitting in the pew, it is also true of some Christian academics and the hosts of some discernment ministries. Discernment requires humility, not just hard work.

For many years, it has become commonplace among some discernment ministries and critics of the modern charismatic movement to show montages of videos exposing members of the movement who appear to be engaged in seemingly wild and unruly behavior. Sometimes these video clips are misleading, isolating a quote or moment from a much longer video that distorts what the person was originally saying or doing. Yet, very often the clips in question are fully within their original context and their analysis of what is happening is perfectly legitimate. The oft repeated joke that "they hang from the chandeliers in that church" is meant to evoke a mental picture of anarchy or unbridled enthusiasm within those churches and movements and sometimes such a description is not that far afield! In some cases, however, an in-between issue arises. The clip is in context, but the observer misunderstands what is happening, either due to theological bias or perhaps even ignorance.

When it comes to the issue of ASCs, one cannot be blamed for misunderstanding the situation. ASCs, on the surface, do look strange, especially to those who are unaccustomed to them or have been predisposed through dogmatic teaching that they must be inherently wrong. Throughout the Bible and church history, many have misinterpreted what is happening to someone who is experiencing an ASC. Pejorative names have often been used to ostracize and diminish those engaged in ASCs. Those familiar with Christian revivalism of the eighteenth and nineteenth centuries and the rise of Pentecostalism in the twentieth century may know of (if only by name and reputation) the "holy rollers" of the holiness movement (found in Methodist and Wesleyan denominations), a term originally coined to make fun of their exuberant manifestations of the Spirit. Similarly, the prophets are sometimes referred to as "madmen" (2 Kgs 9:11; Jer 29:26; Hos 9:7) and probably not just because of the things they say. Outsiders and insiders will naturally use different terms to explain what it is they think is happening.

A number of unique expressions have been used to describe such phenomena throughout Christian history. Some simply refer to them as "enthusiasms," stemming from the Greek phrase *en theos* (from ἐνθουσιασμός/ *enthousiasmos*) which means to be inspired or full of the deity.[3] Others, drawing on the physical symptoms of such experiences, describe it as "fits," "convulsions," or "jerks."[4] Being "slain in the Spirit" is also sometimes used, though this more often refers to the modern practice of a religious authority laying hands on an individual to initiate an ASC where the person suddenly collapses, apparently because of the power of God.[5] Still others have dubbed it variously as being "drunk in the Spirit" or "spiritual intoxication."[6] Additional emic monikers such as being "sloshed," "hammered," "drinking Godka,"[7] and doing "carpet time" have likewise been used to label this practice.[8] The use of alcoholic rhetoric is especially interesting and obviously informs the title of this book. Still, even what one person means when they use the phrase "drunk in the Spirit" may differ from another.

In this book, I use the phrases "spiritual intoxication" or "spiritual drunkenness" to refer broadly to ASCs that often have visible physiological features. Individuals who are spiritually intoxicated will often describe their experience as being "weighed down" or as suddenly perceiving an invisible heaviness on their bodies. Charismatics and Pentecostals have usually interpreted this as a manifestation of God's glory. The Hebrew word for glory (כָּבוֹד/*kavod*) has the semantic meaning of "weighty" or "heavy."[9] Thus, some charismatics suggest that this is to be taken in a literal sense.[10] Spiritual intoxication is thus sometimes accompanied by erratic movements, staggering, prostration, or falling (sometimes violently!) to the ground. Proponents of spiritual drunkenness often cite a number of biblical passages as precedent for their behavior, especially Acts 2 and Eph 5:18. Additionally, those who experience spiritual drunkenness report receiving prophecies or

---

3. LSJ, s.v. "ἐνθουσιασμός"; Taves, *Fits, Trances, and Visions*, 17; ODCC, s.v. "enthusiasm."

4. Chauncy, *Seasonable Thoughts*, 126–29.

5. Burgess, *Pentecostal and Charismatic*, s.v. "Slain in the Spirit."

6. Wigglesworth, *On Spiritual Gifts*, 20. For many other terms and phrases, see Crowder, *Ecstasy of Loving God*.

7. Crowder, "High on Jesus," para. 18.

8. Hannah, "Jonathan Edwards, the Toronto Blessing," 167.

9. Blenkinsopp, *Isaiah 1–39*, 301–2. See Isaiah 17:3–4 and 22:22–14 for examples of wordplays that shows the word "glory" used as "heavy."

10. *NIDOTTE*, s.v. "כָּבֵד."

visions while in this state. Some begin speaking or singing in tongues or repeating biblical terminology or scriptural quotations. In other instances, the recipient simply experiences a kind of euphoria that they report makes them feel closer to God.[11]

Spiritual intoxication is often reported in church gatherings where a perceived spiritual authority, such as a special guest-speaker, is present. It is often believed in these circles that being in the presence of such a person, especially being prayed over or touched by the speaker, will transfer some kind of divine power to the recipient, resulting in spiritual drunkenness. Missionary Rolland Baker, for example, can be seen in one video touching those present, resulting in the recipient collapsing in a form of apparent ecstasy.[12]

Despite the seeming chaotic nature of these manifestations, church groups often contain this enthusiasm within broadly defined boundaries, allowing for emotional expression, but also for orderly conduct. In addition, many "holy drinkers" seem to be able to control their ASC. In some contexts, those who are perceived as out of control may be reprimanded or guided into a softened expression of their ecstasy so that regular teaching, preaching, and worship can continue while not simultaneously quenching the Spirit. The Christian mystic John Crowder, for example, can be seen in one video in a form of ecstasy one moment, but is still able to preach to his audience seemingly sober at other times.[13]

It is important to realize that not all ASCs resemble drunkenness. In fact, some people can experience an ASC in a relatively calm and almost imperceptible manner to observers. The overlap between ASCs and drunkenness can be seen in surface level features like the loss of regular motor function (e.g., falling down) and behavior that is seen as foolish, such as prophetic sign acts, loud and abrupt vocalizations, and other phenomena to be explored in this book. The use of alcoholic language to refer to an ASC is not as uncommon as one may think and is not confined to one denomination or movement. Onlookers commonly report those experiencing religious enthusiasm as looking like drunkards. In one notable instance during the revivals of Jonathan Edwards, John Wesley, and George Whitefield, the physical manifestations were interpreted by onlookers as drunkenness just as in Acts 2. Devereux Jarratt (1733–1801), commenting on the issue of multiple people praying simultaneously, states of these meetings:

---

11. For a number of testimonials, see Poloma, *Main Street Mystics*, 3–5, 64–96; and Cely and Beltrán, "Towards a Typification of Motivations."

12. Harvest Sarasota, "Rolland Baker," 4:36–5:16.

13. Stanmanmo59, "Mystic John Crowder Exposed."

The assembly appeared to be all in confusion, and must seem to one at a little distance more like a drunken rabble than the worshippers of God.[14]

Likewise, one early writer records in rhyme the connection between the Methodists' manifestations and Acts 2:

> The Spirit descended and some were offended,
> And said of these men, "They're filled with new wine."
> I never yet doubted that some of them shouted,
> While others lay prostrate, by power struck down;
> Some weeping, some praising, while others were saying:
> "They're drunkards or fools, or in falsehood abound."[15]

Modern examples are easy to find as well. In the previously mentioned video, John Crowder, while preaching at Bethel Church in Redding, California, can be seen talking about "fat Friar Tuck bartender angels" and thanking God for the "drunken glory" while seemingly intoxicated, staggering around the stage accompanied by intermittent laughing, noises, and physical spasms.[16] Another video shows Marty Blackwelder of Rhema Bible Church at a Kenneth Hagin camp meeting flailing his arms, sporadically bending up and down, laughing, and staggering.[17] In another, Stacey Campbell, sometimes referred to as the "shaking prophetess," can be viewed wildly tossing her head from left to right while prophesying otherwise coherently.[18] Still another shows missionary Heidi Baker on stage attempting to preach while continually falling down, spontaneously jerking, and speaking into a microphone face down on the floor.[19] These strange bodily phenomena are viewed by some outside observers and critics as a form of group psychosis (or hypnosis), the work of demonic activity, or outright faking.[20] Despite such criticisms, those within these movements who claim to regularly experience such manifestations understand it to be tangible evidence that God has either overshadowed the individual or taken control of their mental or physical faculties to some extant. According to one survey, 24–27 percent of church attendees at Toronto Airport Christian Fellowship (TACF,

---

14. Bangs, *Methodist Episcopal Church*, 99.
15. Hauser, *Hesperian Harp*, 455.
16. Stanmanmo59, "Mystic John Crowder Exposed," 1:45.
17. Revkeithbarr, "Drunk in the Holy Ghost."
18. Prove All Things, "Shaking Prophetess."
19. Proverbs1:7Truth, "Drunken Delusion," 5:25.
20. MacArthur, *Strange Fire*, 6.

now known as Catch the Fire) meetings claimed to have experienced being drunk in the Spirit.[21]

Many popular Christian musicians and bands have also embraced the language of spiritual intoxication. One striking illustration of this can be seen in the lyrics of the song "Better than Drugs" by the Christian rock band Skillet, which compares God's love to wine and states that God will make the singer intoxicated like someone under the influence of drugs. Similarly, the Christian rapper Lecrae uses the language of being high on drugs in the lyrics of his song "I'm Turnt." In another case, while Jon Rizzo sings the song "Marriage Wine," he asks God to have his love inebriate the audience. Still more niche, Georgian and Winnie Banov, referred to as the "Joy Apostles," regularly preach in a state of spiritual drunkenness, some of which can be heard on the electronic music album *Blisstronica*. While these artists come from distinct theological backgrounds, the language of spiritual intoxication as a metaphor for love or devotion is ubiquitous.[22]

One may be left questioning why Christians would claim to become drunk for or by God? Even those within these traditions have sometimes looked at such an idea as—if not simply bizarre—a blasphemous manifestation or heretical teaching! Being drunk in the Spirit, however, does not refer to drinking literal alcohol or actually becoming intoxicated by some kind of physical substance. Rather, this language is used to describe a religious experience brought on by God either spontaneously or through various spiritual practices or rituals. While charismatics may describe their experiences differently and use diverse terminology, in general they seem to be describing the same thing. What they are experiencing seems to be some kind of trance state or ecstasy that is brought on either unexpectedly or through a series of ritual actions such as singing, dancing, or praying. Spiritual drunkenness is an ASC in which one's natural inhibitions are suspended and they are open to spiritual experiences outside of the norm. Concepts such as "trance," "ecstasy," and "altered state of consciousness" can often be viewed with suspicion, especially by conservative Christians, often being placed in the ranks alongside words like "meditation" and "mystic." This is partly due to a lack of exposure to such concepts and their wider anthropological, psychological, and sociological context within scholarship. One of the ways this book is meant to bridge this gap is by exposing Christians to the wider scholarly conversation about ASCs and how this can help

---

21. See Poloma, *Main Street Mystics*, 67; and "Divine Healing," 34.

22. One can also see this language in the famous Christian artist Carman's song "The Well."

inform our reading of the Scriptures and explain what we are seeing on the ground in the Pentecostal-charismatic movement.

Naturally, those unfamiliar with such odd-looking manifestations have a number of legitimate questions: What is the point of this? Isn't this a lack of self-control? Why would God do something so counterproductive? Is this the influence of demons? These questions deserve carefully studied answers. Some are quick to attack critics as lacking faith or somehow being spiritually inferior to those they are attacking. This attitude only further alienates critics from taking seriously what the Bible says about the topic at hand. Any question about Christian conduct is important. If such manifestations are not from the Spirit, Christian brothers and sisters ought to be able to address such things without being harassed or demeaned. At the same time, if these things are from the Spirit (and the contention of this book is that some indeed are), then charismatics should have biblically founded answers for those honestly inquiring (1 Pet 3:15). Each side is required to suspend their ego when discussing theological topics, especially those that can so easily cause unnecessary division within the body of Christ (1 Cor 8:1).

Why This Book?

Reading any statement or articles of faith document about a specific church or denomination will only give you a gist of the ins and outs of what that community of believers adheres to. If one were to look at the articles of faith of the Wesleyan Church, for example, they would read under the section on spiritual gifts that "the relative value of the gifts of the Spirit is to be tested by their usefulness in the church and not by the ecstasy produced in the ones receiving them."[23] This naturally would raise a series of questions for readers both within and outside that denomination. What is meant by ecstasy? Does it have any value? Should we expect it? Does this mean that the Wesleyan Church affirms ecstasy is from God? Obviously, we would need to do further investigation to find the answers to these questions and, at the end of it, we may find that each individual church gives a different answer. If this is true of one denomination, we must also be considerate that a movement as large as Pentecostalism or the charismatic movement in general will differ widely in their beliefs concerning these topics. As a result, I can offer three reasons why I think a book on this topic is needed at this time.

First, as far as I am aware, there has not been a book exegetically dedicated to this phenomenon in the form of a theology book that is

---

23. Wesleyan Church, "Articles of Religion," 16.238.

accessible to a lay audience.[24] The closest resource is probably Stacey and Wesley Campbell's book *Ecstatic Prophecy* (2008) and Jack Levison's *Inspired* (2013). Other authors that have touched on this subject include the Franciscan priest Raniero Cantalamessa, who wrote a two-volume work titled *Sober Intoxication of the Spirit* (2005) and John Crowder's *The Ecstasy of Loving God* (2008).

Opposing voices on spiritual intoxication should also be noted. Most well-known is probably the works of John MacArthur, including *Charismatic Chaos* (1992) and *Strange Fire* (2013). The Baptist minister David A. Swincer's *Tongues Vol 1: Confused by Ecstasy* (2006; rev. ed. 2011; updated 2021) briefly surveys some of the biblical passages and the scholarship on the topic of trance and ecstasy more broadly. Yet, his actual exegesis of the relevant biblical texts is barely sustained (especially in the Old Testament) and the book reads more of a criticism of scholars who have seen trance and ecstasy in the Bible. Likewise, Hank Hanegraaff's criticism of spiritual intoxication can be found in his book *Counterfeit Revival* (2001) where he lists numerous anecdotes of spiritual intoxication in modern church circles. Additionally, the nondenominational pastor Henry Bechthold's *Pentecostal Fanaticism* (2021) is a diatribe against what he sees as charismatic excesses in the Pentecostal movement.[25]

---

24. Because so many authors use trance, ecstasy, and altered state of consciousness to describe different accounts and thus either add or subtract from the total number of such accounts, it is difficult to be exhaustive with the material. Should one count, for example, all angelic appearances, dreams, etc.? Consider the following remark from Pilch, *Flights of the Soul*, 174: "In almost every chapter of Acts of the Apostles, one or another person enters into trance or another altered state of consciousness, communicates with a being in alternate reality, and learns new information or receives a new direction in life. Luke reports more than twenty such experiences in Acts." Pilch obviously casts the net wider than I do. In this book I will only be covering a handful of such narratives from Acts. On the other hand, Levison, *Inspired*, 71–123, seems to almost downplay ecstasy in his analysis. Indeed, many of the narratives discussed in this book are not even mentioned by Levison and in most cases he does not see ecstasy in many of the same narratives that others do. As a result, detailed exegesis of these passages is needed to allow readers to detect for themselves whether ecstasy is part of the equation in a given narrative.

25. Without wanting to be overly critical, it should be pointed out that these authors' inabilities to work with the relevant primary sources and original languages is apparent. Little to no interaction with Second Temple Jewish texts, Greco-Roman literature, or Ancient Near Eastern (ANE) works can be found in these books and little attention is drawn to any connection between them and the Bible. Linguistic analysis is also commonly either missing or incorrect. Hanegraaff, *Counterfeit Revival*, 200–01, for example, is able to cite Hebrew words, but his sources for their meaning are generically referred to as "Hebrew scholarship" and a random rabbi in Los Angeles! Additionally, no interaction with the Septuagint and other necessary exegetical considerations are taken

Academic books on the topic of ASCs in the Bible, early Christianity, and early Judaism certainly exist, notably Laura S. Nasrallah's *An Ecstasy of Folly* (2003), John J. Pilch's *Flights of the Soul* (2011), Giovanni B. Bazzana's *Having the Spirit of Christ* (2020), and Reed Carlson's *Unfamiliar Selves in the Hebrew Bible* (2022). It is difficult, however, for nonscholars to work through the sometimes-dense academic rhetoric and background information necessary to appreciate their findings. Thus, there is a need within the body of Christ for a book on this topic that is scholarly, primarily Bible-based as opposed to experiential, and still accessible for a lay audience.

Second, bias within theological guilds can sometimes halt productive dialogue on phenomena beyond the norm. As a result, what the Bible says about a topic can be ignored if it is deemed outwardly fringe or weird. Instead of dismissing the manifestations a priori based on its outward appearance, I will dive into the topic from a number of historically chronological and anthropological vantage points in this book.[26]

It is relatively easy to throw out a simple catchall word to categorize a phenomenon and then not give it any further legitimacy as a result. This not only impedes one's own ability to evaluate things based on careful biblical exegesis (specific is terrific!) but can also aid in causing one to become deaf to potentially rational and insightful counterarguments. For example, while the explanation of spiritual intoxication as a form of group hypnosis lauds a neat and tidy rationale for what these manifestations are, it serves more as an exercise in explaining *away* the phenomenon rather than truly explaining it.[27]

in his analysis of various scriptural texts. Likewise, MacArthur, *Strange Fire*, 38, 40, 121, 122–23, 138, 140–41, 148, 223, who only discusses Greek a handful of times (and never Hebrew), cites no lexicons, grammars, or meaningful scholarly works relevant to the discussion. This can hardly be considered academically sensitive discernment.

26. Pilch, *Flights of the Soul*, 6: "Researchers have always realized that no one possesses immaculate perception. Every researcher inevitably begins from a personal perspective within the researcher's own culture. Perhaps there is no other way to begin. That is why comparative studies, such as psychological anthropology, and other anthropological disciplines, are so pertinent to biblical studies. The vast majority of biblical scholars are outsiders to the culture they are investigating. If they do not use a comparative approach, they run the risk of interpreting ancient Mediterranean texts anachronistically and ethnocentrically. Psychologically minded Western interpreters are ever eager to analyze ancient Middle Eastern persons with tools developed in Western culture."

27. A similar tactic was employed in early scholarship of the witch hunts from the sixteenth through the eighteenth centuries in Europe and North America. Explanations include mass hysteria, the use of psychotropic drugs, and economic hardships for the trials. While such explanations have fascinated the modern mind, most scholars of the witch trials view this as a reductive explanation of a highly complex issue. Likewise, such "easy" explanations of what is happening at charismatic churches does not always

My goal is to present a nuanced perspective of what is happening when someone claims to be spiritually intoxicated and if there is any scriptural basis for it. Additionally, I am interested in the *why* of spiritual intoxication. Why, for example, would well-educated, level-headed individuals engage in this seemingly strange behavior? I also wish to explore the *how* of spiritual drunkenness. How exactly do people either induce or participate in this irregular state?

Finally, the Pentecostal-charismatic movement is the fastest growing Christian movement in the world. Thus, we should want to have biblical criteria for understanding what is happening in such a movement. In terms of Christian charity, it is important to hear the other side of an argument, even if you have never heard it before or have been given a caricature of the opposite side's views.

In chapter 1 I define some key terms that we will see throughout this book. What do I mean, for example, when I use the words "trance" and "ecstasy"? Is this language biblical? Why have Christians traditionally been wary of such terminology when discussing spiritual things? Chapters 2–4 will survey the presence of ASCs in the Old Testament. Importantly, I will try to contextualize the relevant passages within their ancient Near Eastern (ANE) context, especially as they relate to prophets/prophecy and the rituals and other factors involved in attaining an ASC. These chapters have been divided up into the three classical segments of the Hebrew Bible: (1) the Torah,[28] (2) the Prophets,[29] and (3) the Writings.[30] Chapters 5–7 survey ASCs throughout the New Testament. Here we will look at some related Greco-Roman and Jewish material and how they can inform our understanding of passages from the Gospels, Acts, and Pauline Epistles. Chapter 8 discusses the biblical instances of counterfeit ASCs, those brought on through illicit means such as occult activities, drugs, and evil spirits. Chapter 9 functions as a brief survey of ASCs throughout church history. Since this book is not meant to be an exhaustive historical account of ASCs, and because other books have addressed that topic, I have attempted to limit the scope of this chapter to what I think are representative figures and events.

---

get at the root of what is happening on the ground. See Oldridge, *Witchcraft Reader*, 1–16.

28. Genesis, Exodus, Leviticus, Numbers, and Deuteronomy.

29. Sometimes divided into the Former Prophets (Joshua, Judges, 1–2 Samuel, and 1–2 Kings), Latter Prophets (Isaiah, Jeremiah, and Ezekiel, the so-called major prophets), and the Book of the Twelve (Hosea, Joel, Amos, Obadiah, Jonah, Micah, Nahum, Habakkuk, Zephaniah, Haggai, Zechariah, and Malachi, i.e., the minor prophets.).

30. Ruth, 1–2 Chronicles, Ezra-Nehemiah, Esther, Job, Psalms, Proverbs, Ecclesiastes, Song of Songs, Lamentations, and Daniel.

Finally, I end with a conclusion that will contain a theological reflection on the connection between ASCs and God's character.

While I have attempted to write in a way that is accessible to a lay audience, this book will be of most use to pastors and seminary students who are interested in the topic of ASCs and the Bible as well as the modern Pentecostal-charismatic movement. Detailed footnotes are given for those who want to dig deeper on any given topic. Since it has been my experience that the average reader will not have immediate access to the many primary sources cited in this book, where possible I have tried to quote at length the relevant portions. Furthermore, I have tried my best to give the dates of those texts when they first appear in the book. Since I do quote from and refer to a number of nonbiblical sources, it should be understood that this is part of the hermeneutical (i.e., interpretive) and exegetical process.[31] Reconstructing the original context of a situation in the ancient past necessitates using all available sources. Additionally, because this book often deals with ancient languages (such as Greek and Hebrew), I have attempted to use both the original script and provide meaningful transliterations afterward.

Finally, I am not necessarily arguing anything radically new in this book. Rather, I am synthesizing data that is sometimes scattered across various disciplines (sociology, psychology, anthropology, neurobiology, etc.) and of which a wide and daunting field of research exists. This book serves more as an exercise in connecting the dots so that those interested in this subject can determine if there is good cause for believing such manifestations are truly from the Spirit.

---

31. For an introduction to hermeneutics and exegesis, see Osborne, *Hermeneutical Spiral*; Köstenberger and Patterson, *Biblical Interpretation*; Gorman, *Elements of Biblical Exegesis*; and Duvall and Hays, *Grasping God's Word*.

1

Trance, Ecstasy, and Other Scary Words

> What makes authentic disciples is not visions, ecstasies, biblical mastery of chapter and verse, or spectacular success in the ministry, but a capacity for faithfulness.
>
> —Brennan Manning, *The Ragamuffin Gospel*

IT IS ALWAYS NECESSARY for Christians from opposite theological perspectives to agree on what they mean when they use certain words. What a Baptist or Pentecostal means when they say they believe in the Trinity, for example, means something completely different than a Jehovah's Witness or Latter-Day Saint (Mormon). In order to have productive and charitable conversations about difficult topics in the Bible and contemporary church life, we must agree on some basic terminology to have meaningful dialogue.

As previously stated in the introduction, charismatic Christians have diverse words and phrases that they use to describe what they are experiencing. This can be referred to as insider or "emic" terminology. An outsider or "etic" onlooker may use different words and phrases to describe what they observe.[1] In the academic discipline of religious studies and the humanities or social sciences in general, scholars use a number of sometimes interchangeable words to describe what they observe. While there are some differences in how a term might be defined, there is general consensus on

---

1. On the use of emic and etic, see Pike, "Etic and Emic Standpoints."

some of the major overlapping themes in the jargon and nomenclature used by scholars.

The terms "ecstasy," "trance," and "altered state of consciousness" (ASC) are largely used interchangeably by scholars. The word trance, for example, is sometimes used in defining what ecstasy is and vice-versa.[2] One can observe this interchangeability in the following definition of the word ecstasy:

> [Ecstasy is] a trancelike state of profound emotionality in which awareness is limited to the object of contemplation. Also loosely used to refer to any exalted state of emotion.[3]

Likewise, another author states:

> From time to time, I will also use the phrase "altered state of consciousness" (or the abbreviated ASC) and the term "trance" as synonyms for ecstasy.[4]

Over the last century, scholars working in different fields of study have developed their own categories and definitions for the words found in this book. This is best summarized by the American scholar of religion Ann Taves:

> Psychiatrists most commonly refer to dissociation (or more distantly hysteria); anthropologists to trance, spirit-possession, and altered states of consciousness; and religionists to visions, inspiration, mysticism, and ecstasy.[5]

Due to this problematic overlap, each writer is forced to explain what they mean by which word. This book is thus not immune to the wider conversation in academia. Because many of these terms have long and complicated histories of use by scholars and lay people alike, I will not go into great detail about their historical developments. Rather, this section is meant to introduce the reader to these terms in a way that is as concise as possible without causing undue confusion or rhetorical exhaustion. For those not accustomed to this language, it is highly recommended you read through the following definitions and explanations. This will allow you to avoid confusion when encountering what can often be uncommon vocabulary in biblical studies.

---

2. L&N, s.v. "ἔκστασις," describes the Greek word for ecstasy thus: "A vision accompanied by an ecstatic psychological state." See also *NIDNTTE*, s.v. "ἔκστασις."

3. Wulff, *Psychology of Religion*, 7–8.

4. Schantz, *Paul in Ecstasy*, 19.

5. Taves, *Fits, Trances, and Visions*, 7.

Ecstasy

When a friend recently asked me what I was researching, they were confused why I would be studying a hallucinogenic drug. Their mistake was humorous, but became a common obstacle when introducing the concept for this book. For some, the only time they have even heard the word ecstasy is in relation to the pharmaceutical of the same name. The drug ecstasy, also referred to as "MDMA" or "Molly," is commonly used at parties, music festivals, and other recreational spaces to induce a sense of euphoria in the user.[6] This idea of euphoria is probably the second most commonly understood meaning of the word ecstasy in popular culture. When someone is discussing a new job prospect they might say, "I was ecstatic when my boss offered me the position." What that person means, of course, is that they were excited, full of joy, or blissful. In other words, they were euphoric. While euphoria may be a part of ecstasy, it still does not quite get to the heart of what we are exploring in this book.

When the word ecstasy is used in spiritual contexts, we can refer to this as "religious ecstasy." But what is religious ecstasy? One way of describing the phenomena is by listing its qualities or particulars. For example, common features of religious ecstasy include: (1) a feeling of intense euphoria, (2) a loss of sense of self (sometimes referred to as transcendence), (3) a sense of connection with a higher power, (4) absorption or oneness with a higher power, (5) unconscious physiological responses, (6) visual and auditory revelations, and (7) time distortion.

We can also speak of the causes or catalysts of religious ecstasy, such as: (1) spiritual practices and rituals, (2) sensory stimulation, (3) psychological or emotional manipulation, (4) drugs, and (5) spirits. Yet, not all of these features are present when someone experiences religious ecstasy, and various methods or factors, often overlapping, may be involved in promoting the ecstatic experience.

The idea of religious ecstasy can sometimes conjure images related to eastern religious traditions and rituals. One may hear the word ecstasy and think of fits of hysteria, such as during the Salem Witch Trials (1692–1693) where some scholars postulate a hallucinogenic fungus was responsible for the strange behaviors of those accused of witchcraft (although this theory is now greatly contested).[7] One may also think of shamanic indigenous religions where people become possessed and shake as evidence that the gods, spirits, or ancestors have made contact with them. Or, we may in our minds

---

6. One thinks, for instance, of the popular 2017 movie *Molly's Game*.
7. See Woolf, "Witchcraft or Mycotoxin?"

picture monks in deep meditation, emptying their minds in order to become one with Brahman, or the universe. Indeed, such portraits of ecstasy may deter us from thinking that such a thing could even be compatible with the Christian Scriptures.

In some contexts, especially when discussing the history of Christian mysticism, ecstasy is explained as a process of the soul's ascent where the devotee goes through a series of stages or levels that end in euphoria or rapture. The word "rapture" here does not refer to the popular end times belief that the church will be snatched away before a seven-year tribulation period. Rather, the word rapture (from the Latin *raptus*) signifies a snatching away of the soul or senses so that the individual becomes overwhelmed with passion for, and experiences strong emotion toward, God, often culminating in visions or a general sense of awe. For example, the New Testament scholar David E. Aune defines ecstasy as follows:

> An abnormal state of consciousness in which revelatory communications (both visionary and auditory) are believed to be received from supernatural beings.[8]

Defining ecstasy this way, however, runs into problems as well. Not all ecstasies involve or result in visions or hearing voices from a supernatural being. Neither do all ecstasies involve a series of sequential levels as seen in later Jewish and Christian mysticism. Additionally, ecstasy can happen through long periods of prayer and meditation or rapidly and unexpectedly. There is no one-size-fits-all when it comes to ecstasy.

Another way of defining ecstasy is through etymology. Etymology is the study of words, their historical development, and the parts that make up individual words. Our English word "ecstasy" is derived from the Greek noun ἔκστασις/*ekstasis* and the verb ἐξίστημι/*existēmi*. The Greek-English lexicon referred to as BDAG[9] supplies two basic definitions for the noun *ekstasis*: "1. A state of consternation or profound emotional experience to the point of being beside oneself" and "2. A state of being in which consciousness is wholly or partially suspended, freq[uently] associated with

---

8. *ISBE*, s.v. "Ecstasy." Aune further delineates the meaning of ecstasy: "Metaphorically they refer to at least three states of mind, each having characteristic behavioral features: (1) mental or psychological distractions such as excitement and astonishment, fear and terror; (2) the pathological mental state of madness or insanity (whether temporary or permanent); and (3) the trancelike state in which people are considered particularly susceptible to communications from supernatural beings. These types of *ékstasis* were distinguished by Philo (*Her*. 249), who was dependent on Plato (*Phaedr*. 244a–245a), though Plato used different terms."

9. BDAG is an acronym formed from the surnames of the four primary scholars responsible for this Greek Lexicon: Bauer, Danker, Arndt, and Gingrich.

divine action, trance, ecstasy." The first idea is often translated as "amazed" or "astonished."[10] The generally esteemed lexicon LSJ even offers the meaning of "drunken excitement."[11] Likewise, the verbal form can mean either "be amazed" or refer to an "inability to reason normally[,] lose one's mind, be out of one's senses."[12] The verb itself is made up of two words: (1) "out of" (ἐκ/ek) and (2) "to stand" (ἵστημι/histēmi). Thus, at a basic etymological level it means to stand outside oneself or to be displaced.[13]

As the reader can probably deduce, no definition of ecstasy is going to be perfect and all-encompassing and will differ from one author to the next. Yet, a general conceptualization of what ecstasy is will be helpful in framing the discussion in this book. When I use the word ecstasy, I refer to an altered state of consciousness in which a person's normative cognition is displaced or disrupted for an indeterminate amount of time. In ecstasy, a person becomes susceptible to outward forces such as God and spirits and often manifests this through spontaneous movements, vocalizations, and other atypical activities, including miraculous feats. Ecstatics can have varying degrees of control over their physical bodies and minds and may receive visions and auditory revelations during these episodes. In some instances, ecstasy is perceived as "frenzy" because of the abnormal and "uncontrolled" actions of the ecstatic. In this regard, ecstasy is differentiated from "trance" by its more overt and dramatic features.

What Did Ecstasy Look Like?

The African apologist Tertullian (second–third century CE) makes use of the etymological meaning of ecstasy as "displacement" when he states that "this power we call ecstasy, in which the sensuous soul stands out of itself, in a way which even resembles madness."[14] Tertullian's claim that ecstasy resembles madness may be surprising, but many authors from the ancient world and contemporary observers attest to abnormal mental and physical states of those experiencing ecstasy. Naturally, we do not have a way to travel to the past and witness people during ecstatic episodes. This includes

10. BDAG, s.v. "ἔκστασις."
11. LSJ, s.v. "ἔκστᾰσις," citing *Nat. d.* 30 by Cornutus Philosophus (first century CE). LSJ, like BDAG, is an acronym formed from the surnames of the three scholars responsible for this Greek Lexicon: Liddell, Scott, and Jones.
12. BDAG, s.v. "ἐξίστημι."
13. For more details on how to avoid interpretive problems with etymology, see Carson, *Exegetical Fallacies*.
14. Tertullian, *An.* 45.

those who experienced ecstasy in the Bible. Thus, we are reliant on passing remarks by ancient authors, adversarial comments from opponents of ecstasy, and other sources for reconstructing what might have been taking place when someone was experiencing ecstasy. In addition to the Hebrew Bible and New Testament, we also have the writings of the Jewish philosopher Philo of Alexandria (first century BCE–first century CE), the Jewish historian Josephus (first century CE), and other nonbiblical works such as the Dead Sea Scrolls and ANE literature to help us in this endeavor. These extrabiblical works will be incorporated into each chapter to flesh out the cultural and religious context in which the Scriptures were written and help shed light on these issues.

What did people living in the ancient world think *ekstasis* looked like? Philo, one of our chief sources for understanding Jewish beliefs during the time of Jesus, lists four kinds of *ekstasis* in his work titled *Who is the Heir?* (Latin: *Quis rerum divinarum heres sit?*). The first form of *ekstasis* Philo mentions is synonymous with madness or insanity "either through old age, or melancholy, or some other similar cause."[15] The second is described as a kind of terror or amazement "from things which happen suddenly and unexpectedly."[16] The third is a restful and still mind "arising when it is inclined by nature to be quiet."[17] The last kind of *ekstasis* is described as "supernatural possession and frenzy."[18] For Philo, prophetic inspiration fell under this final category. The prophet was viewed by Philo as a "musical instrument of God, played and struck by him invisibly."[19] He continues to state that when a prophet is inspired, his natural mind leaves him to make room for the Spirit's communication: "This very frequently happens to the race of prophets; for the mind that is in us is removed from its place at the arrival of the divine Spirit, but is again restored to its previous habitation when that Spirit departs, for it is contrary to holy law for what is mortal to dwell with what is immortal."[20] Naturally, we cannot base what we believe about the way prophets in the Old Testament received messages on the words of Philo who was writing in the first century, far removed from the time of the

---

15. Philo, *Heir* 249. The Greek physician Galen (second–third century CE) explains ecstasy as "a short-lived madness" (ἐστιν ὀλιγοχρόνιος μανία/*estin oligochronios mania*). XIX 462 K. Galen's works are typically referenced using the system formulated by the German physician and medical historian Karl Gottlob Kühn in a twenty-six-volume series called *Medicorum Graecorum opera quae extant*. Volumes 1–22 are all on Galen.

16. Philo, *Heir* 249.

17. Philo, *Heir* 249.

18. Philo, *Heir* 249–50.

19. Philo, *Heir* 259.

20. Philo, *Heir* 265.

Hebrew prophets, though it does tell us something of what Jewish thinkers may have believed or inherited in previous ages.[21]

Another avenue for understanding what prophetic activities looked like in the Hebrew Bible is to look at the verb for "prophesy" (נָבָא/*naba*). Scholars have long debated the origins of the word *naba*. Part of the debate stems from whether the word reflects Akkadian, Arabic, or some other Semitic root.[22] One suggestion is that it reflects a form of ecstatic activity because it may be etymologically connected with the meaning "to bubble forth" or "to gush out." Albrecht Oepke, for example, suggests that the original meaning of *naba* meant something like "to speak with frenzy."[23] Again, it is not surprising that the prophets are often described as madmen (2 Kgs 9:11; Jer 29:26; Hos 9:7).[24] Prominent among these madmen is Saul who, in 1 Samuel, is depicted as acting quite out of the ordinary. Twice the Spirit of God rushes on Saul (1 Sam 10:10; 19:23–24) with the latter instance resulting in him getting naked and laying on the ground prophesying with a group of other prophets all night. It is particularly important to notice that onlookers twice ask the question, "Is Saul among the prophets?" (1 Sam 10:11, 19:24), insinuating that this is just the way prophets sometimes acted. Indeed, many of the standard Hebrew lexicons available today will list ecstasy as a possible meaning for *naba*.[25] Others have argued, however, that an ecstatic element of prophecy cannot be based on etymological clues.[26] As we will see in the following chapters, part of the reason many scholars see *naba* as having ecstatic roots is because many of the times *naba* appears, the prophet(s) in question *is* in a frenzied state. Both the etymological basis and the actual activities of the prophets themselves thus inform us that ecstasy is a likely candidate for understanding *naba*.[27]

---

21. Like Philo, the Christian author Athenagoras of Athens (second century CE) compares the Old Testament prophets to a musical instrument: "The voices of the prophets confirm our arguments—for I think that you also, with your great zeal for knowledge, and your great attainments in learning, cannot be ignorant of the writings either of Moses or of Isaiah and Jeremiah, and the other prophets, who, lifted in ecstasy above the natural operations of their minds by the impulses of the Divine Spirit, uttered the things with which they were inspired, the Spirit making use of them as a flute-player breathes into a flute;—what, then, do these men say? 'The Lord is our God; no other can be compared with Him.'" *Leg.* 9.

22. *DCH*, s.v. "נבא"; *TWOT*, s.v. "נָבָא"; *NIDOTTE*, s.v. "Prophecy."

23. *TDNT*, s.v. "Ἔκστασις, Ἐξίστημι."

24. See Fleming, "Etymological Origins of *nābîʾ*," 217–24, who suggests that it comes from the Syrian word *nābû* (one who invokes the gods).

25. See *HALOT*, s.v. "נבא"; and *DCH*, s.v. "נבא."

26. Eissfeldt, "Prophetic Literature," 142.

27. Later rabbinic texts seem to interpret prophets as generally entering a trance:

Other ancient authors also tell us something of what ecstasy looked like. While in ecstasy, human beings behave in ways that are observably atypical to everyday experience. It is sometimes depicted as convulsions[28] or fits of anger,[29] death,[30] sleep,[31] or as generally being out of one's mind.[32] Although later authors such as Philo perceived ecstasy as an instance of the soul leaving the body, this was not necessarily the understanding of the authors of Scripture. Rather, ecstasy was not a displacement of the individual's soul somewhere else, but of being overwhelmed by the presence of another spiritual force. From this experience, some form of supernatural communication could be shared, whether by viewing the individual's physiological or psychological state, or by listening to their verbal message.

Reading Philo's explanation of ecstasy might be completely foreign to the way you've ever thought about how the prophets of the Bible heard from God. Yet, such an interpretation of how prophecies were received or delivered is not foreign to orthodox Protestants. The Welsh Protestant minister David Martyn Lloyd-Jones, for example, states that "the prophet gave his

---

"'If you have a prophet of God, I will make Myself known to him though a vision to him'—My Divine Presence will not be revealed to him through a clear lens, but rather through a dream or a trance." Midr. Tanchuma, Tzav13.

28. Chalmers, *Religion of Ancient Israel*, 60–61.

29. T. Sim. 4:8 (second century BCE): "For that attitude makes the soul savage and corrupts the body; it foments wrath and conflict in the reason, excites to the shedding of blood, drives the mind to [*ekstasis*], arouses tumult in the soul and trembling in the body."

30. See Bremmer, *Early Greek Concept*, 29–32.

31. T. Reu. 3:1 (second century BCE): "In addition to all is an eighth spirit: sleep, with which is created the [*ekstasis*] of nature and the image of death."

32. Plato, *Phaedr.* 244a–b (fifth–fourth century BCE): "That the former discourse was by Phaedrus, the son of Pythocles (Eager for Fame) of Myrrhinus (Myrrhtown); but this which I shall speak is by Stesichorus, son of Euphemus (Man of pious Speech) of Himera (Town of Desire). And I must say that this saying is not true, which teaches that when a lover is at hand the non-lover should be more favored, because the lover is insane, and the other sane. For if it were a simple fact that insanity is an evil, the saying would be true; but in reality the greatest of blessings come to us through madness, when it is sent as a gift of the gods. For the prophetess at Delphi and the priestesses at Dodona when they have been mad have conferred many splendid benefits upon Greece both in private and in public affairs, but few or none when they have been in their right minds; and if we should speak of the Sibyl and all the others who by prophetic inspiration have foretold many things to many persons and thereby made them fortunate afterwards, anyone can see that we should speak a long time. And it is worth while to adduce also the fact that those men of old who invented names thought that madness was neither shameful nor disgraceful."

message from God in various ways, sometimes in a kind of trance; he was not clear about the mechanism but the message was quite clear."[33]

Despite this, some conservative Christians still scoff at the idea that Israelite prophets experienced ecstasy. The American theologian Leon J. Wood, for example, devotes an entire chapter of his book *The Prophets of Israel* (1979) to discrediting the idea that Israelite prophets were ecstatics. When discussing the importance of comparative religion, he flippantly states that "the conservative scholar, however, who believes that Israel was unique in its world, having been especially called to existence by God and given its Law and instruction supernaturally, places little reliance on this manner of argument."[34]

One is struck by the dismissive and frankly arrogant tone of this comment. With such a treasure trove of resources from both the ancient world and contemporary anthropology, one would be grossly mistaken to ignore such data. Moreover, to suggest that ecstasy is inherently antithetical to Israelite religion is based on a presupposition that ecstasy must involve devious methods to achieve or that it is somehow equated with false religion. But ecstasy does not necessitate either of these things and so such arguments are devoid of meaning.

Trance

Like ecstasy, the word "trance" has been understood differently by scholars depending on their field of research. The English word "trance" itself comes from the Latin word *transeo*, meaning to "pass [over]."[35] Modern readers may have a caricature of trance as looking something like hypnosis or someone lost in thought. Such an idea is not misguided since trance states typically involve a narrowed perception of one's surroundings. The *Concise Oxford English Dictionary*, for example, defines trance as "a half-conscious state characterized by an absence of response to external stimuli, typically as induced by hypnosis or entered by a medium." By comparison, Aune defines trance as:

> An altered state of consciousness, usually experienced by an individual privately, in which extrasensory sights and sounds, or visions and auditions, are experienced.[36]

33. Lloyd-Jones, *God the Father*, 292.
34. Wood, *Prophets of Israel*, 39.
35. Colpe, "Ecstasy," *EC* 2:29.
36. *ISBE*, s.v. "Trance."

On the surface, Aune's definition of trance is not that different from his definition of ecstasy. This makes sense given the tendency for scholars to conflate the two terms. The German New Testament scholar Carsten Colpe's comment, however, that trance is "often defined as the psychological opposite of ecstasy" is helpful.[37]

In popular discourse, trance is, in some ways, the calmer version of ecstasy. Both involve an alteration in consciousness, but one is more rowdy or maverick than the other. Trance states are something that most people can experience. As Ioan M. Lewis explains:

> Trance states can be readily induced in most normal people by a wide range of stimuli, applied either separately or in combination. Time-honoured techniques include the use of alcoholic spirits, hypnotic suggestion, rapid over-breathing, the inhalation of smoke and vapours, music, and dancing; and the ingestion of such drugs as mescaline or lysergic acid and other psychotropic alkaloids.[38]

When it comes to translating and interpretation, it can become difficult in determining whether trance or ecstasy are in mind. Some Bible translations, including the 1890 Darby Bible, the Douay-Rheims Bible, and the paraphrase The Message by Eugene Peterson, translate the word *ekstasis* as "ecstasy," while most all other translations (e.g., NIV, NRSV, ESV, CSB, NLT) have adopted the word "trance" instead. The ESV and NRSV, for example, state in Acts 10:10 that Peter fell into a "trance" (*ekstasis*). This likely strikes readers as confusing. Why would *ekstasis* be translated as "trance" and not "ecstasy"? In one sense, this is an interpretive choice of the translator based on what they perceive Peter's *ekstasis* looked like. As John J. Pilch explains: "What the Greeks called ecstasy, contemporary Westerners call trance, but not every trance is *ekstasis* in the Greek sense of the word. . . . It is the religious context of the experience that determines ecstasy."[39]

In other words, the Greek language did not use two separate words for trance and ecstasy. Rather, they distinguished between different kinds of ecstasy, of which trance is one species.

What then distinguishes trance from ecstasy? In English, we tend to view a trance as a meditative, sleep-like state whereas ecstasy represents exuberant, joyful, highly energetic fervor or frenzy. However, scholars can talk about people falling into a trance while in an ecstasy or being ecstatic while in a trance, and thus the semantic confusion persists. Since the Bible

---

37. Colpe, "Ecstasy," *EC* 2:29.
38. Lewis, *Ecstatic Religion*, 34.
39. Pilch, *Flights of the Soul*, 132.

does not use two different words for these behaviors, we are stuck with attempting to figure out what exactly is happening in a given narrative.

For the purposes of not adding to this confusion, in this book I have made a conscious effort to use the term "trance" when describing a sedated or meditative state (as much as can be discerned). As we will see, many instances of divine revelation are given when the prophet or individual is in a state that is compared with sleep or drowsiness. In these cases, translating the relevant Hebrew or Greek terms as "trance" makes sense. On the other hand, the term "ecstasy" is used when describing the more exuberant or atypical expressions that can accompany divine revelation or contact, notably sudden physical movements or vocalizations. I have maintained the use of the terms ecstasy and trance predominantly because I believe they are authentic representations of the underlying Biblical texts examined, even if we do not have two distinct words present in the Hebrew or Greek text.

Altered State of Consciousness

The term "altered state of consciousness" (ASC) was originally coined by the psychiatrist Arnold M. Ludwig in 1966 and later popularized by the psychologist Charles T. Tart in 1969.[40] Scholars disagree about how to define an ASC, but the following definition represents the basic elements present:

> An altered state is any mental state(s), induced by various physiological, psychological, or pharmacological maneuvers or agents, which can be recognized subjectively by the individual himself (or by an objective observer of the individual) as representing a sufficient deviation in subjective experience of psychological functioning from certain general norms for that individual during alert, waking consciousness.[41]

In other words, an ASC is simply an experience in which one's normative mental processes are either suspended or altered in such a way as to allow them to perceive or experience things not typically accessible or as easily comprehended when in one's natural mental state.[42] While ASC is

---

40. See Ludwig, "Altered States of Consciousness."
41. Garcia-Romeu and Tart, "Altered States of Consciousness," 129.
42. The term "ASC" is used to describe a number of diverse human experiences. Krippner, "Altered States of Consciousness," identifies some twenty ASCs: (1) dreaming, (2) sleeping, (3) hypnagogic (drowsiness before sleep), (4) hypnopompic (semi-consciousness preceding waking), (5) hyperalert, (6) lethargic, (7) rapture, (8) hysteric, (9) fragmentation, (10) regressive, (11) meditative, (12) trance, (13) reverie, (14) daydreaming, (15) internal scanning, (16) stupor, (17) coma, (18) stored memory, (19)

not a term found in the text of Scripture, it is meant to encapsulate what is happening when one is in an ecstasy or trance.

Modern biblical scholarship has for some time now used interdisciplinary methodologies to make sense of certain portions of Scripture. Using cross-cultural studies from the humanities has allowed scholars to read the Bible in a new light. Although this can sometimes be abused in order to justify contemporary ethical sensibilities or political views, many respected Christian scholars have successfully used such methods in teasing out the nuances of the Scriptures. Thus, by looking at ASCs cross-culturally and historically, and noting similar patterns in form and content, scholars are able to extrapolate similar themes in the biblical text that seem best interpreted as ASCs. Thus, throughout this book I use the acronym "ASC" or the phrase "altered state(s)" to refer to both trance and ecstasy in the body of the text.

It might go without saying that some conservative Christians are skeptical or suspicious of such phenomena in the life of the church. One common objection to ASCs by critics is the call to be of "sound mind" or a "sober mind" (1 Tim 3:2, 11; 2 Tim 4:5; Titus 2:2; 1 Pet 1:13; 4:7; 5:8). How can we therefore argue that ASCs, whether in the form of ecstasy or trance, are compatible with the Christian life? This is a foundational question to the very thesis of this book, and so I think it is worth taking time to dispel such concerns.

At a basic level, many of these criticisms stem from a misunderstanding of the Greek terms behind these translations and their wider context. The Greek word translated as "to be of sound mind" or "to be sober minded" is σωφρονέω/sōphroneō.[43] This word was used especially in ancient philosophical circles as a virtue of ethical living with the idea of exercising moderation or restraint and, in some instances, referred to chastity in Jewish, Christian, and pagan sources.[44] Ethical living also appears to be the driving force behind the presence of this word group in early Jewish writings around the time of the New Testament. According to the apocryphal Wisdom of Solomon (first century BCE–first century CE), Solomon prays for God to send wisdom from heaven so that it might guide him "prudently"

---

expanded consciousness, and (20) normal.

43. BDAG, s.v. "σωφρονέω": "To be able to think in a sound or sane manner, *be of sound mind*"; LSJ, s.v. "σωφρονέω."

44. *NIDNTTE*, s.v. "σωφροσύνη"; T. Jos. 4:2: "Publicly she honored me for my self-control [σώφρονά/sōphrona], while privately she said to me, 'Have no fear of my husband, for he is convinced of your chastity so that even if someone were to tell him about you, he would not believe it.'" Cf. 9:2 and 10:2–3.

(σωφρόνως/sōphronōs).⁴⁵ In 4 Maccabees (first century CE), the author states the law was given "to the mind" so that the one who lives according to the law "will rule a kingdom that is temperate [σώφρονα/sōphrona], just, good, and courageous."⁴⁶ Moses is given as an example of someone who exercises σώφρων/sōphrōn when he restrains his anger.⁴⁷ Importantly we are told that "for the temperate [σώφρων/sōphrōn] mind can conquer the drives of the emotions and quench the flames of frenzied [παθῶν/pathōn] desires."⁴⁸ Note that being of a sound mind stops frenzied or passionate "desires"—that is, fleshly impulses of an ethically dubious sort, not ecstatic episodes or ASCs. Other Jewish texts use this word to discuss abstaining from drinking alcohol, using crude language, fighting, slander, and disobeying God's commands.⁴⁹ Josephus, for example, states that "Moses did not make religion a part of virtue, but he saw and he ordained other virtues to be parts of religion; I mean justice, and fortitude, and temperance [σωφροσύνην/sōphrosynēn], and a universal agreement of the members of the community with one another."⁵⁰

Finally, the word can also have the meaning of being reasonable, as in having a mind geared toward understanding rightly. The second-century apologist Justin Martyr, for example, states: "What sober-minded man [σωφρονῶν/sōphronōn], then, will not acknowledge that we are not atheists, worshipping as we do the Maker of this universe."⁵¹

The New Testament uses this word group a total of fourteen times. In a couple of instances, the word seems to have the general meaning of not being insane. Paul uses the word in Acts 26:25 to emphasize that he was not crazy when talking to Festus.⁵²

---

45. Wis 9:11.
46. 4 Macc 2:23.
47. 4 Macc 2:16–18: "For the temperate [σώφρων/sōphrōn] mind repels all these malicious emotions, just as it repels anger—for it is sovereign over even this. When Moses was angry with Dathan and Abiram, he did nothing against them in anger, but controlled his anger by reason. For, as I have said, the temperate [σώφρων/sōphrōn] mind is able to get the better of the emotions, to correct some, and to render others powerless."
48. 4 Macc 3:17.
49. T. Jud. 16:3.
50. Josephus, *Ag. Ap.* 2.170.
51. Justin Martyr, *1 Apol.*13.
52. Keener, *Acts*, 4:3538-39: "Paul's term for 'utter' (ἀποφθέγγομαι), used in the earliest extant Christian literature only in Acts, is associated with inspired speech in at least one (Acts 2:4) and possibly both (2:14) other uses (see comment on these passages). In that very context in Acts 2, such inspiration appeared to some as drunkenness (2:13). Paul's inspiration, however, ought not to be confused with madness (26:24), for he speaks soberly (26:25). 'Words of truth and sobriety' here may be a hendiadys,

This term is also used to describe how a demon-possessed man came back to his senses after being exorcised (Mark 5:15; Luke 8:35). Based on the narrative presented to us, this demoniac was known for howling and cutting himself with stones and apparently running around naked. Evidently, these are not examples of sound-mindedness. Thus, when we see the demoniac delivered, we are told that he was of sound mind and now, thankfully, clothed. Some may point to this example in the Gospels as evidence that an ASC is unbiblical or demonic. Of course, the issue with this is that ASCs can have multiple sources (divine, demonic, or human). Evidently, the demoniac in this story was acting insane because of the demons controlling him. Thus, saying he came back to his senses says nothing about the nature of ASCs brought on by God or Paul's command to be sober minded more generally.

In other instances, Paul seems to use the term to refer to its classical philosophical meaning of ethical living.[53] In Titus, for example, he juxtaposes "ungodliness" and "worldly passions" with Christ's training to the saints to live "self-controlled [σωφρόνως/sōphronōs], upright, and godly lives" (2:11–12).[54] Titus is instructed to be a "model of good works" as he instructs the younger men to be "self-controlled" (σωφρονεῖν/sōphronein), likely a reference to chastity (Titus 2:6–7). Similar instructions are given to the older women of the church who are to teach the younger women to "love their husbands and children, to be self-controlled [σώφρων/sōphrōn], pure, working at home, kind, and submissive to their own husbands, that the word of God may not be reviled" (Titus 2:4–5).

Here, Paul's use of *sōphrōn* "coupled with 'pure' (*hagnas*, i.e., morally pure, chaste) may express Paul's concern for marital fidelity."[55] Likewise, in the various qualifications for overseers in the church, Paul lists among the

---

hence, 'words of sober truth.' Such sobriety could be contrasted with madness, as here. Less relevant, some people in antiquity also spoke of a divinely inspired μανία that was superior to a 'sound mind' (σωφροσύνης, Ael. Arist. *Def. Or.* 53, §17D)." See also Witherington, *Acts*, 749; and Bock, *Acts*, 722–23.

53. The word may also be used of thinking reasonably about matters. In Romans, Paul says that people should not be arrogant in their assessment of themselves, but to "think with sober judgment [σωφρονεῖν/sōphronein], each according to the measure of faith that God has assigned" (12:3; cf. 12:16). *TDNT*, s.v. "Σώφρων, Σωφρονέω, Σωφρονίζω, Σωφρονισμός, Σωφροσύνη," explains: "He is using the term in its classical sense: 'to observe the proper measure,' 'not to transgress the set laws.' . . . But Paul defines this measure as the μέτρον πίστεως which God gives and which is exhibited in integration into the community and concrete service within it."

54. On the connection between Paul's household code and Hellenistic philosophical tradition, see Zöckler, *Tugendlehre des Christentums*, 7–12; and Weidinger, *Haustafeln*, 51–73.

55. Lea and Griffin, *1, 2 Timothy, Titus*, 300.

guidelines that they should be "above reproach, the husband of one wife, sober-minded, self-controlled [σώφρονα/sōphrona], respectable, hospitable, able to teach, not a drunkard, not violent but gentle, not quarrelsome, not a lover of money" (1 Tim 3:2–3).[56] Being self-controlled, along with the other virtues listed, seem to be contrasted with unethical behavior like drunkenness, violence, anger, and greed.[57]

First Peter 4:7–8 also connects *sōphroneō* with the importance of living prayerful and loving lives because of the imminence of the end times.[58] That virtuous living is intended here is apparent from the previous verses of the chapter which state that Christians should have the "same way of thinking" as Christ so that one ceases sinning (1 Pet 4:1), not to live for "human passions" (1 Pet 4:2), and not to emulate the gentile practices of "sensuality, passions, drunkenness, orgies, drinking parties, and lawless idolatry" (1 Pet 4:3). The priority of ethical living in light of the end times is a theme in other New Testament texts (Matt 3:2; 4:17; 25:10–13; Rom 13:12; Phil 4:5; Heb 10:25; James 5:8; 2 Pet 3:11; Rev 1:3) and should inform our understanding of what *sōphroneō* is meant to communicate.[59]

Early Christian writers appear to have used this word to refer to Christian ethics as well. The first-century-CE work 1 Clement, for example, states: "As touching those things which befit our religion and are most useful for a virtuous life to such as would guide [their steps] in holiness and righteousness, we have written fully unto you, brethren. For concerning faith and repentance and genuine love and temperance [σωφροσύνης/sōphrosynēs] and sobriety and patience we have handled every argument."[60] Furthermore, in Ignatius's *Letter to the Ephesians* he encourages the community to abide in Christ "in all purity and temperance [σωφροσύνη/sōphrosynē]," to contrast letting "no herb of the devil be found in you."[61] Elsewhere in Christian writings it is used of sexual chastity.[62]

56. In this passage sober-minded and self-controlled are set side-by-side. The word "sober-minded" (νηφάλιος/nēphalios) advocates for moderation with alcohol.

57. Towner, *Letters to Timothy and Titus*, 208, connects Paul's instructions here with Hellenistic ethics and emphasizes that "moral change is central" to the word. Mounce, *Pastoral Epistles*, 173, 391, notes that it can often have a sense of sexual self-control and discipline.

58. See Hiebert, "Living"; and Goppelt, *Petrusbrief*, 282.

59. Achtemeier, *1 Peter*, 294, says, "The verb underlying the first imperative (σωφρονέω) describes the ability to see things clearly for what they are, and hence to act in a way appropriate to the prevailing circumstances, in this instance the imminent consummation of the age."

60. 1 Clem. 62:1–2.

61. Ign. *Eph.* 10.3.

62. Acts Thom. 150; Acts John 59.

An important passage in 2 Corinthians, which will be commented on in a later chapter, should be addressed briefly here too. Paul contrasts ecstasy and sound-mindedness apparently in the context of his opponents:

> We are not commending ourselves to you again but giving you cause to boast about us, so that you may be able to answer those who boast about outward appearance and not about what is in the heart. For if we are beside ourselves [*existēmi*], it is for God; if we are in our right mind [*sōphroneō*], it is for you. For the love of Christ controls us, because we have concluded this: that one has died for all, therefore all have died. (2 Cor 5:12–14)

In 2 Corinthians, Paul criticizes a group he sarcastically refers to as superapostles, who seemingly were an influential group who may have emphasized ecstatic experiences (2 Cor 11:4–5; 12:11). Paul is obviously not against ecstatic experiences since he himself had them (Acts 22:17). Indeed, Paul says that if he and his companions are in an ecstasy, it is *for* God.[63] Rather, Paul is concerned with the improper emphasis on them, especially as supposed proof of hyper-spirituality and as a way of claiming undue authority.[64]

This may be what Paul means when he refers to them boasting about "outward appearance" (i.e., ecstasy) as opposed to "what is in the heart" (i.e., ethical integrity). Throughout these passages, the instructions pertaining to sound-mindedness are predominantly about Christian behavior, not cognitive function. Indeed, the only three places where a contrast is made between rational cognition and irrationality is in the case of the demoniac in the Gospels, Paul in Acts, and Paul's statement in 2 Cor 5. Yet, obviously in these cases, the Bible is not saying anything of the inherent value or moral weight of such experiences. Paul is not suggesting that individuals should not have ASCs, as he himself and Peter did. Paul's major concern is regarding ethical behavior, not manifestations of the Spirit. Obviously, being in an ASC is not an excuse for acting inappropriately or unethically. One, for example, can see how individuals may fake ASCs in their faith communities as a way to elevate themselves or draw attention to themselves in the assembly for their own gain. When one is overcome by God, the fruit of an ASC is that they make godly decisions, choices, and judgments on matters of faith

---

63. Paul here uses the so-called dative of advantage. See Porter, *Idioms*, 98.

64. *TDNT*, s.v. "Σώφρων, Σωφρονέω, Σωφρονίζω, Σωφρονισμός, Σωφροσύνη": "In 2 C. 5:13 Paul sets the conduct of the pneumatics in contrast to σωφρονέω. Here, too, the concern for the community which faith imposes is illustrated by the example of the apostle. Sober devotion to one's brother corresponds to ecstasy before God. For this puts into effect the love of Christ which consists in His self-sacrifice and which at the same time demands sacrifice from Christians, 2 C. 5:14."

and practice. But being "sober minded" does not in and of itself mean that a person experiencing an ASC is somehow not obeying Paul's command.

Automatism

In his definition of trance, former professor of psychology at Wheaton College David M. Wulff states it is

> a state of profound absorption frequently accompanied by vocal and motor automatisms that in some contexts are interpreted as signs of spirit possession.[65]

Wulff's definition introduces a number of new terms such as "automatisms" and "spirit possession," which themselves are debated among academics, but are helpful for getting a handle on what kind of features are present during an ASC. While automatism is not a common term used among everyday Christians, it is a useful categorical label for understanding the physical and vocal manifestations of those experiencing a trance or ecstasy.[66]

Automatism comes from the Greek word αὐτόματος/*automatos* and is where we get our English word "automatic."[67] Its meaning relates to something happening of its own accord without an obviously observable agent affecting it. It is used, for example, in the instance when the gates of a city opened by themselves for Peter in Acts 12:10. In Josh 6:5 LXX the conquest of Jericho is described as follows: "When they shout, the walls of the city will collapse spontaneously [*automatos*], and all the people will go in, rushing, each headlong into the city."[68]

---

65. Wulff, *Psychology of Religion*, 29–30.

66. On the general topic of automatisms, see especially Wegner, *Illusion of Conscious Will*, 93–135. Fenwick, "Automatism, Medicine," 4, defines automatism as follows: "An automatism is an involuntary piece of behaviour over which an individual has no control. The behaviour itself is usually inappropriate to the circumstances, and may be out of character for the individual. It can be complex, coordinated, and apparently purposeful and directed, though lacking in judgement. Afterwards, the individual may have no recollection, or only partial and confused memory, of his actions."

67. BDAG, s.v. "αὐτόματος"; LSJ, s.v. "αὐτόμᾰτος."

68. Compare the use of the term in Xenophon, *Hell.* 6.4.7 (fourth century BCE): "Besides this, they were also somewhat encouraged by the oracle which was reported—that the Lacedaemonians were destined to be defeated at the spot where stood the monument of the virgins, who are said to have killed themselves because they had been violated by certain Lacedaemonians. The Thebans accordingly decorated this monument before the battle. Furthermore, reports were brought to them from the city that all the temples were opening of themselves [*automatos*], and that the priestesses said that the gods revealed victory."

Likewise, Job 24:24 LXX talks about "an ear of corn falling off on its own [*automatos*] from the stalk." The author of the Jewish apocryphal book Wisdom of Solomon talks about the Egyptian plague of darkness as follows: "Nothing was shining through to them except a dreadful, self-kindled [*automatos*] fire" (17:6).[69] The opposite of *automatos* is ἑκούσιος/*hekousios*, which is doing something of your own volition.[70] Paul, for example, states in Phlm 14 that "I preferred to do nothing without your consent in order that your goodness might not be by compulsion but of your own accord [*hekousios*]."[71] The Septuagint (LXX) uses the word to refer to the "freewill offering" mentioned in Leviticus: "But if he offers a vow or a freewill offering [*hekousios*] as his offering, on whatever day he presents his offering, it must be eaten on the next day" (7:6 LXX).[72]

Automatism in our context refers to the involuntary movements or speech of a person while in a trance state or ecstasy. When a doctor checks your reflexes and you spontaneously kick your leg forward, this is an example of what is sometimes called "motor automatism."

Another example includes sleepwalking, in which your unconscious mind is moving your body without your direct knowledge. Another form, "verbal automatism," includes spontaneous speech of differing kinds, such as praise, prophecy, or glossolalia (speaking in tongues). Automatism is a neutral academic term that says nothing of the origins of such motions or speech acts. Such manifestations could be the product of divine, demonic, or human activity. When the priests were unable to stand because "the house of the Lord, was filled with a cloud . . . for the glory of the Lord filled the house of God" (2 Chr 5:13–14), this may indicate a motor automatism. Similarly, the demoniac in Mark 9:18 is thrown into convulsions against his will. It is likewise possible to read Elisabeth's outburst when she "was filled with the Holy Spirit" and "exclaimed with a loud cry" (Luke 1:41–42) as a form of verbal automatism.

It is often argued that automatisms cannot be from God based on passages in the New Testament concerned with "self-control" (e.g., Gal 5:23).

---

69. Compare the use of fire also in Herodotus, *Hist.* 2.180.1 (fifth century BCE): "It happened in the reign of Amasis that the temple of Delphi had been accidentally [*automatos*] burnt."

70. BDAG, s.v. "ἑκούσιος"; LSJ, s.v. "ἑκούσιος"; L&N, s.v. "ἑκούσιος,"; *TDNT*, s.v. "ἑκούσιος."

71. Fitzmyer, *Philemon*, 112.

72. Cf. T. Dan 4:6: (second century BCE): "If you lose something, by your own action [*hekousios*] or otherwise, do not be sorrowful, for grief arouses anger as well as deceit." 1 Macc 2:42 uses the verbal form ἑκουσιάζομαι/*hekousiázomai*: "Then there united with them a company of Hasideans, mighty warriors of Israel, all who offered themselves willingly [*hekousiázomai*] for the law."

If self-control is a fruit of the Spirit, how can we even suggest that the Spirit would make people do things seemingly out of control? This logic, much like the issue of being sober minded, is based on a faulty understanding of the underlying Greek text. The self-control being spoken of by Paul is not about automatisms, but again about ethics. The Greek word translated "self-control" in English Bibles is the Greek word ἐγκράτεια/egkrateia. This word is used in ancient Greek philosophical works,[73] contemporary Jewish texts from around the turn of the era, and early Christian works with ethical ramifications.

In the fourth century BCE, Xenophon used this word in the explicit context of ethical living: "But the greatest blessing that befalls the man who yearns to render his favorite a good friend is the necessity of himself making virtue his habitual practice. For one cannot produce goodness in his companion while his own conduct is evil, nor can he himself exhibit shamelessness and incontinence and at the same time render his beloved self-controlled [ἐγκρατῆ/egkratē] and reverent."[74] Similarly, Plato discussed how the use of alcohol will cause young men to lose self-control because of their literal inebriation which in turn would lead to debauchery.[75] Indeed, it is said that "self-control [ἐγκράτεια/egkrateia] is the foundation of every virtue recommended and practiced by Socrates."[76]

Jewish writers also understood the word in this sense. Philo says that God has given humanity self-control so that they are not dominated by the avaricious appetite for food, slander, and sex.[77] In one instance, Philo contrasts self-control with "devotion to pleasure" (φιληδονίας/philēdonias).[78] He also refers to it as the "most useful of all virtues."[79] Josephus, in a well-known passage about the ascetic Jewish group that produced the Dead Sea Scrolls, writes:

> These Essenes reject pleasures as an evil, but esteem continence [ἐγκράτειαν/egkrateian], and the conquest over our passions, to be virtue. They neglect wedlock, but choose out other persons' children, while they are pliable, and fit for learning; and esteem them to be of their kindred, and form them according to their own manners. They do not absolutely deny the fitness

---

73. *TDNT*, s.v. "Ἐγκράτεια (ἀκρασία), Ἐγκρατής (ἀκρατής), Ἐγκρατεύομαι."
74. Xenophon, *Symp.* 8.27.
75. Plato, *Resp.* 390b.
76. Xenophon, *Mem.* 1.5.
77. Philo, *Worse* 101ff; cf. Philo, *Spec. Laws* 2.195.
78. Philo, *Abraham* 24.
79. Philo, *Spec. Laws* 1.173.

of marriage, and the succession of mankind thereby continued; but they guard against the lascivious behavior of women, and are persuaded that none of them preserve their fidelity to one man.[80]

The word *egkrateia* is sometimes used in contexts of sexual ethics. In the work Testament of Naphtali (second century BCE), for example, we read: "For there is a season for a man to embrace his wife, and a season to abstain [ἐγκρατείας/*egkrateias*] therefrom for his prayer."[81] Similarly, Paul uses the verbal form of this word to refer to abstaining from sex in 1 Cor 7:9: "But if they cannot exercise self-control [ἐγκρατεύονται/*egkrateuontai*], they should marry. For it is better to marry than to burn with passion." Elsewhere, self-control is understood generally as not indulging one's basic human urges,[82] rigorous training (Acts 9:25), and later Christian works use it in reference to general ethical behavior.[83]

---

80. Josephus, *J.W.* 2.120–21.

81. T. Naph. 8:8.

82. Sir 18:30 (second century BCE): "Do not follow your base desires, but restrain your appetites"; 4 Macc 5:34 (first century CE): "I will not play false to you, O law that trained me, nor will I renounce you, beloved self-control [*egkrateia*]"; Wis 8:7 (first century BCE–first century CE): "And if anyone loves righteousness, her labors are virtues; for she teaches self-control [*sōphrosynēn*] and prudence, justice and courage."

83. 1 Clem. 30:3 (first century CE): "Let us therefore cleave unto those to whom grace is given from God. Let us clothe ourselves in concord, being lowly-minded and temperate [ἐγκρατεύομαι / *enkrateuomai*], holding ourselves aloof from all backbiting and evil speaking, being justified by works and not by words"; 1 Clem. 35:2: "Life in immortality, splendour in righteousness, truth in boldness, faith in confidence, temperance [*egkrateia*] in sanctification! And all these things fall under our apprehension"; 1 Clem. 62:2: "For concerning faith and repentance and genuine love and temperance [*egkrateia*] and sobriety and patience we have handled every argument, putting you in remembrance, that ye ought to please Almighty God in righteousness and truth and long-suffering with holiness, laying aside malice and pursuing concord in love and peace, being instant in gentleness; even as our fathers, of whom we spake before, pleased Him, being lowly-minded towards their Father and God and Creator and towards all men"; 1 Clem. 64: "Finally may the All-seeing God and Master of spirits and Lord of all flesh, who chose the Lord Jesus Christ, and us through Him for a peculiar people, grant unto every soul that is called after His excellent and holy Name faith, fear, peace, patience, long-suffering, temperance [*egkrateia*], chastity and soberness, that they may be well-pleasing unto His Name through our High-priest and Guardian Jesus Christ, through whom unto Him be glory and majesty, might and honour, both now and for ever and ever. Amen"; Barn. 2:2 (first–second century CE): "The aids of our faith then are fear and patience, and our allies are long-suffering and self-restraint [*egkrateia*]"; Herm. Mand. 8.6–9 (first–second century CE): "'Be thou temperate, therefore, and refrain from all these things, that thou mayest live unto God, and be enrolled among those who exercise self-restraint [*enkrateuomai*] in them. These then are the things from which thou shouldest restrain thyself. Now hear,' saith he, 'the things, in

The opposite of *egkrateia* is ἀκρατής/*akratēs* or ἀκρασία/*akrasia*. Jesus criticizes the Pharisees for such a lack of self-control when he says: "Woe to you, scribes and Pharisees, hypocrites! For you clean the outside of the cup and the plate, but inside they are full of greed and self-indulgence [ἀκρασίας/*akrasias*]" (Matt 23:25). Likewise, Paul in 2 Tim 3:3 states that in the last days people will be "without self-control" (ἀκρατεῖς/*akrateis*) alongside a long list of vices. That Paul understands the word *egkrateia* as ethical in nature seems to be corroborated by its appearance in Acts 24:25 where "self-control" is used in parallel with "righteousness" (δικαιοσύνη/*dikaiosynē*). Finally, in 2 Pet 1:5–6, self-control is listed alongside commands to live out the Christian faith with "virtue" (ἀρετή/*aretē*).

In light of these examples, it seems best to understand Paul's list of spiritual fruit(s) as having to do with controlling our bodies in a holy way. In First Corinthians, Paul uses the analogy of athletic training as a metaphor for exercising self-control in one's life so that he won't be "disqualified" (1 Cor 9:25–27). For Paul, this disciplining of the body is meant to instruct Christians who may be tempted to "desire evil" like the ancient Israelites (1 Cor 10:1–6). Thus, the argument that self-control does not allow for automatisms is simply incorrect. Evidently, many people in the Bible did seemingly lose control of their bodies. Abraham, Adam, and Daniel fall into trances, Saul prophesies naked all night long on the ground, and many others fall or spontaneously blurt out prophetic oracles or cries by the Spirit of God.

Spirit Possession

Christians who hear the term "spirit possession" are likely quick to relegate this to the realm of the demonic. Indeed, demon possession is one form of spirit possession, but it is not the only kind. Spirit possession is another neutral term that is related to ASCs. Eric Eve explains it as follows:

> "Spirit possession" is a category that encompasses demonic possession, but includes many other things besides. Demon possession is the form of spirit possession that a particular society

---

which thou shouldest not exercise self-restraint [*enkrateuomai*], but do them. Exercise no self-restraint [*enkrateuomai*] in that which is good, but do it.' 'Sir,' say I, 'show me the power of the good also, that I may walk in them and serve them, that doing them it may be possible for me to be saved.' 'Hear,' saith he, 'the works of the good likewise, which thou must do, and towards which thou must exercise no self-restraint [*enkrateuomai*]. First of all, there is faith, fear of the Lord, love, concord, words of righteousness, truth, patience; nothing is better than these in the life of men. If a man keep these, and exercise not self-restraint [*enkrateuomai*] from them, he becomes blessed in his life.'"

regards as pathological, an illness that needs to be dealt with. But spirit possession can also include phenomena that particular societies evaluate positively, including shamanism (or more generally, spirit control) and spirit mediumship. In connexion [sic] with the New Testament the potential interest of spirit possession extends beyond demonic possession into fields such as glossolalia, inspirited prophecy and the ability to heal and work miracles.[84]

Spirit possession as a category of human experience has been hotly debated and often has resulted in many methodologies, models, and categories created by scholars to understand what it is, how it happens, and why it occurs. While some Christians may find this strange and simply ask, "What's complicated about it?" spirit possession involves more than the Hollywood representation of people speaking in guttural voices, levitating, or having special knowledge. Does, for example, Janice Boddy's definition of "the hold exerted over a human being by external forces or entities more powerful than she," adequately explain what spirit possession is?[85] How should one go about defining it?

Spirit possession is often understood in social terms. In his influential work *Ecstatic Religion: A Study of Shamanism and Spirit Possession* (1971), Lewis differentiates between two major forms of spirit possession: "peripheral" and "central."[86]

Central spirit possession is understood as possession experienced by the dominant social group while peripheral spirit possession affects those on the fringes of society and thus represents a method for resisting or combatting those of the dominant group. Of the latter, one may immediately think of the sometimes-eccentric activities of the biblical prophets, living on the margins of society and fighting against the corrupt priesthood or ruling elite. Indeed, ecstatic activity representative of Spirit possession among Israel's prophets could plausibly be interpreted within Lewis's binary: the false prophets, propped up by the upper class vs. the true prophets of God that fight for the marginalized on the outskirts.

Spirit possession is often a feature of those who experience trauma, especially as a result of colonization.[87] The reason for this connection may be the dissociative trauma response undergone by victims as a means to

---

84. Eve, *Jewish Context*, 368.
85. Boddy, "Spirit Possession Revisited," 407.
86. Lewis, *Ecstatic Religion*, 30.
87. See Rothenberg, *Spirits of Palestine*; Stoller, *Embodying Colonial Memories*; Hüwelmeier, "Spirit Writing in Vietnam"; and Crosson, "What Possessed You?"

process or deal with that trauma, though this is debated.[88] It is not possible here to go into detail of all that this entails, such as the connection between mental health and spirit phenomena, and other related topics. Yet, it is important to understand that at an anthropological level, spirit possession and social factors are often intertwined and should inform our view of this phenomenon more broadly.

One working definition of spirit possession is supplied by the anthropologist Vincent Crapanzano:

> Spirit possession can refer to a spectrum of experiences in which the person involved negotiates with or is overcome by a force such as an ancestor, deity, or spirit that employs the human body to be its vehicle for communicating to human communities.[89]

The idea of negotiation is noteworthy. Spirit possession differs from culture to culture. How one interprets these spirits (whether as deceased ancestors, animistic spirits, demons, etc.) changes how one negotiates with these spirits and in turn affects the possession experience. While most Western Christians immediately associate spirit possession with witchcraft, uncontrolled frenzy, or mental derangement, this is not always the case cross-culturally. In various contexts, people seek to become spirit possessed, sometimes through appeasing the spirit(s) in question, so that they can reap some benefit. Various cultures frequently differentiate between beneficial and harmful forms of spirit possession. As Bazzana explains: "'Possession' does not always manifest itself as the complete surrendering of self-control but entails several alternative articulations of the relationship between 'hosts' and 'spirits.'"[90]

The word "possession" or "possessed" also carries ambiguity. Who is doing the possessing? We typically conceive of the spirit possessing the human. Yet, as Bazzana states:

> When one attends more closely to the grammatical and semantic peculiarities of the English phrase "spirit possession," it becomes clear that it enshrines a potentially productive ambiguity. Understanding it as meaning that "spirits" possess (and as a matter of fact, control) their human "hosts" is not the only interpretive option. In fact, one might as well take the label

---

88. Schaffler et al., "Traumatic Experience and Somatoform."
89. *ER*, s.v. "Spirit Possession."
90. Bazzana, *Having the Spirit*, 17.

"spirit possession" to mean that "hosts" do possess (and thus, to a certain extent, control) their "spirits."[91]

In other words, spirit possession can refer to either the spirit possessing the human or the human possessing the spirit, or some mix of both. Although this may greatly expand and, in some instances, distort the picture of spirit possession in the biblical text, I think Bazzana is right in pointing out the usefulness of this ambiguity. It will be incumbent on the reader to determine in what sense spirit possession is occurring in a given passage and what this can tell us about ASCs more generally.

Scholars sometimes consider spirit possession a form of artistry or theater.[92] By this it is meant that there is a cultural and religious script that one is consciously or subconsciously aware of and can be imitated. It is important here, however, to note that this does not mean all spirit possession is fake (although some instances certainly are). Rather, it means that whether or not a spirit is really involved in the possession experience, the person still acts in ways understood to be spirit possession by them and/or their audience. Indeed, they may still enter an altered state of consciousness and have involuntary physical spasms, among other features.

Spirit possession is, in one sense, a basic human experience that anyone is capable of, though more frequently in areas and tribal cultures where beliefs in spirits pervade (animism). In a landmark study, the anthropologist Erika Bourguignon found that over 90 percent of cultures around the world demonstrate ASCs and over 50 percent are witness to various forms of spirit possession.[93]

While many non-Christian cultures view spirit possession as potentially causing negative side effects such as sickness, in other cultures spirit possession can be seen as positive or desired, elevating the individual during certain ritual and religious contexts. Children in southeastern Côte d'Ivoire, for example, drum, dance, and chant in order to become possessed by nature (*boson*) spirits.[94] Likewise, practitioners of Haitian voodoo seek spirit possession to facilitate advice and healing.

Two categories of trance are proposed by Bourguignon: "possession trance" and the more generic "trance." She explains it as follows: "We have found it useful to group these into two broad types: (1) states interpreted

---

91. Bazzana, *Having the Spirit*, 17.

92. Levack, *Devil Within*, 141–68.

93. Bourguignon, "World Distribution and Patterns." To better understand spirit possession from an anthropological view, see Bourguignon, *Religion*; and Goodman, *Ecstasy, Ritual*.

94. Duchesne, "Children's Game."

by the societies in which they occur as due to possession by spirits (termed "possession trance" [PT]), and (2) states not so interpreted (termed "trance" [T]).[95] Such a distinction is important. One can enter a trance without the aid of spirits. Likewise, someone can be influenced by spirits but not exhibit the atypical symptoms often associated with possession. How one interprets the cause of the trance is culturally determined. According to Bourguignon, possession trance is marked by "alterations or discontinuity in consciousness, awareness, personality, or other aspects of psychological functioning."[96] Some forms of trance, such as what Bourguignon calls "visionary trance" are quite passive, whereas possession trance is a more "overt, often highly active performance."[97]

Naturally, Christians tend to interpret all invading spirits as demons, but the Bible also speaks of instances where a person becomes possessed by God's Spirit. This form of Spirit possession is expressed in different ways and in different forms in the Hebrew Bible. Some kind of spontaneous Spirit possession takes place through the charismatic abilities of the judges (Judg 3:10; 6:34; 11:29; 13:25; 14:6–19; 15:14–15). God's Spirit temporarily or permanently possesses people in leadership roles such as with Saul and David (1 Sam 10:6–10; 11:6; 16:13–14).

Bourguignon identifies what is probably obvious to most—that possession experiences can be generally categorized as either positive or negative.[98] Lewis, on the other hand, prefers the binary of controlled and uncontrolled or solicited and unsolicited.[99] These latter categories, however, are somewhat problematic when applied broadly to the Bible. While demonic possession obviously can be categorized by Christians as negative or uncontrolled, possession by God's Spirit at times likewise seems to be unsolicited and uncontrolled, such as the aforementioned Saul or even the prophet Ezekiel.

Indeed, in many instances, prophets suddenly have the Spirit come upon them (Num 24:2; 1 Sam 19:20–24; 2 Kgs 3:15; 2 Chr 20:14). The terminology for these experiences in the Hebrew Bible includes stating that the Spirit "was upon" (עָלָיו/ʿālāyw), "clothed" (לבשׁ/lbš),[100] "stirred" (פעם/pʿm),[101] and

95. Bourguignon, *Religion*, 12.
96. Bourguignon, *Possession*, 8–9.
97. Bourguignon, *Religion*, 15.
98. See Bourguignon, "World Distribution and Patterns."
99. Lewis, *Ecstatic Religion*, 49.
100. Judg 6:34 LXX has either "strengthened" (ἐνεδυνάμωσεν/enedynamōsen) or "clothed" (ἐνέδυσεν/enedysen) depending on the manuscript.
101. Judg 13:25 LXX has "go together" (either συνεκπορεύεσθαι/synekporeuesthai or συμπορεύεσθαι/symporeuesthai depending on the manuscript).

"rushed/forced" (צלח/ṣlḥ)[102] the individual. The choice of these words makes sense. A person who has the Spirit "come upon" them suggests that they are being overcome by or overpowered by the Spirit.[103] The Spirit-possessed person can also be said to be "clothed" by God, that is, God either puts them on like a garment, or the individual puts on God. Most interesting is the idea that God's Spirit "rushes upon" (ṣlḥ) individuals. The Hebrew word ṣlḥ has several meanings. In one verbal form (the *hiphil*), it often means "to succeed." Trees ṣlḥ or "thrive" (Ps 1:3; Ezek 17:9), weapons ṣlḥ or "prosper" (Isa 54:17), and journeys ṣlḥ or end as planned (Judg 18:5). In another verbal form (the *Qal*), the meaning of ṣlḥ includes "to penetrate" or "to force entry." The word is used in 2 Sam 19:17 to talk about a group that "rushed down" to the Jordan river. It is also used in Amos 5:6 to refer to God breaking out "like fire" to destroy his opponents. The word ṣlḥ may therefore indicate a forceful entry into the human body, perhaps evidenced by observable phenomena such as supernatural feats or frenzied behavior (e.g., 1 Sam 19:20–24).

The New Testament likewise contains diverse ways of expressing Spirit possession. One can "receive" or "take grasp of" (λαμβάνω/*lambanō*) the Spirit (John 20:22; Gal 3:2), have the Spirit "placed upon" (τίθημι ἐπί/*tithēmi epi*) or "be upon" (εἰμί ἐπί/*eimi epi*) them (Matt 12:18; Luke 2:25; Acts 1:8), be "filled" (πίμπλημι/*pimplēmi*) with the Spirit (Luke 1:15, 41, 67; Acts 2:4; 4:8; 4:31; 9:17; 13:9; 13:52; Eph 5:18), be "given" (δίδωμι/*didōmi*) the Spirit (Luke 11:13; John 3:34; 7:39), have the Spirit "dwell" (μένω/*menō*) in them (John 14:17; Rom 8:9, 11), have the Spirit "intercede" (ὑπερεντυγχάνω/*hyperentynchanō*) for them (Rom 8:26), host the Spirit as a temple (1 Cor 3:16), and become "joined" (κολλάω/*kollaō*) with the Spirit (1 Cor 6:17).

The idea of being possessed by God is used in some contemporary charismatic Christian contexts. Both John Crowder and Heidi Baker, for example, talk about being possessed by God, an expression meant to reflect submission and rendering control over to God as a form of obedience.[104]

---

102. 1 Kgdms 10:6, 11:6, and 16:13 LXX translates ṣlḥ as "spring/leap" (ἐφαλεῖται/ *ephaleitai*).

103. This and similar phraseology appears of spirit phenomena affecting humans, such as ritual impurity (Lev 15:24) and curses (Deut 29:20).

104. Also consider the following explanation of divine possession by Julius Pollux (second–third century CE), *Onom*. 1.15–18: "If somewhere there might be a prophetic spirit, the topic would include being full of the god, inspired, possessed, under divine influence, and taken hold of by a god. Just as the man delivering an oracle also is described as possessed by a god and moved by a god, frenzied, full of the god, transforming by the god, the spirit would speak a prophetic vapor, a miraculous breath, a divine breeze, a prophetic wind, and a voice of divination. The verbs used for such things befalling a man include to be possessed, to be taken hold of, to be inspired, to be frenzied, to be filled with the god. Being inspired means cacophony. The nouns

In this book, I use the term Spirit possessed (with a capital S) to refer to someone who is possessed by God's Spirit or, to follow Bazzana's proposal surrounding the ambiguity of the phrase spirit possession, someone who possesses God's Spirit. Otherwise, I use the term spirit possessed (with a lowercase s) or demon possessed to indicate that some other spirit is at work. Obviously not everyone who simply has the Spirit of God experiences trance, ecstasy, or ASCs. Yet, in some instances this is surely the case, and so Spirit possession becomes a useful category to explain why someone is having such an experience.

The Septuagint

The Septuagint is an ancient Greek translation of the Hebrew Bible. It is important to understand what the Septuagint is as it will become apparent that its translators had a particular interpretation of various words and narratives from the Hebrew text, especially as it related to trance and ecstasy.[105] The Septuagint is called such because of a legend (whether totally historical or not) preserved in the writings of Josephus, Philo, later rabbinic sources, and a work called the *Letter of Aristeas* (third century BCE–first century CE). These various sources reveal that seventy (sometimes seventy-two) Jewish translators were tasked by the Greek king Ptolemy II Philadelphus (285–246 BCE) to translate the Hebrew scriptures into Greek for his library collection. The Latin term "Septuagint" is often abbreviated with the Roman numerals LXX (L = 50 + X = 10 + X = 10 = 70). Hence, when a text is referred to as "Exodus LXX," for example, this means that it is the Greek version of Exodus under discussion, rather than the traditional Hebrew (sometimes called Masoretic) text. The Septuagint was produced between the third century BCE and the first century CE, but copies of the text date from various time periods. The Septuagint is preserved mainly in three later codices (books) called Codex Sinaiticus (mid-fourth century CE), Codex Vaticanus (early to mid-fourth century CE), and Codex Alexandrinus (early fifth century CE);

---

for this concept include possession, descent of a god, trance, possession by a spirit, divine inspiration, inspiration by a spirit, frenzy, being moved by a god, being seized, enthusiasm. Just as also the adverbs, under inspiration of a god, by inspiration of a spirit, by possession, under enthusiasm, by divine inspiration, by divine frenzy." Special thanks to Barry Hofstetter who supplied this translation (August 2017) in the academic Facebook group Nerdy Biblical Language Majors (formerly Nerdy Language Majors), https://www.facebook.com/groups/NerdyLanguageMajors/.

105. For introductions to the Septuagint, I invite readers to consult the following: Dines, *Septuagint*; Marcos, *Septuagint in Context*; and Jobes and Silva, *Invitation to the Septuagint*.

some Dead Sea Scrolls manuscripts (second century BCE–first century CE); and later medieval manuscripts. In addition to the Septuagint, three other Greek versions of the Old Testament exist called Aquila (second century CE), Theodotion (second–third century CE), and Symmachus (early third century CE), named after the men who produced them.[106]

In summary, the Septuagint is one of our earliest witnesses of how Jews interpreted the narratives we are going to analyze throughout this book. This of course does not mean that the Septuagint's interpretation is the "correct" one.[107] Rather, I believe it will help the reader to see that these interpretations are not simply modern inventions or eisegesis, but have a historical precedent within biblical interpretation. Additionally, the Septuagint will aid us in lexical study of a word's probable connotations. Finally, the Septuagint was produced by various authors over several centuries, which gives us multiple voices of interpretation, not a monolithic perspective.

Conclusion

Having looked at a number of terms that will be recurring throughout this book, we can now turn our attention to the Hebrew Bible and New Testament. Prayerfully explore these stories with an open mind to learn and consider the possibilities of God's Spirit in the life of the Christian and how this might manifest. I encourage those who may be resistant to the interpretations offered in this book to ask themselves why they may have never heard such explanations of certain passages. Is it due to a lack of exposure to alternative theological camps? Is it simply that this is a foreign topic that is not often discussed in your church circles? Is it because some commentaries make no mention of these features? Or is it because it just seems weird? Whatever the reason, my hope is that, if nothing else, you will be able to read some of these stories with fresh eyes.

---

106. Other sources for the Greek Old Testament exist as well, including the Lucianic text produced by Lucian of Antioch (ca. 240–312 CE) and a six-columned work called the *hexapla*, produced by Origen of Alexandria (ca. 185–ca. 253 CE), though few examples of the latter exist.

107. A perfect example exists in Ps 115:2 LXX (Ps 116:11), where the psalmist says, "I said in my entrancement [*ekstasis*], every person is a liar." The LXX is translating the Hebrew word חָפַז/*châphaz*, which means something like "amazement" or "alarm." This confusion in the Septuagint lead Augustine to comment, "By trance he means fear, which when persecutors threaten, and when the sufferings of torture or death impend, human weakness suffers. For this we understand, because in this Psalm the voice of Martyrs is heard. For trance is used in another sense also, when the mind is not beside itself by fear, but is possessed by some inspiration of revelation." *Enarrat. Ps.* 116, 8.

2

Getting Tipsy with the Torah

> For I tell you this: one loving, blind desire for God alone is more valuable in itself, more pleasing to God and to the saints, more beneficial to your own growth, and more helpful to your friends, both living and dead, than anything else you could do.
>
> —Anonymous, *The Cloud of Unknowing*

IT IS QUITE POSSIBLE that, depending on what translation(s) of the Bible you have read, you have never even noticed the presence of trance or ecstasy within the First Testament. This is an unfortunate predicament, but not because Bible translators have been trying to downplay these elements within the text. Indeed, biblical scholars and ancient readers have recognized these features of the text for millennia. Bible translations are, generally speaking, created through committees with multiple teams working on different books all trying to offer an informed, consistent, but accessible translation for general audiences.[1]

As a result, interpretive choices must be made, whether to conform to good English style, and to some degree an adherence to traditional liturgical sensibilities such as Psalm 23 or the Lord's Prayer. Indeed, there are a number of interconnected and complicated factors involved in Bible

---

[1]. The most comprehensive, up-to-date book on the topic is Mark L. Strauss's *40 Questions About Bible Translation*.

translation and interpretation, particularly in the passages we will look at in these chapters.

One of the first problems we run into is that there are some words that have multiple meanings in their original languages. Additionally, some words are simply unknown to modern interpreters. The Old Testament was written in Hebrew (and some Aramaic). When a word is used only a few times in Scripture, biblical scholars rely on lexical studies from other related languages to help determine their meaning (a word that only appears once in the Bible is referred to as a hapax legomenon). In order to ascertain the meaning of some Hebrew terms, scholars rely on other Semitic languages such as Akkadian, Syriac, Ugaritic, Arabic, and Ethiopic to shed light on the potential definition of a word. Scholars also look closely at the Septuagint, the Greek translation of the Old Testament, to see how the Greek translators understood a Hebrew term, which may help uncover a word's meaning.

Another problem with discussing ASCs in the Bible is that, in most cases, the Scriptures do not give us detailed accounts of the physiological or psychological effects that someone endures while experiencing an ASC. Thus, we are stuck with teasing out some of these details based on what is recorded. Certain phrases and prepositions help us make sense of how a trance state or ecstasy was initiated, but it does not always tell us how it manifested aesthetically.

Whatever we might find in the Scriptures, there will still be debate about its interpretation among Christians based on their presuppositions of how the Spirit operates. Thus, even though I believe there is compelling evidence for trance and ecstasy in the Bible, individual readers will need to decide for themselves what to make of the present analysis. Thus, we must figure out based on contextual clues what the Bible says about trance and ecstasy. In the following chapters I have attempted to cover every relevant passage in the Hebrew Bible that speaks to this subject and have synthesized the findings here. I have tried to maintain a chronological reading of the texts. In other words, while some studies of trance and ecstasy would typically start with the story of Saul in 1 Sam 10 and 19, I have instead situated those narratives within the broader narrative of the Hebrew Bible. I have done this primarily to show that, even if the story of Saul were not present, we would still have evidence for trance and ecstasy in the Old Testament. Saul's narratives certainly give us a prolonged window into the psychological and physiological activities of one experiencing these phenomena, but they are not the cornerstone on which to build a theological system. Indeed, as I will show, a preponderance of episodes from the Hebrew Bible touch on the topics of trance and ecstasy, many of which have been seemingly ignored or overlooked by proponents and opponents of spiritual drunkenness alike!

Trance and Ecstasy in the Ancient Near East

When discussing the Hebrew Bible, scholars often try to contextualize the narratives and events within their ANE context. The ANE is a modern way of speaking about the geographical locations that correspond to events found in the Old Testament. These include regions like Egypt, Mesopotamia, Assyria, and Babylon. Israel serves as a land bridge between Asia, Africa, and Europe, and travel between them would have involved passing through Israel. Due to the geographical situation of Israel, international trade and dialogue between various religious and cultural traditions was unavoidable.[2] Over the course of the last two centuries, archaeological digs in these regions have unearthed important documents for understanding the worldview of the people who lived in these areas. Hundreds of thousands of Akkadian and Sumerian cuneiform (meaning "wedge-shaped," i.e., the process by which these languages were written) tablets as well as Egyptian, Ugaritic, and Aramaic writings have been made available to further our understanding of the Hebrew Bible. In addition to creation accounts, law codes, and flood stories, many texts deal with divination, magic, and prophecy.[3]

Among these varied genres, trance and ecstasy surface from time to time. Thus, we can learn something of the ANE conceptualization of what these ASCs involved and how the writers of the Hebrew Bible existed within this general framework. Naturally, we do not want to impose the ANE conceptualization upon the Old Testament. Rather, we want to facilitate a working knowledge of what ancient cultures perceived as trance and ecstasy so that our modern understanding does not infiltrate our interpretation.

ASCs were regularly part of ancient prophetic practice among Israel's neighbors. According to a series of prophetic texts from the eighteenth century BCE, certain prophets at the Syrian city of Mari regularly engaged in trance and ecstasy. One prophet referred to as "the servant of Dagan-malik" is said to go "into a trance" (Akkadian: *mahû*) and speak an oracle.[4] Another text states that an individual referred to as "the ecstatic" (Akkadian: *muḫḫûm* [masculine]; *muḫḫūtum* [feminine]) stood in the temple to deliver their prophetic utterances.[5] Elsewhere, the ecstatic is listed alongside

---

2. On the geography of Israel, see Yohanan, *Land of the Bible*.

3. The best way to access many of these sources is through Sparks, *Ancient Texts*, as well as Arnold and Beyer, *Readings from the Ancient Near East*. For a closer study one should consult Pritchard's scholarly sourcebook *Ancient Near Eastern Texts* (*ANET*) and a similar collection by Hallo and Younger called *Context of Scripture* (*COS*).

4. *ANET*, 630.

5. *ANET*, 631.

a series of occult specialists: "A prophet, an ecstatic, a dream-interpreter."[6] Ecstatics could be in one of two states, *šaqālum* (balance or equilibrium) or *imaḫḫi* (ecstasy, trance, frenzy, or altered state of consciousness.)[7] Ecstatic prophecies at Mari were not nonsensical, but "intelligible and grammatical, often of high literary quality and sometimes marked by striking similes and metaphors."[8]

ASCs were often understood as a god or deity possessing or touching the individual.[9] In the Egyptian work Journey of Wen-Amon to Phoenicia (eleventh century BCE), for example, we read that a god "seized one of his youths and made him possessed" so that he was in a "frenzy" that night.[10] Elsewhere, those who are in ecstasy are viewed as crazy.[11] Ecstatics were often made fun of by their contemporaries, evidenced by a number of satirical Sumerian texts that have been found.[12] One Egyptian text called The Instruction of Amen-Em-Opet (tenth–sixth century BCE), for example, instructs people not to tease the blind, dwarves, or the lame, but also "a man who is in the hand of the god (i.e., ecstasy)."[13]

The connection between disabilities and ecstasy suggests that their behavior looked like insanity to onlookers. Indeed, people often assumed that epileptic seizures were actually a form of possession by the gods, which suggests that sporadic movements and convulsions were a normative and

---

6. *ANET*, 535. The word for the office of ecstatic (*muḫḫûm*) comes from a root that means "to rave" or "to become frenzied." See Craghan, "Mari and Its Prophets," 39. Additionally, Tibbs, "Possession Amnesia," 31, notes that "the Sumerian lexical equivalent is *lú-an-dib-ba-ra*, 'one who has been seized by a god.'"

7. Foster, "Ecstatic Speech," 430–31.

8. Foster, "Ecstatic Speech," 431.

9. Steinert, "Ecstatic Experience," 373: "Thus, ˡúan-né-ba-tu '(person) afflicted by heaven' and ˡúAN-dib-ba-ra 'one struck by a passing god' refer to the idea that these performers were under the influence or control of a deity when in trance"; cf. *COS* 1.153: "The exorcist with his ritual did not appease divine wrath. What bizarre actions everywhere. . . . Like one possessed (?), who forgot his lord, who casually swore a solemn oath by his god: I, indeed, seemed (such a one)!"

10. *ANET*, 26; cf. *COS* 1.41: "Now while he was offering to his gods, the god took hold of a young man [of] his young men and put him in a trance. He said to him: 'Bring [the] god up! Bring the envoy who is carrying him.'"

11. Sometimes likened to *ṭēmu* (madness or loss [lit. change] of reason). For example, according to the Babylonian creation myth *Enūma Eliš*: "When Tiāmat heard this, she went into frenzy [lit. she turned into a female ecstatic] and lost her reason [*maḫḫūtiš ītemi ušanni ṭēnša*]. Tiāmat cried aloud and fiercely, All her lower members trembled beneath her [*šuršiš malmališ itrurā išdāšu*]." See Steinert, "Ecstatic Experience," 373.

12. Foster, "Ecstatic Speech," 437.

13. *ANET*, 424–25.

observable byproduct of ASCs in the ancient world.[14] According to some sources, the possession state left the ecstatic in a kind of amnesia, unable to recall what they had said.[15]

The Persian prophet Zarathustra (sometimes called Zoroaster) who established the Iranian religion Zoroastrianism sometime in the mid- to late second millennium BCE has also been viewed as an ecstatic by scholars. According to one apocalyptic work, "Zoroaster reflected that he had seen (it) in a pleasant sleep granted by Ahura Mazda: 'I am not restored from the sleep,' and he took both hands, rubbed his own body: 'I have slept a long time and I am not restored from the pleasant sleep, granted by Ahura Mazda.'"[16] This "pleasant sleep" is interpreted by most scholars to refer to a form of trance.[17]

In two other Zoroastrian texts, a certain Vištaspa is instructed to drink a cup of wine mixed with hemp, seemingly to induce the trance state.[18] Still another work records that the soul of a certain Viraz "went from the body to the peak of Daiti, (over) the Činvat bridge and came back the seventh day and night and went into the body. Viraz rose up as if he arose from a pleasant sleep, thinking of Vohu Manah and joyful."[19]

Once again, the presence of the pleasant sleep and the journey of the soul from its body to a distant location suggests that what has been experienced is a form of trance.

While an exhaustive account of trance and ecstasy in the ANE cannot be produced here, these representative examples should suffice in communicating the common thread of ASCs within the prophetic tradition.[20]

14. Hippocrates, *Morb. sacr.* 1: "Men regard its nature and cause as divine from ignorance and wonder, because it is not at all like to other diseases. And this notion of its divinity is kept up by their inability to comprehend it, and the simplicity of the mode by which it is cured, for men are freed from it by purifications and incantations. ... And I see men become mad and demented from no manifest cause, and at the same time doing many things out of place; and I have known many persons in sleep groaning and crying out, some in a state of suffocation, some jumping up and fleeing out of doors, and deprived of their reason until they awaken, and afterward becoming well and rational as before, although they be pale and weak; and this will happen not once but frequently. And there are many and various things of the like kind, which it would be tedious to state particularly."

15. See Haldar, *Associations of Cult Prophets*, 25; and Tibbs, "Possession Amnesia," 31.

16. *Bahman Yašt* III, 12-13, in Hultgård, "Ecstasy and Vision."

17. See Hultgård, "Ecstasy and Vision," 16.

18. *Denkart* VII, 4:84–86 and *Pahlavi Rivayat* XLVII, 27–32, in Hultgård, "Ecstasy and Vision."

19. *Book of Artay Viraz* III, 1–4, in Hultgård, "Ecstasy and Vision."

20. For more, see Stein et al., *Routledge Companion to Ecstatic Experience*; and

Entering into an ASC facilitated contact between the prophet and the deities with whom they wanted to communicate.

While we do not want to impose superficial similarities between Israel's prophets and those of her neighbors, we must at least be aware of the widespread use of ASCs among ANE prophets. We should not think that Israelite prophets simply mimicked or borrowed these activities for their own purposes. Rather, we should see trance and ecstasy as a cross-cultural and widespread human experience. In the same way that non-Israelite nations had prophets, Israel too had prophets. And whether trance and ecstasy were a part of that activity ought to be based on the text of Scripture itself. That being said, it would be misguided to ignore the seemingly universal presence of ASCs within global religions as a whole. Both extremes will result in obscuring the text. With these caveats in mind, we may now turn to the text of the Hebrew Bible.

Patriarchs of Trance

In 1688, a young teenage girl named Isabeau Vincent from the southeastern province of Dauphiné in France began preaching and prophesying in her sleep. Vincent was eventually arrested, but not before her preaching style had spread to hundreds of other children.[21] Vincent was part of a group known as the Camisards, a French Protestant movement in an area known as the Cévennes, which revolted against the religious persecution under the reign of King Louis XIV. The Camisards were a unique Christian group. Often criticized for their ecstatic prophesying and trance-induced preaching, they soon became known as the "French Prophets."

Sometimes referred to as "sleeping-preachers" or "trance-preachers," the phenomenon of people falling into a deep sleep before suddenly delivering an eloquent sermon was not confined to France. Protestants delivering oracles in such a state became popular in Germany, Switzerland, Scandinavia, and various parts of Africa and North America.[22] In the United States, for example, Amish Mennonite men such as Noah Troyer (1831–1886) and John D. Kauffman (1847–1913) began preaching in an unconscious state and the group established from these preachers still exists today.[23] One instance of a young woman in the 1800s sleep-preaching in Massachusetts is worth quoting in full:

Nissinen, "Prophetic Madness."

21. Garrett, *Origins of the Shakers*, 26–27; Joutard, *Légende des Camisards*, 26.
22. See Voipio, *Sleeping Preachers*; and Garrett, *Spirit Possession*.
23. Hiller, "Sleeping Preachers," 19–26.

In London, in 1815, there appeared a book titled *Remarkable Sermons by Rachel Baker, and Pious Ejaculations, Delivered During Sleep*, by Dr. Mitchell, M.D., Professor of Physic, the late Dr. Priestly, LL.D., and Dr. Douglass. On the title-page of the book are the following words, "Several hundreds every evening flock to hear this most wonderful Preacher, who is instrumental in converting more persons to Christianity, when asleep, than all other ministers together whilst awake." This book gives an account of a girl who was born at Pelham, Mass., in 1794. At the age of seventeen she became a religious melancholic, and later in the same year she fell into a trance and talked about her fear of hell. This continued for two months, at the end of which time she seemed to be converted and her mind was calmed. From this time on she began to preach and to pray in her trances, in such a manner that those who knew her well declared that her readiness and fluency far exceeded her waking state. Her trances occurred almost every evening and lasted for forty-five minutes, beginning and ending with slight epileptiform symptoms, and passing off into natural sleep for the rest of the night. When she awoke she was unable to remember anything that had taken place during her trance.[24]

These stories are certainly strange and perhaps hard to believe, yet hundreds of such accounts have permeated Protestant circles for over three hundred years. What should one make of them? The connection between trance and sleep serves as a springboard to discuss similar phenomena in the Hebrew Bible. While we do not have accounts of biblical patriarchs or prophets delivering lengthy homilies during their nap times, supernaturally imposed sleep-like trances for the purposes of divine communication are present. In fact, we do not need to read far in the biblical text to encounter such ASCs.

Adam in Gen 2 and Abraham in Gen 15 both have what appear to be trance-like experiences. Such a claim regarding these well-known passages may surprise some readers of the Bible who have read these sections of Genesis ad nauseam. While most English translations do a great job of communicating God's word, there will always be nuances or meanings from the original languages that sometimes get glossed over. In the cases of Adam and Abraham, I and many other scholars believe this to be the case.

In the Genesis creation account, Adam enters an ASC. According to Gen 2:21, God is said to have "caused a [תַּרְדֵּמָה/*tardēmâ*] to fall upon the man, and while he slept took one of his ribs and closed up its place with

---

24. Cutten, *Psychological Phenomena*, 58.

flesh." I have purposely left the relevant Hebrew term untranslated. Most translations choose to render this word as "deep sleep" (e.g., NIV, ESV, NLT, KJV). Several words are used in the Hebrew Bible for sleep.

The typical word for sleep is שֵׁנָה/šēnâ. This word does not carry any special meaning and even in cases where God does speak to someone in a dream where this word is used (Gen 28:16; Dan 2:1; and perhaps Zech 4:1), the presence of this word does not indicate anything overtly supernatural. The second word for sleep is יָשֵׁן/yâshên. Like šēnā, this word carries no inherently different meaning than regular sleep, though it can be used euphemistically of death in some contexts. The third word for sleep is נוּם/ nûm. This word is usually paired with yâshên and so its meaning is likely synonymous.

Unlike these three words, tardēmâ requires further investigation. Both the noun tardēmâ and the related verb רָדַם/rādam are each used only seven times in the Hebrew Bible, and tardēmâ is used six of those seven times in instances where supernatural activity is present. I quote these passages here while keeping the term tardēmâ untranslated:

> As the sun was going down, a [tardēmâ] fell on Abram. And behold, dreadful and great darkness fell upon him. (Gen 15:12)

> So David took the spear and the jar of water from Saul's head, and they went away. No man saw it or knew it, nor did any awake, for they were all asleep, because a [tardēmâ] from the Lord had fallen upon them. (1 Sam 26:12)[25]

> For the Lord has poured out upon you a spirit of [tardēmâ], and has closed your eyes (the prophets), and covered your heads (the seers). (Isa 29:10)

> Amid thoughts from visions of the night, when [tardēmâ] falls on men, dread came upon me, and trembling, which made all my bones shake. A spirit glided past my face; the hair of my flesh stood up. (Job 4:13–15)

> In a dream, in a vision of the night, when [tardēmâ] falls on men, while they slumber on their beds, then he opens the ears of men

---

25. Gen. Rab. 17: "There are three slumbers: the slumber of sleep, the slumber of prophecy, and the slumber of a trance. The slumber of sleep—'the Lord God cast a deep slumber upon the man, and he slept.' The slumber of prophecy—'it was when the sun was setting, and a deep slumber fell upon Abram' (Genesis 15:12). The slumber of a trance—'No one saw, and no one knew, and no one awoke, as they were all asleep, because a deep slumber from the Lord had fallen upon them' (1 Samuel 26:12). The Rabbis said: There is also the slumber of foolishness, as it is written: 'For the Lord poured upon you a spirit of deep slumber' (Isaiah 29:10)."

and terrifies them with warnings, that he may turn man aside from his deed and conceal pride from a man. (Job 33:15-17)

Slothfulness casts into a [*tardēmâ*], and an idle person will suffer hunger. (Prov 19:15)

The term *tardēmâ* is thus used in contexts of visions/dreams (Gen 15:12; Job 4:13-15; 33:15-17),[26] sleep-like punishments (1 Sam 26:12; Isa 29:10),[27] and perhaps in one case as a form of lethargy (Prov 19:15).[28] In the two cases of *tardēmâ* used in Genesis and Job 33:15-17, God initiates the *tardēmâ* to communicate important truths or work miracles. In the other cases, the *tardēmâ* is used to punish Israel's enemies and perhaps even of a demonic encounter (Job 4:13-15). Thus, *tardēmâ* is a neutral word that is only positive or negative depending on context.

---

26. Hartley, *Book of Job*, 134, suggests that in such instances *tardēmâ* refers not to a deep natural sleep but to a "stupor that God causes to fall on a person, blocking out all other perceptions, in order that the person may be completely receptive to the divine word." See also Lindblom, "Theophanies in Holy," 91-106, esp. 94.

27. Dahood, "Hebrew-Ugaritic Lexicography," 391-92, argues for a superlative use of *yhwh* with *tardēmâ* so that it emphasizes the nature of the "deep sleep" rather than showing Yahweh as the agent of the *tardēmâ*. Stoebe, *Erstes Buch Samuelis*, 467, argues, however, that the presence of the *tardēmâ* likely is meant to emphasize David's "charismatic" (German: *charismatische*) figure in 1 Sam 26:12. Cf. 3 Macc 5:11-12: "But the Lord sent upon the king a portion of sleep, that beneficence that from the beginning, night and day, is bestowed by him who grants it to whomever he wishes. And by the action of the Lord he was overcome by so pleasant and deep a sleep that he quite failed in his lawless purpose and was completely frustrated in his inflexible plan."

28. One uncommon use of *tardēmâ* is often interpreted as referring to laziness or lethargy (Prov 19:15). As Garrett, *Proverbs, Ecclesiastes, Song of Songs*, 171n361, wonders: "It is somewhat difficult to see how תַּרְדֵּמָה, 'deep sleep,' is equivalent to going hungry." In an attempt to make sense of this, Dahood, *Proverbs and Northwest Semitic Philology*, 40, suggests that *tardēmâ* here should be translated as "bedroom," indicating that the person is asleep and thus lazy. I do not find Dahood's suggestion convincing, nor do I think that *tardēmâ* is awkwardly placed in this sentence as per Garrett. If *tardēmâ* encapsulates a sleep-like state that reflects various forms of ASCs, it is possible to understand it here as a form of daydreaming. The individual, who we might say is "spacing out," to use a modern colloquialism, dreams about possible futures, but does not work, and so goes hungry. The word *tardēmâ* also appears once in a fragmentary line from Dead Sea Scroll 4Q425 4 ii, 2 in the context of offering praise to God. It is possible that *tardēmâ* here reflects a belief that trance or ecstasy was permissible in giving thanks to God. It is also possible that because line 1 mentions fleeing something, that it is relying on the meaning found in Proverbs that one should avoid laziness. Aquila renders the word *tardēmâ* in Gen 2:21; 1 Sam 26:12; Prov 19:15; and Isa 29:10 as καταφορά/*kataphorá* which in some nonbiblical texts (usually medical) has the rare meaning of lethargy. In the noncanonical Psalms of Solomon (first century BCE), for instance, the word *kataphorá* is also used of lethargy: "I slipped for a short time, in the lethargy of those that sleep far from God." Pss. Sol. 16:1.

The seven biblical references where the verbal form *rādam* appear are as follows:

> But Jael the wife of Heber took a tent peg, and took a hammer in her hand. Then she went softly to him and drove the peg into his temple until it went down into the ground while he was [*rādam*] from weariness. So he died. (Judg 4:21)

> At your rebuke, O God of Jacob, both rider and horse [*rādam*]. (Ps 76:6)

> He who gathers in summer is a prudent son, but he who [*rādam*] in harvest is a son who brings shame. (Prov 10:5)

> I fell into a [*rādam*] with my face to the ground. (Dan 8:18)

> Then I heard the sound of his words, and as I heard the sound of his words, I fell on my face in [*rādam*] with my face to the ground. (Dan 10:9)

> Then the mariners were afraid, and each cried out to his god. And they hurled the cargo that was in the ship into the sea to lighten it for them. But Jonah had gone down into the inner part of the ship and had lain down and was [*rādam*]. So the captain came and said to him, "What do you mean, you who [*rādam*]? Arise, call out to your god! Perhaps the god will give a thought to us, that we may not perish." (Jonah 1:5–6)

The term *rādam* is often translated as "be asleep" (Judg 4:21; Prov 10:5; Jonah 1:5), though elsewhere it clearly means something like "stunned" or "enraptured" (e.g., Ps 76:6).[29] In other passages, *rādam* is best explained as an ASC where divine communication with humans can take place. The NRSV and NET translate *rādam* in both Dan 8:18 and 10:9 as "fell into a trance," which seems to accurately reflect what is happening as opposed to "fell into a deep sleep" (ESV, NIV, CSB, KJV, NASB) or "fainted" (NLT).[30]

The connection between sleep and trance creates an obvious parallel, like how sleep is sometimes used euphemistically of death (Ps 13:3; John 11:13).[31] In the same way that someone can metaphorically speak of "sleep-

---

29. *TDNT*, s.v. "Θάμβος, Θαμβέω, Ἔκθαμβος, Ἐκθαμβέομαι." The German New Testament scholar Georg Bertram goes as far as to translate these words as "magical sleep," though the term "magic" tends to have a pejorative connotation and has not been widely adopted.

30. The verb *rādam* appears in 4Q242 3, 5 in reference to someone who speaks to another who is "[*rādam*] in a spirit." Here *rādam* is situated alongside נום/*nwm* (slumber). The presence of the phrase "in spirit/in a spirit" (ברוח/*brwḥ*) may indicate some kind of ASC.

31. Cf. Sir 30:17: "Death is better than a life of misery, and eternal sleep than

ing the sleep of death" (Ps 13:13; cf. John 11:13), one can speak of trance as a form of sleep that one must be awakened from. Zechariah, for example, while experiencing a vision states, "The angel who talked with me came again and woke me, like a man [כאיש/ke'ish] who is awakened out of his sleep" (Zech 4:1).[32] The preposition כ/k attached to the word for "man" (איש/ish) is meant to introduce a simile. Zechariah was not in fact asleep but was experiencing a dream-like state in the form of a trance in which being "awakened" makes rhetorical sense.[33] Similarly, Jonah is said to have fallen into a *rādam* and needs to be woken up by the ship's captain (Jonah 1:5). The use of the verb *rādam* suggests that Jonah may have entered a trance state during the storm, which makes more sense than his ability to literally sleep through it.[34] While in a trance state, the person appears to the observer as if they were asleep or drowsy, thus the link between these two ideas and words makes logical sense and explains why such a lexical range exists. Here is a modern analogy: we may think of the commanding word "sleep" used by hypnotists today. While the hypnotist tells the individual to sleep, what they really mean is "be hypnotized." The patient enters an ASC, but from the outsider perspective it looks as though it is a form of sleep. Thus, even though the word "sleep" can denote natural slumber, depending on the context of when the word is used, a different state of consciousness may be envisioned. A similar understanding of the words *tardēmâ* and *rādam* is likely in order to grasp what is happening in passages where these terms appear. Tertullian says of Adam: "Thus, in the beginning, sleep was preceded by ecstasy, as we read: 'God sent an ecstasy upon Adam, and he slept'. Sleep brought rest to the body, but ecstasy came over the soul."[35]

The earliest extant interpretation of the Genesis account's use of *tardēmâ* comes from the Septuagint. The Jewish translators rendered Gen 2:21 (LES) as follows: "So God laid a trance [*ekstasis*] upon Adam and put him to sleep; and he took one of his ribs and filled up the flesh in the place of it."[36] The Hebrew word for *tardēmâ* is thus translated with the Greek word

---

chronic sickness."

32. Boda, *Zechariah*, 274.

33. Likewise, according to Elihu in the book of Job, God warns people to turn from evil by speaking to them "in a dream, in a vision of the night, when [*tardēmâ*] falls on mortals" (Job 33:15). In this instance, *tardēmâ* most obviously refers to having a dream (cf. Job 20:8; Isa 29:7; Dan 2:19; 7:7, 13).

34. Stuart, *Hosea-Jonah*, 458.

35. Tertullian, *An.* 45.1.3.

36. NETS: "And God cast a trance upon Adam, and he slept, and he took one of his ribs and filled up flesh in its place" (Gen 2:21). The translators of the Septuagint were inconsistent in how they translated the words *tardēmâ* and *rādam*. In some

for "trance/ecstasy" in this instance.[37] One may think of this supernaturally induced trance as a kind of anesthetic used to keep Adam from feeling the physical sensations associated with such a surgery. More likely, however, the *tardēmâ* indicates that Adam was experiencing some kind of vision. Old Testament scholar John Walton explains this option as follows:

> Michael Fox adds the insight that the word [*tardēmâ*] pertains to "untimely sleep or stupefaction, not to normal sleep at night." . . . From these data it is easy to conclude that Adam's sleep has prepared him for a visionary experience rather than for a surgical procedure. The description of himself being cut in half and the woman being built from the other half (Gen 2:21–22) would refer not to something he physically experienced but to something that he saw in a vision. It would therefore not describe a material event but would give him an understanding of an important reality, which he expresses eloquently in Genesis 2:23. . . . The vision would concern her identity as ontologically related to the man.[38]

This ASC in Gen 2 is referred to in the same verse as a form of sleep (*yâshên*), a term which is sometimes connected to prophetic dreams (Gen 41:5; 1 Kgs 19:5) or supernaturally induced sleep (1 Sam 26:12).[39] Whatever the case, Adam's normal senses were changed or nullified so that God could perform a miracle.[40]

---

instances *tardēmâ* is rendered with the Greek words "stupefaction" (κατάνυξις/*katanyxis*; Isa 29:11 LXX), "fear" (φόβος/*phobos*; Job 4:13–15; 33:15–17 LXX), or "amazement" (θάμβος/*thambos*; 1 Sam 26:12 LXX). Likewise, *rādam* is translated variously as "amazed/ecstatic" (ἐξίστημι/*existēmi*; Judg 4:21 LXX), "doze" (νυστάζω/*nystazō*; Ps 75:7 LXX), "sleep" (κοιμάω/*koimaō*; Dan 8:18 LXX), and in some instances is not translated at all (Dan 10:9 LXX)! Based on such a variety of translation choices, it seems evident the Septuagint translators were hard pressed to know exactly what was entailed in each occurrence. Such variety further lends support to the idea that *rādam* and *tardēmâ* encompass more than just natural sleep. Rather, a wide range of states of consciousness are supposed by these words depending on their context. See Thomson, "Sleep," and the entries in LEH and GELS.

37. GELS, s.v. "ἔκστασις"; LEH, s.v. "ἔκστασις."

38. Walton, *Lost World*, 79–80.

39. Rad, *Genesis*, 84: "A 'deep sleep' falls upon man, a kind of magical sleep that completely extinguishes his consciousness. The narrator is moved by the thought that God's miraculous creating permits no watching. Man cannot perceive God 'in the act,' cannot observe his miracles in their genesis; he can revere God's creativity only as an actually accomplished fact. Thus, even Abraham had to sink into fear and insensibility before God's coming (ch. 15.12), and Moses could not see God's face but only 'God's back' (Ex. 33.18–23)."

40. Delitzsch, *New Commentary on Genesis*, 1:142, argues that this is not an "ecstatic

How then should we translate *tardēmâ* in Gen 2:21? The Orthodox Jewish Bible chooses to render the verse using the Hebrew term transliterated into English with a parenthetical translation of "deep sleep": "And Hashem Elohim caused a tardemah (deep sleep) to fall upon the adam, and he slept; and He took from one of his tzalelot (sides, ribs), and closed up the basar in the place thereof." Old Testament scholar John Goldingay goes as far as to translate *tardēmâ* as a "coma."[41] While a coma certainly conveys the surgical element of the text, it may not be the most appropriate. Instead, I believe following the Septuagint's translation of "trance/ecstasy" is appropriate and conveys what is probably happening in the narrative. Thus, we might translate the Hebrew text as follows: "And Yahweh God caused a trance to fall upon the human and he slept." Here, *tardēmâ* is in parallel with sleep, which describes the physiological features of the trance.

Adam is not the only biblical character to experience *tardēmâ*. Like Gen 2:21, the Greek version of Gen 15:12 (LES) refers to the *tardēmâ* that Abram falls into as a trance: "About the time of the setting of the sun, an [*ekstasis*] fell upon Abram, and behold, a great dark fear fell upon him."[42] While Adam undergoes a sleep-like experience, Abram has "dreadful and great darkness" fall upon him (Gen 15:12). While in this state, Abram is able to hear God's voice and see the manifestations of a smoking pot and flaming torch passing between the animals that he had cut (Gen 15:17), symbols of God's covenant agreement. Gen 15:1 states that God spoke to Abram in a vision, which suggests that this latter section in Gen 15:12–21 is also meant to describe a visionary experience. The Hebrew word used for "vision" in Gen 15:1 is מַחֲזֶה/*maḥăzeh*, which one standard Hebrew lexicon even defines as "vision, in the ecstatic state."[43] The other places this term appears include Balaam's vision of God in Num 24:4, 16 and the visions of false prophets in

---

sleep" nor a "trance," though his reasons for concluding this are unclear. His main argument seems to be that since Adam does not receive an oracle and because the Greek translators Aquila and Symmachus translate the word *tardēmâ* differently than the Septuagint, that this proves Adam is not being put into a trance. This is difficult to accept given the other instances where *tardēmâ* most certainly means a trance state, even within Genesis. The lack of an oracle being received has nothing to do with whether or not a trance state was induced. Trance states do not always lead to oracles, though they are a feature of some.

41. Goldingay, *Genesis*, 117.

42. Gen 17:3 and 17:17 state that Abram falls on his face when God appears to him and in the latter instance begins to laugh. Although this passage has been used as a proof text for ASCs in the Bible (especially to justify the phenomena of being "slain in the Spirit"), it is difficult to know whether motor automatisms are present.

43. BDB, s.v. "מַחֲזֶה"; cf. *HALOT*, s.v. "מַחֲזֶה"; *DCH*, s.v. "מַחֲזֶה."

Ezek 13:7. In the case of Balaam I argue elsewhere in this chapter that he too experienced an ASC.

It is worth emphasizing that this reading of the Adam and Abraham narratives are not modern inventions based on contemporary cross-cultural religious studies or denominationalism. Both early Jewish and Christian interpreters were able to see that trance was part of the equation. Philo interprets Abraham as "being thrown into a state of enthusiasm and inspired by the Deity."[44] Likewise, Philo says of Adam that God "'cast a deep trance upon Adam, and sent him to sleep.' He speaks here with great correctness, for a trance and perversion of the mind is its sleep. And the mind is rendered beside itself when it ceases to be occupied about the things perceptible only by the intellect which present themselves to it."[45] The Christian bishop in Lycia, Methodius of Olympus (260–312 CE), uses Adam's trance state as an analogy for the desire men have to beget children and thus the desire Christ has for the church: "Leaving His Father in heaven, [Jesus] came down to be 'joined to His wife;' and slept in the trance of His passion, and willingly suffered death for her, that He might present the church to Himself glorious and blameless."[46] Other Christian writers likewise make these connections, including John Chrysostom (ca. 349–407 CE),[47] Severian of Gabala (ca. 355–ca. 425 CE),[48] and Didymus the Blind (ca. 313–398 CE).[49]

44. Philo, *Heir* 258.

45. Philo, *Alleg. Interp.* 2.31–33: "And when it is not energizing with respect to them it is asleep. And the expression, 'it is in a trance,' is very well employed, as it means that it is perverted and changed, not by itself, but by God, who presents to it, and brings before it, and sends upon it the change which occurs to it. For the case is this:—if it were in my own power to be changed, then whenever I chose I should exercise this power, and whenever I did not choose I should continue as I am, without any change. But now change attacks me from an opposite direction, and very often when I am desirous to turn my intellect to some fitting subject, I am swallowed up by an influx contrary to what is fitting: and on the other hand, when I conceive an idea respecting something unseemly, I discard it by means of pleasant notions while God by his own grace pours into my soul a sweet stream instead of the salt flood. It is necessary therefore, that every created thing should at times be changed. For this is a property of every created thing, just as it is an attribute of God to be unchangeable. But of these beings who have been changed, some remain in their altered state till their final and complete destruction, though others are only exposed to the ordinary vicissitudes of human nature; and they are immediately preserved."

46. Methodius, *Symp.* 3.8.

47. Chrysostom, *Hom. Gen.* 15.7: "It wasn't simply drowsiness that came upon him nor normal sleep."

48. Severian, *On the Creation of the World* 5.8: "Even if one is deeply asleep, he will awake from the pain."

49. Didymus, *In Gen.* 189: "A trance came upon him, then, a trance not like derangement but wonderment and the change from visible things to invisible. The Apostle says,

The idea that Adam and Abraham experienced trances also makes sense within the context of them being viewed as prophets. Abraham is described as a prophet in Gen 20:7 and, as we will see, ASCs were a common feature of prophetic experience. In some early Jewish and Christian texts, Adam too is depicted as a prophet.[50] In the work Life of Adam and Eve (first century BCE–second century CE), Adam recounts his visit to the heavenly paradise and sees God sitting on his throne.[51] Josephus states that Adam made a "prediction that the world was to be destroyed at one time by the force of fire, and at another time by the violence and quantity of water."[52] Ephrem the Syrian (fourth century CE) argues that Adam spoke in a "prophetic way" while in a "vision in sleep."[53] Likewise, in a work known as the *Recognitions of Clement* (second–fourth century CE), a lengthy discussion between Clement and Peter takes place about Adam being a prophet.[54] Tertullian states that Adam prophesied about Christ and the church because "he experienced an accident of the spirit, for an ecstasy fell upon him, a power of the holy spirit, effecting prophecy."[55] Such a description of Adam makes sense within the context of him experiencing an ASC and Christian use of the Septuagint and it also reveals that the general understanding of Adam experiencing an ASC was not foreign to Christian authorities.

These accounts tell us not only some of the methodology God chooses to incorporate in his interactions with humans, but perhaps also that the biblical authors were comfortable with such experiences. Communication with the gods in the ancient world often involved ASCs. Why would this God be any different? Of course, there are differences—important ones! As we will see in the following story of Joseph, Yahweh is not like the other gods, even if he speaks to people in similar ways.

---

for example, 'For whether we are beside ourselves for God, or whether we are in our right mind for you,' suggesting not that we are insane for God, but that even if we are transported by contemplation beyond human things, we do so for God, as David also says, 'I said in my trance, Everyone is a liar.' In other words, being beside himself and having become divine, he says of other people that they are liars, while he himself is no longer human on account of a share in the Holy Spirit."

50. See Gladd, *From Adam and Israel*, 35–36.
51. LAE 25:1–3.
52. Josephus, *Ant.* 1.2.3.
53. Ephrem, *On Genesis* 2.13.2; cf. Clement, *Strom.* 1.135.3.
54. Rufinus, *Clem. Recogn.* 1.47.
55. Tertullian, *An.* 11.4.

The Cup of Intoxication

Anyone familiar with the story of Joseph, perhaps even through DreamWorks's animated movie *Joseph: King of Dreams* (2000) or Tim Rice and Andrew Lloyd Webber's musical *Joseph and the Amazing Technicolor Dreamcoat* (1974), probably remembers the role that Joseph's cup plays in the narrative. Through trickery, Joseph has his steward slip a cup into his youngest brother's bag, only to turn around and accuse him of theft and then eventually reveal himself to be the family's long-lost brother! Indeed, the story of Joseph is filled with betrayal, deception, and miracles, but also ASCs.

After being sold into slavery by his brothers, Joseph is taken to Egypt and eventually thrown into prison, only to be elevated within the Egyptian court after his special abilities become known. In the Hebrew Bible, Joseph is depicted as especially adept at oneiromancy (dream interpretation).[56] In addition to his own dreams (Gen 37:5–11), he is able to interpret those of the chief cupbearer (Gen 40:9–15), chief baker (Gen 40:16–18), and Pharaoh himself (Gen 41:14–36). Yet, there is another art that Joseph appears to be proficient in:

> Is it not from this [silver cup] that my lord drinks, and by this that he *practices divination*? (Gen 44:5; emphasis added)
>
> What deed is this that you have done? Do you not know that *a man like me can indeed practice divination*? (Gen 44:15; emphasis added)

Twice, Joseph is purported to have the ability to practice divination using a cup. The Hebrew word used here for divination is נָחַשׁ/*naḥaš* and the associated word for a practitioner of divination is used in prohibitions against sorcery: "There shall not be found among you anyone who burns his son or his daughter as an offering, anyone who practices divination or tells fortunes or interprets omens [מְנַחֵשׁ/*mənaḥēš*], or a sorcerer or a charmer or a medium or a necromancer or one who inquires of the dead, for whoever does these things is an abomination to the Lord" (Deut 18:10–12; cf. Lev 19:26). It is elsewhere listed among various occult practices (Num 23:23; 2 Kgs 17:17; 21:6; 2 Chr 33:6). The word is similar to the Hebrew word for "serpent" (נָחָשׁ/*nāḥāš*; Gen 3:1–4; Num 21:7) and the word "whisper/charm" (לְחַשׁ/*lāḥaš*). The technical word used for Joseph's form of divination is "scrying," a catchall term for divination by peering into crystals, mirrors,

---

56. In a fragmentary portion of 4Q458 13, 1–2, Joseph is mentioned alongside the Hebrew verb *rādam* at least twice as well as with the phrase "the prophecy" (הנבואה/*hnbw' h*; 4Q458 15, 2).

or other reflective surfaces.⁵⁷ When using water, the practice is called hydromancy, lecanomancy (divination using a bowl), or tasseomancy (reading tea leaves).⁵⁸

In the ancient world, ASCs were often induced so that a person practicing divination was more receptive to communication from and possession by spirits. Consider the following extract from the work of the Neoplatonist Iamblichus (third–fourth century CE):

> You state that there are many who grasp the future by means of divine possession and divine inspiration and that they are awake as far as their ability to act and their sense perceptions are concerned, but not really conscious or not as conscious as before. I also want to show, in this context, the characteristics of those who are truly possessed by the gods. For if they submit their whole life as a vehicle, as a tool, to the gods who inspire them, they either exchange their human life for a divine life or else they adjust their life to the god and do not act according to their

---

57. Nilsson, *Greek Piety*, 146: "Scrying was done by gazing at the surface of water, a method . . . which reminds us of modern crystal-gazing. A medium, an innocent boy, was chosen after he had been tested and found suitable. . . . The medium, with his eyes shut or bandaged, lay on his belly, with his face over a vessel containing water. Thereupon certain ceremonies were gone through which led up to the trance into which the medium passed by staring at the surface of the water, wherein he saw the beings summoned up by the magician, and then gave answers to the questions asked."

58. Augustine, *Civ.* 7.35 (fifth century CE; drawing on the work of Varro, *Antiquitates rerum divinarum* [first century BCE]): "For Numa himself also, to whom no prophet of God, no holy angel was sent, was driven to have recourse to hydromancy, that he might see the images of the gods in the water (or, rather, appearances whereby the demons made sport of him), and might learn from them what he ought to ordain and observe in the sacred rites. This kind of divination, says Varro, was introduced from the Persians, and was used by Numa himself, and at an after time by the philosopher Pythagoras. In this divination, he says, they also inquire at the inhabitants of the nether world, and make use of blood; and this the Greeks call νεκρομαντείαν [*nekromanteian*]. But whether it be called necromancy or hydromancy it is the same thing, for in either case the dead are supposed to foretell future things. . . . Now Numa is said to have married the nymph Egeria, because (as Varro explains it in the forementioned book) he carried forth water wherewith to perform his hydromancy. Thus facts are wont to be converted into fables through false colorings. It was by that hydromancy, then, that that over-curious Roman king learned both the sacred rites which were to be written in the books of the priests, and also the causes of those rites,—which latter, however, he was unwilling that any one besides himself should know." Pliny, *Nat.* 37.73 (first century CE): "Anancitis is used in hydromancy, they say, for summoning the gods to make their appearance; and synochitis, for detaining the shades from below when they have appeared." Strabo, *Geogr.* xvi (first century CE): "Among the Persians, the Magi and Necromanteis, and besides these the Lecanomanteis and Hydromanteis; among the Assyrians, were the Chaldæans; and among the Romans, the Tyrrhenian diviners of dreams." See, however, Kákosy, "Divination and Prophecy," 371–73.

own sense perceptions, nor are they awake like those whose senses are completely awake. They do not perceive the future by themselves, nor do they move like those who act on an impulse. They are not conscious in the way they were before, nor do they concentrate their native intelligence on themselves or manifest any special knowledge.... All this goes to show that in their state of divine possession they are no longer in their normal state of consciousness and that they no longer lead the normal life of a person, of a creature, as far as sense perception and volition are concerned. They exchange these for another, more divine kind of life that inspires and possesses them completely. There are many different kinds of divine trance, and divine inspiration operates in many different ways.... As a result, the outward signs of divine possession are manifold as well: movement of the body or of some of its parts, or total lack of any kind of movement; harmonious tunes, dances, melodious voices, or the opposites of these. Bodies have been seen to rise up or grow larger or float in the air, and the opposites of these phenomena also have been observed. The voice [of the person in trance] seemed to be completely even in volume and in the intervals between sound and silence, and then again there was unevenness. In other instances the sounds swelled and diminished, but occasionally something else happened. But most importantly, the medium who draws down a divine being sees the spirit descending, sees how great it is, what it is like, and is able to persuade and control it in mysterious ways.... Those who draw down the spirits without these wonderful experiences are stumbling in the dark, so to speak, and do not know what they are doing, except for certain quite unimportant signs on the body of the person possessed and other trivial manifestations; the full reality of divine inspiration remains hidden to them, and they are without knowledge.[59]

The philosopher Apuleius (second century CE) discusses at some length how young boys were used in divination. Using a combination of music, aromas, lamps, and incantations, boys would be "stirred into a trance [Latin: *soporari*] ... and thus, just as if he was sleeping [Latin: *quodam sopore*], he foretells future matters."[60] Once again, we should note that trance is often interpreted as outwardly appearing like drowsiness or sleep. In the same section, Apuleius differentiates this trance state from the uncontrolled epileptic seizures of a certain boy named Thallus: "For the poor wretch is such a victim to epilepsy that he frequently has fits twice or thrice in one day

---

59. Iamblichus, *De Mysteriis* 3.4–6 (translation from Luck, *Arcana Mundi*, 361–63).
60. Apuleius, *Apol.* 43.

without the need for any incantations, and exhausts all his limbs with his convulsions."[61] This is an important observation. Many ancients were able to discern between fits brought on through mental disorders or diseases and a trance state or ecstasy.

The use of trance in scrying should not be surprising. The logic behind scrying is that, by staring at the reflective surface, the medium is able to picture, whether optically or within their mind's eye, a series of images to interpret.[62]

In one story from the ancient world, Pharaoh Nectanebo(s) (fourth century BCE) is able to "observe the gods" using lecanomancy.[63] Likewise, in an ancient magical spell from Egypt, the following instructions are given to a certain Psammetichos, king of Egypt (seventh–sixth century BCE), on how to use lecanomancy to contact the gods and hear their voice. The spell details how the king should dress, what incantations to recite (including a long string of nonsensical syllables called *Vocae Magicae* and *Nomina Barbara*), what to pour into the bowl, and even a protective spell to use in case things get dangerous![64]

Biblical commentators have often tried to alleviate Joseph of this occult practice, usually by suggesting that Joseph's conversation about the cup

---

61. Luck, *Arcana Mundi*, 285: "The association of prophetic powers with 'madness' seems to be a very old idea among the Indo-European tribes, as the etymology shows, and the descriptions of prophetic trance . . . stress this particular aspect. It should be said, however, that this is only one form of divination; there are forms (e.g., the interpretation of dreams, or astrological forecasts) that do not require—in fact, they preclude—an abnormal state of consciousness."

62. Luck, *Arcana Mundi*, 312: "This technique allows the 'medium' to see a series of hallucinatory moving pictures 'within' the shining object." In early Babylonian cuneiform tablets dating as early as the eighteenth century BCE, instructions are given on how to interpret the future by observing the movement of oil in a dish of water, perhaps through the use of trance states and technical literature. See Tabor, "Babylonian Lecanomancy."

63. Luck, *Arcana Mundi*, 8: "An aid of achieving trance through looking into a bowl filled with a liquid. In trance, he sees his deities and, becoming like them, the whole world."

64. *PGM* IV. 221–34: "Whenever you want to inquire about matters, take a bronze vessel, either a bowl or a saucer, whatever kind you wish. Pour water: rainwater if you are calling upon heavenly gods, seawater if gods of the earth, river water if Osiris or Sarapis, springwater if the dead. Holding the vessel on your knees, pour out green olive oil, bend over the vessel and speak the prescribed spell. And address whatever god you want and ask about whatever you wish, and he will reply to you and tell you about anything. And if he has spoken dismiss him with the spell of dismissal, and you who have used this spell will be amazed." *PGM* stands for *Greek Magical Papyri* (abbreviated from the Latin title *Papyri Graecae Magicae*) that date from the second century BCE to the fifth century CE.

ought to be viewed as a ruse intended to incriminate his brothers further for supposedly stealing the cup that Joseph himself had planted.[65] One commentator, for example, goes as far as to supply a long parenthetical statement, seemingly to expunge Joseph of any wrongdoing, by suggesting that the ruse is simply amplified by him associating himself as one who has been given access to divinatory secrets.[66]

When Joseph says to his brothers that "a man like me" can practice divination, his argument is based on his established ability to interpret dreams and his position within the Egyptian elite, where magicians and occult specialists were common servants in the court (e.g., Gen 41:8). In both Gen 44:5 and 44:15, the Hebrew phrase to describe Joseph's divinatory practices is intensive: "Indeed he divines through divination" so that some suggest hyperbole is being used and thus relegate Joseph's scrying to the realm of hyperbolic deception. This may be plausible, but there is also no reason to think that Joseph did *not* practice scrying either. It is important to note that Joseph's story takes place centuries before the Mosaic prohibitions on divination are implemented. Thus, the stigma associated with such practices may have been less during this period in Israelite history.

The use of divination to communicate with the God of Israel is not unheard of and includes cleromancy/psephomancy (the casting of lots; Lev 16:7–10), the priest's use of the Urim and Thummim (Num 27:21), and Gideon's use of the fleece (Judg 6:36–40). Indeed, Joseph was not the first (nor the last) to inquire of God by divination. According to Genesis, Laban states, "I have learned by divination (*naḥaš*) that the Lord has blessed me because of you" (Gen 30:27). Likewise, Rebekah is said to "inquire" (דָּרַשׁ/*dāraš*) an answer from God (Gen 25:19–26), a term often used of divination, whether communicating with the dead (Deut 18:10–11; Isa 8:19), idols (Isa 19:3), or even the ark of the covenant (1 Chr 13:3).[67] Probably the most drastic form of divination ordained by God is the "bitter water" ritual found in Num 5:11–31. This passage details an elaborate scenario in which a woman is accused of adultery and made to drink a special concoction to prove her innocence. The elements involved include: (1) holy water (5:17),

---

65. Thus Mathews, *Genesis 11:27—50:26*, 799: "There is no instance of this practice in the Joseph narrative . . . and since Joseph's wisdom relies on the interpretation of dreams, it is best understood as part of the elaborate ploy." Sarna, *Genesis*, 304, agrees: "It is not stated that Joseph actually believes in divination. He wants the brothers to think he does."

66. K&D, 1:234.

67. Hamori, *Women's Divination*, 47: "When someone 'inquires of' Yahweh, this is not suddenly a picture of the person 'seeking' God in some abstract sense, but a use of the same terminology as when a person divines by 'inquiring of' other divine sources and objects."

(2) dust from the floor of the tabernacle (5:17), (3) unbinding the woman's hair (5:18), (4) placing a grain offering in her hands (5:18), (5) forcing the woman to take an oath (5:19–22), (6) writing the curses in a book and washing them into the water (5:23), and (7) offering the grain offering she was holding (5:26). If the woman is innocent, nothing will happen, but if she has indeed cheated on her husband, she suffers a curse and something negative happens to her body (the Hebrew is unclear). One wonders why lots could not be cast in such situations!

The biblical text, however, demonstrates a trajectory initiated by God to move away from technical arts of divination.[68] While in the period prior to the Levitical priesthood God allowed people to inquire of him by various means, after the time of the priesthood God speaks primarily through prophets via dreams, visions, and other auditory-visual means. Although the casting of lots is praised as a means of determining God's will or avoiding strife (Prov 16:33, 18:18), the Israelite kings primarily relied on court seers and prophets to discern matters (e.g., 2 Sam 24:11; 1 Chr 25:25; 2 Chr 35:15).[69]

Mark A. Snoeberger rightly notes concerning the prohibitions against various occult rituals in Deut 18 that "unlike the gods of the nations, Yahweh refused to submit to divination by the manipulative whimsy of his creatures; instead, Yahweh himself would determine when and to whom he would reveal his mind, chiefly through prophets of his own choosing (so vv. 15–22)."[70] Yet, we must also consider the very real possibility, as with Laban,

---

68. Some clarification on this point is necessary. By "technical arts" I mean non-sanctioned divinatory methods. Indeed, it is clear that some of these sanctioned divinatory practices *were* quite elaborate and technical. Likewise, we do not know how exactly the Urim and Thummim were used. As a result, assuming "complex" is somehow equivalent with "occultic" or "taboo" is problematic. As Schantz, *Paul in Ecstasy*, 191, rightly points out, the distinction between Christian "inspiration" and Greco-Roman divinatory "techniques" is a faulty one and that "this distinction is untenable. It is of the same ilk as the accusations that another group performs magic, whereas one's own group uses prayer. As discussed earlier, many types of activities (i.e., 'techniques') are capable of inducing ecstatic states of consciousness. Is fasting not a technique? Is the singing of hymns purely inspiration as opposed to method? The case of Emilio [a Pentecostal] . . . demonstrates the line at which 'inspiration' became 'technique' for one practitioner. At the same time, it also demonstrates the unhelpfulness of such value-laden comparisons. From Emilio's perspective, the ecstasy he sought by squeezing his ribs was as equally 'inspired' by the Holy Spirit as the one he obtained formerly when singing and standing in the midst of other glossolalists who were sufficient driving forces to inspire his own speech."

69. See Wellhausen, *Prolegomena*, 394–95; Nigosian, "Anti-Divinatory Statements"; and Cryer, *Divination in Ancient Israel*, 231–32.

70. Snoeberger, "Old Testament Lot-Casting," 3.

that divination was somehow an effective means of communicating with the God of Israel, even if unsanctioned.

Despite this trajectory, the use of trance and ecstasy was still a valid way of receiving oracles from God, both in the Old and New Testaments. Thus, the simplest reading of Gen 44, I suggest, is that Joseph *did* in fact practice a form of divination, probably lecanomancy or hydromancy, in order to foretell the future or interpret other omens in his career in the Egyptian court. This is descriptive of what Joseph did, not prescriptive of how God wants to communicate to people. This passage in Genesis is not endorsing Christians to go out and purchase divination cups or anything of the sort. Rather, it showcases that God was still able to use this practice to bless Joseph in this context. Like many people in the Old Testament who had less than "kosher" means of entreating God, Joseph's scrying is best interpreted within this rubric. Part of scrying involved inducing a trance to interpret the images that appear within the reflective surface, and so we may reasonably assume that Joseph engaged in such a state as well.

There is still more to this story though. The translation of "chief cupbearer" in Gen 40 may, to our senses, conjure images of a servant tasting the king's drink to detect poison, while the "chief chef" makes us think of someone in charge of pastries. We are told that the two were thrown into prison because they "committed an offense" against Pharaoh. We are not told the infraction, but it is probable that they were not imprisoned for doing a bad job preparing meals, but because of their respective occult duties in Pharaoh's court.[71] Oinomancy (divination using wine) and aleuromancy (divination using flour) were known during this period, and it is likely that magic was one of many dual roles played by employees of the court.[72] Later in the twelfth century BCE, for example, there is evidence that butlers sat as judges with the king, presumably using their divination to help with decision making.[73] Thus, the author of Genesis may have wanted to establish Joseph as the ultimate diviner as opposed to the two Egyptian court officials. It is Joseph's God who can interpret dreams with accuracy. It is Joseph's God who can give clarity to the obscure. And it is Joseph's God who can speak to someone even while in a trance, staring into a cup.

---

71. Often the messages given through aleuromancy were negative, which may suggest why the baker was imprisoned. See Oshima, *Babylonian Poems*, 234n272.

72. See Nougayrol et al., *Ugaritica V*.

73. Sarna, *Understanding Genesis*, 35–37; Davis, "Divination in the Bible."

Miriam and Music

Charismatic congregations are no strangers to dancing. This is especially true of South American and African congregations where, if a church meeting ends without dancing, has one really gone to church? Indeed, men and women dancing in the front of the auditorium and waving flags of variously colored fabrics during times of music and singing is commonplace among some congregations. Sometimes after very intense times of worship, congregants will fall to the ground as if asleep and later confess that they experienced visions from God or prophetic words for other members of the church. In many charismatic churches today, dancing is accompanied by other artistic expressions such as painting. These artists (both painters and dancers) express various prophetic symbols through specific colors and postures, sometimes described as a form of spiritual warfare. Dancing and prophecy were often connected within the ANE as well, and the dancing of modern charismatics is situated in a long line of biblical and historical examples.

Qohelet, the "preacher" of Ecclesiastes, states that there is a "time to dance" (Eccl 3:4). The psalmist declares that God has "turned for me my mourning into dancing" (Ps 30:11) and that we are to praise God with dancing (Ps 149:3, 150:4). We use dance to communicate, find mates, and build social bonds, and it is not surprising that God gave us the gift of dance. The first individual we meet in the Bible who is recorded as dancing is Moses's sister, the prophetess Miriam. I think it is prudent to spend some time analyzing a claim I have seen in both scholarly literature and mainstream Christian books.[74] This claim is that Miriam was an ecstatic prophetess. While I do not think there is enough evidence to substantiate this view one way or the other, I do think it is practical to at least analyze what can be said about why people have suggested this interpretation.

The Talmud (ca. fifth–sixth century CE), a collection of rabbinic interpretations of the Jewish oral law, identifies at least seven women from the Hebrew Bible as prophets: "Sarah, Miriam, Deborah, Hannah, Abigail, Huldah, and Esther."[75] Of these seven women, Miriam, Deborah, Hannah,

---

74. See Scharbert, *Exodus*, 66; and Newsom and Ringe, *Women's Bible Commentary*, 36.

75. On Esther being a prophet, the Rabbis argue in b. Meg. 14b: "Esther was also a prophetess, as it is written: 'And it came to pass on the third day that Esther clothed herself in royalty' (Esther 5:1). It should have said: Esther clothed herself in royal garments. Rather, this alludes to the fact that she clothed herself with a divine spirit of inspiration. It is written here: 'And she clothed herself,' and it is written elsewhere: 'And the spirit clothed Amasai' (1 Chronicles 12:19). Just as there the reference is to being enclothed by a spirit, so too Esther was enclothed by a spirit of divine inspiration."

and Huldah (and we could perhaps add Rebekah, Gen 25:19–26) are the most likely to have engaged in ASCs, though the evidence for each varies considerably. It may be difficult to imagine how such a depiction of Miriam can be garnered from the short passages concerning her in Exodus and Numbers. Indeed, it is primarily her function in Exodus where she is viewed by some as engaging in ecstatic behavior. After the Israelites successfully escape captivity in Egypt, joyful singing erupts among the people, first instigated by Moses. We are then told:

> Miriam the prophetess, the sister of Aaron, took a tambourine in her hand, and all the women went out after her with tambourines and dancing. And Miriam sang to them: "Sing to the Lord, for he has triumphed gloriously; the horse and his rider he has thrown into the sea." (Exod 15:20–21)

Prophecy in the Bible is often connected with the use of instruments (1 Sam 10:5–6; 1 Kgs 3:15–16; 1 Chr 25) and many scholars argue that this music was used to induce an ASC.[76]

We will see a specific instance of this concerning the prophet Elisha later, but we should also note that one of the main reasons for viewing Miriam as an ecstatic is the presence of a tambourine in Exodus and the use of instruments among ecstatic prophets in 1 Sam 10 and 19, which we will cover in more detail later as well.[77]

Viewing Miriam as an ecstatic is not a new and vogue interpretation. Philo interprets Moses's and Miriam's singing as "inspired/ecstatic" (ἐνθουσιώδης/*enthousiōdēs*).[78] Additionally, he compares the siblings to a group known as the Therapeutae whom he describes as engaging in a form of drunken ecstasy.[79] Scholars of religion have commonly noted that ritual

---

76. Williamson, "Prophetesses in the Hebrew Bible," 73: "Probably the most consistent element in the portrayal of the prophetess is the association with inspired singing with accompanying instruments and dancing, suggestive of feverish enthusiasm if not necessarily ecstasy."

77. See Stökl, *Prophecy in the Ancient Near East*, 58.

78. Philo, *Contempl. Life* 87. For references tying in music, ecstasy, and ἐνθουσιώδης/ *enthousiōdēs* and similar cognates, see the entries in *GELS*, LEH, and LSJ.

79. Their choir singing is described by Philo, *Contempl. Life* 89–90, as follows: "Thus they continue till dawn, drunk with this drunkenness in which there is no shame, then not with heavy heads or drowsy eyes but more alert and wakeful than when they came to the banquet. . . . So much then for the Therapeutae, who have taken to their hearts the contemplation of nature and what it has to teach, and have lived in the soul alone, citizens of Heaven and the world, presented to the Father and Maker of all by their faithful sponsor Virtue, who has procured for them God's friendship and added a gift going hand in hand with it, true excellence of life, a boon better than all good fortune and rising to the very summit of felicity."

dancing and music was a primary mechanism for inducing ASCs.⁸⁰ The 1985 book *Music and Trance: A Theory of the Relations Between Music and Possession* by Gilbert Rouget (originally published in French as *La musique et la transe: Esquisse d'une théorie générale des relations de la musique et de la possession*) covers a wide range of traditions where this phenomenon is observable. In ancient Syria and Mesopotamia, the word for "ecstatic" derives its etymology from the hurling or whirling dances they performed to work themselves into an ASC.⁸¹

Thus, the use of music and dance by Miriam and the women in Exodus may have also induced an ASC, but there is no way to be sure since the passage is so short and nondescript.

There may be good reasons not to interpret Miriam's singing and dancing as a form of ecstasy, since the two other passages that mention women dancing and singing with timbrels are best viewed as a form of excited, joyous singing about military victory (Judg 11:34; 1 Sam 18:6). Some have argued that because Miriam is referred to as a "prophetess" in this passage, and since the substance of her song is not seemingly prophetic, there must have been something else that characterized the dancing and singing, namely ecstasy.⁸² The major pitfall of such an argument is that this is the first time Miriam is properly introduced to us and so calling her the prophetess seems more of an introductory remark rather than a statement about the substance of the dancing and singing.⁸³ Moreover, just because a prophecy does not seem prophetic does not mean that it is not an inspired utterance. Miriam did not need to foretell some future event or call out the sins of Israel in order to sing prophetically. Whether the singing was spontaneously led by the Spirit or some other mechanism of prophetic revelation is certainly on the table.

It is worth noting that the earliest nonbiblical texts dealing with Miriam construe her as a visionary of some kind. Philo has been mentioned above, but there is also the work *Visions of Amram* (fourth-third century BCE) found among the Dead Sea Scrolls.⁸⁴ Miriam is described in this work as having access to a special kind of knowledge called רז/*raz* or "mystery"

---

80. See, for example, Plutarch, *Amat.* 16 (*Mor.* 758EF; first–second century CE): "Now the prophetic part of enthusiasm derives itself from the inspiration of Apollo possessing the intellect of the soothsayer; but Bacchanal fury proceeds from Father Bacchus. And with the Corybantes ye shall dance."
81. See Sonik and Steinert, eds., *Routledge Handbook of Emotions*, 260.
82. See Tervanotko, *Denying Her Voice*, 50, 59; and Propp, *Exodus 1–18*, 546–49.
83. See Hamori, *Women's Divination*, 61–63.
84. 4Q546 12, 4.

in Aramaic.[85] Miriam's access to this mystery is similar to other prophetic figures in Second Temple Jewish literature such as Enoch, Methuselah, Noah, and especially Daniel. Additionally, Miriam is mentioned in the first-century-CE Latin work Liber antiquitatum biblicarum (English: Book of Biblical Antiquities, abbreviated as LAB) where she experiences a dream-vision.[86] These texts suggest that Miriam was considered a visionary figure in early Judaism and may have engaged in ASCs to communicate with God. Yet, they do not tell us anything about the historical Miriam found in Exod 15, and with that we must be content and not press beyond.

My hope in covering Miriam in this book is to demonstrate that not every claim of ecstatic experience made by biblical scholars is necessarily convincing nor warranted. Relying on later interpretations of biblical characters is also not the primary method one should be using to deduce what their historical counterparts actually did. While continuity of interpretation certainly aids in making a case, it is not as important as the textual evidence presented in Scripture itself. In the case of Miriam, too little exists to demonstrate either way that she engaged in ecstatic dancing.

Yet, even if Miriam is not an ecstatic, this does not mean that modern Christian dancers do not experience genuine ASCs. Indeed, Christian ecstatic dance has been going on for centuries.[87] Research has shown that dancing, regardless of faith affiliation, can induce ASCs.[88] What one experiences within that state is subject to discernment, but the ecstatic episode itself is not necessarily up for debate. Dancing itself, apart from any supernatural activity, can provoke ecstasy.[89] Thus, whether one experiences prophetic revelation or simply an enhanced feeling of euphoria is dependent on whether God chooses to speak through someone during an ASC. Something that will be repeated throughout this book is that not all prophetic messages require an ASC and not all ASCs require prophetic messages. Revelation and ecstasy are two distinct, but often intertwined, phenomena.

85. *DCH*, s.v. "רָז."

86. LAB 9:10: "And the spirit of God came upon Miriam one night, and she saw a dream and told it to her parents in the morning, saying, 'I have seen this night, and behold a man in a linen garment stood and said to me, Go and say to your parents, Behold he who will be born from you will be cast forth into the water; likewise through him the water will be dried up. And I will work signs through him and save my people, and he will exercise leadership always.' And when Miriam told of her dream, her parents did not believe her."

87. See Van Oort, "Spirit Moves"; Bloomfield, "Pentecostalism"; and Jennings, "Imagining Jesus."

88. See Papadimitropoulos, "Psychedelic Trance."

89. See Fasullo et al., "Innate Human Potential"; Simons et al., "Psychobiology of Trance: I"; and Ervin et al., "Psychobiology of Trance: II."

High on God?

In 2013, the Canadian-American magazine *VICE* produced a twenty-eight-minute documentary titled "Getting Drunk on God" in which they interviewed Red Letter Ministries leader Brandon Barthrop.[90] Throughout the documentary, Barthrop uses physical substances such as frankincense and essential oils to help induce a state of trance or ecstasy and even refers to his house church as "the crack house." In various videos, Barthrop and others can be seen doing invisible lines of cocaine out of Bibles, pretending to smoke invisible joints, or injecting invisible needles into their arms to get high on Jesus or the Holy Spirit, which he and others interpret as a method for inducing ecstasy.

I encourage readers to investigate Barthrop and Red Letter Ministries further to determine why I and countless others within the charismatic movement reject this ministry and movement. However, it is important to engage with some of the arguments at the beginning of this section so that we do not wrongly conflate Barthrop's position with what is possibly a biblical practice.

The particular word we are interested in this section is "entheogen" (from the Greek words ἔνθεος/*entheos* and γίνομαι/*ginomai*), which refers to any form of chemical substance used to induce a trance or ecstasy for religious purposes.[91] Common substances include the indigenous use of peyote and psilocybin mushrooms (magic mushrooms). By partaking in these drugs, hallucinatory visions could be achieved to see ancestors, gods, or other spiritual beings. Most famously, in 1970 the English archaeologist and Dead Sea Scrolls scholar John M. Allegro (1923–1988) wrote the book *The Sacred Mushroom and the Cross* where he argued that Christianity originated as a shamanic cult in which Jesus was not the son of God, but a code for psychedelic mushrooms! Naturally, Allegro's revisionist analysis of early Christianity was met with overwhelming criticism and rejection, leading one scholar to state it was "possibly the single most ludicrous book on Jesus scholarship by a qualified academic."[92] Still, because of media sensation and Allegro's perceived authority in the academy, the idea that psychedelics were the origins of Christianity and, by extension, Israelite religious history (including Moses's burning bush experience among others) has proliferated popular internet culture and the mythology refuses to die out. Thus, Barthrop and other "holy tokers" have similarly argued that the

---

90. VICE, "Getting Drunk on God."
91. BDAG, s.v. "ἔνθεος"; BDAG, s.v. "γίνομαι."
92. Jenkins, *Hidden Gospels*, 180.

incense burned in the tabernacle and Jerusalem temple were psychoactive and helped facilitate coming into contact with God.[93]

Such claims seem ridiculous on the surface, but there has actually been a string of scholars who have held this position. The Polish anthropologist Sula Benet (1903–1982) was the first major proponent of this theory and argued that the Hebrew phrase קְנֵה־בֹשֶׂם/qənē-bōśem (usually translated as "aromatic cane" [NRSV] or "fragrant calamus" [NIV]) used in the prescription for anointing oil in Exod 30:22–25 should be translated as "cannabis"![94] More recently, a 2020 report found that residue of cannabis had been found in two eighth-century-BCE limestone monoliths that archaeologists interpret as altars within a Judahite shrine. The presence of Δ9-tetrahydrocannabinol (THC), cannabidiol (CBD), and cannabinol (CBN) mixed with other substances such as animal dung for burning has led some researchers to suggest that this incense altar was used to induce a trance state.[95] These new findings have reawakened to a certain extent the belief that Israelite cultic activity was heavily centered around an entheogen experience where God was contacted via hallucinogenic means.[96]

It is important to note that many of the standard lexicons and other scholars have not even entertained Benet's translation. Additionally, the residue from a couple of eighth-century altars tells us little about prescribed Israelite law or that this was common practice. Yet, there is good reason to think that the use of incense and anointing oil may have helped facilitate trance states, even if cannabis was not the substance used.[97]

The Swiss classicist Georg Hans Bhawani Luck (1926–2013) notes that the ingredients given in Exod 30 (a mix of myrrh, onycha, galbanum, and

---

93. For incense in Israel, see Nielsen, *Incense in Ancient Israel*; and Heger, *Incense Cult in Ancient Israel*.

94. Benet, "Early Diffusion." Later rabbinic texts have also been interpreted as referring to cannabis. See Warf, "High Points." On page 422 Warf states: "Psychoactive cannabis is mentioned in the Talmud, and the ancient Jews may have used hashish."

95. Arie et al., "Cannabis and Frankincense."

96. For an overview of ancient use of incense, see Dannaway, "Strange Fires."

97. Luck, *Arcana Mundi*, 487: "The holy oil, used to anoint priests, kings, and sacred objects, is also specified in chapter 30 of the Book of Exodus. To judge from the ingredients, it is also psychoactive, but probably to a lesser degree than the incense formula. It consists of: 1. Pure myrrh, the oleo gum resin from Commiphora myrrha 2. Sweet cinnamon, probably from the dried bark of Cinnamomum zeylanicum 3. Sweet calamus, most likely from Acorus calamus, but another name is "fragrant cane," which could be from Cymbopogon martini 4. Cassia, probably from the bark of Cinnamomum cassia or Cassia lignea, but other plants, such as Aucklandia costus, Castus speciosus, and Saussurea lappa have also been proposed. Myrrh, as mentioned above, may be considered an inebriant or a mild narcotic, while the psychoactive properties of sweet calamus (asarone) are well established."

frankincense) were a "very sophisticated psychoactive incense blend, the results of centuries of research and experiment, one would assume. The formula may have been developed in the temples of Egypt to produce visions of a deity in trance."[98] Indeed, frankincense, myrrh, and other gum resins were used throughout the history of religion to induce trance.[99]

Based on the ingredient list and the mention that God will "meet with you" (Exod 30:6) when the incense is burned, Luck states that this "should be taken in the strictest, literal sense. God will appear to the priest who uses the sacred substance in the proper way."[100] This interpretation is further strengthened by the presence of incense in Lev 24:5–9. In this passage, incense is to be sprinkled over the showbread as a אזכרה/'azkarah. This word is likely connected with the Akkadian word zakaru—that is, "to call upon a deity" (i.e., an invocation).[101] Additionally, the "strange fire" (Exod 30:9) that is not to be offered is thus interpreted by Luck as offering incense outside of the prescribed time in a way to circumvent divine communication.

We must say a few words about identifying plants and other substances in the Hebrew Bible. Often when reading English translations, words used for plants, gemstones, colors, and other categories seem oddly specific or perhaps obtusely vague. This is because sometimes we do not actually know the meaning of a particular Hebrew word and are relying on later translations (e.g., the Septuagint, Syriac, etc.) to reconstruct the probable meaning of that word. Thus, there is significant debate about the identification of many of the specific substances listed in the incense and oil ingredients of Exod 30.

---

98. Luck, *Arcana Mundi*, 487.

99. See Moussaieff et al., "Incensole Acetate"; and Luck, *Arcana Mundi*, 474.

100. Luck, *Arcana Mundi*, 487: "But the sanctions against any frivolous, casual use are formidable, just as they were in ancient Greece and no doubt in Egypt. By its very nature, an 'entheogen' is surrounded by taboos, because it gives access to the deity, and the tremendous power it transmits must be controlled. Among all the detailed instructions preserved in the Book of Exodus, there is not a single reference to an 'aroma pleasing to the Lord.' The pleasant, aromatic scent is associated with the epiphany of the deity, as in ancient Greece, because the deity appears in the cloud of aromata covered by human beings. But the incense burned on the shiny surface of the altar has only one function, the most important of all: to bring down the Lord. If this interpretation is right, it may give a new understanding of the Gospel account of Jesus' nativity (notably Matthew 2:11). The three Magi offer gold, frankincense, and myrrh to Jesus. The symbolism of these gifts has been understood in many different ways, but there may be a connection with the incense cult of the Old Testament."

101. Nielsen, "Ancient Aromas," para. 6: "Burning incense produced a soothing odor, pleasing to the deity, thus attracting and appeasing the deity at one and the same time."

The quantity of anointing oil is striking. The 1500 shekels of fragrance (500 of myrrh, 250 of cinnamon, 250 of cane, and 500 of cassia) would have weighed about 38 pounds.[102] It is especially interesting that God describes the anointing oil as a "perfume," since "sweaty bodies were to be avoided in the tabernacle among God's servants the priests (thus the linen garments, as explained by Ezek 44:17–18), and likewise the odor of smelly bodies was to be offset by perfume, at least symbolically."[103] Yet, at the same time, God prohibits people from using this same recipe to make actual perfume because it is meant to be "holy" (Exod 30:36).

We now return to the question at hand: were the priests in the Old Testament getting high as some have suggested? I do not think so. Rather, I think what is more probable is that, like the use of music, rhythmic movement, and other methods of achieving trance or ecstasy, the presence of incense (and smoke in general) may have helped in reaching such states, but the priests were not intoxicated or stoned in our modern sense of someone smoking marijuana.[104]

The imagery of smoke and divine communication is not foreign to the biblical text. According to several passages, God would manifest himself as a pillar of cloud/smoke over the tabernacle (Exod 40:36; Num 9:17; 14:14) and when God wanted to communicate with Moses, the pillar descended (Exod 33:9–11; Num 12:5; Deut 31:15). The presence of the cloud probably had a dual function. First, it obscured God's face from Moses so that he would not die (Exod 33:18–20), but secondly it also obscured Moses's mental faculties from outward distractions or perhaps even facilitated a trance state so that his attention and receptiveness to God's voice was more amicable.[105] The use of cloud/smoke imagery is also used when God discusses how he speaks to prophets in the book of Numbers and comes down in a pillar of smoke (12:5–9). This obscuring of God's face here serves an ironic function. While Miriam and Aaron protest that they too are prophets like Moses, God's intentional obscurity and the fact that he tells them that prophets other than Moses only hear from him in riddles and visions and dreams is meant to showcase that God's method of communication is

---

102. Stuart, *Exodus*, 643.

103. Stuart, *Exodus*, 643–44.

104. See Goodman, *Ecstasy*, 35; Kleinman, *Patients and Healers*, 344; and Hadidi, *Zar*, 43, 106.

105. Pilch, *Flights of the Soul*, 68: "In the ethnographic literature, clouds are often a metaphor for shamanistic journeys . . . the fogs are related to the clouds. Both are gray or white in color, which is neurological evidence of brain activity characteristic of an ASC experience."

typically also obscure.¹⁰⁶ It is also notable that we have examples of people receiving visions while inside or near the temple. Zechariah in Luke 1, for example, is said to experience a vision of an angel while burning incense on the altar. Likewise, Paul falls into a trance while praying at the temple (Acts 22:17), and this may also be the case of the prophet Amos (9:1).

In conclusion, the use of incense, especially the presence of frankincense and myrrh, strongly suggests that there was to some degree a manipulation of the mental faculties of the priests offering it. This is best interpreted, I argue, as inducing a trance state where prophetic oracles and other instructions could be more readily transmitted to the human recipient. Because of the nature of this ritual, God erected various prohibitions and boundaries around who could offer this incense and at what times. This is best explained as a means of limiting competing prophetic voices and establishing Moses as the head prophetic figure within the Israelite assembly. Moreover, since those serving in the Levitical priesthood likely were the most educated (requiring the ability to read and write to some extent), this may have allowed visionary experiences to remain primarily in the realm of the elite, establishing a kind of authoritative prophetic caste among the academic and deterring potential error.

Ecstatic Elders

In 1996, after many years of exhaustive ministry in Mozambique, Africa, and suffering with double pneumonia, Heidi Baker checked herself out of the hospital and flew to Toronto, Canada, to attend a meeting at what was then called Toronto Airport Christian Fellowship. At that point in its history, the church had made international news, with people travelling from all over the world to experience the revival taking place. This event became known as the "Toronto Blessing" and was understood by those in attendance as a contagious, transferrable blessing that started in Toronto but was carried throughout the world. Unique manifestations took place during the days of the revival, some of which garnered extreme criticism from those outside. Despite this, when Heidi entered the building, she took a deep

---

106. Noth, *Numbers*, 96: "The divine teaching about the uniqueness of the relationship between Moses and God, with which Aaron and Miriam are rebuked, obviously derives, in the context of the Pentateuchal narrative, from 11.14–17, 24b–30. If, with these latter remarks, ecstatic 'prophecy' had posited the 'spirit' of Moses as its ultimate origin . . . then the divine address of ch. 12, which is brought about by the appearance of Aaron and Miriam, will be intended to avert the conclusion that Moses had been nothing more than an '(ecstatic) prophet'. He was *much more*; Yahweh had made him his intimate confidant." See also Levine, *Numbers 1–20*, 341–44.

breath and was completely healed of her pneumonia. She then reports the following experience:

> When I was in Toronto once, I was on the floor seven days and seven nights under the power of the Holy Spirit. I was unable to move in my own strength. I couldn't even lift my head, and I had to be carried everywhere, even to the restroom! I couldn't eat or drink by myself. It was almost like being a quadriplegic. The Body of Christ had to take complete care of me. When I was thirsty, the Lord had to speak to someone to come and pour water down my throat. This was really difficult for someone as active as me, and I felt like I was going to die. The Lord told me that's exactly how He wanted me! Dead. He would then raise me from the dead. During this time God was wooing me deeper in to His heart and showing me how I could do nothing without Him, and I could do nothing without His Body. I was learning about dependence on Him and inter-dependence in His beloved Bride. We were all created to be in family and can do nothing without each other.[107]

Heidi reports that after this experience, God formed a team around her and her husband, Rolland, and a revival hit the area where they were ministering. Healings, multiplication of food, and other miracles became commonplace. Her dependance on the body of Christ became a central philosophy of their organization, Iris Global. This seemingly bizarre and intense manifestation thrust them into becoming one of the largest humanitarian agencies working in the country and thousands of churches were born from this. Interestingly, this ASC that she endured has parallels to a story found in the book of Numbers.

Numbers pictures a very tired and burned-out Moses. Due to the complaints of his fellow Israelites, God has Moses gather seventy elders to work with the people and help with the burden of leading. Once the people are gathered, the following is reported:

> Then the Lord came down in the cloud and spoke to him, and took some of the Spirit that was on him and put it on the seventy elders. And as soon as the Spirit rested on them, they [hitnabbē]. But they did not continue doing it. (Num 11:25)

This account has often been suggested to be evidence that the seventy elders experienced a form of ecstasy. A major part of the debate centers around one Hebrew word in this passage: התנביא/*hitnabbē*. Most translations

---

107. Baker, "Primacy of Love," para. 20.

render this phrase as "they prophesied" (e.g., ESV, NASB, NIV, KJV). Others, though, note there is likely an ecstatic element to this verb. The CEV and the GNT, for example, render it as "they started shouting like prophets." The JPS Contemporary Torah translates it as "they spoke in ecstasy."[108]

The debate regarding *hitnabbē* has taken form over the last century.[109] The major players in the early years, Gustav Hölscher and Bernhard Duhm, both published theories about the role that ecstasy played in Israelite history. In the early 1900s, only a few documents from the ANE were readily accessible to academics, but a picture of the inner workings of prophetic experience was beginning to be examined. Scholars since then have gone back and forth about what to make of the verb *hitnabbē*, though the increased publication and distribution of ANE material has certainly shown evidence that ecstasy clearly was part of prophecy around Israel. Still, while many scholars have noted that this word likely represents "exuberant" (i.e., ecstatic) behavior,[110] others have argued that its meaning ranges depending on the context,[111] or that ecstasy is not in view at all.[112]

It is worth noting that understanding *hitnabbē* as referring to ecstatic behavior is not a minority view.[113] Every major Hebrew lexicon offers ecstasy as an interpretation of this word. An exhaustive account of the scholarly debate on this passage is not feasible here, but a close reading of the text is appropriate to see if ecstasy is indeed a possibility. Concerning the word *hitnabbē* in this passage, however, Timothy R. Ashley best summarizes the issue as follows:

> It is hard to know exactly what is meant here . . . it [*hitnabbē*] means, literally, "to act the prophet." In such passages as 1 Sam. 10 and 19 the verb is clearly connected with behavior that might be called abnormal or, better, "ecstatic." In other passages the verb just as clearly indicates speaking Yahweh's word without any hint of such behavior. Can any choice be made here, the only passage in the Pentateuch to use the verb? Since the text itself gives no message or word from Yahweh derived from this prophesying, the more natural meaning seems to be the former, i.e., that these elders behaved in some way that accredited them as prophets. They were under the influence of Yahweh's Spirit,

---

108. Stein et al., *Contemporary Torah*, 235.

109. For a history of the scholarship, see Adam, "He Behaved Like a Prophet."

110. Wenham, *Numbers*, 109; cf. Ashley, *Numbers*, 158.

111. Wilson, "Prophecy and Ecstasy," 336; Uffenheimer, "Prophecy, Ecstasy, and Sympathy," 263.

112. Levison, "Prophecy in Ancient Israel."

113. See especially the analysis of Carlson, *Unfamiliar Selves*, 110–15.

which had been upon Moses. More specific than this we cannot be.[114]

I too think there are good reasons for interpreting what is happening in this narrative as a form of ecstasy. First, as noted by Ashley, the Hebrew word *hitnabbē* is used of ecstatic behavior elsewhere, and even those who disagree with Num 11:25 being such an instance will admit this (e.g., 1 Sam 10:5–13; 18:1; 19:20–24; 1 Kgs 18:29). That *hitnabbē* is recognized as having this connotation, and since no specific message is recorded by the elders here, ecstasy seems to be a more likely candidate for the meaning. Additionally, group ecstasy is known from the ancient and modern world.[115] This fact further suggests that a group-induced ecstasy is the more probable meaning behind *hitnabbē* in this account. Second, that God descends in a cloud is reminiscent of what we have just witnessed in the case of the incense altar and the priests—that divine communication often happens through cloud/smoke motifs meant to induce trance. Third, the elders *hitnabbē* when God's Spirit is placed "on" (עַל/*al*) them and "rests" (נוח/*nuach*) on them. This parallels Acts 2 where the Spirit rests on the disciples, a narrative where ecstasy is a probable interpretation.[116] Fourth, Num 11:25 states that "they did not continue doing it," but the NIV better captures the meaning: "But they did not do so again." If *hitnabbē* is interpreted as a form of ecstasy, such a statement makes better sense than simply not prophesying again. If the meaning is that the elders never prophesied again, this raises the question as to why God would cause them to prophesy here away from the congregation of Israel. For what purpose? Since their job was to aid Moses in administration, God's Spirit empowering them, evidenced by ecstasy, seems more likely. As the Jewish biblical scholar Jacob Milgrom states: "The function of their ecstasy is not to render them prophets—their ecstatic state is never again repeated—but to provide divine validation for their selection as leaders."[117]

---

114. Ashley, *Numbers*, 158.

115. See, for example, Long, "Social Dimensions of Prophetic Conflict," 36.

116. K&D, 1:698: "הִתְנַבֵּא, '*to prophesy*,' is to be understood generally, and especially here, not as the foretelling of future things, but as speaking in an ecstatic and elevated state of mind, under the impulse and inspiration of the Spirit of God, just like the 'speaking with tongues,' which frequently followed the gift of the Holy Ghost in the days of the apostles. But we are not to infer from the fact, that the prophesying was not repeated, that the Spirit therefore departed from them after this one extraordinary manifestation. This miraculous manifestation of the Spirit was intended simply to give to the whole nation the visible proof that God had endowed them with His Spirit, as helpers of Moses, and had given them the authority required for the exercise of their calling."

117. Milgrom, *Numbers*, 89.

Finally, within the narrative of Num 11, ecstatic behavior makes much more sense than generic prophesying.[118] Two men, Eldad and Medad, who remained at the camp are also given portions of God's Spirit and begin to *hitnabbē*. Upon witnessing this, a young man runs to Moses to tell him what is happening. Joshua hears the news and informs Moses to tell them to stop. Ecstatic manifestations likely were interpreted as indicating prophetic leadership.

Thus, Joshua's concern was that Moses's unique authority would be compromised. Yet, Moses tells him, "Are you jealous for my sake? Would that all the Lord's people were prophets, that the Lord would put his Spirit on them!" (Num 11:29). The ecstatic behavior was not, therefore, an outward sign intended for usurping spiritual authority or drawing attention to oneself as a prophetic leader. Rather, it was a manifestation of God's presence within the covenant community.

Importantly, this ASC of the elders was meant to alleviate Moses of the stress of leading the entire Israelite people. It became visibly apparent that God was empowering the elders to lead, and thus Moses became dependent on God's covenant people. This theme of unity among the chosen people speaks to the function of the Holy Spirit within the church as well. In the example of Heidi Baker above, her ASC experience and the subsequent outpouring in Mozambique facilitated a sense of shared values and purpose, which resulted in massive revival among syncretistic Muslims. God's purpose of outpouring the Spirit is for Christians to love one another and work side by side, and so the presence of ASCs in the context of new ministry endeavors seems to be consistent with the general flow of Scripture.

Balaam's Assessment

The sorcerer Balaam does not seem like the person to look to as an example of good religious experiences. Yet, just as God was able to speak through a donkey, he too is able to speak through Balaam, both in the oracle he presents and his explanation of what he experiences. While hired to curse the Israelites, Balaam soon becomes Spirit possessed: "And Balaam lifted up

---

118. Levison, *Inspired*, 76–77, argues that the elders being ecstatic "makes no sense" if the purpose is to aid Moses in administrative tasks. This line of reasoning is confusing. An initial ecstatic experience to demonstrate God's distribution of the Spirit does not undermine their function for later administrative tasks, especially since they "did not continue doing it" (Num 11:25). Indeed, the point seems to be that this ecstatic outburst did *not* interfere with their assigned task as it was not ongoing. Additionally, if "unbridled ecstasy," as Levison refers to it, is not in view, a trance state accompanying the vision may account for the verb *hitnabbē*.

his eyes and saw Israel camping tribe by tribe. And the Spirit of God came upon him" (Num 24:2). This last phrase, "the Spirit of God came upon him," is almost identical to what is found in a number of other passages where ecstasy is present (e.g., 1 Sam 10:10; 11:6; 16:13; 18:10; 19:23; 1 Chr 12:18). The words he then speaks are not his own, but inspired utterances from God's Spirit.

Within the oracle, Balaam explains some of the physiological experiences he undergoes while being Spirit possessed:

> The oracle of Balaam the son of Beor, the oracle of the man whose eye is opened, the oracle of him who hears the words of God, and knows the knowledge of the Most High, who sees the vision of the Almighty, falling down with his eyes uncovered. (Num 24:16)

There are a number of important elements to observe in this short passage. We must note that Balaam describes himself as a "man whose eye is opened." This is not simply a metaphorical statement for understanding. Previously, God is said to have "opened the eyes of Balaam" in order for him to see the angel standing in the way. In other words, Balaam's eyes were opened in that he was having a visionary experience ("who sees the vision of the Almighty"). He was able to actually see that which was previously invisible. We see that Balaam describes himself as "him who hears the words of God" and that he has received knowledge from God. Whether Balaam is literally hearing auditory messages to repeat in his oracles is unclear, but he is somehow able to confer divine information.

Finally, Balaam describes himself as "falling down with his eyes uncovered." Interestingly, the KJV actually translates this passage as "falling *into a trance*, but having his eyes open" (emphasis added). The Septuagint translates it as "sleep" (ὕπνος/*hupnos*).[119] This has led the LES translators to interpret the phrase as meaning that it was like Balaam was experiencing a visionary dream state: "Who saw visions of God as in a dream, his eyes being open." Likewise, the NETS translators render it "one who sees a divine vision, in sleep when his eyes had been uncovered." The Septuagint itself, as well as the English translations of the Septuagint, are all working from the same Hebrew word: נפל/*naphal*. *Naphal* is the generic verb for "fall," but because of the poetic context of the oracle, translations have taken different views on how to render it. The reason for connecting *naphal* to trance and ecstasy in this passage, however, makes sense. Balaam is Spirit possessed, experiencing a vision, and speaking oracles from God. Based on

---

119. LEH, s.v. "ὕπνος."

other similar accounts in the Bible, we should not be surprised that Balaam should be understood as in an ASC.[120] The word *naphal* is also used when describing Adam and Abram's trance states.

But let us turn to the crux of interpreting this passage as literal falling while in ecstasy or trance. When Balaam's eyes are opened and he sees the angel, "He bowed down and fell on his face" (Num 22:31). Is this not what he is then referring to in his oracle? Is he not simply falling down in reverence and fear? On the surface this may appear so. However, the English words translated as "bowed down" (קדד/*qadad*) and "fell" (שחה/*shâchâh*) are not used the same way *naphal* is. The Hebrew words in Num 22:31 are used specifically in the context of worship or showing honor, whereas *naphal* is not. Thus, the narrative of Num 22:31 is not relevant for interpreting what is happening with *naphal* in Num 24:2.[121]

Early Jewish interpreters seem to have considered Balaam as being in a state of ecstasy as well. Philo, for example, states that Balaam "became inspired, the prophetic spirit having entered into him . . . he became like the interpreter of some other being who was prompting his words, and spoke in prophetic strain."[122] Likewise, Josephus states that Balaam spoke "by the divine spirit" and mentions how the "Spirit of God seizes" people and importantly how God "puts such words as he pleases in our mouths, and such discourses as we are not ourselves conscious of."[123]

Some critics of ecstasy have suggested that these moments are evidence of divine judgment, not of divine favor. Setting aside the examples of trance and ecstasy where this is demonstrably not the case (such as with Adam and Abraham), in the specific instance of Balaam this also makes little sense. According to Num 24:1, Balaam's oracle begins with him noticing "that it pleased the Lord to bless Israel." Balaam is not under judgment or acting in disobedience at this point. Rather, he is actively doing the opposite. Balaam specifically is said to "not go, as at other times, to look for omens" (Num 24:1), but instead turns to bless Israel. It is after this point that God's Spirit comes upon him again and he experiences the ASC.

---

120. The *Greek Magical Papyri* record a "charm of Solomon that produces a trance" though the title of this spell literally translates to "Solomon's Collapse," which is interpreted by Betz as some kind of "ecstatic seizure." *PGM* IV. 850–929.

121. Cole, *Numbers*, 416: "In this case the Spirit of God came upon the prophet, and he may have entered into an ecstatic trance in the manner of Saul (1 Sam 10:6) or Micaiah (1 Kgs 22:10–23)."

122. Philo, *Moses* 1.277.

123. Josephus, *Ant.* 4.119.

While many may scoff at charismatics using Balaam as an example of ecstasy in which someone actually falls down, there are good reasons for interpreting these passages as just that.[124]

I suggest one of the main reasons people have not adopted this particular reading is because they have been predisposed to mock the idea outright before delving into the text itself. If we can accept that one of the most significant messianic prophecies (Num 24:15–17) came from the mouth of a pagan magician, is it really that difficult to believe that he was also in an ASC?[125]

Conclusion

This chapter has attempted to introduce readers to a series of narratives in the Torah that deal with ASCs. In some instances, lexical, historical, and contextual clues help aid us in demonstrating that ASCs are present in the text. In other instances, such as with Miriam, there is little to no evidence that such experiences are present. Although in such instances the term "ecstasy" or "ecstatic" may be thrown around too loosely when discussing these narratives, there are nevertheless good exegetical grounds for interpreting other events as ASCs.

Some ASCs are imposed on individuals by God, such as with Adam and Abraham. In other cases, ASCs seem to be self-induced, such as with the use of incense by the priesthood or through scrying as with Joseph. More examples of this dichotomy (imposed vs. induced) regarding ASCs will be explored in the following chapters as well and, as we shall see, there do not seem to be any prohibitions against the induced form. Induced ASCs may include prophetic revelation or feelings of euphoria, but they are not necessary. Likewise, revelation may include ASCs, but not always.

---

124. Levison, *Inspired*, 75, for example, portrays the issue of Balaam's prophecy as "a laconic description of inspiration, though hardly a description of ecstasy, and Balaam's opening words (24:3–4) do not clarify the nature of his experience, due in part to difficulties in the Hebrew text." Evidently, I believe that by working through the Hebrew text and how it was understood by later traditions such as the Septuagint, Josephus, and Philo, we can come to a clearer picture of Balaam's experiences.

125. In a letter written by Jerome (fourth–fifth century CE), the translator of the Latin Vulgate version of the Bible, he recalls a conversation with a woman named Fabiola who asked him, "How came it that the soothsayer Balaam in prophesying of the future mysteries of Christ spoke more plainly of Him than almost any other prophet?" (*Epist.* 77.7). Jerome simply replies that he tried as best he could to answer.

3

Getting Plastered with the Prophets

> Souls and memories can do strange things during trance.
> —Bram Stoker

ACCORDING TO THE APOSTLE Paul, the purpose of prophecy is for people's "upbuilding and encouragement and consolation" (1 Cor 14:3) and is a "sign for . . . believers" (1 Cor 14:22). Yet, when one looks at the landscape of Christianity today, it is easy to see dissenting voices claiming that prophecy is distracting, divisive, or demonic.

Indeed, it is not difficult to look at examples of modern charlatans fleecing the flock under the guise of prophetic inspiration or justifying the most heinous of actions with the excuse "God told me." Others may see contemporary charismatics vying for attention with louder and more spectacular manifestations to outshine other churchgoers. For those who believe in the continuation of the gift of prophecy, it is often troubling to see the misuses, abuses, and disdain shown for this manifestation of the Spirit.

This chapter focuses on a collection of texts called the Nevi'im or "Prophets." It is not just prophets, however, that we will be analyzing. A number of characters not explicitly called prophets engage in prophetic activity and, as we shall see, often experience ASCs. In some instances, these ASCs are so dramatic that the onlookers within the biblical text are confused at what is happening as well! The German Old Testament scholar Hermann Gunkel (1862–1932), was one of the first in the field of biblical studies to raise the question of religious experience when thinking about the prophets of the Hebrew Bible.[1] He believed that the way of understanding the prophets was primarily through ecstasy:

> When such an ecstasy seizes him, the prophet . . . loses command of his limbs; he staggers and stutters like a drunken man; his ordinary sense of what is decent deserts him; he feels an impulse to do all kinds of strange actions . . . strange ideas and emotions come over him . . . he is seized by that sensation of hovering which we know from our own dreams.[2]

The early prophets of Israelite history, according to Gunkel, were frenzied ecstatics (1 Sam 10:1–13; 19:18–24; 2 Kgs 3:14–15; 9:11; Isa 28:7; Jer 29:26; Hos 9:7; Mic 2:11) and he argues that this eventually evolved into a more rational form of prophecy that one finds in the literary or classical prophets of the eighth century BCE onward. Much has been written since Gunkel. Modern scholars, equipped with new tools and archaeological finds, challenge this explanation of the development of Israelite prophecy.[3] The works of John J. Pilch, Reed Carlson, and others mentioned in the introduction to this book are excellent examples showcasing how ecstatic phenomena persisted among prophets beyond the eighth century BCE.

Deborah and Divination

The only people explicitly called "prophets" in the Torah are Abraham, Moses, Aaron, and Miriam (we could add the seventy unnamed elders of Israel and Eldad and Medad to the list). We can assume other prophets must have existed, since Deut 13 and 18 give instructions on how to discern true and false prophets, but we are not privy to their names and activities. The next named prophet in the Bible is Deborah. Like Miriam, Deborah also engaged in public singing and acted as both a prophet and judge for the Israelites, and there is considerable debate about what exactly her roles entailed.[4] For our purposes, the portion of interest is that Deborah "used to sit under the palm of Deborah between Ramah and Bethel in the hill country of Ephraim, and the people of Israel came up to her for judgment" (Judg 4:5). Whether she was meting out civil justice in a court scenario or delivering ad hoc

---

1. Gunkel, *Propheten*.
2. Gunkel, "Secret Experiences," 428.
3. For a summary, see Petersen, "Defining Prophecy"; cf. Wilson, "Prophecy and Ecstasy."
4. Block, *Judges, Ruth*, 191–97.

prophetic oracles, Deborah has often been described as an ecstatic by some scholars.[5]

Of a truth, there are some reasons for thinking Deborah was an ecstatic, though they range in degrees of plausibility. Here, I want to take time to be exhaustive for two purposes: (1) much has been written speculating on the character of Deborah and the nature of ancient Israelite prophecy and (2) it is important to see the limitations of comparative beliefs and practices from the ANE and the Bible. Just because we can find something that seems comparable doesn't mean we can therefore infer a one-to-one scenario.

The most compelling reason for inferring Deborah entered an ASC has to do with the use of trees in prophecy and divination elsewhere in the Bible and the ANE more broadly. In Judg 9:37, a אֵלוֹן מְעוֹנְנִים/' ēlôn məʿônənîm is mentioned as an oracular tool.[6] The Hebrew phrase here is variously translated as "Diviners' Oak/Tree" (CEB, ESV, NIV, NLT), "the oak tree of the fortune tellers" (GNT), and even the lengthy rendering "the tree where people talk with the spirits of the dead" (CEV)!

The Hebrew words themselves point toward some kind of tree used for divination, though the method is unclear. The Hebrew word מְעוֹנְנִים/məʿônənîm comes from the word עָנַן/'nn which is often translated as "to practice soothsaying" or "to interpret omens."[7]

God often communicated to people under or near trees in the Old Testament. The most obvious examples include God's appearance to Abraham by the oaks of Mamre (Gen 18:1), Moses and the burning bush (Exod 3:4), and the angel of the Lord's appearance to Gideon under a terebinth (Judg 6:11). In one particular case, David seems to inquire of God when to go out to battle, only to be told to wait until he hears "the sound of marching in the tops of the balsam trees" (2 Sam 5:24). This case in 2 Samuel may find a parallel in Judg 4:14: "And Deborah said to Barak, 'Up! For this is the day in which the Lord has given Sisera into your hand. Does not the Lord go out before you?' So Barak went down from Mount Tabor with 10,000 men following him."

---

5. Yoder, *Power and Politics*, 67. See also Elkins and Treu, *Bible's Top 50 Ideas*, 177.

6. I disagree with Spronk, "Deborah, A Prophetess," 236–37, who argues that Deborah was a necromancer due to this connection between Judg 4:5 and 9:37. See Osborne, "Biblical Reconstruction of the Prophetess," 207–9. Stökl, "Female Prophets," has argued based on parallels to ANE prophets that Deborah fits the image of a *āpiltum* (prophetess) rather than a *maḫḫūtum* (female ecstatic). Kupitz and Berthelot, "Deborah and the Delphic Pythia," have tried to connect Deborah with the Greek Delphic Pythia.

7. *DCH*, s.v. "עָנַן I"; *HALOT*, s.v. "עָנַן"; BDB, s.v. עָנַן II."

That Deborah knew that God had gone out may be due to similar reasons, the movement of the trees. Thus, the use of trees in general may indicate Deborah's prophetic practices.

Oddly, in the notes of the *NKJV Cultural Backgrounds Study Bible* (2017) it states: "Of all of the divination procedures known from the ancient world, there is no suggestion of trees used as divinatory mechanisms."[8] This is simply incorrect. Caroline J. Tully's article "Understanding the Language of Trees: Ecstatic Experience and Interspecies Communication in Late Bronze Age Crete" in *The Routledge Companion to Ecstatic Experience in the Ancient World* (2022) offers various forms of evidence to the contrary. Even within the Hebrew Bible, this form of divination must have been common enough for the prophet Hosea to say, "My people inquire of a piece of wood, and their walking staff gives them oracles. For a spirit of whoredom has led them astray" (4:12). While the ESV translates the Hebrew word עֵץ/'*ēṣ* here as "a piece of wood," and the NIV (unhelpfully) as "wooden idol," the word can simply mean "tree." Its parallelism with the Hebrew word מַקֵּל/*maqqēl*, translated variously as "walking staff" (ESV), "divining rod" (NRSV), or "diviner's wand" (NASB), suggests a form of dendromancy (divination using trees) or rhabdomancy (divination using a rod/dowsing).[9]

Dendromancy is not unheard of from the ancient world.[10] According to one source known as the Ba'al Epic, a certain individual communicates with a "word of tree," understood by some scholars as the divinatory practice of interpreting the sounds of the wind rustling through the tree.[11] Elsewhere, two texts from the ancient city of Knossos mention a "Priestess of winds,"

---

8. Keener and Walton, *NKJV Cultural Backgrounds Study Bible*, 35.

9. A form of dendromancy may also be present in Ezek 8:17, which states: "Behold, they put the branch to their nose." Pilch, *Flights of the Soul*, 18: "The gesture is more plausibly interpreted as a method of inducing an alternate state of consciousness." This practice is similar to one recorded by Epiphanius about a group known as the Tascodrugites or "peg snouts." *Pan.* 48:14.

10. For examples of dendromancy in Hellenism, see Stiles, "Making Sense of Chaos."

11. *KTU* 1.3:3:15–34: "Let your feet hasten towards me, let your legs hurry to me! For I have a word that I would say to you, a message that I would repeat to you: a word of tree and whisper of stone, the sighing of the heavens to the earth, of the deep to the stars, I understand the thunder which the heavens do not know, a word unknown to men, and which the multitudes of the earth do not understand. Come, and I shall reveal it in the midst of my divine mountain, Saphon, in the sanctuary, on the mountain of my inheritance, in Paradise, on the height of victory." Cf. *KTU* 1.1.3:10–14; 1.7:30–34. *KTU* stands for the German *Keilalphabetischen Texte aus Ugarit* and is the standard title for a collection of the cuneiform texts from Ugarit found in works like Wyatt, *Religious Texts from Ugarit*, the translation I've quoted from here. The word "cuneiform" refers to a kind of writing that used wedge-shaped impressions (usually by use of a reed) into clay tablets that were baked to preserve the script. See Wyatt, *Word of Tree*, 181.

perhaps the title of such an interpreter.[12] In her article, Tully examines a series of icons that represent a ritual known as tree-pulling and agrees with other scholars that "the figures all display a particular body posture, generally agreed to depict movement, which has been interpreted as depicting ecstatic frenzy, caused either through the consumption of psychotropic substances and/or frenetic dancing."[13]

Impressively, modern studies of individuals participating in these bodily postures were shown to evoke visions and feelings of ecstasy.[14] It is also worth noting that of icons depicting dendromancy, women appear twice as often as their male counterparts, which may add weight to the idea that Deborah is one in a line of women who were part of such activities.

One way to enter a trance using trees involves observing patterns of light produced as the wind rustles the branches. This phenomenon is referred to variously as "flicker vertigo" or the "Bucha effect," which refers to the photosensitive disorientation that produces a trance-like state or seizure often experienced by helicopter pilots due to the rapid speed of the helicopter's spinning wheels.[15] Clearly sunlight is not being filtered this quickly through tree branches at the same speed as a helicopter, but the presence of light patterns in general has been show to aid in facilitating an ASC.[16]

Another facet that may point toward an interpretation of Deborah as using ASCs is her designation as the "wife of Lappidoth" (לַפִּידוֹת אֵשֶׁת/'ēšet lappîdôt).[17] The Hebrew name Lappidoth is otherwise unattested in ancient literature, which may mean that this is not identifying Deborah as a wife of some man named Lappidoth (the Hebrew word for "woman" and "wife" are identical). The word lappidoth is the plural form of the word "torch" (לַפִּיד/lappîd). Thus, some scholars have suggested the alternate translation "woman of torches,"[18] perhaps with the sense of "a fiery woman."[19] This

---

12. KN Fp 1.10, 13.3, discusses payment to a female "auger" (qerasiya) and "the Priestess of the winds" (anemoiyereya). KN refers to a fifteenth-century-BCE tablet found in Knossos (Crete) written in a syllabic language designated as "Linear B." See Chadwick and Killen, "Linear B Tablets from Knossos."

13. Tully, "Understanding the Language of Trees," 475.

14. Kennedy, "Embodying Visions"; McGowan, "Experimenting with Embodied Archaeology"; Peatfield and Morris, "Dynamic Spirituality."

15. Cushman and Floccare, "Flicker Illness."

16. Bartossek et al., "Altered States"; Amaya et al., "Effect of Frequency."

17. Kashow, "Lappidoth," EBR 15:827–28: "The feminine plural ending, -ôt, used on a personal name, though rare, is attested (see, e.g., Naboth, 1 Kgs 21:1; Jeremoth, 1 Chr 7:8)."

18. b. Meg. 14a suggests that Deborah had the nickname "woman of torches" because she used to make wicks for the candles of the sanctuary.

19. One rabbi named Naḥman in the Talmud equates Deborah's name with the idea

designation makes etymological sense, especially when connected with Barak, whose name in Hebrew means "lightning." Another suggestion has been to understand "torches" here as referencing pyromancy, a catchall term for divination using fire.[20] By staring into the fire, observing the smoke (capnomancy), the movement of the flames, or other methods, pyromancers would interpret these subtle signs to receive oracles.[21]

Trance was likely a common feature of such pyromantic activities as it is in most forms of scrying. Modern practitioners of pyromancy readily admit that this is the case within their own personal practice.[22] Many of us are aware of the hypnotic state we lull ourselves into staring at a campfire during a summer evening.[23]

The name Deborah itself may also be of importance. While Deborah is literally the Hebrew word for "bee" (דְּבוֹרָה / dəbôrâ), some scholars have suggested her name is derived from another Hebrew word such as "lead" (דבר/dbr).[24] Alternatively, the name may be connected to the verb "speak" (דבר/dbr), a reference to Deborah's prophetic role in Israelite life. That Deborah is connected with the word "speak" could potentially point toward her utterances, a by-product of an ASC. Yet, I think such an etymological link between Deborah's name and these two verbs is most probably a misstep. Josephus, for example, simply connects her name to the Hebrew word for "bee."[25] John C. Yoder, drawing on the meaning of "bee" suggests a connection between Deborah's name and her prophetic activity:

> The association with Rebekah would have heightened Deborah's prominence as a diviner. Deborah's name, which means "honeybee," may offer additional insight into her particular appeal. In Isa. 8:19, the prophet speaks of the whirring and chirping of diviners. The reference may be to the utterances coming out of the mouths of seers overtaken by ecstatic seizures that bridged the gap between the temporal and supernatural worlds. Perhaps the whirring and chirping of ecstatic expressions was Deborah's trademark.[26]

---

of haughtiness (b. Meg. 14b). See Ackerman, *Warrior, Dancer, Seductress, Queen*, 38.

20. Sasson, *Judges 1–12*, 250, 255.
21. See, for example, Hough, *Fire as an Agent*, 182–84.
22. See, for example, Salicrow, *Path of Elemental Witchcraft*.
23. For a contemporary example see Dahl, *Marvellous Story of Henry Sugar*.
24. Hess, "Name Game."
25. Josephus, *Ant.* 5.200.
26. Yoder, *Power and Politics*, 67.

One final passage deserves consideration. In Judg 5:12 we read: "Awake, awake, Deborah! Awake, awake, break out in a song!" Because this statement is in parallelism with the line "Arise, Barak, lead away your captives," some have taken "awake" and "arise" to express the same idea—that is, to be stirred into action. I argue, however, that it is possible to understand this line as referring to Deborah being in a sleep-like trance state that she must be roused out of. The Hebrew word used of Barak to "arise" (קום/*qum*) is militaristic in focus. Deborah, on the other hand is called to "awake" (עור/ *or*) and sing a song.[27] Elsewhere in the Old Testament, God himself is petitioned to "awake" as if he were sleeping and inactive (Ps 7:7, 44:24). As noted previously, the connection between natural sleep and the trance state is typical.

The earliest extant interpretation we have of Deborah comes from Liber antiquitatum biblicarum, a work we looked at when discussing Miriam. Deborah calls on Barak to go to battle, explaining that she has seen (in a vision?) the constellations and lightnings ready to fight against Sisera. In this text, the people sing a song imploring Deborah to sing so that "a holy spirit awake in you."[28] This is to confirm her prophetic experience. The meaning of this phrase could be interpreted as a form of visible ecstasy, though like Miriam, this tells us nothing of the historical Deborah. The presence of lightning in the equation is obviously not a case of ceraunoscopy (divination using lightning and/or thunder), but a wordplay on Barak's name which has the same meaning. Nor should we interpret her prophetic insights of the constellations as a form of astrology (sometimes called astromancy, aeromancy, or roadomancy).[29]

What should we conclude from all of this? Was Deborah participating in some form (or forms) of divination similar to Joseph's use of a lecanomancy? Of the passages considered, the presence of Deborah under the tree seems like the best candidate for interpreting Deborah as an ecstatic. But even then, this is an extrapolation based on other instances of dendromancy found in the Hebrew Bible and the ANE. It could simply be that Deborah enjoyed the shade! Yet, if a cumulative case can be made, all of these

27. It is interesting that the Talmud suggests that Deborah lost her prophetic spirit through self-glorification and that the call for her to "awaken" indicates her need to recover it (b. Pesah. 66b).

28. LAB 32.14.

29. Cf. Pirqe R. El. 52 (eighth–ninth century CE): "From the day when the heavens and earth were created, the sun, the moon, and the stars and the constellations were ascending to give light upon the earth, and they did not come into contact with one another until Joshua came and fought the battles of Israel. It was the even of the Sabbath, and he saw the plight of Israel lest they might desecrate the Sabbath, and further, he saw the magicians of Egypt compelling the constellations to come against Israel."

elements taken together may suggest ecstatic activity. Additionally, her title as a "female prophet" (נְבִיאָה / nəbîʾâ), may point toward ecstasy based on the etymology to "bubble forth," especially in a premonarchic Israelite context.

Is Hannah Hammered?

One of the clearest parallels we have between drunkenness and ASCs in the Hebrew Bible is the story of Hannah in 1 Samuel. Unable to conceive children naturally, Hannah prays to God near the temple in Shiloh. While she is praying, Eli the high priest observes her and mistakenly reprimands her: "How long will you go on being drunk? Put your wine away from you" (1 Sam 1:14). Drunkenness at cultic cites was often a problem in Israel (Judg 9:27; 21:21–23; Isa 28:7).[30] Yet, Hannah is not drunk as he supposes! Why then would he think this was the case?

I do not think this is an example of sexism, in which Eli just assumes that her behavior is "hysterical" and akin to drunkenness, though Eli's discernment abilities are certainly questionable.[31] Instead, I think that Hannah was experiencing an ASC that, on the surface, resembled drunken behavior.

In a 2018 article, the scholar and Episcopal minister Reed Carlson argued that the exchange between Hannah and Eli in 1 Sam 1:12–18 is an example of religious ecstasy being mistaken for drunkenness.[32] Carlson argues this position based on linguistic issues that rely on an understanding of ANE conceptions of physiology. Consider, for example, how the Hebrew phrase אִשָּׁה קְשַׁת־רוּחַ / ʾiššâ qəšat-rûaḥ in 1 Sam 1:15 is translated with metaphorical terms in various translations:

> I am a woman deeply troubled. (NRSV)
> I am a very unhappy woman. (NJPS)
> I am very discouraged. (NLT)
> I am a woman of a sorrowful spirit. (KJV)
> I am a woman with a broken heart. (CSB)

Carlson chooses to translate the phrase literally as "I am a woman of hard spirit" and argues that rendering the Hebrew phrase so metaphorically in English translations is due to a modern conception of human anatomy. Elsewhere, Hannah prays with her "mind/heart" (לֵב/lb; 1:8, 13; 2:1) and "throat/self/soul" (נֶפֶשׁ / nepeš 1:10, 15). Carlson states that "since we are

---

30. Kim, *1 Samuel*, 17; Ackroyd, *First Book of Samuel*, 25.
31. Auld, *I & II Samuel*, 31, suggests that maybe this is an issue with Eli's sight.
32. Carlson, "Hannah at Pentecost."

here engaged with an ancient anatomy, none of these words should be seen as corresponding to anything that might be found in a contemporary medical textbook. The fact that Hannah's psychological state is described by means of narrating the components of her body as hypostasized third parties should make this point clear. It should also make us pause and reconsider how Hannah's 'spirit' (רוח) may be functioning here."[33] Carlson's point is that what is being viewed here is the psychological state which Hannah finds herself in. This language, he argues, is typical of other "spirit language" in the Old Testament where ASCs are the likely meaning.

Interpreters have often read this story as Hannah quietly praying in her heart while silently mouthing the words of her prayer. Yet, as the Swedish Old Testament scholar Gösta Ahlström has noted: "A quiet, tranquil, or silent prayer would certainly not have been mistaken for drunken behavior."[34] Indeed, the verb used here of Hannah's drunkenness is תִּשְׁתַּכָּרִין/ tištakkārîn, the Hithpael form of "drunk" (שׁכר/škr).[35] This form of škr appears only once in the Hebrew Bible, and the NRSV and many lexicons thus translate it as "make a drunken spectacle of yourself." Hannah's behavior must have been observably similar to drunkenness to illicit such a response. This idea is strengthened by Hannah telling Eli not to consider her a בַּת־בְּלִיָּעַל / bat-bəliyyāʿ al, translated variously as "wicked woman" (NIV; NLT), "worthless woman" (ESV), and even "daughter of Belial" (KJV). The phrase probably means something akin to "scoundrel" or "troublemaker," thus making the connection between drunken rabble and her prayers even more interesting. Carlson thus concludes: "Given these clues above, it is best to think of Hannah as engaging in something other than quiet, respectful prayer—something we may tentatively label as 'trance', for lack of a better term."[36] While the word "ecstasy" fits the picture better than "trance" in this instance, I think Carlson's general conclusion is correct.

Having spoken to a number of Protestant pastors about this passage, I have been quite confused at the responses to this idea. When asking why Eli thought Hannah was drunk, ministers I have engaged with have responded with three general answers: (1) prayers were always vocalized during this time period and therefore this silent prayer seemed odd to Eli;[37] (2) ec-

33. Carlson, "Hannah at Pentecost," 251.

34. Ahlström, "1 Samuel 1.15," 254.

35. The Hithpael is often described as the "reflexive" form of the Piel stem. The Piel stem is thought to be the more "intensive" form of the Qal stem (which represents the "basic" verbal stem of the Hebrew verb system). See, for example, GKC, 141, 149–50.

36. Carlson, "Hannah at Pentecost," 253.

37. Smith, *1 & 2 Samuel*, 45, for example states that "silent prayer was unusual at the time."

stasy cannot explain the phenomenon because this is a modern idea being read back into the text and should not be accepted; (3) Hannah was overly emotional.[38] Because I suspect many will reject the interpretation of Hannah being ecstatic using one of the following three reasons above, I want to respond to them here.

The first argument, namely that prayers were always vocalized during this time in Israelite religious life, cannot be substantiated with any evidence. Despite having heard this claim made many times anecdotally, there is no known ancient source suggesting this and, to me, it represents a special pleading used to escape the inevitable interpretation offered by Carlson.

The second argument, that this is a new idea and therefore must be wrong, is also historically incorrect. The hypothesis of Hannah being in prophetic ecstasy is not a niche modern interpretation but is one of the oldest interpretations of the narrative. In his work titled *On Drunkenness*, Philo notes that Hannah's name means "grace" in Hebrew and then makes the following observation: "Whatever soul is filled with grace is at once in a state of exultation, and delight, and dancing; for it becomes full of triumph, so that it would appear to many of the uninitiated to be intoxicated, and agitated, and to be beside itself [ἐξεστάναι/*exestanai*]."[39] Philo thus directly connects Hannah with ecstasy. Hannah is elsewhere interpreted as a prophet in early Judaism. Philo himself calls her a prophetess who is "possessed by a divinely sent impulse."[40] Likewise, the Jewish oral traditions contained in the Talmud state:

> Hannah was a prophetess, as it is written: "And Hannah prayed and said, My heart rejoices in the Lord, my horn is exalted in the Lord" (I Samuel 2:1), and her words were prophecy, in that she said: "My horn is exalted," and not: My pitcher is exalted. As with regard to David and Solomon, who were anointed with oil from a horn, their kingship continued, whereas with regard to Saul and Jehu, who were anointed with oil from a pitcher, their kingship did not continue. This demonstrates that Hannah was a prophetess, as she prophesied that only those anointed with oil from a horn will merit that their kingships continue.[41]

Some other evidence is worth noting as well. The Old Greek version of 1 Samuel adds the phrase "Here I am, Lord" (Ἰδοὺ ἐγώ, κύριε/*Idou egō*,

---

38. Tsumura, *First Book of Samuel*, 100, suggests Eli interpreted Hannah's actions as "mild derangement." Cf. Murphy, *1 Samuel*, 35.

39. Philo, *Drunkenness* 146; cf. Chrysostom, *Anna* 1.

40. Philo, *Dreams* 1.254.

41. b. Meg. 14a.

kyrie) to Hannah's conversation with Elkanah, a phrase curiously used of Abraham (Gen 22:1, 7, 11), Isaac (Gen 27:18), and Jacob (Gen 31:11), especially in the context of theophanies. Positioning Hannah's character within this theophanic framework makes sense if she was interpreted as engaging in trance. Additionally, in an early fragment of 1 Samuel from the Dead Sea Scrolls, Hannah specifically refers to Samuel as a Nazarite in 1 Sam 1:22.[42] Thus, the connection between Hannah and Samuel's spiritual leadership leads Carlson to state: "Ultimately, Hannah, who is herself a practitioner of trance, shows herself to be the true forebear of Samuel both naturally and in terms of office."[43] Moreover, the New Testament authors also likely recognized Hannah as a prophetic figure. Mary's spontaneous song known as the Magnificat (which we will look at in a later chapter) is heavily influenced by the song of Hannah, and it is telling that both the mothers (Luke 1:35, 41, 47) and sons (Luke 1:15, 80; 3:22; 4:1) found in this typological picture are said to be indwelled with the Spirit.

The final argument, that Hannah was overly emotional and that is what made Eli think she was drunk, is a confusing one. Crying and blubbering may occur when you are drunk, but they are objectively very different-looking frames of mind. Additionally, we ought to take the narrator's comment in 1 Sam 3:1 that "the word of the Lord was rare in those days; there was no frequent vision" more seriously. When the young Samuel begins hearing God in his sleep, it takes Eli awhile to discern that God was speaking to him (1 Sam 3:8).

Perhaps the reason Eli is so unequipped at interpreting what is happening to Hannah is because this was not a common occurrence in Israel during this time period. We may find such a story analogous to what has happened in some contemporary Christian circles. Those who often do not see spiritual phenomena are either overly skeptical of their origins or, like Eli, completely misinterpret what is happening.

In conclusion, I think Carlson's argument is a convincing one and makes sense of all of the data found in the exchange between Hannah and Eli. Emotional intensity and focus on a goal could easily develop into a form of ecstasy or trance where the individual's natural inhibitions are cast aside and they appear quite unusual to outsiders.

---

42. 4Q51.
43. Carlson, "Hannah at Pentecost," 256–57.

Saul Among the Prophets

1 Samuel 10:5–13 and 1 Samuel 19:23–24 are the standard go-to passages concerning ASCs in the Old Testament.[44] If we are looking for clear-cut examples of religious ecstasy, these are the passages to consider.[45] The first passage, 1 Sam 10:5–13 is a narrative that describes how Saul became anointed as king by the prophet Samuel.[46] After pouring oil on his head, Samuel states:

> "After that you shall come to Gibeath-elohim, where there is a garrison of the Philistines. And there, as soon as you come to the city, you will meet a group of prophets coming down from the high place with harp, tambourine, flute, and lyre before them, *hitnabbē*. Then the Spirit of the Lord will rush upon you, and you will *hitnabbē* with them and be turned into another man. Now when these signs meet you, do what your hand finds to do, for God is with you. Then go down before me to Gilgal. And behold, I am coming down to you to offer burnt offerings and to sacrifice peace offerings. Seven days you shall wait, until I come to you and show you what you shall do." When he turned his back to leave Samuel, God gave him another heart. And all these signs came to pass that day. When they came to Gibeah, behold, a group of prophets met him, and the Spirit of God rushed upon him, and he *hitnabbē* among them. And when all who knew him previously saw how he prophesied with the prophets, the people said to one another, "What has come over the son of Kish? Is Saul also among the prophets?" And a man of the place answered, "And who is their father?" Therefore it became a proverb, "Is Saul also among the prophets?" When he had finished *hitnabbē*, he came to the high place. (1 Sam 10:5–13)

---

44. For an excellent treatment of these passages, see Firth, "Is Saul Also Among?"

45. While the majority of scholars have adopted the view that early Israelite prophets engaged in prophetic ecstasy or trance, there are some scholarly voices that have opposed it. Adam, "He Behaved Like a Prophet," argues that Saul's ecstasy was actually a ruse in contrast to the other prophets. Adam's argument is based on a textual analysis of differences between the Niphal and Hithpael form of the Hebrew verb for prophesy (נבא/*naba*). He suggests that the Hithpael is used in these contexts to communicate that the individual doing the action is pretending or disguising themselves through their actions. Thus, Saul was not really in an ecstasy according to Adam, he simply acted like he was in one. While he does not view ecstasy as the normative form of prophecy in ancient Israel, he does not deny its existence. For a similar treatment of this issue, see Wilson, "Prophecy and Ecstasy."

46. DeMaris, "Possession, Good and Bad," 16, views Samuel's anointing of Saul as a ritual action that facilitated Spirit possession.

This passage offers an important look into the elements of ecstatic experience. I have left the pertinent Hebrew word untranslated once again: התנביא/*hitnabbē*. This word, which we analyzed briefly before when dealing with the elders of Israel, is derived from the verb "prophesy" (נָבָא / *naba*). It may be tempting, therefore, to simply translate this as "prophesied" as other versions have opted to do (e.g., NIV, ESV, NASB, KJV). Yet, consider how the following Bible translations render 1 Sam 10:6:

> Then the spirit of the Lord will possess you, and you will be in a prophetic frenzy [*hitnabbē*] along with them and be turned into a different person. (NRSV)

> The spirit of the LORD will rush upon you, and you will join them in their prophetic ecstasy [*hitnabbē*] and will become a changed man. (NAB)

> Suddenly the spirit of the LORD will take control of you, and you will join in their religious dancing and shouting [*hitnabbē*] and will become a different person. (GNT)

One is immediately struck by how different these translations are from the "traditional" renderings found elsewhere. What is the reason behind this? The simple answer is that the NRSV and other translations are recognizing that something beyond prophesying is occurring in this passage. There are good reasons for such an approach.

First, *hitnabbē* is used elsewhere in instances where "prophesying" generally makes little sense contextually, but where an ASC makes narrative sense (e.g., 1 Sam 18:10 discussed next). The narrative indicators of group prophesying accompanied by music fits the picture of religious ecstasy in this context. Additionally, Samuel states that this experience will be one of three "signs" (אות/*oth* [singular]; אותות/*othoth* [plural]) that will accompany Saul. The word for "sign" is used of the plagues of Egypt (Exod 4:8, 8:19, 12:13), the [rain]bow (Gen 9:12, 17), and the mark (sign) given to Cain (Gen 4:15), among other things. This implies that some kind of visible sign allowed the onlookers and Saul to see this as a fulfillment of Samuel's words. That they "saw" (ראה/*ra'a*) Saul's behavior further strengthens this connection.[47]

Second, the language used by Samuel of what Saul will experience lends to this word being understood as a form of ecstasy. 1 Samuel 10:6 suggests that Spirit possession will cause such an experience for Saul: "Then the Spirit of the Lord will rush upon you, and you will [*hitnabbē*] with them

---

47. Isbell, "Origins of Prophetic Frenzy," 66.

and be turned into another man." This "rushing" (צלח/*ṣlḥ*) of the Spirit is the same word used in Judges for when the Spirit empowers supernatural feats by Gideon (Judg 6:34), Jephthah (Judg 11:29), and Samson (Judg 14:6, 19; 15:14), but also of Saul leading the Israelites into battle (1 Sam 11:6). The idea of being "turned into another man" may conjure the modern idea that he will simply change and become a "better" person fit for God's calling. In English we may use the expression "I'm a new man" or "he's really grown as a person." Yet, in the context of an ASC experience, the point of becoming a different person is that your behavior and thoughts are overshadowed.[48] In the same way that the demoniacs in the New Testament were changed from being insane to rational people through Jesus's exorcisms, it is also true that the ASC experience causes one to go from one personality to another. Thus, for Saul to become a new person, in this case appearing as a prophet, is not just a colloquial way of expressing that he has matured, but that he has literally taken on a new personality, that of the Spirit that is possessing him. This new personality is exhibited, not by speech (what one typically thinks of when hearing the word "prophesying"), but by ecstasy.

Third, the audience's reaction to the behavior of Saul and the other prophets when they *hitnabbē* makes more sense if ecstasy is in view. When those "who knew him previously saw" Saul *hitnabbē* with the other prophets they ask three important questions. First, they ask "What has come over the son of Kish?" (1 Sam 10:11). This question makes sense if they are observing a physical manifestation similar to the other prophets that identify Saul among them. The second question, "Is Saul also among the prophets?" only serves to further the previous point. Saul acts as prophets sometimes act: in a frenzy. A similar sentiment is shared by the famous *Epic of Gilgamesh*: "[Be] furious, like a prophet (*āpilum*) g[o into f]renzy!"[49] As the Finnish theologian and expert in prophecy from the ANE states: "This passage suggests that the altered state of consciousness of a prophet (*āpilum*) was taken for granted."[50]

The final question asks about Saul's lineage: "And who is their father?" Saul's father, Kish, was not a prophet. In the Old Testament, prophets were often thought to be part of a prophetic guild or assembly who were led by a head prophetic figure deemed the father of their movement. Thus, the prophets were sometimes called "sons of the prophets" (1 Kgs 20:35; 2 Kgs 2:3–15; 4:1, 38; 5:22; 6:1–2; 9:1; Amos 7:13). That Saul is the son of Kish and

---

48. Heard, "Biblical Composition," 120–22, notes that prophetic ecstasy often did not accompany speech. Rather, the possession experience itself was the divine communication.

49. See Nissinen, *Ancient Prophecy*, 174.

50. Nissinen, *Ancient Prophecy*, 175.

not the son of one of these head prophetic figures causes the audience to question his lineage.

Finally, 1 Sam 10:13 states that "when he had finished [*hitnabbē*], he came to the high place" which suggests that, like the elders of Israel who stopped their ecstatic prophesying, Saul's ecstasy was only temporary.

The second passage under consideration takes place after a victorious battle against the Philistines. Saul becomes jealous of the people's praise for David and he becomes angered:

> The next day a harmful spirit from God rushed upon Saul, and he [*hitnabbē*] within his house while David was playing the lyre, as he did day by day. Saul had his spear in his hand. And Saul hurled the spear, for he thought, "I will pin David to the wall." But David evaded him twice. Saul was afraid of David because the Lord was with him but had departed from Saul. (1 Sam 18:10–12)

Unsurprisingly, the Septuagint drops these verses completely, skipping from verse 9 to verse 12.[51] This harmful spirit rushes on Saul just as the Spirit of Yahweh rushed on him, but the result of the *hitnabbē* is different.[52] Here, Saul "prophesying" some divine oracle makes little sense.[53] Most translations render it as something like "raved" (ESV, NASB), "rave . . . like a madman" (NLT), "raged" (NAB), or "acting like a crazy man" (CEV).[54] Such a translation makes sense. Evidently, the harmful spirit was not causing Saul to utter some false prophetic words, but to physically act in an erratic manner. His violent assaults on David are best understood as an ASC where he was not in his right mind. The American Old Testament scholar, Ralph Klein, in his commentary on 1 Samuel, translates the passage as, "The next day an evil spirit from God rushed on Saul and he became ecstatic in the midst of the house."[55]

The final passage under consideration reads as follows:

---

51. Origen, *Princ.* 3.2.1, states that the evil spirit "suffocated" or "strangled" (Latin: *effocare*) Saul.

52. On the nature of the spirit in this passage, see Stokes, "What Is a Demon."

53. Bodner, *1 Samuel*, 196, agrees Saul is ecstatic, but that his *hitnabbē* also contains some unspoken content: "Just as Saul is hurling his spear at the harpist, the reader is given another glimpse of his thoughts: 'I will strike through David and into the wall!' Even though Saul is 'prophesying,' this utterance will not find fulfillment in the story."

54. Rowley, "Nature of Prophecy," 6: "On the philological side it is incontestable that the verb [*hitnabbē*] . . . commonly means 'to behave in an uncontrolled manner.'"

55. Klein, *1 Samuel*, 184.

> Then Saul sent messengers to take David, and when they saw the company of the prophets prophesying, and Samuel standing as head over them, the Spirit of God came upon the messengers of Saul, and they also [*hitnabbē*]. When it was told Saul, he sent other messengers, and they also [*hitnabbē*]. And Saul sent messengers again the third time, and they also [*hitnabbē*]. Then he himself went to Ramah and came to the great well that is in Secu. And he asked, "Where are Samuel and David?" And one said, "Behold, they are at Naioth in Ramah." And he went there to Naioth in Ramah. And the Spirit of God came upon him also, and as he went he [*hitnabbē*] until he came to Naioth in Ramah. And he too stripped off his clothes, and he too [*hitnabbē*] before Samuel and lay naked all that day and all that night. Thus it is said, "Is Saul also among the prophets?" (1 Sam 19:20–24)

This narrative has a number of important features relating to ecstasy. We first note that the prophet Samuel is present. As mentioned in the introduction, ASCs can become more commonplace when a perceived spiritual authority is present. Additionally, there is a group of prophets there, which suggests that group ecstasy and music were part of the process of them entering an ASC.[56] A similar instance of group ecstasy seems to be present in 1 Kgs 22:10: "Now the king of Israel and Jehoshaphat the king of Judah were sitting on their thrones, arrayed in their robes, at the threshing floor at the entrance of the gate of Samaria, and all the prophets were [*hitnabbē*] before them." We should also take note that the Hebrew word גַּם/*gam* is present in 1 Sam 19:24. This word *gam* means "also" or "too." That means the other prophets were *also* prophesying naked all day and night. The picture of prophets strung out on the ground in ecstasy is very similar to an ANE prayer offered to the god Nabû: "I invoked you, Nabû—accept me, o mighty one! I have humbled myself among the people, I have abased myself to the ground. I became affected like a prophet, what I do not know I bring forth."[57]

The idea of someone prophesying naked on the ground for an entire day certainly paints a caricature of what modern thinkers may consider when they hear the term "ecstatic" used in relationship to prophesying. Such ecstasy appears to be uncontrolled, brought on by God's Spirit—that is to

---

56. Greenbaum, "Societal Correlates of Possession Trance," 42: "Possession trance may be an individual or a group phenomenon. It may be induced by drugs, music, or other methods external to the individual, or it may be a spontaneous manifestation by the person possessed. It may be a phenomenon restricted to a particular status or role (for example, a diviner, medium, priest) or it may occur at random in the society. In all cases however, the phenomenon is accepted within the society as a trance induced by a spirit entering the person possessed, and not as an individual psychological aberration."

57. Nissinen, *Ancient Prophecy*, 175.

say that this ecstasy was not self-induced, even if music was present.[58] It is necessary to stress that this ecstatic prophesying is not the result of the "harmful spirit" seen in 1 Sam 18. Rather, it is the Spirit of God (1 Sam 19:23). Once again, the onlookers of this event ask the question, "Is Saul also among the prophets?" (1 Sam 19:24), which would make little sense if the other prophets did not typically act in such a way.[59]

Saul's ecstasies are of value because they not only demonstrate a psychological change in Saul, but also describe to some extent the physiological features of those ecstasies. Additionally, we are able to witness ecstasy induced by both God and by a harmful spirit. Surprisingly, it is God's Spirit that causes Saul to fall on the ground naked, not the harmful spirit. Naturally, this does not mean that every ecstasy where a person rolls about on the floor is genuine or of divine origins, but this should caution us against assuming that ecstatic outbursts where atypical behavior is exhibited must, by default, be demonic.

Going Berserk

Between November 1990 and December 2021, the Japanese author and illustrator Kentaro Miura produced one of the bestselling manga of all time, titled *Berserk* (Japanese: *Beruseruku*). The manga follows the story of a warrior named Guts who experiences a number of traumatic episodes throughout the series, and at various points enters forms of ecstatic rage in order to win fantastical battle scenarios. In other words, Guts goes berserk. You have likely heard the word "berserk" used to describe someone who has lost control and is rampaging, emotionally unstable, or violent. The word comes from the German *berserkergang* (going berserk) which describes the practice of Indo-European warriors entering an ASC prior to battle.

---

58. Long and Sneed, "Yahweh Has Given," 69: "The Dtr dealt with the tension between the potentially threatening facets of ecstasy and its necessity for legitimation by distinguishing between two types of ecstasy: controlled and uncontrolled. . . . Saul exemplifies the uncontrolled aspects, when he is filled with the evil spirit and needs music for relief, and when, under its influence, attempts to kill David with a spear (1 Sam. 18). Elijah and Elisha represent the controlled kind of ecstasy, and our story has Elisha acting in a very controlled manner. The details of ecstasy are carefully avoided and the emphasis is set on the incubation's effectiveness. This careful balancing act of the Dtr is also characteristic of the next important sociological facet of our story."

59. Grudem, *Gift of Prophecy*, 199, suggests that we should not take accounts such as Saul's "involuntary prophesying" as evidence of a class of roaming ecstatic prophetic bands, but he does not provide an exhaustive reason why. He points to 1 Sam 10:5–13 and states that there is no "involuntary ecstatic experience," but does not address the presence of the verb *hitnabbē*.

Warfare, both in the ancient and modern world, often incorporated complex magical rituals to aid warriors and the community. This kind of battle tactic is variously called "war magic" or "shamanic warfare," among other terms.[60] The term "shamanism" is used by anthropologists and historians to speak generally of particular practices within religious systems rather than a religion in and of itself. In other words, "shamanism" is a scholarly term used for the purposes of categorization or shorthand description.[61] The literature on the topic of shamanism is daunting and scholars often debate whether it is a useful term, though there is agreement on some facets. Shamanism differs between cultures and religious systems, despite sharing some common features such as communication with and control of spirits and ASCs.[62] Its most distinguishing feature, however, is the control the shaman demonstrates over his consciousness. As T. Craig Isaacs explains:

> During the trance, the shaman is seemingly in control of him- or herself, and also is not manipulated by the spirits against his or her will. Rather, the shaman works with the spirits and can actually be said to be more the possessor of spirits than possessed by them. Thus the shaman's state of ecstasy is thought to be different from that of other trance-like states commonly seen as possession.[63]

This key differentiation has led the American anthropologist Michael Harner to refer to this as the "shamanic state of consciousness."[64]

Some older European shaman-warriors would hype others into a state of ecstasy through various means, apparently with the result that fire and blades would not even hurt them![65] The use of ASCs allowed warriors to bypass pain, amplify their strength, increase trust within the group, and blocked the normative psychological guilt associated with killing.[66] Even in modern times, American soldiers sometimes use heavy metal and rhythmic dancing to achieve trance states prior to missions.[67] In one article, the German ethnologist Heidi Behrend explored the connection between spirit possession and war in northern Uganda. There, spirit mediums were used during times of war and persecution. In some instances, these

---

60. Farrer, "Cross-Cultural Articulations."
61. Hultkrantz, "Definition of Shamanism"; Siikala, "Siberian and Inner Asian."
62. See Pilch, *Flights of the Soul*, 113–14.
63. Isaacs, *In Bondage to Evil*, 74–75.
64. Harner, *Way of the Shaman*, 26.
65. Wade, "Going Berserk," 24, 29–30.
66. Jordania, *Why Do People Sing*, 98.
67. Pieslak, *Sound Targets*.

mediums would take part in rallying warriors together into a form of trance or ecstasy.[68] In another context, the Weenhayek people of Gran Choco engaged in ritual drinking bouts administered by a *hiyaawu'* (shaman) before military campaigns. Accordingly, they believed that the "fermentation constituted a process where divine forces gathered, and the intoxication that followed was a kind of communion with these forces, where they took possession of the human beings that drunk the beer . . . and reinforced them or protected them e.g., during the war raid they were about to embark upon."[69] Those possessed by the warrior spirit (*caboclo*) in Brazil sing songs called *sotaque* through the possessed: "Let us make war, *caboclo*, Let us make war, warrior."[70] Even being in the presence of someone in a trance or ecstasy may have been enough to cause a contagious outpouring. Luck, for example, asks: "Is it conceivable that the mere sight of persons in trance can induce a kind of trance in those who are not directly affected by any psychoactive substance? In some cultures, this is almost certainly the case."[71]

We should not be surprised that such a "magical" method employed in modern wartime would also be present in the ancient world. One immediately can think of Balaam who was hired by King Balak to curse Israel so that they might be given the upper hand. Likewise, when King Mesha discovers that he is losing the battle with Israel, he sacrifices his son with the result that "there came great wrath against Israel" (2 Kgs 3:27).[72] Perhaps the figure of Deborah fits within this tradition too.[73]

Scholars have variously attempted to describe biblical characters as shamans, such as Moses,[74] Isaiah,[75] and even Jesus.[76] In the field of biblical studies, the terms "shaman" and "shamanism" have slowly been incorporated into the conversation of ecstatic experiences and religious authoritative figures, though it still likely shocks first-time readers to hear these

---

68. Behrend, "Power to Heal."
69. Alvarsson, "Shamanism and Armed Conflict," 245.
70. Wafer, *Taste of Blood*, 77
71. Luck, *Arcana Mundi*, 482.
72. This action is variously interpreted as the Moabites pacifying their god Chemosh (Jones, *1 and 2 Kings*, 2:400; and Hobbs, *2 Kings*, 39–41), a psychological method of motivating the Moabite armies (Honeycutt, "2 Kings," 3:235), or as a means of persuading Israel to stop attacking (Wiseman, *1 & 2 Kings*, 202; Keil, K&D 3:307; and Patterson and Austel, "1, 2 Kings," 817–19).
73. For additional examples, see Ehrenreich, *Blood Rites*.
74. Jones-Hunt, *Moses and Jesus*.
75. Landy, "Shamanic Poetics."
76. See Craffert, *Life of a Galilean Shaman*.

categories used in reference to biblical characters and events.[77] Its usefulness as a category aside, it is worth observing some cross-cultural similarities between shamanic warfare and what is found in a handful of biblical episodes.

Battle-trance appears to have been a feature of war among the Israelites.[78] Unlike the surrounding people groups who relied on shamanism, alcohol, or hallucinogenic drugs to induce these ASCs, the Israelites relied on God's Spirit to empower them in battle. Throughout the book of Judges, for example, God's Spirit comes upon people to empower them in battle. These Spirit-possessed warriors were given supernatural strength to accomplish insurmountable achievements in battle. Consider the following examples:

---

77. See Craffert, "Towards a Post-Colonial Reflection."

78. Although unclear, Joshua may have been one of these ecstatic warriors as well. According to Num 27:18, Joshua is said to be "a man in whom is [a/]the [s/]Spirit [אִישׁ אֲשֶׁר־רוּחַ בּוֹ/'iš ' ăšer-rûaḥ bô]." Moses is then instructed to lay his hands on him. Curiously, in Deut 34:9, the chronology is different: "Joshua the son of Nun was full of the spirit of wisdom [מָלֵא רוּחַ חָכְמָה/mālē' rûaḥ ḥākmâ], for Moses had laid his hands on him." That Joshua is said to have a/the s/Spirit prior to Moses laying hands on him may suggest Spirit possession used in military pursuits. It is only after Moses lays hands on him to give him a different "spirit of wisdom" that he is able to then give proper leadership to the Israelites. LAB 20.2–3 retells the story so that God tells Joshua to "take his [Moses'] garments of wisdom and clothe yourself, and with his belt of knowledge gird your loins, and you will be changed and become another man. Did I not speak on your behalf to Moses my servant, saying, 'This one will lead my people after you, and into his hand I will deliver the kings of the Amorites?' And Joshua took the garments of wisdom and clothed himself and girded his loins with the belt of understanding. And when he clothed himself with it, his mind was afire and his spirit was moved." The language of becoming "another man" is obviously drawn from Samuel's words to Saul, a reference to the ecstasy that he would eventually experience. Milgrom, *Numbers*, 235, summarizes the issue and addresses the shortcomings of some interpretations of this passage: "A number of interpretations have been suggested [regarding what spirit is being referred to in Num 27:18]: (1) 'spirit of wisdom,' mentioned in Deuteronomy 34:9. However, wisdom, according to that passage, comes to Joshua as a result of his investiture; here it is clear that he qualifies as Moses's successor because he already possesses the spirit; (2) 'spirit of prophecy,' supported by the example of the elders who begin to prophesy upon receiving Moses's spirit (11:17, 25). However, Joshua never becomes a prophet and before his investiture is just a military officer (Exod. 17:9–13) and Moses's aide-de-camp (Exod. 24:13; 32:17); (3) 'spirit of skill,' supported by the examples of Bezalel whom God 'endowed with a divine spirit of skill, ability, and knowledge in every kind of craft' (Exod. 35:31; cf. 31:2) and of Joseph, endowed with the skill of dream interpretation (Gen. 41:38). This 'spirit,' then, would refer to Joshua's endowed talent (not acquired skill), attested by his military success; (4) 'spirit' as a synonym for 'courage,' as in Joshua 2:11 and 5:1. This courage manifests itself in his victory over the Amalekites (Exod. 17:9–13), and it is exemplified by his willingness to stand up for God and Moses in the scout episode—for which he is nearly stoned (14:6–10), as alluded to in 26:65. Either of the latter two explanations is acceptable."

The Spirit of the Lord was upon [' ālāyw] him [Othniel], and he judged Israel. He went out to war, and the Lord gave Cushan-rishathaim king of Mesopotamia into his hand. And his hand prevailed over Cushan-rishathaim. (Judg 3:10)

But the Spirit of the Lord clothed [lbš] Gideon, and he sounded the trumpet, and the Abiezrites were called out to follow him. . . . So Gideon and the hundred men who were with him came to the outskirts of the camp. . . . And they blew the trumpets and smashed the jars that were in their hands. . . . And they cried out, "A sword for the Lord and for Gideon!" Every man stood in his place around the camp, and all the army ran. They cried out and fled. When they blew the 300 trumpets, the Lord set every man's sword against his comrade and against all the army. (Judg 6:34; 7:19–22)

Then the Spirit of the Lord was upon [' ālāy] Jephthah, and he passed through Gilead and Manasseh and passed on to Mizpah of Gilead, and from Mizpah of Gilead he passed on to the Ammonites. (Judg 11:29)

Then the Spirit of the Lord rushed upon [ṣlḥ] him [Samson], and although he had nothing in his hand, he tore the lion in pieces as one tears a young goat. (Judg 13:24)

And the Spirit of the Lord rushed upon [ṣlḥ] him, and he went down to Ashkelon and struck down thirty men of the town and took their spoil and gave the garments to those who had told the riddle. (Judg 14:19)

Then the Spirit of the Lord rushed upon [ṣlḥ] him, and the ropes that were on his arms became as flax that has caught fire, and his bonds melted off his hands. And he found a fresh jawbone of a donkey, and put out his hand and took it, and with it he struck 1,000 men. (Judg 15:14–15)

One unusual case of Spirit possession and military warfare involves David. While Saul and the Israelite judges seemingly have one-time instances of the Spirit coming upon them to empower them in military victory, when David is anointed by Samuel "the Spirit of the Lord rushed upon [ṣlḥ] David from that day forward" (1 Sam 16:13). As Klein states, David's elevation is signalled by the "superiority" of his long-lasting "spirit possession."[79] This appears to be some kind of permanent indwelling similar to the New Testament teaching of the indwelling Holy Spirit. Rather than the few instances of the judges and Saul who only had the Spirit rush upon him twice,

---

79. Klein, *1 Samuel*, 162.

David's life is marked by the continual empowerment of the Spirit. As Andrew E. Steinmann notes, "Yahweh's Spirit continued to rush upon David from that day forward. Apparently the coming of the Spirit upon David was manifested in a recognizable way."[80] He does not, however, mention what this manifestation was, and one is left to wonder if it is just an assumption on the part of Steinmann. Yet, there are good reasons to think that observable signs of Spirit possession were prominent in David's life.

The presence of the word ṣlḥ (to rush or to penetrate) in 1 Sam 16:13 is found also in the cases of Samson's supernatural strength and of Saul's prophesying (1 Sam 10:10) and military campaign (1 Sam 11:6). The same verb is used of the "evil spirit" that rushes upon Saul, causing him to prophesy or "rave" (1 Sam 18:10). That this verb is connected with charismatic spirit phenomena should inform us of interpreting David's experience as well. Indeed, once David becomes Spirit possessed, he is able to perform some kind of exorcistic musical ritual on Saul (1 Sam 16:23), defeat the giant Goliath (1 Sam 17), defeat various armies such as the Philistines (1 Sam 18:5; 19:8; 23:1–5) and Amalekites (1 Sam 30:16–31), and make use of the prophetic powers of the ephod (1 Sam 23:6–12; 30:7–8), as well as to speak an oracle on his deathbed (2 Sam 23:1–2).[81] David's military expertise is so extreme that Saul gets mad at David because the women sing that "Saul has struck down his thousands, and David his ten thousands" (1 Sam 18:7).

In addition to individuals being Spirit possessed to accomplish military victory, we also have evidence that God empowered groups of Israelite soldiers as well, potentially through trance or ecstasy. First Samuel records what appears to be an example of this kind of phenomenon:

> And the Spirit of God rushed upon Saul when he heard these words, and his anger was greatly kindled. He took a yoke of oxen and cut them in pieces and sent them throughout all the territory of Israel by the hand of the messengers, saying, "Whoever does not come out after Saul and Samuel, so shall it be done to his oxen!" Then the [pāḥad] of the Lord fell upon the people, and they came out as one man. (1 Sam 11:6–7)

First Samuel 11:6 states that upon seeing the Israelite army weeping, Saul becomes Spirit possessed and is filled with anger. He then performs a prophetic sign indicating that if the people do not go out to battle, they will

---

80. Steinmann, *1 Samuel*, 311.

81. Klein, *1 Samuel*, 26–27, 214; cf. Albright, "Ephod and Teraphim," 39, 42. Tsumura, *First Book of Samuel*, 534, interprets the ephod as some kind of image. David also records an instance of him defeating lions and bears (1 Sam 17:34), though this occurs prior to his explicit anointing by the Spirit.

suffer judgment.[82] The Israelites are then overcome by God and go out to battle in unity against their enemies. Once again, I have left the relevant Hebrew word untranslated. The Hebrew word פַּחַד / *pāḥad* is typically translated as "fear," "dread," or "awe" and this is certainly the case in most instances (Job 4:14; 21:9; Jer 30:5; 48:44).

It appears several times in the context of holy war as well (2 Chr 14:13; 17:10; Jer 49:5). In the Greek version of this passage, *pāḥad* is translated with the word *ekstasis*. This has lead two English versions of the Septuagint to translate it quite differently:

> And the *astonishment* of the Lord came over the people of Israel, and they cried out as one man. (LES; emphasis added)

> And a *transport* from the Lord came upon the people of Israel and they came out to battle as one man. (Brenton; emphasis added)

While elsewhere in the Old Testament the fear of the LORD falls on the enemies of God (2 Chr 17:10; Isa 2:10, 19, 21), in 1 Sam 11:7 and 2 Chr 14:13 the fear of the LORD falls on Israel to empower them for battle. Prior to this battle, Saul was anointed king and Spirit possessed after meeting with a band of prophets (1 Sam 10:5–13). Once Samuel calls the people to rally under Saul's leadership, Saul goes to Gibeah and is joined with "men of valor whose hearts God had touched" (1 Sam 10:26). There are only a few times within the Hebrew Bible where God is said to touch people. These include when God puts Daniel into a trance (Dan 8:18, 10:16), when God touches Jeremiah's mouth to be his prophet (Jer 1:9), and when God wrestles with Jacob (Gen 32:25, 32). All of these instances use the same Hebrew word for touch (נגע/*ngʿ*). God's touching of people is directly connected with theophanies elsewhere, which suggests that 1 Sam 10:26 ought to be read in light of this. In other words, it is not simply a metaphorical way of saying God changed their mind to follow Saul, but like elsewhere in the Hebrew Bible, God seems to have given them a prophetic revelation of some sort.

Based on the presence of Spirit possession here and elsewhere in passages concerning war throughout the Hebrew Bible, language centered around unity and divine intervention, and the context of battle-trance throughout various cultures and time periods, it makes sense to interpret 1

---

82. McCarter, *I Samuel*, 203: "Ancient parallels, moreover, suggest that the threat might have been more direct, wishing that the people themselves, not their oxen, would be slain, for the practice of dismembering an animal to muster the troops seems to have had its origin in covenant-making ceremonies, which often involved dismemberment of animals accompanied by an oath ('May I suffer the fate of these animals if I am not true to the terms of this agreement!')."

Sam 11:7 as an example of such a battle trance. The historian and World War II veteran William H. McNeill (1917–2016) in his book *Keeping Together in Time: Dance and Drill in Human History* (1995) spends a significant amount of space discussing the use of trance and ecstasy in military and religious contexts and concludes regarding this narrative in 1 Samuel that "these passages make it clear that Saul's military leadership was closely connected with ecstatic, collective prophecy."[83]

Other passages related to warfare might suggest ASCs as well. Numbers 6 gives a series of instructions for those wanting to take on what is referred to as a "Nazirite vow." Although Num 6 assumes a form of self-admission to the vow, the two characters typically associated with the Nazirite vow in the Hebrew Bible (Samson and Samuel) are both made Nazirites by their parents. The word Nazirite itself comes from the Hebrew word נזר/ *nzr*, meaning "to separate."[84] The vow involves separating oneself to God for an indeterminate amount of time.[85] Additionally, it prohibits the individual from partaking in alcoholic substances (including eating grapes), cutting their hair, and coming into contact with a corpse. It is never explicitly stated why one would take on a Nazirite vow in the first place, but the places where Nazirites appear in the Hebrew Bible are often in the context of charismatic or ecstatic activity, either in warfare or prophecy.

We have already noted the many cases in which Samson becomes Spirit possessed in order to accomplish amazing feats (Judg 13:24; 14:19; 15:14–15). His strength is attributed to him bearing the stereotypical long hair of the Nazirite (Judg 16:17). This has led the German Old Testament scholar Walther Eichrodt to describe the activity of ancient Nazirites as "similar to those of the 'battle ecstasy' found among other peoples—notably in the case of the Nordic 'berserker.'"[86] In fact, Judg 5:2 may preserve a reference to Nazirite warriors as part of Deborah's army: "When locks are long in Israel, when the people offer themselves willingly—bless the Lord!" (NRSV).[87] The idea here seems to be that the long flowing hair of the Nazirites was a sign of military blessing and success.

It is compelling that both men and women could take on the Nazirite vow. In the context of warfare, female Nazirites could potentially have acted as prophets, much like Deborah herself. Military activity connected with

---

83. McNeill, *Keeping Together in Time*, 69.

84. *HALOT*, s.v. "נזר."

85. The Mishnah states that a Nazirite vow that is not given a determinate amount of time by the individual lasts for a total of thirty days (m. Naz. 1:3).

86. Eichrodt, *Theology of the Old Testament*, 305.

87. Milgrom, *Numbers*, 356.

the Nazirites also appears in 1 Maccabees. While preparing for battle, Judas Maccabeus gets the army to fast and then "stirred up the Nazirites who had completed their days."[88] Although the Nazirites are not explicitly stated to partake in the battle, that they are called upon to add some kind of divine favor to Judas's army is of note.[89]

Samuel is also often considered a Nazirite, although the term is never actually used of him in the Hebrew Bible. His mother, Hannah, is said to make a vow placing Samuel in service to God, with the specific note that "no razor shall touch his head" (1 Sam 1:11). Clearly, this is the marked sign of the Nazirite vow. The assumption that Samuel was perceived to be a Nazirite is corroborated by the Hebrew version of Sirach which explicitly refers to him as a "Nazirite of the Lord in prophecy."[90] Samuel, like Samson, is also referred to as a "judge" and serves as a military instructor of sorts (1 Sam 7:6, 15). In one instance, while Samuel offers a young lamb for the Israelites, the Philistines who begin attacking while this ritual is underway are sent into a "confusion" by God and defeated (1 Sam 7:9–10). In another dramatic episode, Samuel is said to have "hacked Agag to pieces before the Lord in Gilgal" (1 Sam 15:33) after Saul wrongly spared his life.[91]

In addition to his participation in contexts of warfare and violence, Samuel is otherwise known for his impeccable prophetic skill. We are told that "Samuel grew, and the Lord was with him and let none of his words fall to the ground" (1 Sam 3:19; cf. Luke 2:52). Especially important is that Samuel is present with the other prophets, Saul's servants, and the king himself as they fall into ecstasy (1 Sam 19:20–24). Although Samuel is not explicitly stated to become frenzied himself, it is reasonable to think he might have.[92]

A connection between prophets and Nazirites is overtly made in Amos 2:11–12:

---

88. 1 Macc 3:49.

89. Chepey, *Nazirites*, 42–46.

90. Sir 46:13.

91. The Hebrew term translated as "hacked to pieces" (שׁסף/šsp) is a hapax legomenon and its meaning is still uncertain. The Vulgate translates it as *frusta concidit* (cut into pieces). In the Hebrew of the Mishnah, the word is used of separating or dividing. See *NIDOTTE*, s.v. "שָׁסַף."

92. The Hebrew phrase עֹמֵד נִצָּב/'ōmēd niṣṣāb in 1 Sam 19:20 causes some difficulty in how to understand Samuel's posture in this narrative. Most translations, however, take this phrase not to refer to literal standing, but as a reference to Samuel's authoritative position over the group of prophets. Thus, it is not out of the question to see Samuel here as engaging in prophetic ecstasy, perhaps as the one inspiring the others to engage in such activity. See McCarter, *I Samuel*, 329.

"And I raised up some of your sons for prophets, and some of your young men for Nazirites. Is it not indeed so, O people of Israel?" declares the Lord. "But you made the Nazirites drink wine, and commanded the prophets, saying, 'You shall not prophesy.'"

That these two groups are linked suggests that Nazirites may have engaged in prophetic activity which was sought to be halted by their opponents.[93] Thus, in the same way that the prophets are told not to prophesy, the enemies of God gave wine to the Nazirites to thrust them out of their vow so that they might not give oracles, especially related to judgment for disobedience. Forcefully abolishing the Nazirite vow clearly had negative repercussions, such as Samson's loss of strength when his hair was cut. Further evidence for a connection between the Nazirite vow and prophecy comes in Prov 31:1–9. There, an "oracle" (מַשָּׂא/*maśśā'*) is recorded of King Lemuel's mother to the "son of my vows" (Prov 31:2).[94] The word used for "vow" (נֶדֶר/*neder*) here is the same used in Num 6 regarding the Nazirite vow.[95] Of particular note is that this oracle speaks at length about the proper use of alcoholic substances, which may have been of special interest to a woman who had taken on a Nazirite vow or bestowed one upon their child in order to become pregnant.[96]

Collectively, the references to Spirit possession among some of Israel's warriors as well as the seemingly charismatic nature of the Nazirite vow suggest that, to some extent, ASCs were a common occurrence during warfare. Whether the ASCs influenced prophetic activity during wartimes or by empowering soldiers, God is seen as the source of Israel's military victories.

---

93. Wolff, *Joel and Amos*, 170: "In Deuteronomy and in the Deuteronomistic History the expression 'to raise up' (קום hip il) also denotes the induction into office of prophets (Dtn 18:15, 18), judges (Ju 2:16, 18), deliverers (Ju 3:9, 15), priest (1 Sam 2:35), and king (1 Kgs 14:14)." See also Eidevall, *Amos*, 118; and Carroll R., *Amos*, 175–76.

94. Fox, *Proverbs 10–31*, 885.

95. *NIDOTTE*, s.v. "נֶדֶר."

96. Hannah explicitly takes on a "vow" (*neder*) in 1 Sam 1:11 so that she might conceive. Thus, it is not just that she made Samuel a Nazirite, but she herself seems to have taken on a vow as well, perhaps the vow of a female Nazirite. This may explain why Hannah adamantly dismissed Eli's accusation that she was drunk. Longman, *Proverbs*, 20–21, contends that the issue of alcohol in Prov 31 is mostly relevant to righteous governing.

Eccentric Ecstatics

Prophets in the Hebrew Bible often performed sign acts that today we would look at with great suspicion. While not all of these necessarily reflect ecstatic activity, it does help demonstrate that atypical behavior did reflect genuine prophetic activity. Ezekiel, for example, is instructed to: (1) eat a scroll (Ezek 3:1), (2) play with a miniature army set (Ezek 4:1–3), (3) lay on his side for a total of 430 days (Ezek 4:6–9), (4) cook food over human feces (Ezek 4:12–15), (5) cut off his hair and burn some of it (Ezek 5:1–4), (6) pack all of his belongings and pretend he was moving every day (Ezek 12:1–7), (7) dig through a wall with his bare hands in the middle of the night (Ezek 12:7), (8) violently shake while eating food (Ezek 12:18), and (9) remain emotionally numb when his wife passes away (Ezek 24:16–18). Similar activity can be found in other prophetic literature. God instructs various prophets to: (1) wear a yoke around their neck (Jer 27:2), (2) bury underwear and dig it up once it has been soiled (Jer 13:1–7), (3) marry a "whore" (Hos 1:2), and (4) walk around naked for three years (Isa 20:2–4).

Without wanting to conflate distinct prophetic figures from diverse time periods and historical situations, one feature that is worth exploring further is the way God's supernatural touch initiates an ASC. Throughout the Bible, the phrase "the hand of Yahweh" (יַד־יְהוָה / *yad-yəhwâ*) has two primary uses. First, it is used when God is against something, whether a sinful generation (Deut 2:15), Israel (Judg 2:15), the Philistines (1 Sam 7:13), or false prophets (Ezek 14:9). It is most often used in contexts of war, where God is against a particular nation or people.[97] The second use describes when God's miraculous powers are on display. John the Baptist, for example, is viewed by the people with great wonder because "the hand of the Lord was with him" (Luke 1:66). Likewise, the men of Cyprus who were displaced after Stephen's martyrdom preach about Jesus and "the hand of the Lord was with them, and a great number who believed turned to the Lord" (Acts 11:21).

At least eleven times the prophets in the Hebrew Bible are said to have the hand of the Lord come upon them to inspire prophetic activity (1 Kgs 18:46; 2 Kgs 3:15; Isa 8:11; Jer 25:17; Ezek 1:3; 3:14, 22; 8:1; 33:22; 37:1; 40:1), which most scholars interpret to be a "rather specific reference to an ecstatic or trance state, though these terms harbour their own ambiguities."[98] In one startling example, Elijah is able to outrun the chariot driven by king Ahab

---

97. In other instances, God's hand is upon the nation of Israel so that they have a sense of unity (e.g., 2 Chr 30:12). The mechanics of this are unclear but may be similar to what we have seen in the context of holy war.

98. Roberts, "Hand of Yahweh," 245.

for some twenty-seven miles: "The hand of the Lord was on Elijah, and he gathered up his garment and ran before Ahab to the entrance of Jezreel" (1 Kgs 18:46).[99] This strange feat is accomplished after Elijah prophetically hears the sound of rain (1 Kgs 18:41) and ascends Mount Carmel only to put his face between his knees.[100] After seven bouts of intense prayer, God sends rain (1 Kgs 18:45). Such a meditative stance may have helped to induce an ASC and may have been part of what led to Elijah's possession by God's Spirit in 1 Kgs 18:46.[101] It is also important to interpret Elijah's actions in light of what has just occurred in 1 Kgs 18. Elijah's contest with the prophets of Baal may also involve an ecstatic element. As Elijah mocks them, the prophets cut themselves until blood gushes out and "as midday passed, they [*hitnabbē*] until the time of the offering of the oblation" (1 Kgs 18:29). Again, the word *hitnabbē* here indicates some form of ecstatic prophesying, which Bible translations render as "raved" (ESV, NRSV, NLT, NASB), "frantic prophesying" (NIV), and even "ecstatic frenzy" (NET). Indeed, an Akkadian text from Ugarit mentions how the ecstatic prophets (*muḫḫûm*) "drench themselves in their own blood."[102]

If this is the case, Elijah's actions on Mount Carmel in 1 Kgs 18:41–46 are a further validation of his true prophetic gifting, evidenced by God now hearing his prayer to send rain after previously sending fire from heaven.[103]

Elijah's disciple, Elisha, experiences a number of Spirit-related phenomena.[104] He is asked to prophesy by the king of Israel. To accomplish this task, Elisha calls for a musician and once the music was played "the hand of the Lord came upon him" (2 Kgs 3:15). We have seen elsewhere that prophecy was often accompanied by music, likely with the intention of entering

---

99. David-Néel, *Magic and Mystery*, 184, notes how Tibetan lamas practice a form of ecstatic running called *lung gom pa*, suggesting that running while in an ASC may have cross-cultural import. See also Wilson, *Depression and the Divine*, 64–66, who makes a compelling case for interpreting Elijah as an ecstatic.

100. DeVries, *1 Kings*, 217, says that Elijah "ecstatically hears" the future rain.

101. Cogan, *I Kings*, 444.

102. Cogan, *I Kings*, 441; Sweeney, *I and II Kings*, 228.

103. Wray Beal, *1 & 2 Kings*, 244.

104. According to 2 Kgs 2:9, Elisha requests that "there be a double portion of your spirit on me." The phrasing of this passage is curious. Is Elisha asking for God's Spirit to be on him or does he want Elijah's spirit? The answer appears in 2 Kgs 2:15: "The spirit of Elijah rests on Elisha." Sir 48:12 likewise interprets this as Elijah's human spirit: "When Elijah was enveloped in the whirlwind, Elisha was filled with his spirit. He performed twice as many signs, and marvels with every utterance of his mouth." Is this an example of metonymy, where the spirit being referred to is simply the spirit associated with or possessed by Elijah (i.e., God's Spirit)? On the passage in Sirach, see Wright, "With a Spirit of Understanding."

a trance or stirring people into prophetic ecstasy.[105] Despite many scholars adopting an ecstatic interpretation of this account,[106] others seem reticent about inferring from this narrative that Elisha has entered an ASC or that the music was the catalyst for such a state.[107] If Elisha is not in an ASC, one is left to wonder what the point of mentioning the calling for a musician was for and what to do with the ubiquitous cross-cultural evidence of music being used to induce ASCs.[108] Additionally, one would need to explain what the connection is between the presence of music and the hand of God falling on Elisha. Are we to interpret this as a mere coincidence?[109] Elsewhere, Elisha is referred to as "the madman" (הַמְשֻׁגָּע/hamšuggāʿ; 2 Kgs 9:11), a term elsewhere used of the "man of Spirit" (Hos 9:7) and false prophets (Jer 29:26), which may suggest ecstatic or frenzied behavior.

Another strange event involving Elisha must also be considered. Upon Naaman's leprosy being healed, one of Elisha's servants—a man named Gehazi—attempts to fleece Naaman for a financial gift as appreciation for his healing. Upon Gehazi's arrival back home, Elisha asks where he has been, to which Gehazi denies having gone anywhere. What follows is a curious statement by Elisha: "Did I not go with you in spirit (לֵב/lēb) when someone

---

105. Stökl, *Prophecy in the Ancient Near East*, 56–57: "In one of the two texts for the Eštar ritual, two alternatives are described depending on the actions of a *muḫḫûm* [ecstatic]: either he raves, in which case the musicians are required to sing a certain lament, or he remains in equilibrium (i.e. does not go into ecstasy) and the musicians are sent away."

106. See Parker, "Possession Trance," 283.

107. Wray, *1 & 2 Kings*, 314; Wiseman, *1 & 2 Kings*, 225.

108. Pilch, *Flights of the Soul*, 36: "Research conducted by associates of the Cuyamungue Institute, which has been investigating ASCs since its founding in 1970, has shown that those who practice deity-oriented ecstatic trance often feel a pressure at the top of the head when the trance begins.... The ancients may well have been describing this same feeling by the phrase 'the hand of God.'"

109. The arguments put forward by Wood, *Prophets of Israel*, 48–49, that the instruments had an alternative use, that "music that produces ecstasy, however, is not played while one walks along," and that one minstrel "could hardly stir up a type of music to induce an ecstatic state" are unconvincing. How does one explain the many cases of people falling into ASCs while walking (and running!) to music in modern times (David-Néel, *Magic and Mystery*, 184)? Additionally, the assumption that one musician could not play in such a way to induce an ASC seems to be based on nothing more than special pleading. Even many modern charismatics can attest to experiencing ASCs while listening to someone strum on an acoustic guitar or otherwise. We are also not privy to how long the musician played and so monotony in Elisha's case may have been present. While Wood thinks that an ecstatic interpretation of Israelite prophecy is unwarranted and a misinterpretation of the text, in my opinion it seems that it is the nonecstatic interpretations that stretch credulity.

left his chariot to meet you?" (2 Kgs 5:26 NRSV). How did Elisha's spirit or heart go with Gehazi?[110]

Many commentators not so conveniently either completely ignore this detail or leave it unexplained.[111] One chapter later Elisha is able to tell "the king of Israel the words that you speak in your bedroom" (2 Kgs 6:12). Did Elisha see Gehazi and the king of Syria in an ecstatic vision or some kind of out-of-body experience?[112] Early Christian writings also speak of some kind of spirit travel. Tertullian, for example, states in the context of a martyr that "though the body is shut in, though the flesh is confined, all things are open to the spirit. In spirit, then, roam abroad; in spirit walk about, not setting before you shady paths or long colonnades, but the way which leads to God. As often as in spirit your footsteps are there, so often you will not be in bonds. The leg does not feel the chain when the mind is in the heavens."[113]

Other authors, such as Athanasius, envisage a kind of dream-like travel of the soul or spirit.[114] John of Lycopolis appears to a woman in a dream and instructs her, "Always fear the Lord and do not ask for more than is owed to you for your just deserts. Therefore, let it be enough for you to see me in your dream; do not ask for more."[115] Some prophets seem to be translocated throughout the Bible. In 1 Kgs 18:12, for example, a prophet named Obadiah states that "as soon as I have gone from you, the Spirit of the Lord will carry you I know not where. And so, when I come and tell Ahab and he cannot find you, he will kill me." Although Elijah is not explicitly teleported in this passage, the assumption seems to be that this was a common enough occurrence for Obadiah to be concerned. Likewise, Ezek 3:14–15 has the prophet being transported by the Spirit and Philip is physically teleported in Acts 8:38–40.

---

110. The Hebrew does not include the phrase "with you" but it is in the Septuagint. The suggestion of André, "Ecstatic Prophecy," 197, that the text reads, "My heart has not left me," is difficult to accept since the interrogative can be implied without the use of the particle. See GKC §150a.

111. Park, *2 Kings*, 72; Hobbs, *2 Kings*, 67–68; Cogan and Tadmor, *II Kings*, 66; Brueggemann, *1 & 2 Kings*, 337; House, *1, 2 Kings*, 274.

112. On this topic, see Craffert, "Heavenly Journeys," 393–98.

113. Tertullian, *Mart.* 2.9–11.

114. Athanasius, *C. Gent.* 31.5: "When the body is lying on the earth, man imagines and contemplates what is in the heavens. Often when the body is quiet, and at rest and asleep, man moves inwardly, and beholds what is outside himself, travelling to other countries, walking about, meeting his acquaintances, and often by these means divining and forecasting the actions of the day. But to what can this be due save to the rational soul, in which man thinks of and perceives things beyond himself?"

115. Rufinus, *Inquiry About the Monks in Egypt*, 67.

Yet, in the case of Elisha, this seems to be more a matter of translocation of his spirit, not his physical body. In such instances, a trance state best accounts for these supernatural events.

In the book of Ezekiel, the prophet has the hand of the LORD come upon him multiple times as well.[116] In some instances, the hand of Yahweh is "upon" (עַל/ʻal) him (Ezek 1:3; 3:22; 33:22–23) or "falls" (נפל/naphal) on him (Ezek 8:1), while in other instances the prophet seems to be Spirit possessed (Ezek 2:2) or transported (Ezek 3:14; 37:1; 40:1–2).[117] According to Ezek 1:1, the prophet experiences the heavens being "opened" and seeing "visions of God" (מַרְאוֹת אֱלֹהִים / marʼwt ʼĕlōhîm).[118] Visions of the sky opening are not uncommon in the Bible (1 Kgs 22:19; 2 Chr 18:18; Matt 3:16; Mark 1:10; Rev 4:1). One notable example is when the sky opens during Jesus's ascension to heaven (Acts 1:2–7). In the ancient world, people believed that portals existed in the sky that one could travel to via various rituals or that a god or spirit could communicate through that portal.[119] When Jacob has his visionary experience of the ladder in the book of Genesis, for example, he emphatically states that "this is none other than the house of God, and this is the gate of heaven" (Gen 28:17).[120] Thus, the Hebrew Bible often refers to

---

116. Jeremiah too is said to receive God's words when "the LORD put out his hand and touched my mouth" (Jer 1:9).

117. Witmer, *Jesus, the Galilean Exorcist*, 56: "That spirit possession or trance was experienced among prophetic groups and by individuals in the Hebrew Bible is suggested by the frequency with which expressions such as, 'the word which I saw' [Amos 1:1], 'the word which came/was to me' [Hos 1:1; Joel 1:1; Mic 1:1; Zeph 1:1], 'the spirit entered into me' [Ezek 2:2, 3:24], 'the hand of the Lord fell upon me' [1 Kgs 18:46; 2 Kgs 3:15; Isa 8:11; Jer 15:17; Ezek 1:3; 3:13, 22; 8:1; 33:22; 37:1; 40:1], 'the spirit lifted me up' [Ezek 8:3; 11:1, 24; 43:5], and 'the heavens were opened and I saw visions of God' [Ezek 1:1], occur within the narrative. Visions were also common among Hebrew prophets. While Isaiah's famous temple vision is perhaps the best known of these, other prophets, in particular, Jeremiah, Ezekiel, and Amos, were also recognized for their visions. Visions need not necessarily imply spirit possession. However, in several cases the same prophets who reported visions also appear to have experienced some kind of ecstatic trance. In the cases of Jeremiah and Amos, these included images of coming disaster, which were at times accompanied by physical and psychological distress [Jer 1–4; Amos 7–9]. Ezekiel's chariot vision and vision of bones coming to life also utilize language associated with ecstatic trance, and his spirit travels exhibit clear parallels to the soul journeys described by shamans across cultural traditions."

118. Pilch, *Flights of the Soul*, 34, takes the Hebrew phrase here as a genitive so that it reads "divine visions," suggestive of Ezekiel's entrance into an ASC.

119. Pilch, *Visions and Healing*, 18. Cf. the science fiction/horror movie *Event Horizon* alongside *Contact*.

120. T. Levi 5:1: "And thereupon the angel opened to me the gates of heaven, and I saw the holy temple, and upon a throne of glory the Most High." 3 Macc 6:18: "Then the most glorious, almighty, and true God revealed his holy face and opened the heavenly gates, from which two glorious angels of fearful aspect descended, visible to all but the

God's place of habitation as in the sky (Deut 26:15; 1 Kgs 8:43; 2 Chr 18:18; 30:27; 36:23; Ezra 1:2; Job 22:12–14; Ps 11:4; Isa 14:13–14).[121]

Ezekiel's vision seems to fit the model of what ethnographers and anthropologists refer to as a "Sky Journey," an ASC found almost universally across time and cultures.[122] Various methods can be used to induce these states, though as Pilch argues: "While many sky journeys in ancient literature involve some sort of technique on the part of the visionary, others come at God's initiative and an initiative from alternate reality. They are spontaneous. Presumably, if God can initiate such an experience, then God created all human beings with that capability."[123] In his analysis of Ezek 1:4–28, Pilch concludes that the descriptive features of Ezekiel's visionary experience, especially mentions of lights and geometric shapes—"brightness" (v. 4), "fire flashing" (v. 4), "gleaming metal" (v. 4), sparkling "burnished bronze" (v. 7), "burning coals of fire" (v. 13), bright fire (v. 13), "lightning" (vv. 13, 14), "gleaming . . . beryl" (v. 16), and "shining . . . crystal" (v. 22)—are typical neurological features known from research on the stages of ASCs.[124]

Motor automatisms seem to be present in Ezekiel as well. Instances of the prophet falling down are recorded (Ezek 1:28; 3:23–24; 43:3–5; 44:4) and we will discuss these in the following chapter. One specific example, however, will draw our attention here. Ezekiel 3:22–27 mentions (1) experiencing the hand of Yahweh (v. 22), (2) falling down (v. 23), (3) having the Spirit enter him (v. 24), (4) being set down by the Spirit (v. 24), (5) being "bound" by cords by God (v. 25; 4:8), (6) having his tongue "cling" to the roof of his mouth (v. 26), and (7) having his mouth opened by God (v. 27). Scholars have debated whether these are to be taken as metaphors or purely symbolic actions, or as genuine physical symptoms imposed by God, though the latter seems to be the predominant view.[125] Zimmerli states that "in its content we must note that after the clear command of v 24b which the prophet was to obey . . . things are mentioned in vv 25–27 which have nothing to do with the prophet's own choice, but are simply to be suffered by

---

Jews." See also 2 Bar. 22:1; 3 Bar. 2:1–7; 11:1–6; 1 En. 14:15; and Mart. Ascen. Isa. 10:24.

121. Pilch, *Flights of the Soul*, 169: "In the Greek tradition, the opening was over Delphi. In the Israelite tradition, the opening was over Jerusalem."

122. Sheils, "Cross-Cultural Study"; Winkelman, "Altered States of Consciousness," 411.

123. Pilch, *Flights of the Soul*, 64.

124. Pilch, *Flights of the Soul*, 36: "To see a bright color is a definite sign that one is in an ASC. Indeed, this color characterizes the first of three possible stages of ecstatic trance."

125. Block, *Ezekiel 1–24*, 155; Blenkinsopp, *Ezekiel*, 32; Broome, "Ezekiel's Abnormal Personality," 272–92; Zimmerli, *Ezekiel 1–24*, 160.

him."[126] Unlike in the New Testament where demoniacs are said to be mute (Matt 9:32; 12:22; Mark 9:17, 25; Luke 11:14) and rigid (Mark 9:18), here it is God himself causing his own prophet to exhibit these symptoms! The overlap in these experiences is accounted for by the fact that automatisms themselves do not indicate their source. Thus, an onlooker is unable to determine the cause of an automatism based on outward appearances.

---

126. Zimmerli, *Ezekiel 1-24*, 159.

4

Getting Wasted with the Writings

> When indeed God stopped my most perfectly wise song as I prayed many things, he also again placed in my breast a delightful utterance of wondrous words. I will speak the following with my whole person in ecstasy.
>
> —Sibylline Oracles 2:1–4

THIS CHAPTER WILL BE our final look at instances of ASCs in the Hebrew Bible. It begins by looking at a series of verbal automatisms found in the books of 1 and 2 Chronicles. We will then move on to the incorporation of prophetic music used in the sanctuary and the prophetic role of the Psalms. After this, a treatment of the "glory cloud" and motor automatisms found in Exodus, Ezekiel, and Chronicles is supplied. Finally, as we transition to the New Testament, it will be advantageous to make some general comments on Second Temple Jewish interpretations of biblical characters such as Ezra and Enoch.

Chronicling Verbal Automatisms

We have already seen elsewhere, such as with the example of Balaam (Num 24:2) or with some groups of prophets (1 Sam 10:6), that when God's Spirit comes upon a person, they often begin spontaneously speaking.¹ We may also add to this that some form of verbal automatism was probably present when the evil spirit from God was sent upon Saul in 1 Sam 18:10. Throughout 1 and 2 Chronicles, God's Spirit moves on people to have them spontaneously speak, often in the form of prophetic oracles. This form of Spirit phenomena is best described as a kind of verbal automatism whereby the speaker is compelled to speak as a reflex of being overcome by the Spirit.

In 1 Chr 12:17-19, when David's mighty men visit him in Ziklag, the Spirit² "clothed" (לבשׁ/*lbš*) the chief of the thirty, a man named Amasai, making him speak.³

Within the narrative, David has questioned whether they have come as allies or foes, and Amasai's spontaneous response quells his doubts about their allegiance. What is remarkable about Amasai's response, however, is that it is a collage of phrases and themes meant to reverse the hostile remarks against David elsewhere in 1 Samuel and 1 Kings.⁴

Thus, Amasai's automatic reply to David through the Spirit solidifies in David's mind their loyalty and that God is with him despite his enemies.

Other occurrences of verbal automatism appear in 2 Chronicles. According to one passage: "The Spirit of God clothed Zechariah the son of Jehoiada the priest, and he stood above the people, and said to them . . ." (2 Chr 24:20). Again, note that the Spirit coming upon the individual is immediately followed by speech. Zechariah, unfortunately, is not given a warm welcome and is promptly stoned "in the court of the house of the Lord" (2 Chr 24:21). This Zechariah seems to be the same one mentioned by Jesus in Matt 23:35 during a scathing speech against the religious leaders.⁵ The prophetic activity of this Zechariah and his untimely death must been perceived as quite major since, according to the apocryphal work Lives of the Prophets (first century CE), after his death "visible portents occurred in the Temple, and the priests were not able to see a vision of angels of God or

---

1. Ecstatics from ancient Assyria are called variously *zabbu/zabbatu* (frenzied one) and *raggimu* (shouter). See Foster, "Ecstatic Speech," 438.

2. Knoppers, *1 Chronicles 10-29*, 559, notes that it is not "the Spirit" but "a spirit" since the Hebrew lacks the article. He therefore translates the phrase as, "Then a spirit enveloped Amasai." 556.

3. Johnstone, *1 Chronicles 1—2 Chronicles 9*, 162, states that "God himself" was "controlling the response"; Knoppers, *1 Chronicles 10-29*, 564, refers to this event as "possession."

4. Williamson, "We Are Yours, O David," 174.

5. Levin, *Chronicles*, 210–11.

to give oracles from the *Dabeir*, or to inquire by the Ephod, or to answer the people through Urim as formerly."[6]

In another instance, when the Moabites, Ammonites, and Meunites come against king Jehoshaphat for war, "the Spirit of the Lord came upon Jahaziel the son of Zechariah, son of Benaiah, son of Jeiel, son of Mattaniah, a Levite of the sons of Asaph, in the midst of the assembly. And he said . . ." (2 Chr 20:14–15).

Jahaziel's genealogy is of particular interest. He is a descendant of Mattaniah, a member of the sons of Asaph, a prophetic group known for using music in their prophesying (1 Chr 25:1), a practice we have already noted is connected with ASCs. That Jahaziel is not a prophet but a Levite has led some scholars to argue that the presence of Spirit possession here is meant to acknowledge that Jahaziel was not one of the typical court prophets.[7]

One final example like this occurs earlier in 2 Chronicles: "The Spirit of God came upon Azariah the son of Oded, and he went out to meet Asa and said to him . . ." (2 Chr 15:1–2). Interpreting this as verbal automatism is more difficult since Azariah moves from one location to another while in a state of Spirit possession and, although ecstasy could still be a component, the spontaneous nature of the speaking is less clear.

Jewish writers of the postexilic period, of which 1 and 2 Chronicles are a product, were seemingly comfortable with the idea of verbal automatism. This is evident from nonbiblical sources as well. In a work from the apocrypha called Susanna (an addition to the biblical book of Daniel), for example, when the titular young woman Susanna is falsely accused of sexual immorality and led to her execution, we read that "God stirred up the holy spirit of a young lad named Daniel, and he shouted with a loud voice, 'I want no part in shedding this woman's blood!'"[8] Verbal automatism was no doubt part of prophetic practice in the ANE, evidenced by the "bubbling forth" of the prophets.

---

6. Liv. Pro. 23:1–2.

7. Schniedewind, *Word of God in Transition*, 70–74, 116–17.

8. Sus 45–46 (NRSV). The LES, following a different manuscript tradition, puts it as such: "The messenger gave, as he was commanded, a spirit of insight and understanding to a young man, Daniel. And Daniel, stirring up and dividing the gathering, and taking a stand in the midst of them, said 'In such a way as this, O foolish sons of Israel, are you not examining this closely nor recognizing the plain truth, that they killed a daughter of Israel?'"

Music in Chronicles

The connection between music and prophecy is pronounced in 1 and 2 Chronicles:

> David and the chiefs of the service also set apart for the service the sons of Asaph, and of Heman, and of Jeduthun, who prophesied with lyres, with harps, and with cymbals. The list of those who did the work and of their duties was: Of the sons of Asaph: Zaccur, Joseph, Nethaniah, and Asharelah, sons of Asaph, under the direction of Asaph, who prophesied under the direction of the king. (1 Chr 25:1–2)

> The singers, the sons of Asaph, were in their place according to the command of David, and Asaph, and Heman, and Jeduthun the king's seer; and the gatekeepers were at each gate. They did not need to depart from their service, for their brothers the Levites prepared for them. (2 Chr 25:15)

These passages may imagine a prophesy-on-command situation where the prophet prophesies at the command of the king and the musicians under the command of Asaph, though it is possible that it means that they prophesied under the employment or direct oversight of their employer or leader.[9] There is also some debate about what it means to "prophesy with" the varying instruments. Ralph W. Klein states: "This clause suggests that the musical instruments *accompanied* the prophetic activity, but the Hebrew could also be construed to mean that the playing of the musical instruments was itself an act of prophesying."[10] Likewise, John W. Kleinig argues that the singing of psalms was a "prophetic proclamation."[11]

Other scholars variously interpret what is happening as musical improvisation[12] or ecstasy.[13] That instrumental accompaniment was used to induce prophetic ecstasy may find support in the fact that Jahaziel, whom we have already discussed, is said to become Spirit possessed in the assembly and is directly associated with the musical family of Asaph.

Stökl suggests a historical development that involves the prophets being split into two categories:

---

9. Dirksen, "Prophecy and Temple Music."
10. Klein, *1 Chronicles*, 480.
11. Kleinig, *Lord's Song*, 18.
12. Ehrlich, *Randglossen zur Hebräischen Bibel*, 350; Rad, *Geschichtsbild des chronistischen Werkes*, 114–15; Galling, "Königliche und nichtkönigliche," 73.
13. Slotki, *Chronicles*, 133.

At some point, presumably in the aftermath of the destruction of Jerusalem, when the term נביא started to be used for Jeremiah, either during his lifetime or afterwards, something like the following process must have happened: the roles of a court-diviner and that of the ecstatic combined to form a new role, that of a messenger-type prophet, such as we find them in most of the writing prophets. At the same time, a different development saw the musical side of the ecstatic groups of נביאים transferred to the temple musicians, which is how we meet them in 1–2 Chronicles.[14]

If Stökl is correct, this would mean that music accompaniment was specifically used for inducing ASCs and would certainly be in line with what we encounter with Elisha in 2 Kings. The move toward prophetic music in the temple suggests a concern for revelation within Israelite religion during this time. The ability for the king, but also the general populace, to have access to prophetic ministry may have been seen as advantageous for everyday life affairs. First Samuel 9, for example, recounts the story of how Saul and his servant track down a goat that had gone astray by means of seeking out the prophet Samuel. We are told that "formerly in Israel, when a man went to inquire of God, he said, 'Come, let us go to the seer,' for today's 'prophet' was formerly called a seer" (1 Sam 9:9).

Evidently, day-to-day issues were brought to a prophet so that they could find answers to common questions or concerns. While itinerant prophets may have aided in this concern, others likely lived locally and were apparently brought gifts as appreciation for their services (1 Sam 9:7). In addition to these prophets, having a series of professional prophets working in the temple complex further allowed those travelling to the temple to inquire of them.

The presence of music alongside prophetic ministry probably acted as a natural method for the prophets to enter an ASC and respond to individual queries.

David's Automatisms?

King David sometimes is involved in prophetic activity that may involve motor and verbal automatisms. According to 2 Samuel, David speaks an "oracle" (נְאֻם/nəʾ um) on his deathbed (23:1), the typical Hebrew word used of prophetic oracles elsewhere.[15] Additionally, he states that "the Spirit

---

14. Stökl, *Prophecy in the Ancient Near East*, 175.
15. *DCH*, s.v. "נְאֻם"; BDB, s.v. "נְאֻם"; *HALOT*, s.v. "נְאֻם."

of the LORD speaks by me; his word is on my tongue" (23:2).¹⁶ Because of the poetic nature of this passage, it is difficult to know whether Spirit possession is envisioned here, though it seems likely.¹⁷ There is some evidence to see Spirit phenomena at play that may include verbal automatism. First, many features of David's oracle here find parallels in the songs of Hannah and the oracle of Balaam, both of whom we have suggested may have also experienced ASCs.¹⁸ Second, the Septuagint translates 2 Sam 23:3 as God commanding David to "speak a parable" (παραβολὴν εἰπόν/*parabolēn eipon*) and it seems like God is the one speaking through David. Third, David is frequently interpreted as being a prophet, both in the New Testament (e.g., Acts 1:16, 2:30), Josephus,¹⁹ and later rabbinic Judaism.²⁰ Fourth, while most English translations say that the Spirit spoke "by" (ESV, KJV, NASB) or "through" (NRSV, NIV, CSB, NLT) him, David is said to literally have Yahweh's Spirit speak "in" (בְּ/*b*) him.

The Hebrew preposition here may indicate a state of Spirit possession.²¹ Similar phraseology is used of Joseph "in whom is the Spirit of God" (אֱלֹהִים בּוֹ/' *ĕlōhîm bw*; Gen 41:38) because of his divinatory prowess. Likewise, the prophet Micaiah is assaulted and asked, "How did the Spirit of the LORD go from me to speak to you?" (2 Kgs 22:24; cf. 2 Chr 18:23).

The transference of the Spirit seems to assume temporary Spirit possession as a method of engaging in prophetic vision and explication.

The connection between scribal activity and Spirit possession should be considered as well as David engages in what seems to be motor automatism. In one notoriously difficult passage from 1 Chr 28:19 we read the following:

> "All this," David said, "I have in writing as a result of the LORD's hand on me, and he enabled me to understand all the details of the plan." (NIV)

> "All *this*," said David, "The LORD made me understand in writing by *His* hand upon me, all the details of this pattern." (NASB)

---

16. Psalm 156 col. 1:14 (second–first century BCE?): "You prophesied through your spirit by the mouth of your servant"; Psalm 156 col. 2:5: "I saw a vision and all his prophecies"; cf. Psalm 156 col. 3:10. Translations from Charlesworth and Allen, *Psalm 156*.

17. Anderson, *2 Samuel*, 268, suggests that "ecstatic behavior" is not in view here but does not explain why.

18. See Firth, *1&2 Samuel*, 525–26.

19. Josephus, *Ant.* 6.8.2.

20. b. Sotah. 48b.

21. *TDNT*, s.v. "רוּחַ in the OT," lists this passage as an example of ecstasy.

> "All this he made clear to me in writing from the hand of the LORD, all the work to be done according to the plan." (ESV)

> All this he wrote down, by the hand of the LORD, to make him understand it—the working out of the whole design. (NAB)

> "All this, in writing at the LORD's direction, he made clear to me—the plan of all the works." (NRSV)

> David concluded, "By the LORD's hand on me, he enabled me to understand everything in writing, all the details of the plan." (CSB)

These translations offer completely different senses of what this verse entails. Is it, as the CSB and NASB imply, that David was given understanding of a writing that already existed? Or, is it as the ESV and NIV suggest that this writing was produced by God's hand being on David? Klein translates it as follows: "All this was in a document—since the hand of Yahweh was upon him—that made clear all the details of the plan."[22] In this case, his translation makes clear that the plan was produced through divine intervention: "Despite several uncertainties in the phraseology, two things seem clearly intended by this verse: the plan for the temple and its furnishings was contained in a written document, and this plan had divine authorship even if it was mediated through David. According to the Chronicler the plans for the temple were not just ideas David had dreamed up."[23] This is similar to what we find in the case of Moses receiving the plans of the tabernacle (Exod 25:9, 40; 27:8). That scribes were often thought of as inspired is evident from a section in the apocryphal work Sirach:

> How different the one who devotes himself to the study of the law of the Most High! He seeks out the wisdom of all the ancients, and is concerned with prophecies; he preserves the sayings of the famous and penetrates the subtleties of parables; he seeks out the hidden meanings of proverbs and is at home with the obscurities of parables. He serves among the great and appears before rulers; he travels in foreign lands and learns what is good and evil in the human lot. He sets his heart to rise early to seek the Lord who made him, and to petition the Most High; he opens his mouth in prayer and asks pardon for his sins. If the great Lord is willing, he will be filled with the spirit of understanding; he will pour forth words of wisdom of his own and

---

22. Klein, *1 Chronicles*, 516.
23. Klein, *1 Chronicles*, 527.

give thanks to the Lord in prayer. The Lord will direct his counsel and knowledge, as he meditates on his mysteries.[24]

Another biblical scribe who is later pictured as prophetically inspired is Ezra. We are told that Ezra "was a scribe skilled in the Law of Moses that the Lord, the God of Israel, had given, and the king granted him all that he asked, for the hand of the Lord his God was on him" (Ezra 7:6). A little later in this same chapter, Ezra states that "I took courage, for the hand of the Lord my God was upon me, and I gathered leaders from Israel to go up with me" (Ezra 7:28). It is easy to read these two statements in Ezra as meaning something like "God's favor was with me."[25] Again, however, the only time the phrase is used in a way comparable to this is in military contexts or warnings against disobedient nations, and both of these uses also appear in Ezra (8:22, 31). Additionally, we must note the difference within the Hebrew text in these passages. Ezra 7:6 and 28 both refer to the "hand of Yahweh" not the "hand of God."[26]

Ezra is almost universally interpreted as a visionary prophetic figure in early Jewish and Christian literature.[27] In the work 4 Ezra (part of the work 2 Esdras), he falls down and must wait so that his "soul recover[s] the spirit of understanding"[28] and elsewhere has his "mouth opened"[29] by God and immediately begins speaking.[30] These seem best interpreted as motor and verbal automatisms. Additionally, one passage contains the Latin phrase *et ventilatus est spiritus meus valde*, which may be translated as "and my spirit was greatly lifted up," and echoes the many instances of ASCs in Ezekiel.[31]

Jews around the time of Jesus believed the Psalms contained prophetic content. The Aramaic paraphrase (called a Targum) of Psalms (first–sixth century CE) frequently mentions David as a prophet or as prophesying (14:1; 18:1; 45:16–18; 103:1).

Likewise, the Qumran community viewed David's writing as prophetic: "All these he [David] spoke through (the spirit of) prophecy which

---

24. Sir 38:34—39:7.
25. See Breneman, *Ezra, Nehemiah, Esther*, 128.
26. Cf. Ezra 7:9.
27. Works dating from the first to the ninth century CE that picture Ezra as a visionary prophet include: 4 Ezra (first century CE), the Greek Apocalypse of Ezra (second–ninth century CE), the Vision of Ezra (fourth–seventh century CE), Questions of Ezra (date unknown), and Revelation of Ezra (prior to ninth century CE).
28. 2 Esd 5:22.
29. 2 Esd 9:28.
30. See Stone, *Fourth Ezra*, 119–24; and Merkur, "Visionary Practices."
31. 2 Esd 3:3.

had been given to him from before the Most High."³² Interpretive works (called Pesharim) from Qumran also treat the Psalms like prophecies. One work called 4QPsalms Pesher³, for example, interprets Ps 37 as a prophecy fulfilled in the community's own time. Jesus states that the Psalms also have prophetic significance in the fulfillment of his earthly ministry: "These are my words that I spoke to you while I was still with you, that everything written about me in the Law of Moses and the Prophets and the Psalms must be fulfilled" (Luke 24:44).

Although this is a cumulative case, given the interpretations of the character of David in later periods as a prophet, the near ubiquitous meaning of the phrase "the hand of the LORD" in the context of scribal and prophetic activity, and statements made about David in the New Testament, it seems probable to interpret David as engaging in verbal and motor automatisms brought on through Spirit possession.

David the Ecstatic?

In addition to automatisms, David is sometimes depicted as being (or pretending to be) an ecstatic. In one instance, upon fearing for his life before the king of Gath, David "changed his behavior before them and pretended to be insane in their hands and made marks on the doors of the gate and let his spittle run down his beard" (1 Sam 21:13).³³ As a result, King Achish states that David is a "madman" and that he already does not "lack madmen" (1 Sam 21:15). While this could be interpreted as a denigrating comment toward the king's court staff, it may be that these madmen do not refer to "insane" individuals or subpar employees, but to prophets. In other words, Achish already has a host of court prophets and does not need another one interrupting him with their ecstatic activity. The Septuagint's rendering is also telling: "And he changed his face before him, and he put on an act in that day, and he drummed on the doors of the city and gestured with his hands and fell against the doors of the gate, and his spittle ran down on his beard. And Anchous said to his servants, 'Look, see an epileptic man [ἐπίλημπτον/*epilēmpton*]; why did you bring him to me? Indeed, do I lack epileptics [ἐπιλήμπτων/*epilēmptōn*], that you have brought him to have an epileptic fit [ἐπιλημπτεύεσθαι/*epilēmpteuesthai*] before me? This fellow shall

32. 11Q5 XXVII, 11.

33. The Hebrew word הלל/*hll*, translated as "to be insane" in 1 Sam 21:14, also has a synonym with the meaning of "praise" elsewhere (Ps 22:23; Isa 38:18). Auld, *I & II Samuel*, 264, argues that this is not coincidental. The idea seems to be that praise can sometimes look like erratic behavior to "outsiders." Cf. Payne, *I & II Samuel*, 113.

not come into the house'" (1 Sam 21:13-15 NETS). That David is portrayed as an epileptic suggests that David is not acting insane but rather like an ecstatic, which typically has features reminiscent of epilepsy such as falling, drooling, and erratic behavior. We saw earlier that, in some texts, ecstatics are not to be made fun of or treated with contempt.[34] Thus, the king has David leave unharmed since violence against an ecstatic was seen as taboo.

Some Psalms, both canonical and noncanonical, depict David as being ecstatic as well. Psalm 31:22 and Ps 116:11 in most English translations say that David spoke either in his "alarm" or "haste" (חפז/ḥpz). The Septuagint translates both instances as ἐκστάσει/ekstasei. Some later Christians, relying on the Septuagint, therefore deduced that David was speaking "in ecstasy." Augustine, for example, drawing on Ps 31:22 says, "'I said in my ecstasy.'— What saidst thou in thine ecstasy?—'I am cast away from the sight of Thine eyes.' For it seems to me as if he who said this had lifted up his soul unto God, and had been carried beyond himself."[35] Elsewhere, however, he interprets the same idea in Ps 116:11 as referring to fear.[36]

David may have also produced songs in ecstasy. Psalm 7:1 titles the song a "[שִׁגָּיוֹן/šiggāywōn] of David." This word only appears in one other instance in Hab 3:1 where it appears in the plural form: "A prayer of Habakkuk the prophet, according to [שִׁגְיֹנוֹת/šigyōnôt]."[37] Lexical entries on šiggāywōn define it variously as "wild, passionate song, with rapid changes of rhythm,"[38]

34. *ANET*, 424–25.

35. Augustine, *Serm.* 2.16 (NPNF[1] 6:263); cf. Augustine, *Enarrat. Ps.* 42:17: "'Why hast Thou rejected me?' 'Rejected' me, that is to say, from that height of the apprehension of the unchangeable Truth. 'Why hast Thou rejected me?' Why, when already longing for those things, have I been cast down to these, by the weight and burden of my iniquity? This same voice in another passage said, 'I said in my trance' (i.e., in my rapture, when he had seen some great thing or other), 'I said in my trance, I am cast out of the sight of Thine eyes.' For he compared these things in which he found himself, to those toward which he had been raised."

36. Augustine, *Enarrat. Ps.* 116:8: "'I said in my trance, All men are liars' (ver. 11). By trance he meaneth fear, which when persecutors threaten, and when the sufferings of torture or death impend, human weakness suffereth. For this we understand, because in this Psalm the voice of Martyrs is heard. For trance is used in another sense also, when the mind is not beside itself by fear, but is possessed by some inspiration of revelation."

37. Evidence from the prayer/song of Habakkuk itself may point toward ecstasy as well. Habakkuk mentions in the first person that "I saw the tents of Cushan in affliction; the curtains of the land of Midian did tremble" (Hab 3:7), which suggests a visionary experience. Language that expresses features typical of ASCs are likewise found. The prophet states his "body trembles" and "lips quiver" and that his legs "tremble" (Hab 3:16). Additionally, he states that "His brightness was like the light; rays flashed from his hand" (Hab 3:4). Bright lights are often associated with ASCs.

38. BDB, s.v. "שִׁגָּיוֹן."

or a "song of ecstasy."³⁹ The Septuagint renders it as a "Psalm" (Ψαλμὸς/ *Psalmos*), while the Syriac Peshitta circumvents the problematic term by not translating it at all! Some Latin versions (called the *versio juxta Hebraicum*) translate it as "*pro ignoratione David*"—that is, "for the ignorance of David." Likewise, in Hab 3:1 the word is translated by the Latin Vulgate as "for the ignorances" (*pro ignorantia*). This same meaning is shared by Aquila, Symmachus, and Theodotion, the three other major translations of the Septuagint. "Ignorance," in this case, could possibly be interpreted as an ASC whereby the mental faculties are not fully engaged in a traditional sense. Various proposals for its meaning based on similar words from Semitic languages have also been given.⁴⁰ Some have proposed it stems from the Akkadian word for "lamentation" (*šigû*). Others have argued that the word is etymologically related to the Hebrew verb שָׁגָה/*šāgâ*, which means "to go astray" or "to swerve" or "to stagger" such as with alcohol (Isa 28:7), perhaps as a song of an ecstatic.⁴¹ An Arabic word meaning "to stimulate great excitement" (*sajā(w)*) is also suggested (though lexigraphy in this area is uncertain).

In the noncanonical Ps 156, we are told that "on the fourth (day) in the month of Iyyar, in the spirit, I (David) saw the Holy vision and all his prophecies."⁴² Being "in the spirit" is differentiated from seeing the vision and the prophetic portents, which suggests that it is describing the state David is in—that is, an ASC. In Matt 22:43 David is understood to produce Ps 110 "in the Spirit" (ἐν πνεύματι/*en pneumati*), a phrase elsewhere used of ecstatic experiences that will be explored in the next chapter.

Rudolf Pesch refers to David's experience as an "apocalyptic formula" (German: *apokalyptische Formel*) typical of prophets like Ezekiel and John of Patmos.⁴³

Conclusion

Pre- and postexilic writings mention verbal and motor automatisms and perhaps ecstatic activity. Likewise, various instances in the Hebrew Bible concerning David picture him as an ecstatic and perhaps as undergoing automatisms. Depending on how one chooses to interpret this evidence, it may be that David engaged in ASCs, perhaps as a method for inspiration to

---

39. *DCH*, s.v. "שִׁגָּיוֹן I."
40. For a history of interpretation, see *HALOT*, s.v. "שִׁגָּיוֹן."
41. Sellin, *Zwölfprophetenbuch*, 2:406.
42. Psalm 156 col. 4:16.
43. Pesch, *Markus-Evangelium*, 2:253.

produce music. The connection between music, prophecy, and cultic worship suggests that ASCs were linked to musical accompaniment and musical professionals. Nothing in the text suggests that such activity became rarer over time or that these experiences were somehow aberrant. In the following chapter we turn our attention to the New Testament where ASCs abound. Thus, if anything, there is not a decrease, but an increase of ASCs in the life of God's people.

5

Gin and Gospels

> The Son of Man came eating and drinking, and they say, "Look at him! A glutton and a drunkard, a friend of tax collectors and sinners!" Yet wisdom is justified by her deeds.
>
> —Matthew 11:19

It is unfortunately commonplace for Christians to put little stock in the stories of the Hebrew Bible in formulating a picture of religious experience. This is especially true when it comes to the miraculous and supernatural. How often have you seen a sea split in half? When was the last time your bones raised someone back to life? Such a view of the Hebrew Bible is lamentable, especially since the New Testament is grounded in the Jewish Scriptures and the same God who put people into trances and ecstasies back then continued to do the same in the New Testament.

While it may be easy to think of John receiving the visions of Revelation in a trance, Christians tend to gloss over many other biblical characters who experienced ASCs. Peter and Paul are explicitly said to fall into *ekstasis* in the book of Acts. Jesus's family members try to remove him from a crowd because he was *existēmi*. Many others cry out uncontrollably when the Spirit comes on them. As we will see, there is no shortage of ASCs within the New Testament.

The following three chapters divide the New Testament portion of our study into the Gospels, the Acts of the Apostles, and the Letters of Paul.

Treatment of other passages from the General Epistles and Revelation are sprinkled throughout. Our investigation begins, however, with a short Greek phrase.

En Pneumati

What does it mean for someone to be "in the Spirit"? It is perhaps easy to perceive this as a statement about being in union or agreement with God. One may otherwise interpret it as a way of expressing a figurative locale that Christians find themselves in. For example, one could say they are "in" God or "in" the Spirit as opposed to "in" the world. In both cases, this idea of the expression "in the Spirit" seems to be rooted in particular passages from Paul's letters, such as Romans: "You, however, are not in the flesh but in the Spirit, if in fact the Spirit of God dwells in you. Anyone who does not have the Spirit of Christ does not belong to him" (8:9), or Colossians: "He [Epaphras] has made known to us your love in the Spirit" (1:8).

There is, however, another way that the phrase "in the Spirit" is used. Scholars such as Clint Tibbs[1] have helpfully demonstrated that the Greek phrase ἐν πνεύματι/*en pneumati*, translated as "in [a/the] s/Spirit," is used in some places to refer to ASCs, not just as a way of juxtaposing virtuous and unethical living.[2] Jacob Kremer puts it succinctly that "ἐν πνεύματι [*en pneumati*] came to be a t.t. [technical term] for prophetic ecstasy."[3] In

---

1. Tibbs, "Mediumistic Divine Possession," 182: "The prepositional phrase *en pneumati* is quite varied in the NT. In reference to 'holy spirit' it appears 56 times in diverse contexts including baptism (Matt 3:11; Mark 1:8; Luke 3:16; John 1:33; 1 Cor 12:13), praying (John 4:23,24; 1 Cor 14:15; Jude 20), circumcision (Rom 2:29), a state of mind (Rom 8:9; 9:1), elation (joy) (Rom 14:17), sanctification (Rom 15:16; 1 Cor 6:11), ministry (2 Cor 6:6), justification (Gal 3:3), awaiting hope (Gal 5:5), living (Gal 5:16, 25), and guidance (Gal 5:18). In all of these cases, the phrase is rendered in English as 'in/by the Spirit' suggesting some kind of presence of 'the spirit' in the lives of Christians. In other contexts, the phrase *en pneumati* describes the experience of visionary phenomena had by John (Rev 1:10; 4:2; 17:3; and 21:10). Here, *pneumati* does not refer to 'holy spirit' but rather to a spiritual reality/realm into which John enters 'in spirit' outside of his body in order to have visionary experiences (cf. 2 Cor 12:13)."

2. Holloway, *Philippians*, 65–66: "Christ-believers are 'in the Spirit' because the Spirit is 'in them': 'you are not in the flesh but in the Spirit [ἐν πνεύματι] *since* the spirit of God dwells in you [ἐν ὑμῖν]' (Rom 8:9a). To be 'in the Spirit' means to be permanently possessed by the divine spirit: 'since *we live in the Spirit* [ζῶμεν πνεύματι], let us also walk in the Spirit' (Gal 5:25). By analogy, then, to be 'in Christ' would mean to be permanently possessed by Christ. This conclusion is supported by the fact (1) that for Paul Christ was himself now a 'spirit' (1 Cor 15:45; cf. 2 Cor 3:17) and (2) that Paul often used 'the spirit of God' and 'the spirit of Christ' interchangeably."

3. EDNT, "πνεῦμα," 3:119.

what follows, we will look at instances of this phrase in Second Temple Jewish texts, rabbinic literature, later Christian writings, and finally the New Testament.

Second Temple Judaism

Sections from the Septuagint, Pseudepigrapha, and Dead Sea Scrolls suggest that the phrase "in the Spirit" is used either of prophetic inspiration or more specifically of ASCs. In the Septuagint, the phrase *en pneumati* is used in two passages from Ezekiel where ASCs are obvious. Ezekiel 11:24 (NETS) states: "And a spirit took me up and brought me to the land of the Chaldeans, into the captivity, in a vision, in a divine spirit [בְּרוּחַ/bərûaḥ | ἐν πνεύματι/en pneumati], and I ascended from the vision that I saw."[4] Likewise, during the prophet's vision of the valley of dry bones: "The hand of the Lord came upon me, and the Lord brought me out in a spirit [בְּרוּחַ/bərûaḥ | ἐν πνεύματι/en pneumati] and set me in the midst of the plain, and this was full of human bones" (Ezek 37:1 NETS).[5] We have already noted that the phrase "hand of the Lord" is a typical expression of an ASC in the Hebrew Bible.

In 1 Enoch, during one of his visionary tours, Enoch encounters an angel named Saraqa'el who is "one of the holy angels who are (set) over the spirits of mankind who sin in the spirit [τῷ πνεύματι ἁμαρτάνουσιν/tō pneumati hamartanousin]."[6] George W. E. Nickelsburg suggests that this may be a Christian alteration relating to blasphemy against the Holy Spirit found in the Gospels, a case where spirit possession is at the forefront.[7] Another possible way to interpret Saraqa'el's role is that he punishes those who prophesy falsely while in an ASC, a sentiment shared by the Christian work the Didache.

---

4. Olley, *Ezekiel*, 299: "In conclusion, the reader is reminded that all of this was 'in a vision', in a trance-like state. The vision had begun while 'the elders of Judah were sitting before me' (8:1), the 'hand of Lord' no doubt causing him to fall (cf. 2:1; 9:8). Now 'I got up from the vision' (MT: 'the vision went up from me') and he speaks to them, to the 'captivity' amongst whom God has already said he will be 'a little sanctuary' (see v. 15)."

5. Olley, *Ezekiel*, 489: "A nuance different to MT's 'spirit of Yahweh' is provided by B's syntax, 'Lord led me out by a spirit/wind' which to Greenberg suggests an event that is 'real rather than visionary' (1997: 742) (but P967 Q, ἐν πνεύματι κυρίου), although B's consistent use of the abbreviation leads the reader to nevertheless think of the Spirit." Micah too is described as being *en pneumati* as he contrasts himself with the false prophets that Israel has followed: "Otherwise I will replenish strength in the spirit [אֶת־רוּחַ/eth-ruah | ἐν πνεύματι/en pneumati] of the Lord, and of judgment and of dominance to declare to Iakob his impious acts and to Israel his sins." (Mic 3:8 NETS).

6. 1 En. 20:6.

7. Nickelsburg, *1 Enoch*, 296.

The Dead Sea Scrolls often discuss the inspiration of God's Spirit in the life of the prophets or of individuals being given a spirit by God using the Hebrew phrase ברוח/*brwh* (in a/the s/Spirit). A work called 4QVision and Interpretation, for example, preserves a fragmentary mention of such a prophetic experience:[8] "And now, I, th[ese things] in the spirit (בְּרוח/*brwh*) [...] you, and the or[acle] (המ[שא/*hm*[*sh*') will not fail, [and] not [will be du]mb [...] the oracle (המשא/*hmsh*'), and concerning the house of [... the] vision (חז[ה/*h*]*hzwn*), f[or] I have [se]en."[9] Here, being "in the spirit" is connected with an oracle, likely received and/or communicated while in an ASC.

Another scroll, 4QInstruction[b], gives a series of guidelines for living and serving in the community including the following: "[Do not se]ll your soul for money. It is better that you are a servant in the spirit (ברוח/*brwh*), and that you serve your overseers for nothing."[10] Being a "servant in the spirit" may suggest prophetic activity. The scroll called The Community Rule, for example, mentions that the "prophets have revealed through his holy spirit (ברוח קודשו/*brwh qwdshw*)"[11] and another work called 4QNon-Canonical Psalms B mentions similarly that "by his spirit (ברוחו/*brwhw*) prophets «were given» to you to teach you and show you."[12]

Lastly, a portion from the Hodayot or Thanksgiving Hymns reads: "And I, the Inst[ructor, have known you, my God, through the spirit (ברוח/ *brwh*) which you gave in me, and I have listened loyally to your wonderful secret] through [your holy] spirit. [You have opened within me knowledge of the mystery of your wisdom, the source of your power, ...]."[13] Here, the instructor (משכיל/*mshkyl*) is given a spirit by which he accesses secret knowledge.

It is not always clear whether the sense of the preposition ב/*b* in these passages should be translated as "in" or "by" or "through" or something of the like, or whether this distinction even matters. The inspiration of the s/Spirit (it is not evident if it is God's or the human spirit that is in view in each passage)[14] may have involved ASCs regardless.

---

8. In the quotes that follow from the Dead Sea Scrolls, parentheses are my inclusion of the Hebrew and brackets indicate reconstructed text from the original source material.

9. 4Q410 1.7–9.

10. 4Q416 2 2.17

11. 1QS 8.16.

12. 4Q381 69 4; cf. 1QS 1.3; 1QpHab 2.9, 7.5; 4Q166 2.5; and 4Q292 2 4.

13. 4Q427 8 ii, 12–13.

14. See Sekki, *Meaning of Ruach at Qumran*.

Rabbinic Literature

In later rabbinic texts, the phrase "in the holy spirit" is used generally of those authoring Scripture or the prophetically inspired. A priest should not consult the Urim and Thummim, for example, unless he "speak with Divine Spirit" (בְּרוּחַ הַקּוֹדֶשׁ/*beruah haqqodesh*) and who has the "Divine Presence" (שְׁכִינָה/*shekhinah*) on him.[15] Rabbi Meir says, "Everywhere where it says (in the Scriptures), 'He replied and said such-and-such,' the person concerned speaks in the holy spirit."[16] In a commentary on the Song of Songs, Rabbi Yudan bar Simon states that the "Divine Spirit [רוּחַ הַקֹּדֶשׁ/*ruah haqqodesh*] rested upon him [Solomon] and he composed these three books: Proverbs, Song of Songs, and Ecclesiastes."[17] In the same work, a theoretical debate is brought up about whether to listen to the author of Ecclesiastes. The conclusion is that if "he [Solomon] had said them according to his opinion (his own discretion), you should have tilted your ears and heard them, and all the more so since he spoke them in the holy spirit."[18]

It is important to note that when the rabbis talk about the "Holy Spirit," they are not referring to the Christian conception of the Holy Spirit as a member of the Trinity, but as the empowering charismatic force that animates the prophet and writers of Scripture. Note, for example, the names given to the Holy Spirit in one rabbinic text: "By ten names was the Holy Spirit called, to wit: parable, metaphor, riddle, speech, saying, glory, command, burden, prophecy, vision."[19] This connection between the Holy Spirit and revelation is made explicit in the Tosefta (third–fourth century CE), a collection of supplementary Jewish legal material related to the Mishnah:

> When the latter prophets died, that is, Haggai, Zechariah, and Malachi, then the Holy Spirit came to an end in Israel. But even so, they made them hear [Heavenly messages] through an echo. M'SH Š [the story is told concerning]: Sages gathered together in the upper room of the house of Guria in Jericho, and a heavenly echo came forth and said to them, "There is a man among you who is worthy to receive the Holy Spirit, but his generation is unworthy of such an honor."[20]

---

15. b. Yoma 73b.
16. Qoh. Rab. 7:2.
17. Shir Rab. 1:1.
18. Shir Rab. 1:1.
19. 'Abot R. Nat. A.34.
20. t. Sotah 13:3.

In addition to generic inspiration, the phrase "in the holy spirit" is also used in the context of visions. The Talmud records Hezekiah saying "I saw in the holy spirit that no excellent children would come from me."[21] Likewise, Rabbi Aqiba "looked in the holy spirit (in the power of his prophetic gift) and said to his students, 'Whoever has a daughter of age, go and give her as a wife!'"[22] King David also "saw in the holy spirit (as a prophet)."[23] Additionally, in a Cairo Genizah text that contains songs attributed to David, the following is mentioned as a preface to the fourth song: "On the fourth (day) of the month Iyyar I surveyed in the spirit in a holy vision and (in) all His prophecies and I prayed before the face of the Lord."[24] That being in the spirit is paralleled with having a holy vision and prophecy is further evidence that the phrase "in the spirit" refers to an ASC.

Early Christianity

Later Christians used the phrase *en pneumati* to speak of ASCs as well, especially as they relate to prophecy. In one early Christian work called the Didache (ca. second century CE), instructions are given on discerning between true and false prophets.[25] These discernment tips are mostly centered around the ethical behavior and greed of the prophet and the author makes use of the phrase *en pneumati* throughout:

> Not everyone who speaks [*en pneumati*] is a prophet but only the one whose behavior is the Lord's. So the false prophet and the prophet will be recognized by their behavior. No prophet who orders a meal [*en pneumati*] eats of it himself; if he does, he is a false prophet.... You shall not listen to anyone who says [*en pneumati*], "Give me money, or something," but if he is asking that something be given for others who are in need, let no one judge him. (11:8-9, 12).

The author of the Didache prefaces his instructions with the following warning: "Do not test any prophet who speaks [*en pneumati*], and do not judge him, for all sins will be forgiven, but this sin will not be forgiven."[26] A

21. b. Ber. 10a.
22. Lev. Rab. 21 (120C).
23. Midr. Ps. 22 § 7 (92B).
24. Bauckham et al., *Old Testament Pseudepigrapha*, 270.
25. Niederwimmer, *Didache*, 53: "In sum, the date of the *Didache* is a matter of judgment. An origin around 110 or 120 c.e. remains hypothetical, but there are as yet no compelling reasons to dismiss this hypothesis."
26. Didache, 11:7.

person speaking *en pneumati* should not be viewed with disdain. Yet, it is obvious that not all prophets are true prophets. In this case, the sign of an ASC might have compelled the Didache's audience to give food or money to an itinerant prophet. Thus, ethical conduct must be used to judge the prophet's character instead and whether or not they should be honored in the community.[27]

Related to this, there are instances where Christian prophets and false prophets seem to become possessed by various spirits that need to be discerned:

> Beloved, do not believe every spirit [παντὶ πνεύματι/*panti pneumati*], but test the spirits [πνεύματα/*pneumata*] to see whether they are from God, for many false prophets have gone out into the world. By this you know the Spirit of God: every spirit [πᾶν πνεῦμα/*pan pneuma*] that confesses that Jesus Christ has come in the flesh is from God, and every spirit [πᾶν πνεῦμα/*pan pneuma*] that does not confess Jesus is not from God. This is the spirit of the antichrist, which you heard was coming and now is in the world already. Little children, you are from God and have overcome them, for he who is in you is greater than he who is in the world. They are from the world; therefore they speak from the world, and the world listens to them. We are from God. Whoever knows God listens to us; whoever is not from God does not listen to us. By this we know the Spirit of truth and the spirit of error. (1 John 4:1–6)

In the context of speaking about true and false prophets, John states that there are multiple spirits, both good and evil, that can possess a person and have them speak. As Georg Strecker explains, "Our text differs from what has gone before in speaking not about the Holy Spirit but about human beings who are guided by different spirits."[28] In other words, this does not appear to be referring to discerning corporeal manifestations of angels, demons, or other spiritual beings, but of prophets speaking through various kinds of spirits. The focus is thus on the person speaking by means of the spirit indwelling them. This sentiment is shared in the Christian text Shepherd of Hermas:

---

27. Niederwimmer, *Didache*, 178–82. Clement of Alexandria, relaying the apocryphal words of the prophet Zephaniah quotes: "The Spirit of the Lord took me, and brought me up to the fifth heaven, and I beheld angels called Lords; and their diadem was set on in the Holy Spirit [ἐν πνεύματι ἁγίῳ/*en pneumati hagiō*]; and each of them had a throne sevenfold brighter than the light of the rising sun; and they dwelt in temples of salvation, and hymned the ineffable, Most High God." *Strom.* 5.11.77.

28. Strecker, *Johannine Letters*, 132.

> For every spirit [πᾶν γὰρ πνεῦμα/pan gar pneuma] which is given from God is not asked questions, but has the power of the Godhead and speaks all things of itself [ἑαυτοῦ/heautou], because it is from above, from the power of the Divine spirit.... So when the person who has the spirit of God [ὁ ἔχων τὸ πνεῦμα τὸ θεῖον/ho echōn to pneuma to theion] enters the assembly of just men who believe in the divine spirit, and prayer is made to God by the assembly of those men, then the angel of the prophetic spirit [ὁ ἄγγελος τοῦ πνεύματος τοῦ προφητικοῦ/ho angelos tou pneumatos tou prophētikou] that rests upon that person fills the person, who, being filled with the holy spirit [πληρωθεὶς ὁ ἄνθρωπος τῷ πνεύματι τῷ ἁγίῳ/plērōtheis ho anthrōpos tō pneumati tō hagiō], speaks to the whole crowd as the Lord wishes. Thus the divine spirit is revealed. Such is the power of the Lord with regard to the divine spirit.[29]

In addition to the Hebrew and Greek phrases analyzed above, Latin texts use identical phraseology to indicate ASCs. The early church father Tertullian, for example, speaks of possession amnesia experienced by the apostle Peter during the transfiguration and uses the equivalent Latin phrase *in spiritu* for *en pneumati*:

> Now, it is no difficult matter to prove the rapture [*amentiam*] of Peter. For how could he have known Moses and Elias, except (by being) in the Spirit [*in spiritu*]? People could not have had their images, or statues, or likenesses; for that the law forbade. How, if it were not that he had seen them in the Spirit [*in spiritu*]? And therefore, because it was in the Spirit [*in spiritu*] that he had now spoken, and not in his natural senses, he could not know what he had said.[30]

Elsewhere, Tertullian records the following communication with a Montanist where the word for ecstasy and the phrase *in spiritu* are linked (here translated as "ecstatic vision" by the translators of the *ANF* series):

> We have now amongst us a sister whose lot it has been to be favoured with sundry gifts of revelation, which she experiences in the Spirit by ecstatic vision [*ecstasin in spiritu*] amidst the sacred rites of the Lord's day in the church: she converses with angels, and sometimes even with the Lord; she both sees and hears mysterious communications; some men's hearts she understands, and to them who are in need she distributes remedies. Whether

---

29. Herm. Mand. 11.5, 9–10.
30. Tertullian, *Marc.* 4.22.5.

it be in the reading of Scriptures, or in the chanting of psalms, or in the preaching of sermons, or in the offering up of prayers, in all these religious services matter and opportunity are afforded to her of seeing visions. It may possibly have happened to us, whilst this sister of ours was rapt in the Spirit [*in spiritu*], that we had discoursed in some ineffable way about the soul.[31]

Other Latin Christian texts are relevant to this discussion. The famous account of the martyr Perpetua (second century CE), for example, states that she was "in the Spirit and in an ecstasy [*in spiritu et in extasi*]."[32] The Gospel of Pseudo-Matthew records an apocryphal tale of Jesus entering a school and being "led by the Holy Spirit, He took the book out of the hand of the master who was teaching the law, and in the sight and hearing of all the people began to read, not indeed what was written in their book; but He spoke in the Spirit [*in spiritu*] of the living God, as if a stream of water were gushing forth from a living fountain, and the fountain remained always full."[33] Finally, Cyprian (third century CE) states that "in the spirit [*in spiritu*]," the apostle "foresaw this praise of courage and firmness of strength; and, attesting your merits by the commendation of your future doings."[34]

New Testament

In line with the various examples highlighted above, the phrase *en pneumati* can also be used of ASCs in the New Testament.[35] John is four times said to be *en pneumati* (Rev 1:10, 4:2, 17:3, 21:10)[36] while experiencing his rev-

31. Tertullian, *An.* 9.

32. *Passion of Saints Perpetua and Felicity* 6.3 (ANF 3:705).

33. Ps.-Mt. 39.

34. Cyprian, *Epist.* 56 2. This work is listed as *Epistle* 60 in some printed editions of the Latin text.

35. See *TDNT*, s.v. "Ἐν": "Since the conception of the Spirit is itself imprecise, the Spirit may easily be identified with the state produced by Him. The idea is also local, but not fluid, when the two basic orientations of existence, ἐν σαρκί and ἐν πνεύματι, are opposed to one another (R. 8:8 f.). Here there is little trace of the fluid and ecstatic element. The Spirit is the constantly active principle of ethical life. The transition from the ecstatic to the pneumatic is important not merely for the ethical consequences (cf. also R. 9:1; 15:16; ἐν πνεύματι πραΰτητος, Gl. 6:1; 2 C. 6:6 with ἐν γνώσει κτλ.), but also for declarations on the proclamation of the gospel (1 Th. 1:5, again with material substantives; 1 Pt. 1:12) and prayer (Eph. 6:18; Jd. 20). In what seems to be a most comprehensive way the demand of Jn. 4:23 f. (προσκυνεῖν ἐν πνεύματι καὶ ἀληθείᾳ) emphasises the correspondence between the absolutely boundless and truly personal being of God and the worship which we are to render Him."

36. Pilch, *Flights of the Soul*, 216–17: "The English phrase 'in spirit' is a 'literal'

elation on Patmos and most scholars point out that such language is likely borrowed from Ezekiel.[37] Paul also uses this terminology in 1 Cor 12-14. In 1 Cor 12:3, for example, he states that "no one speaking [*en pneumati*] of God ever says 'Jesus is accursed!' and no one can say 'Jesus is Lord' except [ἐν πνεύματι ἁγίῳ/*en pneumati hagio*]." The person speaking *en pneumati* is speaking in an ASC.[38] Should someone exhibit signs of being in an ASC (suggesting they are speaking prophetically from God) and curse the name of Jesus, they are to be anathematized. Likewise, Paul states that "if you give thanks [*en pneumati*], how can anyone in the position of an outsider say 'Amen' to your thanksgiving when he does not know what you are saying?" (1 Cor 14:16).[39] Some English translations, such as the ESV, insert the phrase "*your* spirit" (emphasis added) after "give thanks" in this passage, despite it not being in the Greek text, in an attempt to make sense of Paul's statement. Yet, this insertion seems to obscure what Paul means—that is, that the one speaking in tongues speaks in an ASC that is viewed as insanity by outsiders.[40]

The Gospel writers also use this phraseology. During a confrontation with the Pharisees, Jesus asks the following question: "How is it then that David, [*en pneumati*], calls him Lord, saying, 'The Lord said to my Lord, "Sit at my right hand, until I put your enemies under your feet"'? If then David calls him Lord, how is he his son?" (Matt 22:43-45).[41] On the opposite end of the spiritual spectrum, however, the phrase is used by Mark in his description of the demoniac in the Capernaum synagogue: "And immediately there was in their synagogue a man in an unclean spirit [*en pneumati akathartō*]. And he cried out. . . . But Jesus rebuked him, saying, 'Be silent,

---

translation of the Greek ἐν πνεύματι, which occurs three more times in Revelation (4:2; 17:3; 21:10). We can view this statement as an ethnographic report, the cultural interpretation of John's experience." Malina and Pilch, *Social-Science Commentary*, 37, translate this phrase (problematically) as "was in the sky power" and Holy Spirit as "divine sky power" (41) in an attempt to attend to social-scientific vocabulary.

37. See Beale, *Book of Revelation*, 203; and Swete, *Apocalypse of St. John*, 12-13.

38. This may be differentiated from a prophet like Agabus who prophesies "by the spirit" (διὰ τοῦ πνεύματος) in Acts 11:28. The preposition διὰ seems to imply the source of the revelation rather than the method of communication as per ἐν (cf. Isa 30:1 LXX; Acts 21:4; 1 Cor 2:10; 12:8; Eph 3:16). See Porter, *Idioms*, 148-49 (§ 4.5.1 and 4.5.3), 158 (§ 4.8.3).

39. See Tischendorf, *Novum Testamentum Graece*, 2:542-43.

40. Mount, "1 Corinthians 11:3-16."

41. Luz, *Matthew 21-28*, 89n12: "Ἐν πνεύματι suggests a vision, an audition (references in Pesch, *Markus-Evangelium* 2.253) or some other form of inspiration (cf. 2 Esdr 14:22; Acts 1:16; 1 Pet 1:11; 2 Pet 1:21; Heb 3:7)."

and come out of him!' And the unclean spirit, convulsing him and crying out with a loud voice, came out of him" (Mark 1:23, 25–26).[42]

Related to all this, the English theologian Henry Barclay Swete recognized more than a century ago that "the return to a non-ecstatic state [is] described as ἐν ἑαυτῷ [en heautō = 'came to himself']."[43] Such language appears after Peter's trance in Acts 10:17 and after he had a vision of an angel in Acts 12:11.

There are other passages where *en pneumati* is used in the New Testament of what appears to be ASCs that will be dealt with later in this chapter. It is important to note, however, that not every instance of this phrase signals an ASC. One must rely on contextual clues to determine when such an interpretation is warranted. For example, Paul expresses in Rom 15:16 his desire that "the offering of the Gentiles may be acceptable, sanctified by the Holy Spirit [*en pneumati*]." Clearly the offering is not in an ASC. Thus, it is incumbent on the interpreter to prove that an ASC is the most logical or probable understanding. In instances where prophetic inspiration, visions, automatisms, and other Spirit phenomena are present, however, it makes sense to offer an ASC as a plausible reading of the phrase *en pneumati*.

Temple Trances

We briefly observed in previous chapters that, in the ancient world, ASCs within temples were not uncommon.[44] In the Hellenistic (Greek) world too, ASCs were part of some religious activities, especially within temples.[45] Readers have likely heard stories of the oracle of Apollos at Delphi

---

42. Marshall, *Gospel of Luke*, 192: "Since he uses ἐν πνεύματι [*en pneumati*] for possession of the Spirit of God (2:27; 4:1, 14) he substitutes ἔχων [*echōn*; "having"] here (8:27; 13:11; Acts 8:7; 16:16)."

43. Swete, *Apocalypse of St. John*, 13.

44. *ANET*, 87, 143, 150, 624, 631. See Ludwig, "Historical Survey of the Early Roots."

45. Aristides tells of an ASC he experienced in the Asclepian Temple (*Or.* XLVIII, 31–35 = test. 417): "It [i.e., the remedy] was revealed in the clearest way possible, just as countless other things also made the presence of the god manifest. It was like seeming to touch him, a kind of awareness that he was there in person; one was between sleep and waking, one wanted to open one's eyes, and yet was anxious lest he should withdraw too soon; one listened and heard things, sometimes as in a dream [*onar*], and sometimes as in waking life [*hypar* = waking vision]; one's hair stood on end; one cried, and felt happy; one's heart swelled, but not with vainglory. What human being could put that experience into words? But anyone who has been through it will share my knowledge and recognize the state of mind." Cf. Plutarch, *Luc.* 12.1; Philostratus, *Vit. soph.* 1.25.536; Iamblichus, *De Mysteriis.* 3.3; and Athenaeus, *Deipn.* 10.422D.

breathing in vapors to prophesy in an ASC,[46] or perhaps the frenzy of the Bacchae, described as "possessed" and "foaming at the mouth and twisting" their eyes.[47] The ancient tragedian Euripides (ca. 484–407 BCE) states concerning the god Bacchus and his devotees that "this god [Bacchus] is a prophet—for Bacchic revelry and madness have in them much prophetic skill. For whenever the god enters a body in full force, he makes the frantic to foretell the future."[48] And of course, prophetic and visionary experiences within the temple are known from the Hebrew Bible as well (e.g., 1 Sam 3; Isa 6). Such activity in temple complexes makes perfect sense from an ancient worldview. Temples were thought to be places where gods and other spiritual beings often resided, bringing humans into closer contact with them and mediating communication with them. Idols were thought to play host to the god, so that the differences between the god and its idol were often blurred in ancient thought.[49]

In some instances, rituals were performed to have the god come reside in the idol so that cultic actions could be directed toward this physical manifestation of the god.[50] Thus, the presence of ASCs in temple complexes should not strike us as unusual.

In both the Gospel of Luke and Acts, multiple prophetic ASCs are recorded in the temple. According to Luke, the priest Zechariah was chosen by lot to enter the Jerusalem temple and burn incense. We have noted previously the use of incense likely contributed toward the facilitation of ASCs among the priesthood. Zechariah sees an angel "standing on the right side of the altar of incense" (Luke 1:11). It seems obvious that the story of Zechariah and his barren wife Elisabeth is modeled after Abraham and Sarah's account in Gen 15. Here too, a promise is made of procreation and an ASC may be used to communicate the message. When Zechariah doubts the words of Gabriel, he is struck mute, causing the crowd outside to become concerned for his wellbeing (Luke 1:20–21). When Zechariah comes out of the temple, the people conclude that he had "seen a vision" (Luke 1:22). This

---

46. Strabo, *Geogr.* 9.3.5. Plutarch, *Def. orac.* 40, compares this frenzy to drunkenness. The view that the oracle at Delphi was entering ASCs through geochemical fumes has been hotly debated. See, for example, Piccardi et al., "Scent of a Myth."

47. Euripides, *Bacch.* 1120–24.

48. Euripides, *Bacch.* 298–304.

49. Dick, "Mesopotamian Cult Statue."

50. See, for example, Robins, "Cult Statues," 1: "In general, statues in ancient Egypt were places where a non-physical entity—a deity, the royal *ka*-spirit, or the *ka*-spirits of the dead—could manifest in this world. Statues provided physical bodies for these beings and allowed them to be the recipients of ritual actions. In order for a statue to function in this way, it had to undergo the Opening of the Mouth ritual, which vitalized it and enabled it to house the being it represented."

word for "vision" (ὀπτασία/optasia)⁵¹ is used six times of Daniel's visions in the Greek version of Daniel made by Theodotion. It is likewise used of Paul's visions (in or out of the body) recorded in 2 Cor 12:1 and of the early Christian bishop Polycarp, who saw a vision of a burning pillow (69-155 CE), symbolizing his forthcoming martyrdom.⁵²

Upon leaving the temple, Zechariah was expected to recite the Aaronic blessing found in Num 6.⁵³ His muteness obviously prohibited this from happening. Yet, it seems unclear how the people concluded he had experienced a vision. Was it that he somehow communicated to them with a form of sign language (Luke 1:22: "making signs")? Did he write a message to them on a writing tablet (cf. Luke 1:63)?

Some commentators have suggested that the crowd's apparent understanding of Zechariah's experience is not of importance, but rather a narrative necessity.⁵⁴ Yet, there are good reasons why the people may have understood that Zechariah experienced something supernatural in the temple. Josephus records a very similar occurrence of prophetic activity taking place in the temple with the high priest John Hyrcanus II (164-104 BCE) offering incense: "God came to discourse with him [Hyrcanus]; for they say that on the very same day on which his sons fought with Antiochus Cyzicenus, he was alone in the temple as high priest offering incense, and heard a voice, that his sons had just then overcome Antiochus."⁵⁵

Likewise, in a story found in the apocryphal book 2 Maccabees (ca. first century BCE-first century CE), a man named Heliodorus entered the temple treasury where God caused a "great manifestation" of horses and two young men who beat him for entering. We are then told that "when he suddenly fell to the ground and deep darkness came over him, his men took him up, put him on a stretcher, and carried him away—this man who had just entered the aforesaid treasury with a great retinue and all his bodyguard

---

51. ὀπτασία is a rare word, only occurring once outside of the LXX and the NT. In several passages from the LXX, it is obvious the meaning of ὀπτασία is "appearing" rather than a vision (e.g., Esth 4:17 LXX; and Sir 43:1-2, 16).

52. Mart. Pol. 5:2. While Lightfoot's translation inserts the phrase "in a trance," the Greek does not support this, even though *optasia* is used in similar situations. Polycarp's vision was not so much a good omen, as he was burned alive at the stake as a martyr, and ultimately stabbed to death when the flames could not harm him! See also Acts Paul 3, 15.

53. m. Tamid 7:2; Prot. Jas. 24:1f.

54. Fitzmyer, *Gospel According to Luke*, 329: "Luke does not tell us how the crowd could have been so perceptive; but to ask how is to miss the point of his story." Naturally, I disagree. Zechariah's muteness is pivotal to understanding various other elements of the story.

55. Josephus, *Ant*. 13.282.

but was now unable to help himself. They recognized clearly the sovereign power of God."[56] Thus, there was good reason for the crowd to be worried about Zechariah's prolonged stay in the temple and for them to assume that perhaps he had seen a vision (whether for good or bad).[57] Indeed, physical disabilities like blindness, deafness, and muteness are sometimes interpreted as the presence of spirits elsewhere in the New Testament (Matt 12:22; Mark 9:17-27; cf. Acts 13:11).[58] The inability to speak also occurs during Daniel's ASC (Dan 10:15) and Ezekiel's visions (Ezek 3:26, 24:27). Similarly, Heliodorus is unable to speak after his ASC in the temple: "He lay prostrate, speechless because of the divine intervention."[59] Zechariah is thus one in a line of spiritually inflicted mutes. Whether Zechariah was in a form of trance while in the temple, however, is not stated and we can only base its probable presence off of comparative literature, the presence of incense, and the general theme of ASCs in temples.

Another possible instance of an ASC occurs in Luke 2:22-37, once again in the temple grounds. Here, we are introduced to a certain Simeon concerning whom the Holy Spirit was "upon" on at a previous time, informing him that he would not die before seeing the Messiah. The Greek of Luke 2:25 is strange, as it literally reads "s/Spirit was holy upon him" (πνεῦμα ἦν ἅγιον ἐπ' αὐτόν/*pneuma ēn hagion ep' auton*), though Luke clearly wants us to understand Simeon as a prophet.[60] Importantly, Luke tells us that Simeon entered the temple "in the Spirit" (ἐν τῷ πνεύματι/*en tō pneumati*). Simeon, like those in the examples provided above, seems to also have been in an ASC when entering the temple.[61] This reads very similar to Paul's words in

---

56. 2 Macc 3:27-28. Cf. m. Yoma 5:1.

57. Cf. Jub. 32:1; and 2 Bar. 34:1—36:1.

58. Though consider Collins, *Mark*, 435: "The possessing demon is called 'a mute spirit' (πνεῦμα ἄλαλον). Judging from the rest of the narrative, the reason is that the spirit does not speak through the afflicted person; the possession is manifested in physical symptoms. Or the description of the demon may derive from an ancient perception of the symptoms of epilepsy." On the topic of epilepsy, possession, and mute and deaf people, see Temkin, *Falling Sickness*, 40.

59. 2 Macc 3:29.

60. *TDNT*, s.v. "Προφήτης, Προφῆτις, Προφητεύω, Προφητεία, Προφητικός, Ψευδοπροφήτης."

61. See Levison, "Spirit, Simeon." Marshall, *Gospel of Luke*, 119, and Stein, *Luke*, 115, disagree with the idea that Simeon was in an ecstasy. Yet, they do not give any reasons other than the presence of the definite article in the phrase *en tō pneumati* and a parallel use in Luke 4:1 (which could also be interpreted as a form of ecstasy!). It is confusing why this would somehow turn aside an ecstatic reading of the text. Indeed, they do not deal with any of the primary sources on this matter. Even with the article, the phrase is used of what appears to be prophetic Spirit possession (Mark 12:36; Luke 10:21). Likewise, the absence of the preposition ἐν/*en* does not nullify an ASC. In Acts

Acts 20:22–23: "And now, behold, I am going to Jerusalem, constrained by the Spirit [τῷ πνεύματι], not knowing what will happen to me there, except that the Holy Spirit testifies to me in every city that imprisonment and afflictions await me."[62] Simeon's inspired words of praise perhaps indicate a form of verbal automatism similar to Amasai as his spontaneous praise is drawn from themes found in Isa 40–55. After Simeon speaks, Mary and Joseph are visited by another prophetic figure, an elderly woman named Anna. Her devotion of praying, fasting, and constant presence in the temple grounds may suggest that she too experienced ASCs, though Luke does not tell us this explicitly and there is not enough information to come to any meaningful conclusions.[63]

Finally, Paul's ASC in the temple found in Acts is also worth briefly considering. After being arrested by the Jews, Paul defends himself to the tribune. He begins with a biographical sketch of his life and recent conversion to the Way, and amid his explanation he tells us of an ASC he experienced:

> When I had returned to Jerusalem and was praying in the temple, I fell into a trance [*ekstasis*] and saw him saying to me, "Make haste and get out of Jerusalem quickly, because they will not accept your testimony about me." (Acts 22:17–18)

In Paul's trance, he sees and hears the risen Jesus himself (cf. Acts 9:1–19; 26:12–32) who tells him to go to the gentiles. Intense concentration, such as in prayer, meditation, or other spiritual activities, has commonly been shown to induce trance in its practitioners.[64]

Within 1 Corinthians, Paul says his apostolic call was given to him in a vision (9:1, 15:8). Like Abraham's ASC which confirmed the covenantal promise of a future hope for the nations, it is perhaps in parallel to this that Paul's own missionary call in an ASC to the gentiles is to be viewed.

---

of Paul and Thecla 2 (second century CE), a certain Onesiphorus does not know about Paul's physical appearance except by a description of Titus because he had seen Paul "only in the Spirit" (μόνον πνεύματι/*monon pneumati*). The absence of the preposition *en* seems to have not been necessary to indicate a visionary state. See Porter, *Idioms*, 158 (§4.8.5).

62. Nolland, *Luke 1—9:20*, 119.

63. Stronstad, *Charismatic Theology of St. Luke*, 34: "Significantly, in Jewish Antiquities, Josephus reports on three Essene prophets: (1) Judas, who foretold the death of Antigonous (13.311–13); (2) Menahem, who foretold that Herod would become 'king of the Jews' (15.373–78); and (3) Simon, who interpreted a dream of Archelaus to mean that his rule would last ten years (17.345–48). It is tantalizing to speculate that Simon, the Essene prophet, might be identified with the prophet Simeon, who blessed Jesus in the temple (Luke 2:25–35)."

64. Pilch, *Flights of the Soul*, 178.

Likewise, Peter's trance in Acts 10 (explored in the following chapter) is also related to the gentile mission.

Birthing the Miraculous

While preaching in 1995, the evangelist Steve Hill turned his attention to the man who was convulsing on the floor in Pensacola, Florida. Hill informed the audience that the man was "interceding" for their souls with "moanings and groanings and . . . birth pains. He's giving birth to you, friend. He's giving spiritual birth to you" (cf. Gal 4:19).[65]

Most people would not be faulted with immediately asking the obvious question: why was a *man* giving birth during church?

Wesley Campbell, in his book *Welcoming a Visitation of the Holy Spirit* (1996), states that one possible physical manifestation of the Holy Spirit can be "giving birth." By this he does not mean literally bearing a child, but rather he is describing a prophetic sign in which the individual feels as though they are experiencing labor pains as a symbol of God "birthing" new gifts in them or anointing them more generally. In some instances, these individuals will groan or cry out as part of the manifestation. The American sociologist Margaret M. Poloma in her book *Main Street Mystics: The Toronto Blessing and Reviving Pentecostalism* (2003) likewise records her own investigation and interviews of both women (and surprisingly) men who engaged in what she calls "birthing." These individuals reported "feeling burdened by some world problem for which they travailed in prayer."[66] Such ideas are not just from the twentieth century either.

In the Middle Ages, women would sometimes claim that their bloated figure was actually a sign that they were "pregnant with Christ!"[67]

The sight of adults writhing in pain on the floor from supernatural contractions and the idea of women literally expanding is obviously difficult for many to take seriously and I am not suggesting we believe all such accounts. Yet, we should not be so quick to relegate all verbal outcries to the realm of deception or the demonic. While groaning and moaning may not be part of the normative Spirit-filled experience, there are forms of verbal automatism found in the New Testament that ought to be considered.

Luke records instances of loud verbal automatisms in his writings. When Elizabeth is pregnant with John the Baptist, upon Mary's arrival John leaps within the womb and she is "filled with the Holy Spirit" (Luke

65. Hanegraaff, *Counterfeit Revival*, 62.
66. Poloma, *Main Street Mystics*, 85.
67. Graham, "Social Image of Pregnancy."

1:41) and immediately "exclaimed with a loud cry" (Luke 1:42) a blessing to Mary and Jesus. This "loud cry" (κραυγῇ μεγάλῃ/*kraugē megalē*) and related phrases are used inside and outside of the New Testament often in the context of the possessed. The disciple of the bishop Irenaeus, Hippolytus (ca. 160–235 CE), for example, tells of a sorcerer who, "appearing to be borne away under divine influence, (and) hurrying into a corner (of the house), utters a loud and harsh cry, and unintelligible to all . . . and orders all those present to enter, crying out (at the same time), and invoking Phryn, or some other demon."[68] Likewise, in the Gospels we have numerous accounts of demons or demon-possessed individuals who "cry out" (Matt 8:29; Mark 1:23; 3:11; 5:5, 7; 9:26; Luke 4:33, 41; 8:28; 9:39). It is not just Elizabeth, however, who cries out in this narrative. Mary begins singing spontaneously (Luke 1:46–56). Although the phrase "filled with the Holy Spirit" does not appear here, it is clear that this is a prophetic utterance brought on through the Spirit. In fact, Mary's song has many parallels with Hannah's song in the Hebrew Bible, suggesting that there is a typological expectation for us to interpret Mary as engaged in an ASC. Zechariah too becomes "filled with the Holy Spirit" and is explicitly said to speak a "prophecy" (Luke 1:67).

Verbal automatisms are found elsewhere in Luke's writings. Throughout Acts, people are "filled with the Holy Spirit" and speak in tongues (Acts 2:4), speak boldly (Acts 4:8, 31), recount visions (Acts 7:55–60), and rebuke others (Acts 13:9–11). Why is it that Luke recounts so many examples of verbal automatism compared to the other synoptic gospels and John? In general, Luke seems to be more familiar with Jewish and Greco-Roman magical practices.[69] Acts 5:15 and 19:12, for example, describe the miraculous expectations and uses of shadows, handkerchiefs, and aprons.[70]

Moreover, Luke's use of the phrase "finger of God" as opposed to Matthew's "spirit of God" is meant to mirror the miraculous ministry of Moses and Aaron in Exod 8:19 (cf. Exod 31:18; Deut 9:10; Ps 8:4), a ministry contrasted with Egyptian magic, but also reliant on various ritual objects such as Aaron's staff (e.g., Exod 7:8), dust (Exod 8:16), and soot (Exod 9:8). In other words, Luke's Gospel tends to have a major theme of prophetic activity and spirit phenomena compared to the other Gospel accounts. As a result, we should not be surprised that Luke is more likely to record instances of verbal automatism, perhaps a manifestation he was himself well aware of within and without Judaism and Christian circles more broadly.

---

68. Hippolytus, *Haer.* 4.28; cf. Lucian, *Men.* 9.
69. See Garrett, *Demise of the Devil*; and Heintz, "Trois études préliminaires."
70. Keener, *Acts*, 3:2841.

In Rom 8:15 and Gal 4:6, Paul may be drawing on a tradition of verbal automatism when he says that a person who receives the Holy Spirit cries out "Abba! Father!" Yet, many argue that these people are not actually in an ecstatic state when crying out.[71]

Additionally, many have pointed to Rom 8:26 as a proof text for *glossolalia* or Spirit-induced speech: "Likewise the Spirit helps us in our weakness. For we do not know what to pray for as we ought, but the Spirit himself intercedes for us with groanings too deep for words." Instead of using this verse as a proof text for verbal automatisms, some instead argue that we ought rather to view it as a figure of speech that might have a background in the concept of automatism but is not itself an example of it.[72]

The important point, however, is that it is not just evil spirits that cause people to cry out. There is precedent in the New Testament for the Holy Spirit to cause people to spontaneously speak, whether as a form of prophecy, praise, or other utterance.

Fear and Falling

According to P. H. Alexander, in his entry "Slain in the Spirit" in the *New International Dictionary of Pentecostal and Charismatic Movements*: "An entire battalion of Scripture proof texts is enlisted to support the legitimacy of the phenomenon [of being slain in the Spirit], although Scripture plainly offers no support for the phenomenon as something to be expected in the normal Christian life."[73] John MacArthur quotes this entry to infer that even Pentecostal and charismatic scholars disagree with the phenomenon.[74] Yet, Alexander does not mean that people do not fall down by the power of God, or that there are no instances in Scripture of people falling down

---

71. Walter, *TDNT*, s.v. "Κράζω, Ἀνακράζω, Κραυγή, Κραυγάζω": "But what is the meaning of κράζομεν or κρᾶζον in this connection? We cannot accept the view that it denotes ecstatic outcry after the manner of glossolalia. There is no suggestion that man's self-awareness is lost in such prayer. The reference is rather to the Spirit sent εἰς τὰς καρδίας, i.e., to the λαμβάνειν of the Spirit of sonship as distinct from that of bondage. In R. 8:15 an ecstatic understanding is also ruled out by the explanatory statement that the Spirit bears witness to our spirit, i.e., to our personal consciousness, that we are the sons of God. Thus the κράζειν of R. 8:15 is more akin to the calling on God of the Ps. and other parts of the NT. The Spirit, who effects divine sonship, impels us to this." It is interesting, however, that later rabbinic works use the phrase that the Holy Spirit "cries out" (רוח צווחת = πνεῦμα κρᾶζον) as a way of expressing prophetic inspiration (e.g., Mek. DeRabbi Yishmael 15.2.1; and *Rambam on Pirkei Avot* 4:4).

72. See the discussion in Jewett and Kotansky, *Romans*, 521–24.

73. Alexander, "Slain in the Spirit," 1073.

74. MacArthur, *Strange Fire*, 200.

due to supernatural causation. Rather, his point is that the contemporary practice of using a middleman to induce such a state is not attested in the biblical texts, nor is it normative of everyday Christian experience. Indeed, Alexander himself states at the end of his article that "the evidence for the phenomenon of being "slain in the Spirit" is thus inconclusive."[75]

In the previous chapter we looked at instances where motor automatisms may account for people falling down in the presence of God. Several other passages from the New Testament have sometimes been used to support this idea as well. These passages are of varying usefulness in this regard and we will address each in canonical order.

During the transfiguration, Peter, James, and John are covered with a cloud and fall to the ground. The synoptic Gospels (Matthew, Mark, and Luke), however, vary on the details of this event:[76]

> He was still speaking when, behold, a bright cloud overshadowed them, and a voice from the cloud said, "This is my beloved Son, with whom I am well pleased; listen to him." When the disciples heard this, they fell on their faces and were terrified. But Jesus came and touched them, saying, "Rise, and have no fear." And when they lifted up their eyes, they saw no one but Jesus only. And as they were coming down the mountain, Jesus commanded them, "Tell no one the vision, until the Son of Man is raised from the dead." (Matt 17:5–9)

> And a cloud overshadowed them, and a voice came out of the cloud, "This is my beloved Son; listen to him." And suddenly, looking around, they no longer saw anyone with them but Jesus only. And as they were coming down the mountain, he charged them to tell no one what they had seen, until the Son of Man had risen from the dead. (Mark 9:7–9)

> Now Peter and those who were with him were heavy with sleep, but when they became fully awake they saw his glory and the two men who stood with him.... As he was saying these things, a cloud came and overshadowed them, and they were afraid as they entered the cloud. And a voice came out of the cloud, saying, "This is my Son, my Chosen One; listen to him!" And when the voice had spoken, Jesus was found alone. And they kept silent and told no one in those days anything of what they had seen. (Luke 9:32–36)

75. Alexander, "Slain in the Spirit," 1074.

76. Helpful studies on the transfiguration accounts in the Synoptic Gospels include: Murphy-O'Connor, "What Really Happened"; Ramsey, *Glory of God*; Reid, *Transfiguration*; and Stein, "Transfiguration a Misplaced Resurrection Account?"

In all accounts, Jesus speaks with Elijah and Moses, but only Luke records that the disciples were in various stages of sleep and waking. Luke likewise differs in the details of how the cloud affected the disciples. In Matthew, the disciples fall to the ground in fear because they hear God's voice. In Luke, however, the disciples are afraid and then enter the cloud. Mark does not record any falling. Mark's account has Jesus charging the disciples not to divulge "what they had seen" (Mark 9:9), whereas Matthew's Gospel refers to this event as a "vision" (ὅραμα/hórama). That Matthew calls this experience a vision may make sense as to why Luke pictures the disciples as sleepy and may also account for why Matthew has the disciples falling in the first place. François Bovon suggests "their condition should not be described either as sleep or being awake, but a 'second' consciousness that the Hebrew Bible attributes, for example, to Abraham (Gen 15:12) and Daniel (Dan 8:18; 10:9), when God communicates with them."[77] As we have seen elsewhere, visionary experiences could lead to motor automatisms like falling or a state that is described as sleep-like (e.g., Zechariah).

John Nolland notes that "twenty-one of the thirty-eight uses of hórama in the Septuagint are in Daniel, generally in relation to apocalyptic visions."[78] Matthew seems to be attempting to connect the experience of the disciples with that of Daniel. Based on Matthew's account, it is not the cloud itself that is causing the disciples to fall, but rather hearing God's voice, which parallels Dan 10:9. Obvious parallels to the descent of the cloud in Exodus, Ezekiel, and Chronicles are also worth noting since motor automatisms seem to be in view there as well.

Scholars argue about who was experiencing an ASC during the transfiguration. Was it just Jesus? The disciples? Both parties? Jesus states that they saw a vision, which already presumes some kind of ASC, perhaps trance. John Pilch makes a compelling case that both Jesus and the disciples were experiencing an ASC. Drawing on modern social-scientific theories and ancient texts that report simultaneous visionary experiences of multiple people in different states of consciousness, Pilch argues that from "a Mediterranean cultural perspective, it makes plausible sense to interpret the Synoptic account of the transfiguration of Jesus as the report of altered or alternate states of consciousness experienced by Jesus and three disciples. Jesus has his vision; the three disciples have theirs."[79]

The allusions to accounts in Exodus, Ezekiel, Chronicles, and Daniel, along with Luke's description of a sleep-like state and Matthew's mention

---

77. Bovon, *Luke 1*, 377.
78. Nolland, *Gospel of Matthew*, 705n78.
79. Pilch, *Flights of the Soul*, 142.

of the disciples falling and experiencing a vision strongly suggest an ASC (possibly accompanied by motor automatisms) is being reported.

While the Gospel of John does not record the transfiguration, it contains its own peculiar narrative of the guards coming to arrest Jesus falling down:

> Then Jesus, knowing all that would happen to him, came forward and said to them, "Whom do you seek?" They answered him, "Jesus of Nazareth." Jesus said to them, "I am he." Judas, who betrayed him, was standing with them. When Jesus said to them, "I am he," they drew back and fell to the ground. (John 18:4–6)

This strange interaction has prompted various interpretations. Some scholars have proposed that what is occurring is a theophany, some kind of supernatural revelation similar to the transfiguration that causes immediate prostration either out of fear or supernatural power.[80] Others think that this is just some kind of awe-inspired fear due to the boldness of Jesus's words.[81] Still others think that it is "vain to inquire whether the withdrawal and prostration of the band of men was due to 'natural' or 'supernatural' causes."[82]

There may be a good reason to interpret this event as involving motor automatisms. This event may be a fulfillment of various passages from the Psalms, both of which mention enemies falling down. The first is Ps 27:2 (NETS): "When wicked people would approach me . . . they became weak and fell." The second is Ps 34:4 (NETS): "Let them be turned back, rewards, and be put to shame who devise evil against me." Similarly, Ps 55:10 (LES) states: "My enemies will turn around backwards in whichever day I call upon you." Parallel phrases between John and the Septuagint version of Psalms suggest that the authors of the Gospels interpreted them as messianic predictions.[83]

This account also finds a parallel in the apocryphal book of Tobit. After travelling with Tobias for some time, the angel Raphael, disguised as a human, finally reveals his identity: "I am Raphael, one of the seven angels who stand ready and enter before the glory of the Lord." The two of them

---

80. Lindars, *Gospel of John*, 541; Bultmann, *Gospel of John*, 639. Carson, *Gospel According to John*, 578, argues that "theophanies do not depict the worshipper *drawing back* and falling to the ground." Whether such additional details matter in interpreting the account is debatable.

81. Beasley-Murray, *John*, 322–23.

82. Westcott, *Gospel According to St. John*, 1:253.

83. See Haenchen, *John 2*, 165; and Beasley-Murray, *John*, 323.

were shaken; they fell face down, for they were afraid."[84] A textual variant exists within the manuscript tradition so that the final clause reads either "for/because (ὅτι/ *hoti*) they were afraid" or "and (καὶ / *kai*) they were afraid" (my translation). If the latter is preferred, the falling down is not directly tied to the fear and thus could be interpreted as a motor automatism. The explicit mention of Raphael's proximity to God's "glory" (δόξα / *doxa*) may likewise influence how one understands the reason for the falling.

Several early Christian writers interpreted this passage as a supernatural falling as well. Augustine states that Jesus "threw them to the ground" by his "power" to fulfill his words in John 10:18.[85] Likewise, Gregory of Nyssa states that Jesus showed his sovereignty by causing them "to go backward."[86] Most curiously, John Chrysostom states that Jesus "crippled them" temporarily.[87] Evidently, this is not a new interpretation invented by those wishing to proof text passages to legitimize phenomena such as being "slain in the Spirit." Indeed, ancient authors seem to have assumed some kind of supernatural causation for the event.

In addition to Paul's trance state in the temple, his experience on the road to Damascus retold in Acts may be a case of motor automatism as well:

> Now as he went on his way, he approached Damascus, and suddenly a light from heaven shone around him. And falling to the ground, he heard a voice saying to him, "Saul, Saul, why are you persecuting me?" (Acts 9:3–4)

> As I was on my way and drew near to Damascus, about noon a great light from heaven suddenly shone around me. And I fell to the ground and heard a voice saying to me, "Saul, Saul, why are you persecuting me?" (Acts 22:6–7)

> At midday, O king, I saw on the way a light from heaven, brighter than the sun, that shone around me and those who journeyed with me. And when we had all fallen to the ground, I heard a voice saying to me in the Hebrew language, "Saul, Saul, why are you persecuting me? It is hard for you to kick against the goads." (Acts 26:13–14)

The accounts differ in detail, especially concerning who saw and heard what. Additionally, according to Acts 9 and 22 it is only Paul who fell down, while in Acts 26 it is Paul and his companions who fall. Regardless of how

---

84. Tob 12:15–16.
85. Augustine, *Tract. Ev. Jo.* 11.2, 28.2.
86. Gregory, *C. Eun.* 2.11.
87. Chrysostom, *Hom. Matt.* 26:39 (NPNF[1] 9:204).

one deals with these discrepancies, the falling itself deserves careful consideration, especially the account as recorded in Acts 26.[88]

In the third retelling of this experience, Paul includes a saying not previously divulged. The voice speaking to him says, "It is hard for you to kick against the goads." This proverb was used in the context of trying to work against the will of a deity, often with the result that the individual would reap the anger of the god.[89] Scholars typically point to a passage from Euripides's work *Bacchae* as the origin for Luke's usage: "I would sacrifice to the god rather than kick against his spurs in anger, a mortal against a god."[90] The allusion to Bacchic frenzy is significant.[91] The sentiment of this same proverb occurs in a passage from Euripides referring to ecstatic madness, possession by a god, and not wanting "to fight against the god."[92]

Indeed, the fact that Paul is accused of being "out of his mind" in Acts 26:24 only reinforces this theme. These contextual clues may suggest that Luke wants us to read Paul's experience within the paradigm of ecstasy.[93] If this is the case, motor automatisms are not out of place and do not indicate generic prostration, but supernaturally induced falling.

The final passage under consideration in this section is from the apocalypse of John:

> When I saw him, I fell at his feet as though dead. But he laid his right hand on me, saying, "Fear not, I am the first and the last."
> (Rev 1:17)

We already know from Rev 1:10 that John was in an ASC (*en pneumati*). One is left to wonder in what way John experienced the visions. Was it in a trance state where he saw visions within his mind's eye, a waking dream, or through translocation?[94] We are not told. John's falling is obviously drawn from Ezek 1:28, Dan 8:17–18, and Dan 10:8–10.[95] His experience of falling down "as though dead" is paralleled in another New Testament passage. The men set to guard Jesus's tomb, for example, "shake" (σείω / *seiō*) and "became

---

88. Pilch, *Flights of the Soul*, 174–90, offers an analysis of this encounter, yet does not mention "falling down."

89. For references, see Keener, *Acts*, 4:3514n1351.

90. Euripides, *Bacch.* 794–95.

91. See Haenchen, *Acts*, 685n3; Dibelius, *Studies in Acts*, 188–91; and Vögeli, "Lukas und Euripides."

92. Euripides, *Bacch.* 301–29.

93. Lentz, *Luke's Portrait*, 85.

94. See Skaggs and Benham, *Revelation*, 29–30.

95. Beale, *Revelation*, 213; Blount, *Revelation*, 45–46.

like dead men" when encountering the angel (Matt 28:4).[96] As Ulrich Luz puts it: "The external convulsion of the earthquake (σεισμός) is continued in their internal convulsion (ἐσείσθησαν)."[97] This reaction is contrasted with that of the women who came to visit the tomb and, after leaving, bend down to worship Jesus (Matt 28:9).[98] Though some commentators suggest that the guards are simply petrified in a rhetorical sense, a spontaneous fainting or motor automatism is just as likely. That the guards are scared and not the women suggests that the effect of the angel was in mind.

Similar examples in Rev 1:17 appear in early Jewish and Christian texts from around the same time period. In 2 Maccabees, Heliodorus falls to the ground unconscious due to a manifestation of God in the treasury; his friends plead with Onias to pray to God to "grant life" to Heliodorus because he was "lying quite at his last breath."[99] According to the author, he had been "flogged by heaven."[100] Similarly, 4 Maccabees, drawing on this story, records an instance in which Apollonius sees a vision of angels riding horses and "fell down half dead in the temple area that was open to all, stretched out his hands toward heaven, and with tears begged the Hebrews to pray for him and propitiate the wrath of the heavenly army."[101] In a work known as the Testament of Abraham (first–second century CE) an angel is sent to Abraham and upon seeing the supernatural agent "he fell upon his face on the ground as one dead."[102] According to 4 Ezra, the angel Uriel is sent to Ezra and sees him "lying there like a corpse, deprived of my understanding."[103] Using different language, but no doubt describing a similar phenomenon, the Apocalypse of Abraham (first–second century CE) has the titular protagonist report the following: "And behold there was no breath of man. And my spirit was amazed, and my soul fled from me. And I became like a stone, and fell face down upon the earth, for there was

---

96. That physical shaking is in view may be supported by the fact that Matthew uses the same verb in 27:51 regarding the earth shaking and the temple veil ripping. See Nolland, *Matthew*, 1248.

97. Luz, *Matthew 21–28*, 596.

98. According to the retelling of this story in the fourth-century-CE apocryphal work Acts of Pilate (part of a larger work titled Gospel of Nicodemus), the guards twice report being unable to move or speak (Acts Pil. 13).

99. 2 Macc 3:22–34.

100. 2 Macc 3:34.

101. 4 Macc 4:11.

102. T. Ab. [A] 9:1.

103. 4 Ezra 10:29–30; cf. 2 En. 1:7 (first century CE); and Jos. Asen. 14:10 (first century BCE–second century CE).

no longer strength in me to stand up on the earth. And while I was still face down on the ground, I heard the voice speaking."[104]

John is in a long line of visionaries who fall down "as though dead" within Judaism and there seems to be a differentiation between those who prostrate themselves willingly due to fear or reverence and those who are "overwhelmed" by supernatural forces at play.[105] This variance is made explicit in other portions of Revelation. Revelation 19:10 and 22:8 both indicate that John fell down in order to worship. Ironically, in these two instances of volitional reverence, he is told twice that what he is doing is inappropriate![106] Although some critics of the charismatic movement have balked at the idea of these passages being interpreted as motor automatisms, there are actually compelling historical and textual reasons for interpreting them as just that.

Jesus's Journeys

For most Christians, Jesus serves as the pinnacle for emulation. Such imitation ranges from ethics to economic lifestyle and even to miraculous claims of prolonged fasting, raising the dead, and even receiving the marks of Jesus's crucifixion (known as stigmata)! What of ASCs? Does Jesus ever engage in trance or ecstasy? In this section, I will discuss the evidence for this proposal. Some may think there is no evidence at all. Yet in 1903, the German theologian Oscar Holtzmann published an entire book titled *Was Jesus an Ecstatic?* (German: *War Jesus Ekstatiker?*). Clearly there is something to be said! Much of the problem with characterizing Jesus as an ecstatic, however, has been the rather imprecise definition of what ecstasy involves. Are the baptism and transfiguration, as some have argued, examples of ecstasy? In what sense? How can we tell? These questions are not easily answered. In some cases, scholars outright dismiss the possibility that Jesus experienced ecstasy, but for no other reason than the presupposition that the context cannot include it. In many of these cases no sustained exegesis of the relevant passage is presented and one is left wondering: what exactly about the context makes ecstasy such an unlikely candidate?

In this section I argue that four examples can plausibly be read to demonstrate that Jesus experienced ASCs. Mark 3:21 recounts a story in which an anonymous group tries to restrain Jesus under the impression that he is insane or ecstatic. The second example includes a series of accusations that

---

104. Apoc. Ab. 10:2–3.
105. Aune, *Revelation*, 99; Koester, *Revelation*, 247.
106. Cf. Josh 5:14; 4 Ezra 4:11; and Herm. Vis. 1.1.2 and 1.2.1.

Jesus is possessed and, consequently, mad. Third, an instance of an ASC may also be present during Jesus's temptation in the wilderness where he seems to be transported in a visionary context by Satan. Finally, a possible example of verbal automatism may be found in Jesus's spontaneous praise after a visionary experience of seeing Satan fall from heaven.[107]

Mark 3:21

After some time of ministering in the synagogue, praying for the sick, and casting out demons, Jesus arrives home. There, the crowd was so intense that he and those with him were unable to eat. Suddenly, those with him attempt to seize him because they were saying "he is ἐξέστη/exestē" (Mark 3:21).[108] English translations render it variously that Jesus is "out of his mind" (NIV, NLT, ESV) or has "lost his senses" (NASB), others as "he is beside himself" (KJV) or even "he was crazy" (CEV) or "he is insane" (WEB).[109] The word exestē is the aorist form of existēmi which itself is related to the Greek noun ekstasis and thus we must carefully consider what is meant by Mark here.[110]

---

107. Other passages from the Gospels may suggest that Jesus entered ASCs. Pilch, *Flights of the Soul*, 109–23, offers five instances where this might be the case. These include: (1) his baptism, (2) his testing in the wilderness, (3) his walking on the water, (4) his transfiguration, and (5) his resurrection appearances. Pilch devotes brief explanations to three of these, but dives deeper into the transfiguration and postresurrection appearances, as well as Luke's account of Jesus's ascension. In most of these cases it is difficult or impossible to determine whether trance or ecstasy are actually part of the equation and the presence of ASCs in general relies on cross-cultural disciplines to situate them within that context. In some of these examples, Pilch argues that Jesus experienced ASCs, but it seems more likely that it is the disciples who experienced the ASC rather than Jesus. Pilch uses the term ASC to refer generally to the visionary experience, regardless of the presence of trance or ecstasy. For example, when Jesus is transfigured, the disciples were drowsy with sleep and potentially were more susceptible to trance, though Pilch suggests that Jesus too was engaged in an ASC. But this seems less clear unless what is meant is simply that Jesus experienced "alternate reality" through the appearance of Moses and Elijah. Mark's account of the transfiguration has Jesus charging the disciples not to divulge "what they have seen" (Mark 9:9), whereas Matthew's Gospel refers to this event as a "vision" (ὅραμα/hórama).

108. The exact identity of those who have come to seize Jesus is unclear, though his family seems to be implied. See Swete, *Gospel According to St. Mark*, 63.

109. For a detailed conversation on some of the textual issues at play and the varieties of translation choices, see France, *Gospel of Mark*, 165–66 and notes of the NET Bible).

110. Other scholars have taken this approach to the text as well. The careful analysis of Dwyer, *Motif of Wonder*, 105–8 is invaluable, especially his comments about how scholars have overlooked the connection between ecstasy and spirit possession. See also the important article by Neufeld, "Eating, Ecstasy, and Exorcism."

New Testament scholar M. Eugene Boring notes that both "interpreters and scribes who transmitted the [manuscripts] have attempted to soften the obvious meaning."[111] Such softening has come in various forms. First, Matt 12:22–32 and Luke 11:14–23 both contain the so-called Beelzebul Controversy found in Mark, but omit the account of the accusation of him being *existēmi*. Second, Christian scribes were especially disturbed by this accusation, as evidenced by the variations of this passage within the manuscript tradition. Some manuscripts have changed it to "escape" (εξεσταται/ *exestatai*).[112] Others have the Scribes and Pharisees accusing Jesus, not his family.[113] Two manuscripts remove the charge of *existēmi* and instead read "they were adherents of his" (εξηρτηνται αυτου/*exērtēntai autou*).[114] Third, modern scholars have likewise attempted to reorient the passage so that Jesus is not the one viewed as being *existēmi*. Henry Wansbrough, for example, translates the passage as follows: "When they heard it, his followers went out to calm it [the crowd] down, for they said that it was out of control with enthusiasm."[115] In this translation, it is now the crowd that is *existēmi* instead of Jesus! Jerome (fourth–fifth century CE) briefly refers to this passage by stating that "in the gospel we read that even his kinsfolk desired to bind him as one of weak mind."[116]

One should not be surprised by such variation both within manuscripts and the history of interpretation. The idea of Jesus being viewed as out of his normal senses was not something early or even later Christians liked to entertain.[117]

With such controversy surrounding such a small section of Mark, it is no wonder that many contemporary Christian interpreters have not adopted what, to me, seems like the most apparent interpretation: Jesus is exhibiting ecstatic behavior.[118] But again, this is not really a new interpretation. The Latin Vulgate, for example, translates the phrase as "he is on the verge of fury" (*in furorem versus est*). The Latin word *furor* elsewhere has

---

111. Boring, *Mark*, 106.

112. Witherington, *Gospel of Mark*, 154.

113. See Marcus, *Mark 1–8*, 270.

114. Witherington, *Gospel of Mark*, 154.

115. Wansbrough, "Mark III. 21," 233–35. This position has not been accepted by the majority of scholars. See France, *Gospel of Mark*, 165–66.

116. Jerome, *Epist.* 108.19.

117. On the widely accepted view of Jesus's prophetic ecstasy by later Christians as proposed by Erasmus, see Screech, *Laughter at the Foot of the Cross*, 84–89, 98–106.

118. Sanders, *Historical Figure of Jesus*, 151, goes as far as to suggest that "Jesus himself may have displayed erratic behavior."

the meaning of inspired or prophetic frenzy.[119] One ancient Christian commentary on Mark, known as the *Catena in Marcum* (fifth–sixth century CE) interprets the passage in connection with Bacchic frenzy:

> Therefore, when he has chosen them, he comes home, and again a crowd gathers, so that they are not able to eat any bread. "And when they heard, those from beside him went out to restrain him, for they were saying that he had gone out of his mind." Who heard, or from where they went out, he has not described clearly. Therefore, believing that the Evangelist is speaking about the Pharisees and the Scribes, that having heard about him and the crowd around him, being filled by malign influences with Bacchic frenzy in anger, they ran over to restrain him, supposing him to suffer what they themselves suffered. For to suppose that the performer of such wonders, the benefactor of souls, and the teacher of divine wisdom had been driven out of his mind is clear madness and distraction of mind.[120]

In order to demonstrate that ecstatic behavior is a viable interpretation, we must address several key features of this passage: (1) the word *existēmi* itself within the context of Mark, (2) the connection between frenzied behavior and accusations of possession, (3) the verb used for "restrain" (κρατῆσαι/ *kratēsai*) in this passage, and (4) the problem with alternative interpretations.

First, and probably the most obvious argument, is that the word *existēmi* does have the meaning of "lose one's mind." Xenophon of Athens (fifth–fourth century BCE), for example, states that those who are bit by scorpions experience *existēmi*.[121]

In the Septuagint, the word can be used of those who have "lost their senses" with alcohol (Isa 28:7 LXX) and false prophets are referred to by two Greek words for madness: παρεξίστημι/*parexistēmi* and μανία/*mania* (Hos 9:7 LXX). Elsewhere it is used of God's ability to confound Israel's enemies so that they are victorious in battle against them (Exod 23:27 LXX). Most striking is Paul's use of the word in 2 Cor 5:13 where he differentiates between being *existēmi* and being in one's right mind (*sōphroneō*). This use of the verb can likewise be found in visionary contexts such as the Testament of Job: "Who then will not say you are demented [ἐξεστήκεις/*exestēkeis*] and

---

119. See Andrews, *Harper's Latin Dictionary*, s.v. "*furor*."

120. See Lamb, *Catena in Marcum*, 259.

121. Xenophon, *Mem.* 1.3.12: "Don't you know that the scorpion, though smaller than a farthing, if it but fasten on the tongue, inflicts excruciating and maddening pain (ἐξίστησι/*existēsi*)?"

mad [μαίνει/*mainei*] when you say, 'My children have been taken up into heaven!' Tell us the truth now!"[122]

The word *existēmi* appears only four times in Mark (2:12, 3:21, 5:42, 6:51)[123] and can have the meaning of simple "amazement," but we must also consider the surrounding context of Mark to help us give an appropriate translation of what is envisioned here.[124] There are good reasons to view Mark's use of *existēmi* here as referring to a state of ecstasy. If *existēmi* simply means "amazed," this would need to be a reference to either Jesus's teachings or miracles. This raises the question of how this amazement would make people conclude that he needed to be removed from the crowds.[125] Yet, as Boring insists: "That *exestē* must here refer to berserk behavior is clear from its usage elsewhere (e.g., 2 Cor 5:13), by the parallel between what the scribes are saying and what his family is saying . . . and by the strong word

---

122. T. Job 39:13.

123. Sabin, *Gospel According to Mark*, 98, chooses throughout the Gospel of Mark to translate every instance of *existēmi* as ecstasy, even in instances where this doesn't seem to make sense. Mark 5:41–42, for example, translates the raising of a dead girl and the crowd's response as "they were *out of their minds . . . with ecstasy*" (emphasis added).

124. France, *Gospel of Mark*, 167: "Can the offence then be lessened by suggesting a weaker sense of ἐξίστημι? It is true that in its three other uses in Mark (5:42 is the only other active use; in 2:12 and 6:51 the middle is used) it refers to the (laudable) astonishment of those who witnessed Jesus' miracles (Matthew [once] and Luke-Acts also use it in the same sense), but three uses do not establish a presumption in favour of this meaning when (a) the verb is commonly used elsewhere to mean 'be mad' (*TDNT*, s.v. "ἐξίστημι (ἐξιστάνω)"; see especially 2 Cor. 5:13, where it is contrasted with σωφρονέω), and (b) the clause here is in parallel with an accusation of demon possession in v. 22. Nor is it easy to understand why a belief that Jesus was 'amazed' (about what?) should cause his people to want to seize him."

125. Holland, "Meaning of Ἐξέστη," 6–31, attempts to formulate the statement about Jesus in a positive sense, though I am not convinced at his findings for several reasons. First, his interaction with the relevant passages dealing with ecstasy in the Septuagint is problematic. He is mostly concerned with finding examples in the LXX where the relevant word can be understood as "madness." Unable to do so, he assumes that ecstatic frenzy is therefore not in view. No mention is made, however, of the ASCs of Adam and Abraham. Second, while situating the word within Mark's other uses of the term is necessary, this does not mean that language is continually static in every context. The fact that the ecstasy charge is made right before he is accused of possession by Beelzebub ought to inform the meaning of the verb. Finally, examples of *existēmi* meaning "gone mad" are not mentioned and are suggested to not exist (See BDAG, s.v. "ἐξίστημι," for examples). A lack of interaction with Philo and other sources suggests that *existēmi* does in fact have the meaning of going mad with ecstasy. As a result of these factors, I cannot accept Holland's conclusions.

kratēsai [restrain] expressing the family's intent."¹²⁶ Thus, at a lexical level, the word *existēmi* in Mark 3:21 *can* involve ecstatic behavior.¹²⁷

Second, this pronouncement about Jesus's mental state comes right before a narrative in which the Pharisees accuse Jesus of being possessed by Beelzebul (Mark 3:22).¹²⁸ That demoniacs acted in atypical ways has already been established, and thus the parallel between ecstatic fervor and possession should inform our reading of *existēmi*. Indeed, Jesus's response to the religious leaders is telling: "If I cast out demons by Beelzebul [ἐν Βεελζεβοὺλ/ *en beelzeboul*] by whom do your own exorcists cast them out? Therefore they will be your judges. But if it is by the Spirit of God [ἐν πνεύματι θεοῦ/*en pneumati theou*] that I cast out demons, then the kingdom of God has come to you" (Matt 12:27-28). There is a common trope of people mistaking divine Spirit possession and prophetic understanding as madness in both the Hebrew Bible and Second Temple Judaism more broadly.¹²⁹ These include such figures as Hannah, various prophets (2 Kgs 9:11; Jer 29:26; Hos 9:7) and even some Greek philosophers.¹³⁰

Jewish texts from around the time of Jesus also speak of this association. One passage from the work Testament of Benjamin (second century BCE), for example, reads: "Fear the Lord and love your neighbor. Even if the spirits of Beliar seek to derange [ἐξαιτήσωνται/*exaitēsōntai*] you with all sorts of wicked oppression, they will not dominate you, any more than they dominated Joseph, my brother."¹³¹ Likewise, in the context of prophecy, Josephus says of the prophet Jeremiah that "the greater part believed him; but the rulers, and those that were wicked, despised him, as one disordered in his senses [ἐξεστηκότα/*exestēkota*]."¹³²

---

126. Boring, *Mark*, 106.

127. See the comments of Witmer, *Jesus, the Galilean Exorcist*, 111-19, who responds to the claim by Dunn, *Jesus and the Spirit*, 87-88, that Jesus was not ecstatic.

128. Herm. Mand. 11.9 uses the phrase ἔχων τὸ πωεῦμα/*echon to pneuma* which appears to be synonymous in meaning to *en pneumati*. See Tibbs, "Mediumistic Divine Possession," 189.

129. See Screech, "Good Madness in Christendom."

130. Plato, *Phaedr.* 249C-D: "And therefore it is just that the mind of the philosopher only has wings, for he is always, so far as he is able, in communion through memory with those things the communion with which causes God to be divine. Now a man who employs such memories rightly is always being initiated into perfect mysteries and he alone becomes truly perfect; but since he separates himself from human interests and turns his attention toward the divine, he is rebuked by the vulgar, who consider him mad and do not know that he is inspired." Translation from Fowler, *Plato*, 1:480-83.

131. T. Benj. 3:3.

132. Josephus, *Ant.* 10.114.

Philo likewise states this confusion in his work *On Drunkenness*: "Now when grace fills the soul, that soul thereby rejoices and smiles and dances, for it is possessed and inspired, so that to many of the unenlightened it may seem to be drunken, crazy and beside itself [ἐξεστάναι/*exestanai*]."[133] Neufeld states that "the unpredictable behavior of these persons [those who experience spirit possession] made it impossible for the community to control them; so they were often forcibly removed from community life."[134] Thus, the association of prophetic ministry with ecstasy makes sense.

Third, the word "restrain" (*kratēsai*) used in Mark 3:21 can be interpreted within the context of ecstasy. The verb κρατέω/*krateō* is used of taking property by force,[135] emotional instability,[136] the seizing of souls into hell,[137] the casting down of Satan (Rev 20:2), holding back wind (Rev 7:1), and especially of arresting people such as John the Baptist (Matt 14:3), Paul (Acts 24:6), and Jesus (e.g., Matt 21:46).[138] Interestingly, this same verb is used in another text related to Beelzebul. According to the Testament of Solomon, Beelzebul discusses another "ungodly" figure that "holds [κρατεῖ/*kratei*] in his power the race of those bound by me in Tartarus."[139] Thus, the Greek word *krateō* is used in contexts of intense strength or power, often with the sense of forced restraint. If Mark 3:21 infers that it is his family or disciples attempting to restrain him, this may be similar to what one finds of binding demoniacs (e.g., Mark 5:2–3).[140] In fact, upon reading this passage Erasmus posited that Jesus's family "came out with chains to bind him," like a demoniac![141] Likewise, if it is the opponents of Jesus coming to restrain him (as some manuscripts read), this in no way suggests that ecstatic behavior cannot be in view.[142]

---

133. Philo, *Drunkenness* 36 §145–46.

134. Neufeld, "Eating, Ecstasy, and Exorcism," 156.

135. 1 Macc 15:33: "Simon said to him in reply: 'We have neither taken foreign land nor seized [κεκρατήκαμεν/*kekratēkamen*] foreign property, but only the inheritance of our ancestors, which at one time had been unjustly taken by our enemies.'"

136. 4 Macc 6:32: "For if the emotions had prevailed [κεκρατήκει/*kekratēkei*] over reason, we would have testified to their domination."

137. T. Ab. (A) 12:2: "And the angel seized [ἐκράτει/*ekratei*] one soul. And they drove all the souls into the broad gate toward destruction."

138. Cf. Mart. Ascen. Isa. 3:11–12: "But Beliar dwelt in the heart of Manasseh and in the heart of the princes of Judah and Benjamin, and of the eunuchs, and of the king's counselors. And the words of Belkira pleased him very much, and he sent and seized Isaiah."

139. T. Sol. 6:3.

140. Compare the use of binding for arresting in Acts 22:4.

141. Screech, "Good Madness in Christendom," 33.

142. See Painter, *Mark's Gospel*, 67–68.

Finally, while "insane" may be within the semantic domain of consideration for this passage, what is it that is causing his family to assume this about Jesus? Is it his message? His newfound popularity with the masses? What does performing exorcisms, healing the sick, and taking care of the least of these have to do with insanity? Evidently, there could be something Jesus said that was taken as crazy by his family, but it is not recorded in Mark's account (and this story is not repeated in either Matthew or Luke). Was it his overall gospel message? All we are left with is the context that Mark gives us about an accusation of possession by Beelzebul. Ignoring this crucial narrative element will obscure our translation of the Greek verb *existēmi* and, what's more, point us away from a historical-grammatical exegesis of the text in favor of a more "sensitive" reading for many modern Christians.

In conclusion, Jesus's behavior, in some way, is concerning to those around him and prompts accusations of possession. The lexical range of the verb *existēmi* includes ecstatic behavior and the overt connection with possession further emphasizes that this is in view. Additionally, the forceful verb *krateō* suggests physical restraint because of Jesus's mental state is in view. It is not the content of what he says that alerts them to the need to calm him down (indeed, we are not told that Jesus *has* said anything), but rather some pronounced behavior (apparently related to his exorcisms). Although Jesus's behavior is presented in the form of an accusation or misunderstanding by either his opponents or own family and disciples, this does not mean that Jesus did *not* exhibit this behavior. Rather, it reveals that like other parts of his ministry, Jesus is commonly misunderstood, both in terms of the meaning of his message and the source of his teaching and miracles.

Based on these reasons, I offer the following translation of Mark 3:21: "And after hearing him they went out to restrain him. For they were saying 'he is ecstatic.'"[143]

Accusations of Possession

Jesus is frequently accused of being possessed. In addition to Mark 3, the following passages reveal this was a go-to argument of Jesus's enemies:

> "Has not Moses given you the law? Yet none of you keeps the law. Why do you seek to kill me?" The crowd answered, "You have a demon! Who is seeking to kill you?" Jesus answered them, "I did one work, and you all marvel at it. Moses gave you

---

143. See Carlson, *Unfamiliar Selves*, 42.

circumcision (not that it is from Moses, but from the fathers), and you circumcise a man on the Sabbath. If on the Sabbath a man receives circumcision, so that the law of Moses may not be broken, are you angry with me because on the Sabbath I made a man's whole body well? Do not judge by appearances, but judge with right judgment." (John 7:19–24)

The Jews answered him, "Are we not right in saying that you are a Samaritan and have a demon?" Jesus answered, "I do not have a demon, but I honor my Father, and you dishonor me. Yet I do not seek my own glory; there is One who seeks it, and he is the judge. Truly, truly, I say to you, if anyone keeps my word, he will never see death." The Jews said to him, "Now we know that you have a demon! Abraham died, as did the prophets, yet you say, 'If anyone keeps my word, he will never taste death.'" (John 8:48–52)

There was again a division among the Jews because of these words. Many of them said, "He has a demon, and is insane; why listen to him?" Others said, "These are not the words of one who is oppressed by a demon. Can a demon open the eyes of the blind?" (John 10:19–21)

In John 7:19–24, Jesus is accused of possession based on his observation that the crowd wants to kill him. The crowd must either assume that Jesus is paranoid (and thus suffering from demonic delusion) or they are offended by the nature of their hearts being revealed and thus lash out with an ad hoc possession accusation. The crowd is specifically concerned that his teachings are "leading the people astray" (7:12).

Possession is sometimes connected with false teaching, specifically around Sabbath observance. In a text known as the Damascus Document from Qumran, for example, the following instructions are given: "Every /man/ over whom the spirits of Belial dominate, and who preaches apostasy, will be judged according to the regulation of the necromancer or the diviner. But everyone who goes astray, defiling the Sabbath and the festivals, shall not be executed, for it is the task of men to guard him; and if he is cured of it, they shall guard him for seven years and afterwards he may enter the assembly."[144] Whether frenzied behavior typical of possession was also an element in the crowd's accusation of Jesus, however, is not stated.

The crowd's accusation in John 8:48–52 comes after Jesus accuses them of having the devil for a father (John 8:44). Yet, Jesus is not just accused of possession, but also of being a Samaritan. In the New Testament and other

---

144. CD XII, 2–6.

early Christian texts, Samaritans were often connected with practicing magic.[145] The most obvious example is Simon Magus who "practiced magic in the city and amazed the people of Samaria" (Acts 8:9). Justin Martyr discusses Simon in his work *First Apology*, stating that he was a Samaritan from the village of Gitto and that his apprentice, a man named Menander, likewise practiced magic and was also a Samaritan.[146] Jesus likewise is accused of magic in the Talmud: "Jesus the Nazarene practiced magic and led Israel astray."[147] Keener states that "full-scale syncretism may have affected some Samaritans more severely, probably because of the local prominence of Greek Sebaste."[148] The accusation of both being a Samaritan and being possessed may include an accusation of sorcery, which often did include rituals involving frenzied behavior. But again, the crowd seem to be more disturbed by his claim of giving eternal life than by any observable actions on Jesus's part.

Finally, after speaking in parables to the crowds, they conclude "he has a demon and is insane [μαίνεται / *mainetai*]" (John 10:20). There is a division within the crowd, however, about whether this explanation makes sense. The accusation of insanity may derive from a trope within Judaism of the righteous being considered "mad" or "insane" by the wicked, some of which we have noted above. Wisdom of Solomon has the unrighteous saying concerning the righteous that "we thought that their lives were madness [μανίαν / *manian*]."[149]

Once again it is interesting that insanity is connected to demon possession, suggesting that perhaps something atypical was observable besides just the words Jesus spoke. Later hostile Jewish sources against Jesus described him as a demon-possessed madman.[150] John 10:21 offers the coun-

---

145. Borchert, *John 1–11*, 307: "Samaritans were regarded by Jews as half-breed heretics who also (at least later) were associated with demonic/cultic magic"; cf. Bowman, *Samaritan Documents*, 30; see also Müller-Kessler et al., "Inscribed Silver Amulet."

146. Justin Martyr, *1 Apol.* 26.

147. b. Sanh. 107b; Justin Martyr, *Dial.* 69: "And having raised the dead, and causing them to live, by His deeds He compelled the men who lived at that time to recognise Him. But though they saw such works, they asserted it was magical art. For they dared to call Him a magician, and a deceiver of the people."

148. Keener, *Acts*, 1:1515.

149. Wis 5:4; cf. Zech 13:3–6.

150. Luck, *Arcana Mundi*, 64: "Matthew's report that Jesus was taken to Egypt as an infant was used by hostile sources to explain his knowledge of magic; according to a rabbinical story, he came back tattooed with spells. It is also pointed out in the rabbinical tradition that Jesus was 'mad,' which probably means 'emotionally unstable,' one of the characteristics of the shaman, or occasionally 'in a state of trance' (e.g., when receiving a vision). The Gospels speak of the 'descent of the spirit,' the outsiders of 'possession by a daemon,' and both are possibly describing the same mystic phenomenon, the former as Jesus would explain it, the latter in a negative way. It has even been suggested

terargument to those accusing Jesus of having a demon: "These are not the words of one who is oppressed by a demon. Can a demon open the eyes of the blind?" The argument is twofold. The latter argument is based on the benevolent nature of the miracle, since it is assumed that demons do not typically heal the blind. The former argument, that "these are not the words of one who is oppressed by a demon," is worth investigating further.

We must here make an interpretive decision. Is the crowd referring to the form of the speech Jesus is conducting or their substance? If we take the first approach, we can ask how does someone who is demonized speak? According to the New Testament they act fiercely and scream (Matt 8:28; Luke 4:33, 41; Acts 16:16), or (conversely) do not speak at all (Matt 9:32)! In one instance a demon attacks a young boy and "he suddenly cries out. It convulses him so that he foams at the mouth, and shatters him, and will hardly leave him" (Luke 9:39). Yet, if we take the second approach, that it is the substance of his speech, this seems to align with the ongoing debates between Jesus and the Jews (John 7:20; 8:48–49, 52) and the constant accusation of Jesus having a demon where no discussion on his mental state is alluded to. This second interpretation seems to make the most sense given the flow of John's narrative. As a result, it is difficult to see ecstatic behavior as part of the equation in these accusations from John.

Temptation Narratives

The testing of Jesus occurs in all three synoptic Gospels (Matthew, Mark, and Luke). Mark's is the shortest, mentioning only that "the Spirit immediately drove him out into the wilderness. And he was in the wilderness forty days, being tempted by Satan. And he was with the wild animals, and the angels were ministering to him" (Mark 1:12–13). Matthew and Luke both greatly expand this narrative. One of the first differences one immediately notes is that in Mark's account, Jesus is "cast out" or "driven" (ἐκβάλλω / *ekballō*) by the Spirit into the wilderness (a term often used when Jesus drives demons out of the possessed). Both Matthew and Luke change this language to being "led up" (ἀνήχθη / *anēchthē*; Matt 4:1) by the Spirit or being "full of the Spirit" (Luke 4:1). Luke uses the exact phrase that appears as the impetus for Stephen's visionary experience in Acts. Additionally, not only is Jesus first filled with the Spirit, he is then led ἐν τῷ πνεύματι/*en tō pneumati*. This suggests that, for Luke, Jesus's temptation may have existed

---

that Jesus' claim to be 'the Son of God' is a formula used in magical rites by the operator who identifies himself closely with the supernatural power that he invokes."

in an ASC.[151] The presence of self-deprivation from food also suggests that Jesus became susceptible to a trance state. Matthew and Luke both include that Jesus had fasted for forty days and nights (Matt 4:2; Luke 4:2). Luke is explicit that "he ate nothing during those days" (Luke 4:2), which emulates the fasting and ascent of Moses to meet with God in Exodus (24:18, 34:28).

We are also told that Jesus was "brought up" (ἀνάγω / anagō) by Satan in order to show him "all the kingdoms of the world in a moment of time" (Luke 4:5). Matthew's account states that Jesus was "taken" (παραλαμβάνω / paralambanō), though the words likely connote the same meaning (Matt 4:5, 8). This has typically been interpreted by commentators as a visionary translocation rather than physical teleportation.[152] A similar experience occurs in Luke 4:9 where Satan takes him from the mountain to the top of the pinnacle of the Jerusalem temple. These experiences make most sense within the framework of a series of visions. That these visions took place while in a trance state seems probable.

Luke 10:18

There is one final narrative to examine concerning Jesus and ASCs. In Luke's Gospel, after seventy-two of Jesus's disciples return to him and joyfully announce that they were successful in exorcising demons, Jesus tells them "I saw Satan fall like lightning from heaven" (Luke 10:18). This saying has been taken in two different ways, either as a reference to Jesus's primordial observation of Satan's rebellion against God and subsequent punishment,[153] or as a comment about the exorcisms just performed by Jesus's disciples.[154] Another common interpretation has been that Jesus was seeing a vision.[155] This last interpretation makes sense especially given a statement found only a few verses later: "In that same hour he rejoiced in the Holy Spirit ([ἐν] τῷ πνεύματι/[en] tō pneumati) and said, 'I thank you, Father, Lord of heaven

---

151. Cf. Sir 39:6: "If the great Lord is willing, he will be filled with the spirit of understanding [πνεύματι συνέσεως ἐμπλησθήσεται / pneumati syneseōs emplēsthēsetai]; he will pour forth words of wisdom of his own and give thanks to the Lord in prayer."

152. Bovon, *Luke 1*, 143-44; Marshall, *Gospel of Luke*, 171; Stein, *Luke*, 147.

153. Cf. John 12:31; Rom 16:20; and Rev 20:1-3, 10; cf. T. Levi 18:12; T. Jud. 25:3; T. Ash. 7:3; T. Dan 5:10f.; As. Mos. 10:1; and Jub. 23:29. For a history of interpretation on this passage, see Bovon, *Luke 2*, 32-34.

154. Stein, *Luke*, 309.

155. Marshall, *Gospel of Luke*, 428; Creed, *Gospel According to St. Luke*, 147; Bultmann, *Geschichte der synoptischen Tradition*, 113, 174; Grundmann, *Evangelium nach Lukas*, 212.

and earth, that you have hidden these things from the wise and understanding and revealed them to little children'" (Luke 10:21).[156]

In apocalyptic Jewish literature, thanksgiving was sometimes the result of receiving a vision, even while the prophet was in the visionary state. In the case of Daniel, he praises God after receiving a "vision of the night" (Dan 2:19–23). Similarly, in the book of 1 Enoch, Enoch ascends to heaven in a whirlwind, receives several visions, and praises God.[157] The author of a series of noncanonical Hebrew hymns called the Hodayot found among the Dead Sea Scrolls states: "I give [you] thanks, [Lord,] because you have taught me your truth, you have made me know your wonderful mysteries, your kindness towards [. . .] man."[158] Most compelling, however, is a story given by Josephus that he was "in an ecstasy [ἔνθους / enthous]; and setting before him the tremendous images of the dreams he had lately had, he put up a secret prayer to God."[159] Thus, the presence of ecstasy and ASCs preceding or congruent with thanksgiving is attested in Judaism of this period and suggests that Jesus too experienced this pattern.

Conclusion

The physiological features of Jesus are difficult if not impossible to tease out, although it is worth suggesting that the people's desire to remove him from the crowd may have been due to physical signs of Spirit possession and ecstatic behavior. Likewise, it seems likely that Jesus's visionary experiences, brought on through prolonged fasting, involved trance. More problematic are the passages where Jesus is accused of being possessed. In such cases, it

---

156. You will have noticed that the "ἐν/en" is enclosed in square brackets. This is because this passage has multiple readings in the manuscript tradition. In New Testament scholarship, certain readings are given letter ratings to determine whether they were authentic to the original text of the New Testament. This particular reading is given a "C." A "C" in this instance "indicates that the Committee had difficulty in deciding which variant to place in the text." The reading ἐν τῷ πνεύματι/en tō pneumati does appear in a third century papyrus (abbreviated as 𝔓75), the famous Codex Sinaiticus (abbreviated as ℵ [Aleph] or 01), Codex Bezae (abbreviated as Dea or 05), and several other later manuscripts. Here, Marshall concludes, "The strongest external evidence favours variants 1 [ἐν τῷ πνεύματι τῷ ἁγίῳ] and 2 [τῷ πνεύματι τῷ ἁγίῳ], but it is not easy to decide whether ἐν should be included or not" (brackets mine). Marshall, *Gospel of Luke*, 433. We cannot hope to resolve this text-critical issue here, but it should be noted that this may point to yet another instance of Spirit-inspired speech that elsewhere relates to ASCs. See Metzger, *Textual Commentary*, 128. Cf. the NET Bible.

157. 1 En. 39:1–14; 69:26.
158. 1QH[a] XV, 26–27.
159. Josephus, *J.W.* 3.353.

seems to be the content of his speech rather than his behavior that alarms the crowd, although ecstatic phenomena could still be an element. Despite some uncertainty, however, throughout the Gospel accounts, individuals commonly experience motor and verbal automatisms typical of ASCs. Visions, accusations of atypical behavior, and spontaneous prophetic activity are evidence of Spirit-induced ASCs.

6

Alcoholics in the Acts of the Apostles

> These people are not drunk, as you suppose.
>
> —Acts 2:15

MOVING BEYOND THE GOSPELS, the book of Acts is replete with extraordinary movements of the Spirit, demonstrating how ASCs served as a powerful means of divine communication and community transformation in the early church. The narrative begins with the dramatic events of Pentecost (Acts 2:1–13), where the disciples, gathered together, are filled with the Holy Spirit. They begin speaking in other languages, causing astonishment and confusion among the onlookers, some of whom mockingly accuse them of being drunk. This accusation reflects an ancient association between ecstatic spiritual experiences and perceived loss of control, a theme that occurs throughout Acts and connects to broader cultural understandings of ASCs.

Further examples of ASCs occur in the lives of early Christian leaders. Peter, while praying on a rooftop in Joppa (Acts 10:9–16), falls into a trance (*ekstasis*), during which he receives a vision that reshapes the mission of the church by extending it to the gentiles. Paul also experiences ASCs. In Acts 9:3–9, on the road to Damascus, he encounters the risen Jesus in a vision that leaves him blinded and transforms his life mission. Later, while praying in the temple (Acts 22:17–18), he falls into a trance and receives a direct command to take the gospel to the gentiles. Such episodes illustrate how visionary experiences and trances were integral to both Peter and Paul's understanding of the gospel and underscore the role of ecstatic experiences in guiding the early church's leaders.

Additionally, the narrative of Stephen, the first Christian martyr (Acts 7:54–60), provides another example of ASCs and the sharing of the gospel. As he faces execution, Stephen looks up and sees a vision of Jesus standing at the right hand of God. This moment of heightened spiritual awareness not only comforts Stephen but also serves as a testimony to those around him.

Finally, the story of Simon Magus (Acts 8:9–24) offers still another glimpse into ASCs in Acts. Simon is struck by the visible manifestations of the Spirit among the apostles and seeks to purchase this power for his own use. While the text does not explicitly describe the behavior of those receiving the Spirit, Simon's reaction suggests that it involved ecstatic behavior. His misguided attempt to commodify the Spirit underscores the mysterious and uncontrollable nature of these divine encounters.

While there are certainly other passages that could be considered, such as those who begin speaking in tongues (Acts 10:44–48; 19:1–10) or Philip's teleportation (Acts 8:39), the stories noted above will act as an outline for this chapter. Naturally, the very best place to start is at the beginning.

Morning Drinks

Acts 2 is typically understood as the birth of the church. Some see the Pentecost narrative as a reversal of the tower of Babel from Gen 11.[1] Others have seen it as a parallel to Moses receiving the law from Sinai.[2] Neither interpretation concerns us in our present study. Our priority is to answer the following question: Why did those observing the first Christians assume they were drunk? Luke reports that after hearing the newly Spirit-endowed Christians speak in tongues, some of those present at the Pentecost celebration mocked them saying, "They are filled with new wine" (Acts 2:13). Is this an instance of pure mockery or is something else going on?

Some charismatics and Pentecostals have used Acts 2 in conjunction with Eph 5:18 (to be analyzed in the following chapter) as proof texts for the phenomenon of spiritual intoxication. In the case of Eph 5:18, Paul instructs the Ephesian Christians to "not get drunk with wine, for that is debauchery, but be filled with the Spirit" and address each other in songs, give thanks to God, and submit to one another (Eph 5:19–21). Many critics have scoffed

---

1. See, for example, Davies, "Pentecost and Glossolalia"; and Rackham, *Acts*, 19.
2. Knox, *Acts*, 80–84. See also Snaith, "Pentecost."

at the idea of understanding these passages as referring to some kind of ecstatic expression and are often seen as being "appropriated" by charismatics in an attempt to foist their manifestations onto the biblical text. Yet, there are good reasons for understanding Acts 2 as referring to ASCs. This is not uneducated eisegesis or a mishandling of the text of Scripture as some have claimed. Rather, it takes seriously the whole narrative of Scripture and its historical, cultural, and religious context. Indeed, many levelheaded scholars interpret Acts 2 and Eph 5:18 as referring to ASCs and we ought to at least listen to what they have to say before outright dismissing the notion.

Three arguments can be put forward for understanding Acts 2 as recording an instance of group ecstasy: (1) it is logically inconsistent to view the remark as having to do with the content of the speech in Acts; (2) primary sources indicate that people often mistook, or wrongly attributed, ecstasy for drunkenness; and (3) early Christian interpretations of this event seem to point toward ecstasy. We will now work through these three arguments in order.

First, the idea that the crowds were mocking the Christians for the *content* of their speech as opposed to the *method* of their communication makes little sense.[3] Scholars often point to ecstatic speaking as the reason why the disciples were accused of drunken behavior, but the way they go about explaining this connection is somewhat misleading. In some instances, "ecstatic" is equated with "unintelligible" by scholars.[4] George B. Caird, for example, says that the criticisms by onlookers likely have to do with "ecstatic speech."[5] One is left wondering what "ecstatic speech" means in this

---

3. Witherington, *Acts*, 133–34 states: "If simple ecstatic speech was in view here, Luke ought simply to have used the term γλωσσαις, not ετεραις γλωσσαις. It is no argument against this conclusion that when these disciples were heard in the temple courts they were accused of drunkenness. If they were, as Luke tells us, exuberantly praising and speaking and perhaps even singing of the mighty acts of God (v. 11b) at an early hour in the morning, this could have easily prompted the accusation of drunkenness. In short, other things than ecstatic speech could have prompted such a suggestion." Witherington then goes on to argue in a footnote that reliance on parallels from the Testament of Job and general connections between drunkenness and ecstasy in the ancient world cannot help us read this narrative as an instance of group ecstasy because "the subject matter here is prophecy . . . speaking prophecy in the biblical tradition involve[s] intelligible communication, not just ecstasy" (134n16). Witherington's argument is confusing. Clearly there *is* intelligible communication—"we hear them telling in our own tongues the mighty works of God" (Acts 2:11)—and ecstasy is not at odds with such forms of communication.

4. Parsons, *Acts*, 50.

5. Caird, *Apostolic Age*, 60; Keener, *Acts*, 1:852, similarly connects this with Paul's statements in 1 Cor 14:23 since "Paul . . . believed that outsiders would judge tongues-speaking believers insane if no interpretation was provided."

context.⁶ Typically, a connection is made to Paul's explanation of tongues in 1 Cor 14. Yet, what is happening in Acts 2 seems to be demonstrably different at some level: "Some have observed that the miracle at Pentecost was one of hearing not of speaking, in which case Luke may have intended to convey that ecstatic speech was 'translated' by the Holy Spirit into language intelligible to the audience—that is, into whatever language they spoke."⁷ Keener is more guarded in his language: "Many commentators thus find in Acts 2:13's accusation of drunken-like behavior a suggestion of behavior or speech that is ecstatic; at the least (a qualification offered only because 'ecstatic' has been subject to too wide a range of definitions), it suggests an extremely atypical exuberance."⁸ He points out, though, that "it is probably also no coincidence that Paul . . . contrasts being 'filled with the Spirit' with drunkenness (Eph 5:18)."⁹ Mikeal C. Parsons, unclear if intelligible or ecstatic speech was present at Pentecost, suggests that "those gathered there heard in their own languages (2:6–7), but others mistakenly believed the disciples were drunk (2:13), suggesting that at least for some the apostles' speech was unintelligible."¹⁰

The binary of "intelligible" and "ecstatic" is, however, a false dichotomy. Ecstatic does not automatically mean something is unable to be understood. Part of the argument, therefore, has been confused by authors who talk about "ecstatic speech" as if it were unintelligible. It is clear that those in attendance at Pentecost *did* understand what was being said: "We hear them telling in our own tongues the mighty works of God" (Acts 2:11). Not only is the language understandable, the content is expressly known. This does not, contrary to popular belief, discount ecstasy. One can still communicate while in an ASC, even accompanied by extreme motor or even verbal automatisms, and this does not stop onlookers from grasping the message. Pervo, therefore, makes the best (and perhaps more obvious) observation that the crowd's response "would apply to ecstatic speech but makes little

---

6. Considerable debate exists about the connection between Acts 2 and 1 Cor 12–14. Are the tongues being spoken of by Paul the same kind recorded by Luke in Acts? If they are different, in what ways? What criteria should we use to determine if Acts 2 is recording ecstatic activity? While such questions are certainly important to interpreting the text, what seems to be most important in rightly determining what was happening at Pentecost comes not from answering these assorted questions, but from analyzing what Luke himself records. See Martin, "Glossolalia"; Neil, *Acts of the Apostles*, 73; and Williams, *Acts*, 63.

7. Parsons, *Acts*, 50.
8. Keener, *Acts*, 1:853.
9. Keener, *Acts*, 1:852.
10. Parsons, *Acts*, 50.

sense as a reaction to hearing Arabic or Persian and is illogical."[11] That is to say, that it is not the content of the message they are hearing in their own language (this is obviously digestible) that causes the criticism, but the rowdy (ecstatic) activity of the Christians doing the communicating.

A parallel to the Pentecost event and intelligibility can be seen in the works of Lucian of Samosata (second century CE), where he records the following about a false prophet named Alexander:

> In the morning he ran out into the market-place naked, wearing a loin-cloth (this too was gilded), carrying his falchion, and tossing his unconfined mane like a devotee of the Great Mother in the frenzy. Addressing the people from a high altar upon which he had climbed, he congratulated the city because it was at once to receive the god in visible presence. The assembly—for almost the whole city, including women, old men, and boys, had come running—marvelled, prayed and made obeisance. Uttering a few meaningless words like Hebrew or Phoenician, he dazed the creatures, who did not know what he was saying save only that he everywhere brought in Apollo and Asclepius.[12]

The time frame (morning), the explicit mention of ecstatic behavior (frenzy), the presence of foreign languages (meaningless words), and the crowd's ignorance (they did not know what he was saying) are of interest in understanding the crowd's reaction during the Pentecost narrative in Acts 2. The fact that being filled with the Spirit often results in prophetic speech-acts (Acts 4:8, 31; 9:17; 13:9), sometimes tongues (Acts 2:4, 10:46, 19:6), that this is interpreted as madness by outsiders (1 Cor 14:23), and that this is a common feature of being *en pneumati* (i.e., in an ASC), all suggest that Acts 2 is a case of group ecstasy.

Second, as I have tried to map out in this book, trance and ecstasy are found throughout the biblical narrative, and contemporary sources tell us that sometimes this is mistaken as drunkenness or insanity by onlookers.[13] Plutarch states that some women would pluck ivy and chew it, believing that it contained a spirit that caused madness (πνεῦμα μανίας/*pneuma manias*) and ecstasy (ἐξίστησι/*existēsi*) so that it likened "drunkenness without wine to those that have an easy inclination to enthusiasm [ἐνθουσιασμὸν/ *enthousiasmon*]."[14] Elsewhere, he states that when the prophetic spirit is

---

11. Pervo, *Acts*, 68.

12. Lucian, *Alex.* 13–14.

13. For examples between Acts 2 and Greek literature, see Van der Horst, "Hellenistic Parallels."

14. Plutarch, *Quaest. rom.* 112.

"instilled into the body, it creates in souls an unaccustomed and unusual temperament, the peculiarity of which it is hard to describe with exactness, but analogy offers many comparisons. It is likely that by warmth and diffusion it opens up certain passages through which impressions of the future are transmitted, just as wine, when its fumes rise to the head, reveals many unusual movements and also words stored away and unperceived."[15] Still in another instance, Plutarch writes of a certain Bias who says that "if I become filled with his [Dionysus'] spirit I shall compete with less courage."[16] Here, Dionysus being the god of wine is naturally combined with possession of his spirit and intoxication. Lucian of Samosata states that listening to philosophy "produced the same effect on me as wine" and as a result he goes "about like one possessed; I am drunk with the words of wisdom."[17] Iamblichus, who divides ecstasy into two categories, lists one as resembling "the aberrations of intoxication, and to the fury which happens from mad dogs."[18]

Jewish sources likewise make the connection between ASCs and intoxication.[19] Philo, commenting on the story of Hannah, states that "when grace fills the soul, that soul thereby rejoices and smiles and dances, for it is possessed and inspired [βεβάκχευται/bebakcheutai], so that to many of the unenlightened it may seem to be drunken, crazy and beside itself."[20] Philo's use of bebakcheutai (from βακχεύω/bakcheuō), a word that specifically means something like "celebrate the mysteries of Bacchus," is telling.[21] Most striking are his comments in a work called *On Dreams*: "And, when the happy soul holds out the sacred goblet of its own reason, who is it that pours into it the holy cupfuls of true gladness, but the Word [λόγος/logos], the Cup-bearer of God and Master of the feast, who is also none other than the draught which he pours."[22]

Second Esdras also contains a narrative where ecstasy and intoxication may be connected. Ezra is given a cup "full of something like water, but its color was like fire."[23] Immediately, his "heart poured forth understanding, and wisdom increased in my breast, for my spirit retained its memory."[24]

15. Plutarch, *Def. orac.* 40.
16. *Sept. sap. conv.* 4.
17. Lucian, *Nigr.* 5.
18. Iamblichus, *De Mysteriis* 3.25.
19. See Levison, "Inspiration and the Divine Spirit."
20. Philo, *Drunkenness* 146.
21. LSJ, s.v. "Βακχεύω."
22. Philo, *Dreams* 2.248–9.
23. 2 Esd 14:39.
24. 2 Esd 14:40.

Over the course of forty days, Ezra, along with five others, seem to sit in a trance where they are dictated the words to write down in characters they do not understand.[25] This reads as a form of Spirit possession initiated through drinking some heavenly substance likened to wine (cf. Prov 23:31; Rev 14:10).[26] The parallels that both Christians and onlookers could have made to such ideas floating around in the milieu of the first century are obvious.

Finally, early Christians seem to connect ecstasy and the Spirit with intoxication or alcoholic language (the most obvious being Eph 5:18). The sixth-century-CE Christian poet, Arator, for example, refers to the Pentecost event as an "intoxicating teaching of heaven."[27] Scribes were likewise curious about the accusations of drunkenness in Acts 2. One fifth-century manuscript called Codex Bezae (also referred to as D or 05), embellishes the story as follows: "So they [the crowd] were bewildered and perplexed at what had happened, constantly asking one another 'What is this business about?' There were some who made fun of the whole business by announcing: 'all these characters are carrying a heavy load of cheap wine.'" Pervo notes that, in this manuscript, "the participle (lit. "weighed down") suggests slurred rather than excited speech."[28]

John Chrysostom also appears to understand that something other than confusing speech caused the mockers to make accusation of drunkenness. He states that Peter didn't defend himself by saying "they are not drunk, but speak by the Spirit" as this would give the argument too much credence, so he instead quotes the prophet Joel. He thus concludes that "to

---

25. 2 Esd 14:42–48.

26. Myers, *I&II Esdras*, 326, notes that when it says Ezra's "spirit retained its memory," that this is "a reminder of the difference between Ezra and the ecstatics; the former retained consciousness and memory while the latter were generally deprived of both." Myers's analysis of how Ezra is being differentiated from other prophetic figures here is mistaken. The text doesn't seem to be about whether Ezra was ecstatic or not (the assumption seems to be that he was), but whether or not he experienced possession amnesia—a common symptom of ecstasy even within Judaism. Pseudo-Philo, for example, states: "A holy spirit came upon Kenaz and dwelled in him and put him in ecstasy, and he began to prophesy, saying . . . When Kenaz had spoken these words, he was awakened, and his senses came back to him. But he did not know what he had said" (LAB 28.6, 10). Additionally, verbal automatisms may be present in 2 Esd 14:39 since in the Arabic version it states that after drinking Ezra's "mouth uttered wisdom." Cf. Pss. Sol. 8:14: "Because of this God mixed them (a drink) of a wavering spirit, and gave them a cup of undiluted wine to make them drunk."

27. Hillier, *Arator on the Acts*, 28.

28. Pervo, *Acts*, 69n86.

some [of the prophets] the grace was imparted through dreams, to others it was openly poured forth."[29]

Ambrose of Milan (fourth century CE) speaks overtly of the intoxicating effects of the Spirit. He states, for example, that "there is, too, the inebriation that follows on the penetrating rain of the Holy Spirit. We read in the Acts of the Apostles . . . of those who spoke in foreign tongues and appeared, to those who heard them, to be drunk on new wine."[30] Likewise, in the hymn *Splendor Paternae*, Ambrose writes: "And may Christ be food to us, / and faith be our drink, / and let us joyfully imbibe the Spirit's / sober intoxication."[31] As Brian P. Dunkle explains: "The transformation is expressed through the language of 'sober drunkenness' ('bibamus sobriam / ebrietatem Spiritus' (23–4)), which is bestowed by the Holy Spirit. The paradoxical phrase expresses the conviction that the drunkenness of the Spirit brings true sobriety to the soul. The hymn likewise suggests that the soul and the senses, elevated through sacramental 'inebriation,' recognize the transcendent in the rites and Scripture."[32]

To conclude, the mockery of the disciples at Pentecost as being "drunk with new wine" (Acts 2:13) is best understood as a response to their ecstatic behavior rather than the content of their speech. While scholars often attribute this reaction to "ecstatic speech," many mistakenly equate ecstasy with unintelligibility. However, Acts 2:11 indicates that the crowd understood the disciples, hearing them proclaim "the mighty works of God" in their own languages. This suggests that the mockery stemmed from the exuberant and atypical demeanor of the disciples, not from incomprehensible speech.

Historical and cultural parallels support this interpretation. Ancient sources, such as Plutarch, Lucian of Samosata, and Philo, describe how ecstatic behavior—including prophetic utterances, frenzied actions, and heightened spiritual states—was frequently mistaken for drunkenness. For instance, Philo comments on the story of Hannah, noting that those who experience divine grace can appear drunk or insane to outsiders. Similarly, Jewish and Greco-Roman texts connect spiritual inspiration with the effects of intoxication, highlighting the cultural lens through which ecstatic states were interpreted.

In light of all this, the Pentecost narrative aligns with ancient perceptions of ASCs. The crowd's accusation likely reflects their misunderstanding

---

29. Chrysostom, *Hom. Act.* 5 (NPNF[1] 11:32).
30. Translations from Ní Riain, *Commentary of Saint Ambrose*, 47.
31. Translation from Dunkle, *Enchantment*, 222.
32. Dunkle, *Enchantment*, 104.

of the disciples' visible, Spirit-filled excitement, which they misinterpreted through familiar cultural frameworks linking ecstasy to drunkenness.

Open Heavens

Charismatic and Pentecostal Christians often use the phrase "open heavens" to describe a desired atmosphere or ethos of revival, the presence of miracles, and other supernatural events. The African American gospel singer Maranda Curtis, for example, sings a song called "Open Heaven" that discusses such an atmosphere. Likewise, the famous worship band Hillsong sings in one of their songs (also called "Open Heaven (River Wild)") about God's supernatural feats. Numerous books have also been authored with the phrase "open heavens" in the title by prominent charismatic speakers such as Bill Johnson's *Open Heavens: Position Yourself to Encounter the God of Revival* (2021) or Robert Henderson's *Prayers & Declarations That Open the Courts of Heaven* (2018).

The phraseology of "open heavens" is based on a number of biblical passages, including Ezek 1:1, Mal 3:10, Matt 3:16, Mark 1:10, Luke 3:21, John 1:51, and Rev 19:11. Another common term related to this includes "breakthrough." James W. Goll wrote a blog for the magazine *Charisma* called "3 Keys to Open Heavens, Minds and Doors" where he says that "prayer with fasting is a powerful key to making an opening for breakthrough."[33] Are such uses of the phrase "open heavens" biblical? Can we fast to get ASCs or miracles?

Fasting from food has been a common practice among religions across the world throughout history. While these religions have internally diverse views on why someone fasts, all agree that it accomplishes something, whether a display of devotion to a deity, as an impetus for prayers to be answered, the celebration of certain holy days, etc. Even nonreligious individuals engage in fasting for various health benefits or simply to clear their minds. In animistic religions (those religions which believe spirits inhabit every living thing such as trees, rivers, etc.), fasting is often used to help induce ASCs among their ritual specialists, often referred to as shamans.[34]

---

33. Goll, "3 Keys to Open Heavens," line 8.

34. Dunbar, *How Religion Evolved*, 35, 134: "Fasting is common before taking part in shamanic ceremonies, as is exposure to intense heat or cold. Fasting, pain and overheating were associated with the sweat lodges of the Native American tribes of the Great Plains and Midwest.... Sun Dances were always preceded by several days of fasting and dehydration, as well as physically exhausting exercise (for example, long runs, bathing in cold streams) and sensory deprivation, while the ceremony itself involved self-inflicted torture and strenuous dancing to low-frequency chanting and rhythmic

Combined with fasting, prayer and isolation are common elements found to induce the ASC.[35] Daniel, for example, experiences visions after three weeks of mourning and having "eaten no rich food, no meat or wine ... for the full three weeks" (10:3). As Pilch elaborates: "Fasting or nutritional deficits affect serotonin synthesis in the human body and produce emotional disturbances, hallucinations, alterations in cognitive and emotional functioning, and occasionally symptoms that are often interpreted as possession."[36]

According to Acts, Peter fell into a trance while waiting alone on the rooftop as a meal was being prepared:

> The next day, as they were on their journey and approaching the city, Peter went up on the housetop about the sixth hour to pray. And he became hungry and wanted something to eat, but while they were preparing it, he fell into a trance [*ekstasis*] and saw the heavens opened and something like a great sheet descending. (Acts 10:9–11)

While fasting is not explicitly mentioned in the text, there are good reasons to think that Peter had been fasting. The first hint is the time of day. While noon may be a typical mealtime for many of us today, during this time in history in the Roman empire it was decidedly uncommon.[37] It seems probable that Peter was hungry and required food because he had been fasting for a prolonged amount of time. Those preparing the meal must have made a special exception because of this.[38] Our second hint is that Peter is said to be πρόσπεινος/*prospeinos*, which the majority of English translations render simply as "hungry." This word, a hapax legomenon, appears one other time in all known ancient literature in the work *Ophthalmicus Medicus*. This work itself is preserved by the physician Aëtius of Amida (fifth-sixth century CE) and it records the medical knowledge of a man named Demosthenes Philalethes (first century CE). Writing on the issue of eye diseases,

---

drum beats at around three beats per second."

35. One of the greatest resources for parallel literature on the subject is *RAC*, s.v. "Ekstase," 4:944–87, esp. 970; and *RAC*, s.v. "Fasten," 7:447–94, esp. 462–63. *RAC* stands for the German *Reallexikon für Antike und Christentum* (Specialist Dictionary for Antiquity and Christianity), a lengthy encyclopedia that cites various parallels between Christian, Jewish, and pagan sources.

36. Pilch, *Flights of the Soul*, 53.

37. Polhill, *Acts*, 254.

38. Cf. Pervo, *Acts*, 269: "Midday meals were not a normal part of the daily routine in the Roman world. The willingness of Peter's hosts to prepare him food is an indication of his high standing."

Demosthenes tells a patient that should he become *prospeinos* he ought to eat certain prescribed foods.[39]

It is unclear whether *prospeinos* is meant to be understood as a particular medical term (as in, Peter had a medical issue that required him to fast either for long periods or to eat only certain foods, hence the long preparation time), or if it simply implies "very hungry" or something of that sort. In either case, Peter's hunger may not simply be the typical daily hunger, but of someone who has been involved in intensive fasting.

The combination of fasting, isolation on the rooftop, and prayer makes sense as to why Peter was particularly susceptible to receiving a vision while in a trance state. The substance of the vision is also telling. The vision involves Peter being instructed to eat what was considered "unclean" foods according to the Hebrew Scriptures. The vision itself is thus playing on the fact that Peter himself was experiencing physical hunger.

In terms of discernment, it is understandable why Peter hesitates to obey. The experience of the trance state does not itself necessarily validate that what he is hearing is truly from God. Indeed, after the vision, the Spirit explicitly says to him, "Behold, three men are looking for you. Rise and go down and accompany them without hesitation, for I have sent them" (Acts 10:19–20). Peter meets with the centurion Cornelius and concludes from his vision the following: "You yourselves know how unlawful it is for a Jew to associate with or to visit anyone of another nation, but God has shown me that I should not call any person common or unclean" (Acts 10:28). Peter did *not* conclude that he no longer had to obey the Jewish dietary laws. Rather, the vision was symbolic for communing with the gentiles.[40]

Did fasting somehow coax God into giving Peter a trance? Certainly not! In Peter's case, it is explicitly said that the trance came "upon" (ἐπί/*epi*) him, suggesting that it would have happened regardless of his mental state or previous actions. Fasting and other factors may have made him more receptive to experiencing a trance, but we cannot conclude that such ritual activities will automatically induce an authentic visionary experience.

Yet, this does not mean that we should therefore turn up our noses at the idea of fasting to hear from God, even within a prophetic capacity.

What of any outward physical manifestations of the trance? Peter relays the event one chapter later and reports that "I was in the city of Joppa praying, and in a trance I saw a vision" (Acts 11:5). It is important to emphasize that the trance and the vision were not synonymous. The trance was the avenue for the vision to take place. Not all trance states produce

---

39. Dillistone, "Prospeinos," 380.
40. Staples, "Rise, Kill, and Eat"; Thiessen, "Paul, the Animal Apocalypse."

visions and not all visions involve trance states. This is important, because having a vision does not always involve physiological characteristics such as automatisms or a dream-like waking state. Yet, as we have seen from Jewish sources such as Philo, *ekstasis* seems to involve physiological features that are atypical to the observant. The second-century-CE apologist Justin Martyr contrasts the "waking condition" (ἐν καταστάσει/*en katastasei*) with "trance," suggesting that the latter looks inherently different.[41]

Stoned in the Spirit

Elsewhere in Acts, another visionary account of the sky opening takes place with the martyr Stephen. Angered at his speech already, Stephen infuriates the crowd further by claiming that "I see the heavens opened, and the Son of Man standing at the right hand of God" (Acts 7:56). Stephen's vision takes place when he is "full of the Holy Spirit" (πλήρης πνεύματος ἁγίου/*plérés pneumatos hagiou*). Earlier in Acts, Stephen is initially chosen to serve alongside six other men at the behest of the apostles. The criteria for choosing these men included: (1) being of good repute, (2) being full of the Spirit, and (3) being full of wisdom (Acts 6:3).[42] Stephen is prominently mentioned as one who is "a man full of faith and of the Holy Spirit" (Acts 6:5). Others who are said to be full of the Holy Spirit include Barnabas (Acts 11:24), Peter (Acts 4:8), and Jesus (Luke 4:1). In the case of Peter and Jesus, the text seems to imply that this was not simply a way of expressing that they were of noble character.

Stephen is described as "full of grace and power" and someone able to do "great wonders and signs" (Acts 6:8). When those from the Synagogue of the Freedmen approach Stephen, they are unable to oppose him because of "the wisdom and the Spirit with which he was speaking" (Acts 6:10). That both wisdom and Spirit are offered as characteristics of Stephen's speech is curious. The Greek text makes it clear that it is both the content (wisdom) of Stephen's words and perhaps the display (Spirit) of his words that cause the opponents to falter. The wisdom from which Stephen speaks is obviously a reference to Jesus's words in Luke 4:14 and 21:15 in which he promised that the words would be given to speak out against opponents of the gospel.

41. Justin Martyr, *Dial.* 115. "But even if I did, I have shown that if there was a priest named Joshua (Jesus) in your nation, yet the prophet had not seen him in his revelation, just as he had not seen either the devil or the angel of the Lord by eyesight, and in his waking condition, but in a trance, at the time when the revelation was made to him."

42. Acts 6:3 cannot be read as a hendiadys, that is, the expression of a single idea through two individual words. Thus, a construction like "Wisdom of the Spirit" is impossible due to the presence of the distinct definite articles. See Keener, *Acts*, 1:1310.

But do we have here an example of ecstatic speech which also stumps his enemies?[43] Is Stephen speaking *en pneuamti*? The fact that Stephen is described as having the "face of an angel" (Acts 6:15) certainly suggests that something other than an everyday sermon was happening. Indeed, early scribes seemed to think this was the case as well. A number of manuscripts read that Stephen was "in the Holy Spirit" (ἐν πνεύματι ἁγίῳ/*en pneumati hagio*).[44]

The choosing of Stephen to serve seems to have allusions to Gen 41:33–38, where Joseph is described as both "wise" and "in whom is the Spirit of God."[45] As we have already seen, Joseph's ability to scry assumes an ASC experience. Thus, the mention of Stephen being full of the Holy Spirit during his public stoning seems best interpreted as a way of expressing that he was "in the Spirit"—that is, experiencing an ASC. The fact that Stephen is experiencing a vision in and of itself points us toward this reading.

Stephen is not the only martyr to experience ASCs while undergoing pain or torture. In the apocryphal work 4 Maccabees, for example, a man named Eleazar is tortured and flogged. Yet, "the courageous and noble man, like a true Eleazar, was unmoved, as though being tortured in a dream; yet while the old man's eyes were raised to heaven, his flesh was being torn by scourges, his blood flowing, and his sides were being cut to pieces."[46]

In another Jewish-Christian work called The Martyrdom and Ascension of Isaiah (first–second century CE) it states: "And Isaiah was in a vision of the Lord, but his eyes were open, and he saw them."[47]

Magicians and Manifestations

Acts 8:9–25 records an exchange between the apostle Simon Peter and a magician also named Simon (often referred to as Simon Magus). After Philip shared the gospel with the people of Simon Magus's city, he too was converted and followed Philip and was impressed by his miraculous ministry. John and Peter eventually came to Samaria to lay hands on the new converts who had not yet received the Holy Spirit. We are then told that

43. See Pervo, *Acts*, 170.

44. Pervo, *Acts*, 197n11: "The D-Text . . . begins ὁ δὲ ὑπάρχων ἐν πνεύματι ἁγίῳ ('but he, being in the Holy Spirit'). The first is an improvement over the conventional text, in which ὑπάρχων is technically circumstantial. 'To be in the Holy Spirit' is not conventional. It is therefore tempting to view the weakly attested D-Text as original, but note Luke 4:1* (Jesus)."

45. See Faw, *Acts*, 94.
46. 4 Macc 6:5–6.
47. Mart. Ascen. Isa. 5:7.

Simon Magus attempted to purchase this ability so that he too could give people the Holy Spirit. Peter aptly rebukes him. The relevant portion for our aims is that Simon Magus "saw" that the people received the Spirit through the laying on of hands.

What Simon Magus "saw" was not simply the laying on of hands, but the manifestation of the Holy Spirit falling on the people. A number of scholars have proposed that Simon Magus witnessed a form of ecstatic behavior. New Testament scholar James Dunn, for example, argues that "Luke has in mind here an eye-catching display of ecstasy."[48] Likewise, Richard I. Pervo compares this passage with Gal 4:6 and states: "The implication is that the gift of the Spirit produced a perceptible result, such as prophesying and/or glossolalia, some sort of ecstatic behavior."[49] In addition to prophecy and tongues, it is possible that those having hands laid on them experienced visions as well.[50] Even John B. Polhill, professor of New Testament at Southern Baptist Theological Seminary, states that "just what he 'saw,' the text does not say (v. 18). Luke was not interested in the concrete mode of the Spirit's appearance, only in the fact that the Spirit came to the Samaritans in an objective, verifiable fashion. . . . Luke's stress was more on its visibility than its audibility," suggesting that something observable was more likely.[51] The reception of the Holy Spirit in Acts is often accompanied by tongues (10:44–46; 19:6), and though no specific manifestation is recorded here, it is obvious to see why Simon would have desired this ability. Magicians commonly charged money for their services. If Simon could get ahold of such a power, he may have thought that this would bring him great fortune.

Another reason for interpreting what Simon Magus saw as a form of ecstasy has to do with Luke's description of him and his audience in Acts 8:11: "They paid attention to him [Simon] because for a long time he had amazed [*existēmi*] them with his magic." Luke seems to be playing a word game to point the reader to what Simon Magus saw. While he originally made his crowd "ecstatic" (*existēmi*), he is even more amazed when he encounters actual *ekstasis* from those receiving the Holy Spirit.

---

48. Dunn, *Jesus and Spirit*, 188; see also Chrysostom, *Hom. Act.* 18.

49. Pervo, *Acts*, 214.

50. In Herm. Vis. 1.3, the author states that "the spirit caught me away [πνεῦμά με ἔλαβεν/*pneuma me elaben*]," referring to the author experiencing a vision. This phraseology is similar to that of those possessed by spirits in the Gospels (Luke 9:39), Josephus (*Ant.* 4.119), Pseudepigrapha (T. Sol. 17:2–3), *Greek Magical Papyri* (PGM IV. 613), and patristic authors (Justin Martyr, *1 Apol.* 18).

51. Polhill, *Acts*, 219 and n115.

Conclusion

ASCs in Acts reveal the interplay between Spirit phenomena and the early church's mission. From the rambunctious events of Pentecost to the transformative visions of Peter and Paul, these ecstatic experiences were not mere anomalies; they were essential to shaping the beliefs and practices of early Christians. The repeating themes of confusion, dismissal, and awe highlight how ASCs served as catalysts for community transformation and the dissemination of the gospel. Through an analysis of the cultural and historical context of Acts, the ASCs recorded can be viewed within broader Greco-Roman and Jewish understandings of prophetic behavior, thereby shedding light on how such phenomena were perceived and their significance within early Christian praxis.

7

Pinot Noir with Paul

No one understands him, but he utters mysteries in the Spirit.
—1 Corinthians 14:2

Paul's Travels

IN ADDITION TO HIS trance in the temple, Paul also experienced night visions or dreams (Acts 16:9–10; 18:9–10), as well as a vision on the road to Damascus (Acts 9:1–19; 22:3–21; 26:9–18). Pilch argues that the presence of light in Luke's account of Paul's experience is representative of the initial stages of what he labels an "ecstatic trance."[1]

The fact that Paul experiences a voice asking him why he is persecuting the church is also given as evidence that Paul is in a trance state as, according to the work of M. S. Goldman, recent personal experiences are often the subjects of the visionary state while in trance.[2] This section, however, is not about Paul's experience on the road to Damascus, but of an account of being "caught up" into the third heaven in 2 Cor 12:1–10:

> I must go on boasting. Though there is nothing to be gained by it, I will go on to visions and revelations of the Lord. I know a man in Christ who fourteen years ago was caught up to the third heaven—whether in the body or out of the body I do not

---

1. Pilch, *Flights of the Soul*, 181.
2. Goldman, "Expectancy Operation."

know, God knows. And I know that this man was caught up into paradise—whether in the body or out of the body I do not know, God knows—and he heard things that cannot be told, which man may not utter. On behalf of this man I will boast, but on my own behalf I will not boast, except of my weaknesses—though if I should wish to boast, I would not be a fool, for I would be speaking the truth; but I refrain from it, so that no one may think more of me than he sees in me or hears from me. So to keep me from becoming conceited because of the surpassing greatness of the revelations, a thorn was given me in the flesh, a messenger of Satan to harass me, to keep me from becoming conceited. Three times I pleaded with the Lord about this, that it should leave me. But he said to me, "My grace is sufficient for you, for my power is made perfect in weakness." Therefore I will boast all the more gladly of my weaknesses, so that the power of Christ may rest upon me. For the sake of Christ, then, I am content with weaknesses, insults, hardships, persecutions, and calamities. For when I am weak, then I am strong.

This is a notoriously difficult passage to interpret. Colleen Schantz's *Paul in Ecstasy* (2009) is probably the most recent sustained study of this account and her observations about why some scholars have been so reluctant to embrace an ecstatic interpretation are worth considering. Schantz argues that modern academics have primarily obscured the ecstatic element of 2 Cor 12 based on several biases. These include a tendency toward ethnocentric and cognicentric views within New Testament studies,[3] denominational polemics (especially between Roman Catholics and Protestants),[4] and exegetical habits that frequently neglect the importance of mysticism and ecstatic experiences within Paul's writings (especially by pitting Paul against ecstatic abuses within the church and/or by saying that Paul's own ecstasies were flukes and unimportant).[5] Careful introspection, therefore, should be cautioned when attempting to interpret this passage. We do not have access to Paul's personal experience, but we *do* have access to his description of the event.

The idea of people ascending to heaven to receive visions was common in Jewish, Christian, and pagan circles.[6] Most famously, the patriarch Enoch was taken up by God to be given a tour of heaven and hell. His journey is recorded in the nonbiblical Jewish work 1 Enoch, but is also mentioned

---

3. Schantz, *Paul in Ecstasy*, 27–33.
4. Schantz, *Paul in Ecstasy*, 33–37.
5. Schantz, *Paul in Ecstasy*, 38–56.
6. Young, "Ascension Motif."

by the author of the book of Hebrews (11:5) and Jude (14). The prophet Elijah is also recorded as having been caught up in a whirlwind into heaven (2 Kgs 2:11), and of course Jesus too ascended into heaven (Acts 1:9–11). Yet, as Schantz notes, "Although comparisons with Jewish and Hellenistic religious writings provide a broad context in which experience like Paul's makes sense, they fail to account for a number of features; in particular, why Paul is perplexed about his body and conflicted about how to describe his experience. What happens if instead we place Paul among the cross-cultural list of those who have spoken about their ecstatic experiences . . . ?"[7]

Several features of Paul's account in 2 Corinthians suggest ecstatic phenomena. These include the mention of his body and the inability to speak what he had seen. Paul's hesitation for not knowing whether this ascent was simply a visionary experience (out of the body) or actual physical relocation (in the body) is understandable given what we read in Acts 12:9 concerning Peter's unawareness that an angel was actually in front of him.

Evidently, the lines between a visionary experience and the "real thing" were blurred. Likewise, Paul's (seemingly self-imposed) limitation on what he can reveal from the event is typical of ecstatic experiences cross-culturally.[8] It, therefore, has a scientific basis due to the neurological processes involved during ecstasy.[9]

Elsewhere in 2 Corinthians, Paul discusses the topic of ecstasy explicitly. In 2 Cor 5:13–14 he states: "For if we are beside ourselves [*existēmi*], it is for God; if we are in our right mind [*sōphroneō*], it is for you. For the love of Christ controls us." This passage is typically interpreted as being either about religious zeal interpreted as insanity[10] or as ecstasy.[11] The latter is demonstrated in the Douay-Rheims translation: "For whether we be transported in mind [i.e., in an ecstasy], it is to God; or whether we be sober, it is for you." In order to understand Paul's meaning, we must look at the wider context of 2 Corinthians. Throughout 2 Corinthians, Paul addresses the

---

7. Schantz, *Paul in Ecstasy*, 93.

8. Ahlberg, "Some Psycho-Physiological Aspects." The concept of ineffability related to having a vision can also be found in the *Greek Magical Papyri*. In one case, a child is taken to receive a vision and part of the instruction is to state that the "hidden and unspeakable name—it cannot be uttered by human mouth" (*PGM* XIII. 763).

9. See Björkvist, "Ecstasy from a Physiological Point of View."

10. Harris, *Second Epistle to the Corinthians*, 418, connects vv. 12–13 as follows: "We are certainly not promoting ourselves [v. 12a], for (γάρ) whether our words and conduct be thought irrational [v. 13a] or rational [v. 13b], God and you are the ones for whom I speak and work, just as my life is an open book to God and you [v. 11b]" (brackets in the original).

11. See Fee, *God's Empowering Presence*, 329.

prideful ministry of false teachers and a group he sarcastically calls "super-apostles" (2 Cor 11:5, 12:11). This may be the same group mentioned in 2 Cor 5:12 who "boast about outward appearance and not about what is in the heart." Evidently, we must ask what this "outward appearance" is that Paul refers to. Is it hypocritical living? Given that Paul immediately uses the word *existēmi*, we must think carefully about what he is getting at. Paul elsewhere denounces people who are obsessed with "asceticism and worship of angels, going on in detail about visions, puffed up without reason by his sensuous mind" (Col 2:18). He goes on to state that ascetic practices "have indeed an appearance of wisdom in promoting self-made religion and asceticism and severity to the body, but they are of no value in stopping the indulgence of the flesh" (Col 2:23). The "outward appearance" referred to by Paul in 2 Cor 5:12 may include hypocrisy, but perhaps also extreme asceticism and the pursuit of supernatural experiences, including ecstasy. If this is the case, his point seems to be that it is not ecstatic experiences or being a rational orator that make one a great or true apostle but being controlled by Christ's love and motivated by the gospel message. As Garland argues: "Paul may be downplaying the value of ecstatic visions in contrast to his more flamboyant opponents who put great stock in them as part of their apostolic credentials."[12]

If this interpretation of 2 Cor 5 is correct, this further places 2 Cor 12 within the context of ecstasy. Paul's autobiographical sketch serves to contrast his ministry with the false apostles that have been invading the Corinthian church. His boasting about visions in 2 Cor 12 thus serves "to show the Corinthians that he was not at all deficient in ecstatic experiences, as some imagined."[13] In the New Testament, few people are transported bodily, other than Jesus and Philip (Acts 8:39), and this is not in a visionary context, but as a form of levitation and teleportation respectively. The concept of

---

12. Garland, *2 Corinthians*, 275: "He talks of his ecstatic visions in 12:1–7 only reluctantly, while his opponents apparently publicly prided themselves on their celestial revelations. Paul knows, however, that apostles who are forever in a state of frenzied ecstasy will not be much use to a community in need of sober-minded direction. Paul may be saying, 'If we do experience ecstasy, then that is something between us and God [not something to be displayed before others as proof of the spiritual character of our ministry], but if we are in our right mind [and, use reasonable, intelligible speech], that is for your benefit.' The Corinthians' fixation on such things, however, suggests that they would be prone only to criticize Paul for his shortage of thrilling visions. Thrall suggests, 'They might have wished to have seen him in an ecstatic condition, to which they could bear testimony.' They could then vaunt his spiritual bona fides to external critics. Paul responds to such criticism that they can only depend on his sober and rational arguments, not any dazzling religious ecstasy" (brackets original to source).

13. Harris, *Second Epistle to the Corinthians*, 833.

being physically lifted up in a visionary experience can be found, however, in Ezekiel (8:3) and throughout Revelation (4:1–2; 17:3; 21:10).[14]

Whether or not Paul experienced the revelation in the body or not, the fact that he alludes to such experiences and himself elsewhere engaged in a trance state, suggests that he was not averse to the experience, but rather the unnecessary emphasis on such experiences.[15]

Other instances where scholars infer an ecstatic or mystical interpretation of Paul is in Galatians. Paul describes his conversion there as follows: "But when he who had set me apart before I was born, and who called me by his grace, was pleased to reveal his Son [ἐν/*en*] me, in order that I might preach him among the Gentiles . . . " (Gal 1:15–16). The preposition *en* here is sometimes translated with the word "to" in modern English translations (ESV, NRSV, NLT). The NIV and KJV are probably more accurate in translating it as "in."[16]

What then does it mean that Christ was revealed "in" Paul? Scholarship on how exactly to interpret this strange construction is best summarized by the theologian Ernest De Witt Burton: "[Does it refer to a] subjective revelation in and for the apostle or to an objective manifestation of Christ in and through him to others."[17] Theologian Timothy George confusingly states that "some have opted for the subjective, mystical reading of this phrase because they have dismissed out of hand the possibility that Jesus Christ could actually have appeared in person to Paul at a particular place in time."[18] By a "mystical reading" of the text, George is referring to the interpretation that the experience was internal and that Paul did not literally "see" Jesus. Yet, 1 Cor 9:1 and 15:8 seem to suggest that Paul *did* in fact see Jesus.[19] The German New Testament Scholar Hans Dieter Betz says of Paul's statement in Galatians that his "experience was ecstatic in nature, and that in the course of this ecstasy he had a vision (whether external or internal or both—'I do not know, God knows" [cf. 2 Cor 12:2, 3])."[20]

---

14. Aune, *Revelation*, 82–83.

15. Pilch, *Flights of the Soul*, 201–2, suggests that Phil 3:12 can be interpreted as possession: "In social-scientific terms, specialists would say that Paul became as it were 'possessed' by the being he saw . . . one can plausibly surmise from Paul's statements about being 'apprehended,' 'captured,' 'snatched' by God that he did indeed feel the presence of God upon himself giving him fresh insight into God and the identity of Messiah Jesus."

16. See Porter, *Idioms*, 159 (§4.8.6).

17. Burton, *Epistle to the Galatians*, 50.

18. George, *Galatians*, 119.

19. Supported by a debate found in the Ps.-Clem. *Homilies* 17.13–19.

20. Betz, *Galatians*, 71.

If these readings are correct, Paul does not discourage ecstasy, but rather desires to place it within authentic Christian life. While the so-called super-apostles boasted in their ecstatic fits as evidence of their advanced spirituality, Paul argues that such boasting is actually foolishness, not because ecstasy itself is foolish, but because boasting in an outward manifestation is foolish.[21] These are akin to those who become "puffed up" by recounting elaborate visions such as those in the Colossian church.

Crazy and/or Corinthian?

The idea of divinely inspired speech has briefly been addressed above. People in the ancient world (and today) believed that gods, spirits, ancestors, or other outward forces could give revelation to men and women who became possessed by them or who experienced trance states where those spiritual beings communicated to them in visions or other means. We also noted in passing some references to what appears to be spontaneous ecstatic utterances. Such ecstatic speech acts are not uncommon to Judaism around the time of Jesus.[22] According to a work called the Testament of Job (first century BCE–first century CE), Job's daughter is said to have "took on another heart—no longer minded toward earthly things—but she spoke ecstatically in the angelic dialect, sending up a hymn to God in accord with the hymnic style of the angels. And as she spoke ecstatically, she allowed 'The Spirit' to be inscribed on her garment."[23] It is important to observe that the word "ecstatically" is not in the original Greek text of this passage

---

21. Schantz, *Paul in Ecstasy*, 183–84, concludes that "Paul's ecstasy relates positively to his apostleship. First, it is relevant because his superlative visions and journey to heaven presumably gave him some of the content (particularly his certainty that Christ was raised)—and much of the conviction—of the gospel with which he was entrusted as an apostle. Second, through it, Paul brings people into contact with the spirit in ways that are seen to demonstrate their divine election. At the same time, the bumpiness of Paul's discussion in 2 Corinthians 12 is noteworthy: Paul both asserts his superlative ecstatic feats (2 Cor 12:1–4, 7, and 12) and tries to offer weakness as the truer measure of his character. This is not to say that his ecstatic experience was unimportant to him or that ecstatic feats and knowledge played no role in his apostleship; rather it is to say that the complexity of the interplay between Paul's social role and his ecstatic abilities seems to have required negotiation from time to time."

22. Sib. Or. 3.489–91 (first century BCE–first century CE): "When indeed my spirit stopped its inspired hymn the utterance of the great God again rose in my breast and bade me prophesy concerning the earth"; cf. Mart. Pol. 7.3 (second–third century CE): "And on their consenting, he stood up and prayed, being so full of the grace of God, that for two hours he could not hold his peace, and those that heard were amazed, and many repented that they had come against such a venerable old man."

23. T. Job 48:1–3.

but is rather an interpretation supplied by the translator. One manuscript of this text, however, includes the phrase "and at once she was outside her own flesh," which certainly is ecstatic rhetoric and shows that this passage was interpreted by its audience as involving ecstasy. Indeed, the taking on of "another heart" suggests that ecstasy is in view, similar to 1 Sam 10:6, 9.[24] Inspired speech also occurs in the Jewish book of Jubilees. In one passage "the spirit of righteousness descended" into Rebekah's mouth to have her bless Jacob.[25] A similar occurrence happens to Isaac when "a spirit of prophecy came down upon his mouth" in order to bless Levi and Judah.[26] Likewise, 1 Enoch records an instance where Enoch cries out because his "spirit was transformed" and had a "spirit of power."[27] Philo says of Moses that "after a short time he became inspired by God, and being full of the divine spirit and under the influence of that spirit which was accustomed to enter into him, he prophesied."[28]

Additionally, we have covered the instances of what appear to be verbal automatisms both in the Hebrew Bible and New Testament. Naturally, such issues are relevant to the understanding of the gift of tongues found in Paul's letter to the Corinthians, as well as other passages scattered among the books of the New Testament. As Keener notes: "Whether early Christian tongues were 'ecstatic' depends on how one defines 'ecstatic' and on one's further conclusions about the nature of ancient Christian tongues (which, like modern tongues, may have varied in form from one church and individual to another)."[29]

First Corinthians 12–14 is a land mine of exegetical and interpretive issues.[30] We cannot hope to address all of them here, but I do want to draw attention to several important passages that relate to our investigation. We have previously noted how Paul says that people proclaim Jesus's lordship when they are speaking *en pneumati* (1 Cor 12:3). They are therefore able to discern between true spiritual manifestations and false ones based on the

---

24. Compare the words of Montanus found in Epiphanius (fourth century CE): "Behold! Humankind is like a harp, and I strum as a plectrum; humans sleep, I am awake. Behold! The Lord is the one who excites the hearts of humans, the one who gives them a heart." *Pan.* 48.4.1.

25. Jub. 25:9; cf. 1QH^a IV, 17: "[I give] you [thanks] for the spirits which you placed in me" (brackets original to source).

26. Jub. 31:12.

27. 1 En. 71:9–12.

28. Philo, *Moses* 1.175.

29. Keener, *Acts*, 1:811.

30. Thiselton, *Corinthians*, 907–1168; Garland, *1 Corinthians*, 437–528; Fitzmyer, *First Corinthians*, 453–538.

content of their speech, not simply the outward physical signs. Throughout 1 Cor 12, Paul says that the spiritual manifestations (πνευματικά/*pneumatika*) have their source "through" (διά/*diá*) or "according to" (κατά/*kata*) the Spirit (1 Cor 12:4–9). Thus, not all manifestations are products of ecstasy, but some ecstatic states do have their origin from the Spirit, especially the gift of tongues.

The sheer amount of scholarly literature available on the topic of tongues is daunting and there is significant debate about what sources should even be consulted in identifying the socioreligious context of tongues. Should we look to Greco-Roman religions and their divination and magical rites?[31] Should we look to Gnostic or esoteric writings?[32] Does the oracle at Delphi give us a glimpse into glossolalia?[33]

Since an exhaustive exploration into these avenues is outside of the scope of the present book, I want to highlight instead the text of 1 Cor 14 itself.

According to Paul "one who speaks in a tongue speaks not to men but to God; for no one understands him, but he utters mysteries in the Spirit" (1 Cor 14:2). In terms of audience, "tongues" is primarily a vertical expression (to God), not horizontal (not to men). The only time tongues become horizontal is when it is interpreted to edify the church (1 Cor 14:5). The interpreter may be a fellow congregant or the tongues-speaker (1 Cor 14:13). Paul describes tongues as praying or singing with their "spirit" instead of their "mind" (1 Cor 14:14–16). Scholars debate whether Paul is speaking here about the human spirit or the Holy Spirit and whether this points toward some kind of ecstatic expression of tongues.

---

31. Keener, *Acts*, 1:810: "Yet the strings of nonsense syllables found in magical papyri are mostly from the third century or later; more decisively, they are incantations and invocations, not understood as genuine language, not revelatory, and not inviting 'interpretations.'"

32. *Corp. herm.* 1.26.

33. *Heraclidae Fragmentum* 92: "The Sybil with raving mouth uttering her unlaughing, unadorned, unincensed words reaches out over a thousand years with her voice, through the (inspiration of the) god." Cf. Plato, *Tim.* 71f.; and Keener, *Acts*, 1:810: "Although many scholars have accepted other scholars' proposed parallels, careful investigation of the claims limits the concrete values of these parallels. Supposed parallels between tongues (with interpretation, as in Paul) and Delphic incoherency translated by a prophet misunderstand the nature of the Delphic experience; the Pythia spoke ambiguous, obscure oracles, not incoherently (see comment on Acts 16:16). Her supposed glossolalia is 'a product of modern scholarly imagination,' an example of an early Christian idea now read back into its environment. Mystery cults offer no parallels to tongues." See also *TDNT*, s.v. "πνεῦμα, πνευματικός"; Eitrem, *Orakel und Mysterien*, 42; and Delling, *Worship in the New Testament*, 31–41.

One of the main reasons for interpreting tongues as an ecstatic speech act is because of Paul's warning that "if, therefore, the whole church comes together and all speak in tongues, and outsiders or unbelievers enter, will they not say that you are out of your minds [μαίνομαι/mainomai]?" (1 Cor 14:23). Why would Paul give such a warning and why would people conclude that the believers at Corinth were out of their minds? One would scarcely consider a number of people speaking in diverse languages a form of madness. Nor would hearing many voices speaking over one another constitute an accusation of insanity (though we might think it is chaotic). One probable interpretation, therefore, is to view this interpretation of madness as an etic onlooker viewing unbridled mass ecstasy.

Part of Paul's reasoning seems to be that outsiders will interpret these widespread ecstatic experiences as similar enthusiasms found amongst other Greco-Roman religions. The Greek word μαίνομαι/mainomai is used in reference to such religious contexts. According to the author of the apocryphal Wisdom of Solomon, those who worship idols "rave [μεμήνασιν / memēnasin] in exultation, or prophesy lies" (14:28). Likewise, the ancient author Euripides uses the word frequently to denote frenzy from the gods or spirits.[34] Jesus's critics accused him of having a demon and that he was "insane" (μαίνεται / mainetai). Thus, the connection between possession and insanity or manic behavior was commonly understood. The word mainomai is also used by Josephus to refer to the mania of Herod and Sossius's armies who slaughtered infants, women, and the elderly "like madmen" (μεμηνότες / memēnotes),[35] perhaps a reference to battle trance.

Paul is not saying that the ecstasy of the Corinthians is from the same source as those of pagan religions, but that from an outsider's perspective, this is assumed to be the case. This is because, like other religious rituals and experiences, the outward substance of those experiences does not necessarily indicate their source. Paul does not disparage ASCs (he himself engaged in them), but teaches that they, like many things, are meant to be exercised in their proper place. Keener argues for a categorical difference between Christian tongues and pagan ecstasy in that Paul "expects (in contrast to pagan possession trance) the individual believer to maintain control of responses (14:32); also distinctively, for Christian (in contrast to pagan Greek) prophecy, he appears to insist on the need for an accompanying rational component."[36]

---

34. Euripides, *Bacch.* 690–711, 748–68, 1095–1136.
35. Josephus, *J.W.* 1.352.
36. Keener, *Acts*, 1:811.

An alternative interpretation of this data has been given by New Testament scholar Stephen J. Chester. He argues that the outsiders' reaction to the Corinthian church's glossolalia should be interpreted in a positive sense. Chester sees the ecstasy of the Corinthians as proof of God's presence within the congregation. He compares ecstatic states found in other Greco-Roman religious contexts as evidence of divine possession to those witnessed by outsiders in the Corinthian church and posits that unbelievers would have viewed the Christians as divinely inspired and not "crazy" in our modern sense of the term.[37] Thus, according to Chester's interpretation, Paul prefers the Corinthian church to prophesy rather than speak in tongues because, while speaking in tongues may give evidence to outsiders that God is at work within the community, its substance does not articulate the gospel that will lead them to saving faith.[38]

Other passages about praying "in the Spirit" are also relevant to the discussion. In Eph 6:18, for example, Paul instructs the church to be "praying at all times in the Spirit [ἐν πνεύματι/*en pneumati*]."[39] Contextually, this instruction occurs after a prolonged discussion on methods for fighting against evil spiritual forces (what is called in scholarly literature "apotropaism"). Thus, the presence of ecstatic speech is not out of place.[40] Likewise, Jude 1:20 instructs his audience to "pray in the Holy Spirit" (ἐν πνεύματι

---

37. Chester, "Divine Madness."

38. Grudem, *Gift of Prophecy*, 208, argues that we should not look at general prophetic practice in the ancient Mediterranean world to understand Christian prophetic practice. Grudem's argument is that there is an inherent difference between the two, namely that Christian prophets could be tested by their proclamation of Jesus as Lord. This argumentation is confusing for a number of reasons. Christian and pagan prophecy could share similar physiological and psychological features much like music, prayer, and other religious activities share ubiquitous features. Moreover, Grudem seems to undermine his own point. There was a way to discern true and false prophecy, not by looking at ecstatic activity, but by the content of their speech.

39. Elsewhere in Ephesians, Paul states that the mystery of Christ "was not made known to the sons of men in other generations as it has now been revealed to his holy apostles and prophets [*en pneumati*]" (3:5). For Paul at least receiving knowledge about the mystery of Christ *en pneumati* was in the form of a vision on the road to Damascus. In 1 Thess 1:5, Paul tells the Thessalonians that the gospel message "came to you not only in word, but also in power and [*en pneumati hagiō*] and with full conviction."

40. Neyrey, *2 Peter, Jude*, 90; Green, *Jude & 2 Peter*, 121. Schreiner, *1, 2 Peter, Jude*, 483, however, argues that in Jude, like in Ephesians, "The context . . . clarifies that speaking in tongues is not primarily in view," though he does not explain why. Indeed, the presence of various apotropaic methods in Ephesians seems to envision that ecstatic utterances could very much be in view. The "tongues of angels" likewise in 1 Corinthians suggests that angelomorphic rhetoric is being used, similar to what one finds in the Qumran sectarian texts that see the community as participating in the angelic host's praise, a place where demonic activity is thwarted. See Angel, "Maskil, Community."

ἁγίῳ/en pneumati hagiō).⁴¹ In Jude's case, he also uses the phrase "building yourselves up" (ἐποικοδομοῦντες ἑαυτοὺς / epoikodomountes heautous) which is reminiscent of 1 Cor 14:4: "The one who speaks in a tongue builds up himself" (ἑαυτὸν οἰκοδομεῖ / heauton oikodomei). To ignore this lexical similarity is to do an injustice to the text of Jude and the obvious parallel it has to 1 Cor 14.

That Acts 2 narrates the onlooking crowds as accusing the disciples speaking in tongues as being drunk, we may assume that such a similar accusation could have been leveled against those at Corinth. We will return to Acts 2 later, but it is worth emphasizing that those who wish to make the tongues of Acts 2 and 1 Cor 12–14 one and the same will likewise need to grapple with this ecstatic element.

Although I have addressed the issue of self-control and automatisms in chapter 1, select passages from 1 Cor 14 are sometimes used by critics to discredit the place of ASCs in the church⁴² or to say that verbal automatisms are inherently antiscriptural.⁴³ Paul's instructions to the church to only let "two, or at most three, and each in turn" speak in tongues followed by interpretation (1 Cor 14:27), as well as his statement about appearing "crazy" to outsiders in 1 Cor 14:23, are used by critics to indicate that ASCs and any resultant automatisms must be prohibited. Several difficulties with such an interpretation, however, must be addressed.

First, while Paul does address orderly conduct in 1 Cor 14:26–40, it is important to realize that Paul nowhere prohibits automatisms. Thus, the only instruction we can derive from 1 Corinthians about automatisms is that they should not cause disorder during formal church gatherings. In the context of 1 Cor 14:27, the tongue-speaker seems to be addressing the congregation directly as a method for dispensing encouraging revelations or praise (cf. 1 Cor 14:6, 16). That this is Paul's meaning seems to find support in the following verses on the etiquette of prophets who likewise speak in turn (1 Cor 14:29–32).

Second, Paul does not say that the individual *cannot* pray in tongues in the congregation. Rather, "if there is no one to interpret, let each of them keep silent in church and speak to himself and to God" (1 Cor 14:28). The person speaking in tongues is "silent" insofar as they are not disrupting the

---

41. Bauckham, *Jude, 2 Peter*, 113; Dunn, *Jesus and the Spirit*, 239–42. See also Hillyer, *1 and 2 Peter, Jude*, 264.

42. MacArthur, *Strange Fire*, 200.

43. Grudem, *Gift of Prophecy*, 73–74, for example, argues that "the Holy Spirit will subject his inspiration to the prophet's own timing, and thus will never force a prophet to speak out of turn, because it is not in the nature of God to inspire confusion." For a response to Grudem, see Schantz, *Paul in Ecstasy*, 189–90.

formal church service, but they are still speaking (quietly) in tongues to God, as per 1 Cor 14:2.[44] Again, the issue Paul seems to envision is that of multiple people vying for a position to address the entire congregation by interrupting those who were there first.

Third, the unspoken (but clearly inserted) interpretation of this passage by critics is that the individuals are all speaking in tongues sporadically and chaotically, thus interrupting the church service, and that Paul does not want this happening. The reconstruction of what exactly was happening in the assemblies in Corinth is difficult to ascertain and a reader may come away from the text with wildly different ideas based on what they perceive an ASC to look like. Were people yelling out in tongues? Were they flailing around? Or, as has been suggested above, were they simply interrupting others?

Finally, individual experiences of ASCs vary considerably, and scientific research shows that people can control certain facets of these ASCs.[45] Paradoxically, automatisms (which are sometimes perceived as a lack of self-control) can be controlled. I am not referring to the issue of inducing automatisms, but that the experience of Holy Spirit activity can be ethically or unethically exercised. Prophetic inspiration, for example, may be genuine but spoken at an inappropriate time. Speaking over another prophet is not in line with Pauline ethics laid out in 1 Cor 14. It does *not*, however, mean that the prophecy is *untrue*, only that the prophet immaturely exercised their gifting (1 Cor 14:32). Likewise, many who experience motor automatisms are able to contain their physical movements to a certain degree. While Paul envisions some boundaries within the church gathering, his main concern has to do with clear communication. Those who witness the individual in an ASC can assess that God's Spirit is at work, hence the language of "manifestations" of the Spirit in 1 Cor 12.[46]

Denominations and individual churches have divergent views on what is a distraction or not. For some, spotlights, fog machines, and other factors contribute to distraction, while for others they help absorb the member into a state of worship. Thus, the presence of verbal and motor automatisms may be a distraction only to some sectors of the Christian faith. Yet, in many

---

44. Witherington, *Conflict and Community*, 286: "V. 28b may allow speaking in tongues silently or under one's breath even in the assembly."

45. Hilgard, *Divided Consciousness*; Fasullo et al., "Innate Human Potential"; Smith and Messier, "Voluntary Out-of-Body Experience"; Picard and Craig, "Ecstatic Epileptic Seizures."

46. Grudem, *Gift of Prophecy*, 80, argues that "Christian prophecy itself is by nature non-ecstatic" because of Paul's instructions in 1 Cor 14. Yet, he never deals with the phrase *en pneumati* in 1 Cor 12 and elsewhere.

instances, those experiencing verbal and motor automatisms are still able to preach and teach coherent and edifying content.

Based on the following analysis, I suggest that there is biblical space for automatisms. Automatisms are meant to be manifestations of the Holy Spirit and thus act as a form of edification either for the individual or the church. Like other Spirit-empowered activities, they require wisdom in execution.

The unique nature of automatisms (that they are brought on spontaneously) requires sensitivity and biblical congregational teaching that has sometimes been ignored in some streams of the Christian faith. In the same way someone might mock a denomination for incorporating dancing into their worship, we should not be so quick to ignore the biblical evidence for trance and ecstasy and the physiological features that may accompany such states.

Ephesian Ethanol

In our section on Acts 2 it was noted that Eph 5:18 also plays an important role as a common proof text for spiritual intoxication among modern Pentecostals and charismatics. This passage is located within a larger exhortation of ethical conduct and so it is worth reading the passage in full:

> Take no part in the unfruitful works of darkness, but instead expose them. For it is shameful even to speak of the things that they do in secret. But when anything is exposed by the light, it becomes visible, for anything that becomes visible is light. Therefore it says, "Awake, O sleeper, and arise from the dead, and Christ will shine on you." Look carefully then how you walk, not as unwise but as wise, making the best use of the time, because the days are evil. Therefore do not be foolish, but understand what the will of the Lord is. And do not get drunk with wine, for that is debauchery, but be filled with the Spirit [πληροῦσθε ἐν πνεύματι/plērousthe en pneumati], addressing one another in psalms and hymns and spiritual songs, singing and making melody to the Lord with your heart, giving thanks always and for everything to God the Father in the name of our Lord Jesus Christ, submitting to one another out of reverence for Christ. (Eph 5:11–21)

Several reasons for interpreting this passage as having to do with ASCs include: (1) parallels with the cult of Dionysus regarding spiritual intoxication, (2) Jewish and pagan writings that use alcoholic rhetoric in relation to spirit phenomena and ethics, (3) the role of inspired singing in both

Ephesians and parallel literature related to spiritual intoxication, and (4) the idea of being "filled with a/the s/Spirit" (*plērousthe en pneumati*) implies Spirit possession.

First, scholars have often connected Paul's words as a condemnation of Dionysian cult activities where drunkenness, orgies, and ecstatic activity were often linked.[47] As Stanley E. Porter argues, the language used by Paul "would have been suitable and found a reception in the Ephesian context, where the Dionysian cult had been known from before and long after the letter to the Ephesians was written."[48] Indeed, Paul's language invites comparison to passages from Euripides's *Bacchae*. Craig Evans goes on to suggest that in addition to the Ephesian context, Paul may have been dealing with Dionysian influence in Corinth as well since "imbibing the spirit of Dionysus leads to 'madness' and ecstatic speech."[49] The confusion between cultic ecstasy and Christian Spirit possession no doubt made it sometimes difficult for the uninitiated to discern the source of these ASCs: "To both non-Christians and members of the congregation, the external phenomena of inebriation and inspiration looked so similar that one could be mistaken for the other (see Acts 2:13, 15)."[50]

Second, although the connection between alcoholic rhetoric and Spirit possession has previously been addressed in the section on Acts 2, it is worth repeating that such overlap is known from pagan and Jewish writings. Jewish sources speak of the idea of becoming "drunk" on God's wisdom, for example, such as in Sirach: "To fear the Lord is fullness of wisdom; she inebriates mortals with her fruits,"[51] and "Like the vine I bud forth delights, and my blossoms become glorious and abundant fruit. Come to me, you who desire me, and eat your fill of my fruits."[52] A work known as History of the Rechabites (first–fourth century CE) speaks of a group that, after fasting for a lengthy period, are told not to "exalt your heart, saying: 'For forty years I did not eat bread.' For the word of God is more than bread, and the Spirit of God is more than wine."[53] Philo again exemplifies the connection between religious experience and intoxication when he writes that "Melchizedek shall bring forward wine instead of water, and shall give your souls to drink,

---

47. See especially, Rogers, "Dionysian Background of Ephesians 5:18"; Moritz, *Profound Mystery*, 94–95; and Porter, "Ephesians 5:18–19."

48. Porter, "Ephesians 5:18–19," 79.

49. Evans, "Ephesians 5:18–19," 184.

50. Barth, *Ephesians 4–6*, 582.

51. Sir 1:16.

52. Sir 24:17–19.

53. Hist. Rech. 1:4.

and shall cheer them with unmixed wine, in order that they may be wholly occupied with a divine intoxication, more sober than sobriety itself."[54]

By contrast, drinking literal alcohol is linked with the invasion of hostile spiritual forces. According to the Testament of Judah the "spirit of promiscuity has wine as its servant,"[55] and if one "exceeds the limit, the spirit of error invades his mind."[56] Most curious is Judah's statement that "wine reveals the mysteries of God,"[57] which may show a connection between intoxication and ecstatic revelation. Aristotle connects intoxication with the reception of harmful visions: "Sometimes the visions appear confused and monstrous, and the dreams are morbid, as occurs with the melancholic, the feverish, and the intoxicated; for all these affections, being of spirit, produce much movement and confusion."[58] While ethical conduct is certainly the primary issue of which Paul speaks, Evans points out that "his addition of πληροῦσθε ἐν πνεύματι [plērousthe en pneumati] moves the thought away from wisdom themes to the religious and mystical."[59]

The idea that excessive drinking could put one at risk of experiencing negative spiritual influences makes sense within the Ephesian religious context in which Paul writes, but also within broader Jewish concerns about ethics. The issue for Paul is not just ecstatic drinking practices, but that these practices also include other immoral activities. Thus, his instructions to not be drunk, but to be filled *en pneumati*, makes sense, since Christian Spirit possession ought to bring about righteous living (Gal 5:23; 2 Tim 1:7).

Third, the connection between spiritual intoxication and singing also has parallels from ancient sources.[60] Plato speaks of how madness "takes hold upon a gentle and pure soul, arouses it and inspires it to songs and other poetry."[61] Elsewhere he states that wine "renders each man more ready and less ashamed to sing chants"[62] and that Dionysus is one of the three authors of "rhythm and harmony."[63] Lucian states that if one drinks their fill "they too will know Bacchic frenzy" and "then of a sudden he acquires

---

54. Philo, *Alleg. Interp.* 3.82.
55. T. Jud. 14:2.
56. T. Jud. 14:8.
57. T. Jud. 16:4.
58. *Parv. Nat.* 461A; cf. Plutarch, *Mor.* 377D.
59. Evans, "Ephesians 5:18–19," 190.
60. For more examples, see Howell, "Swapping Drinking Songs."
61. Plato, *Phaedr.* 245A.
62. Plato, *Leg.* 2.666C.
63. Plato, *Leg.* 2.672D.

a splendid voice, a distinct utterance, a silvery tone, and is as talkative."[64] Paul's immediate command to sing songs after a statement about abstaining from literal alcohol, but being filled with the Spirit, makes sense within the context of ASCs.

Finally, Eph 5:18–19 seems to imply a state of Spirit possession that results in content, namely inspired speaking, singing, and thanksgiving.[65] The connection of being *en pneumati* and Spirit-induced speech acts found in 1 Corinthians and the Didache should obviously be considered as important parallels. Some scholars, however, have tried to dismiss an "ecstatic" reading of this passage. For example, Neufeld states: "In Ephesians, being *filled with the Spirit* is not focused on ecstatic manifestations of the Spirit, as is the case in 1 Corinthians 14," though he admits "we will miss the energy and enthusiasm that is to pervade the corporate experience of the church if we allow no spillover from the image of intoxication."[66] Rudolf Schnackenburg likewise argues that "what in Philo is described as a condition of the soul (more precisely of the νοῦς [*nous*], the human reason) is in Eph. the effect of the divine Spirit."[67] Part of the rejection of the ecstatic reading of this passage comes from how scholars choose to interpret the phrase *en pneumati* here: "Interpretations of the verse depend on whether 'Spirit' is taken as a reference to the Holy Spirit or to the inner person, the nature of the verb *plēroō*, and the force of the preposition *en*."[68]

If one discounts the cases where *en pneumati* clearly does refer to ASCs, then this would make for a strong position. However, as we have seen, the ideas of spiritual intoxication, possession by spirits, ethical living, and ecstatic singing make sense primarily if read as a statement on ASCs and Christian Spirit possession, especially when read in tandem with parallel ancient sources related to these topics. In fact, other instances of the phrase *en pneumati* in Ephesians may tenably be read as instances of ASCs as well (Eph 2:2, 3:5, 6:18)! Thus, the British New Testament scholar Andrew T. Lincoln argues that Paul's intent is to "contrast between drunkenness and being possessed by the Spirit of God" because both "involve the self coming under the control of an external power, and the states of alcoholic and of religious intoxication were often compared."[69]

64. Lucian, *Bacch.* 5–7.

65. Long, *Kairos*, 172: "These adverbial participles indicate result. As such, they describe what it looks like to be filled with the Spirit. We might be surprised at what is present and what is lacking from Paul's description."

66. Neufeld, *Ephesians*, 239 (emphasis original).

67. Schnackenburg, *Epistle to the Ephesians*, 237.

68. See Brown and Whitehead, *Ephesians*.

69. Lincoln, *Ephesians*, 344.

Conclusion

ASCs occur frequently in the New Testament, especially in the Gospels and Acts, but also in various parts of the Pauline Epistles. In addition to explicit cases of trance and ecstasy, features such as verbal and motor automatisms can be deduced. Additionally, ASCs seem to be a feature of the Corinthian church and perhaps Jesus himself. Based on this evidence, and the fact that ASCs are not immediately always linked to spiritual gifts, it would seem that ASCs represent a biblically orthodox method of experiencing God whether one adheres to cessationist or charismatic theology. The New Testament contains what is a long tradition of ASCs in the Hebrew Bible and suggests that the God who never changes (Mal 3:6) continues to work in such extraordinary ways in the New Covenant.

8

Counterfeit Cocktails

> He does not know what he is saying and doing, for he has fallen into the ecstasy of folly.
>
> —Epiphanius, *Panarion* 48.5.8

WHEN TEACHING A COURSE called Spiritual Conflict Resolution (which might as well be renamed Defense Against the Dark Arts), my students often openly share their experiences with the demonic, though I personally would love to hear more stories about healing and prophecy! Yet, to cover all forms of ASCs in the Bible we must also consider those that are induced through less-than-kosher means—namely, those ASCs that are brought on through drugs, demonic activity, and other means. Admittedly, these are the ASCs that tend to get the most press among Christians. People often huddle around to hear fantastical stories of cross-cultural missionaries returning from the field to discuss cases of demonic possession, witchcraft, and other wild accounts. Ironically, these same Christians tend to be less inclined to listen to or accept stories of possession by God's Spirit, despite there being many examples from the Bible and contemporary accounts of such instances. Indeed, many Christians seem to be very quick to accept stories if they include demons, but not if they include angels!

I obviously think it is important, however, to talk about demon possession and related topics. Exorcism was an essential part of Jesus's earthly ministry and is still something that happens around the globe. The early

Christians were known for their effectiveness at exorcism and one would think that responsible training in this area would filter into seminaries. Alas, this is rarely the case.

Drugs and Magic

The use of drugs and other substances was a decidedly quick method of inducing an ASC for the purposes of divination or other occult practices.[1] We already catch wind of such aberrant altered states in the Greek version of Exod 7:11. There, Pharaoh summons the wise men and "sorcerers" (φάρμακος/*pharmakos*)[2] to deal with Moses's miraculous staff turning into a snake. The Septuagint translates the Hebrew term for sorcerers (כַּשָּׁף/*kaššāp*)[3] here as *pharmakos*. This word is related to the Greek word for "sorcery" or "magic" (φαρμακεία/*pharmakeia*)[4] and is where we get our English word "pharmaceutical."

This suggests that magicians in the ancient world relied on drugs for their sorcery. In the early Christian work Shepherd of Hermas, for example, the author tells the ecclesiastical authorities in the church to "be not ye like unto the sorcerers. The sorcerers indeed carry their drugs in boxes, but ye carry your drug and your poison in your heart."[5]

Evidently, the magicians' use of drugs was limited in power, as we see in the Greek version of Exod 8:18: "But the magicians also *tried to* do likewise by their use of drugs, potions, and spells to bring out the gnats, and yet they were not able."

While the differences between magic and medicine were often blurred in the ancient world, people still differentiated between a druggist/apothecary (φαρμᾰκοπώλης/*pharmakopṓlēs*)[6] and a sorcerer to some extent. The use of potions is listed among a series of tactics used in the ancient world found in a letter from the Neoplatonic philosopher Porphyry (ca. 234–ca. 305 CE). Indeed, Porphyry gives a laundry list of methods people used for entering ASCs for the purposes of divination.[7]

---

1. See Samorini, "Psychoactive Plants"; and Francia, "Plant-Based Potions." For medicinal uses, see Böck, "Mind-Altering Plants."
2. BDAG, s.v. "φάρμακος"; LSJ, s.v. "φάρμακος"; L&N, s.v. "φάρμακος."
3. DCH, s.v. "כשׁף."
4. BDAG, s.v. "φαρμακεία"; LSJ, s.v. "φαρμᾰκείᾱ."
5. Herm. Vis. 3.9.7.
6. LSJ, s.v. "φαρμᾰκοπώλης."
7. Porphyry, *Aneb.* 5–6: "But many, through enthusiasm and divine inspiration, predict future events, and are then in so wakeful a state, as even to energize according

Self-Mutilation

Another method of entering an altered state was through physical self-harm and mutilation.[8] One prayer found at the ancient site of Ugarit states: "The family is assembled to bend down (from grief) before the time, The in-laws stand darkly, My brothers are drenched in their blood like ecstatics [*aḫḫūa kīma maḫḫê damīšunu ramkū*], My sisters sprinkle pressed oil on me."[9] The most obvious example from the Hebrew Bible is that of the prophets of Baal in 1 Kgs 18:26-29 discussed previously. The prophets of Baal are said to "limp" (פסח/*psḥ*)[10] around the altar and "cut" (גדד/*gdd*)[11] themselves with various implements. That this results in them engaging in *hitnabbē* further suggests that this was the method used for inducing such a state.

Likewise, a passage from Zechariah may be read as an instance of physical self-harm being used to induce an ASC. Zechariah 13:2-6 discusses the judgment of false prophets and includes a number of deceptive answers the false prophets give to escape punishment.[12]

In addition to avoiding typical prophetic garb (13:4), the false prophet also states that the "wounds" (מַכָּה/*makkâ*)[13] on his back or chest (the wording is ambiguous)[14] are from the "house of my friends" (13:6).[15]

---

to sense, and yet they are not conscious of the state they are in, or at least, not so much as they were before. Some also of those who suffer a mental alienation, energize enthusiastically on hearing cymbals or drums, or a certain modulated sound. . . . But some energize enthusiastically by drinking water, as the priest of Clarius, in Colophon; others, by being seated at the mouth of a cavern, as those who prophesy at Delphi; and others by imbibing the vapour from water, as the prophetesses in Branchidae. Some also become enthusiastic by standing on characters, as those that are filled from the intromission of spirits. Others, who are conscious what they are doing in other respects, are divinely inspired according to the phantastic part; some, indeed, receiving darkness for a cooperator, others certain potions, but others incantations and compositions: and some energize, according to the imagination, through water; others in a wall, others in the open air, and others in the sun, or in some other of the celestial bodies. Some also establish the art of the investigation of futurity through the viscera, through birds, and through the stars."

8. See Lindblom, *Prophecy*, 5, 8-9, 43, 58-60.
9. See Steinert, "Ecstatic Experience," 373.
10. *HALOT*, s.v. "פסח"; BDB, s.v. "פָּסַח II"; *DCH*, s.v. "פסח II."
11. *DCH*, s.v. "גדד II"; BDB, s.v. "גָּדַד"; *HALOT*, s.v. "גדד I."
12. For more information, see the commentaries of Mark J. Boda and Al Wolters.
13. *DCH*, s.v. "מַכָּה"; *HALOT*, s.v. "מַכָּה."
14. Boda, *Zechariah*, 562-63.
15. Boda, *Zechariah*, 563, suggests that these "friends" or "lovers" (מְאַהֲבַי/*məʾahăbay*) might refer to homosexual pagan prostitution rites.

In a similar vein, an unnamed prophet in 1 Kgs 20:35 referred to as one of "the sons of the prophets" tells another man to "strike me [נכה/ *nkh*],[16] please," using the same Hebrew root found in Zech 13:6. Because the mention of wounds are found in parallel with deceptive practices of false prophets, it seems likely that they were interpreted by their adversaries as the marks of prophetic activity, i.e., blood letting or bruising for ecstatic prophecy.[17] Indeed, Carol L. Meyers and Eric M. Meyers conclude that "the individual who, like Amos, denies being a prophet, and who also dissociates from the clothing or marks of professional and/or ecstatic prophets, would thus be with friends rather than colleagues."[18]

Spirits

ASCs can also be brought on through the activity of spirits. One obvious case of such ecstasy appears in 1 Sam 18:10-11 where an "evil/harmful spirit" from God causes Saul to *hitnabbē*.[19] We may also consider the "slave girl who had a spirit of divination and brought her owners much gain by fortune-telling" (Acts 16:16). This "spirit of divination" or "python" spirit (πύθων/*pythōn*) "would entail a spirit like the one that possessed the Pythia, Apollo's oracular priestess, with what was considered highly reliable prophetic information."[20] The slave girl is also reported to "cry out" (κράζω/ *krazō*), a typical feature of possession (e.g., Mark 1:26).[21]

---

16. *DCH*, s.v. "נכה"; *HALOT*, s.v. "נכה"; BDB, s.v. "נָכָה."

17. Meyers and Meyers, *Zechariah 9–14*, 382: "Deuteronomy 14:1 contains an unambiguous biblical prohibition against self-laceration. However, it uses the root *gdd* (to cut), which is the same verb used of the Baal prophets in the Elijah passage mentioned above, and which also appears in Jeremiah in reference to a funerary custom of self-laceration (Jer 16:6; 41:5; 47:5; cf. Hos 7:14). Because the self-cutting both by the Baal prophets and by mourners apparently involved the flow of blood, the bruising signified by *nkh* would consequently not be included in the behavior prohibited by Deuteronomic law. Indeed, flogging (again, using the root *nkh*) is mandated in Deut 25:2 (cf. Prov 19:29). Thus, the negative connotations of bruising activities as practiced by ecstatic or professional prophets (see Petersen 1977: 35, 71), who are condemned by Second Zechariah for not speaking Yahweh's word, are derived from their association with prophets deemed false." See also Clark and Hatton, *Handbook*, 333–34.

18. Meyers and Meyers, *Zechariah 9–14*, 383.

19. Stokes, "What Is a Demon." Verbal automatisms from a demonic source may be found in Isa 8:19: "And when they say to you, 'Inquire of the mediums and the necromancers who chirp and mutter,' should not a people inquire of their God? Should they inquire of the dead on behalf of the living?"

20. Keener, *Acts*, 3:2422.

21. Cf. T. Sol. 1:12, 3:4; and Seneca, *Dial*. 7.26.8.

In other instances, a person may be in an ASC and experience spiritual activity even if that altered state was not brought on through spirits.

Consider the following passage from Job 4:13–18:

> Amid thoughts from visions of the night,
>> when deep sleep [*tardēmâ*] falls on men,
> dread came upon me, and trembling,
>> which made all my bones shake.
> A spirit glided past my face;
>> the hair of my flesh stood up.
> It stood still,
>> but I could not discern its appearance.
> A form was before my eyes;
>> there was silence, then I heard a voice:
> "Can mortal man be in the right before God?
>> Can a man be pure before his Maker?
> Even in his servants he puts no trust,
>> and his angels he charges with error."

Once again, the Hebrew word *tardēmâ* is being used in the context of visions, leading Marvin H. Pope to translate v. 13 as: "In a nightmare, in a trance, When slumber falls upon men."[22] It is difficult to know whether the spirit here is an "evil" spirit like the demons encountered in the New Testament or a spirit under the command of God (like 1 Sam 18:10–11; 1 Kgs 22:13–28).[23]

Another case of spiritual influence is the case of the necromancer at Endor. According to 1 Sam 28:1–25, a frustrated Saul is unable to hear God's voice through "dreams, the Urim, or by prophets" (v. 6). Despite him having driven out all the experts at divination from Israel (v. 3), Saul, in disguise, meets with a woman skilled in the art of necromancy in order that she might bring up the prophet Samuel for him. The Hebrew text refers to her as a "woman medium" (בַּעֲלַת־אוֹב/*baʻălat-'ôb*) or, more literally a "ghostwife."[24]

Although the exact identification of what this kind of spirit is remains elusive, similar titles for divination experts from the ANE suggest necromancy involving ancestral spirits is in view.[25] Possession through medium activity is also implicitly suggested in Lev 20:27 which may be translated as

---

22. Pope, *Job*, 34.

23. Harding, "Spirit of Deception."

24. McCarter, *I Samuel*, 417. Auld, *I & II Samuel*, 321, 325–26, offers "a bottle-mistress," suggesting that a bottle was used in divination much like a crystal ball.

25. *DDD*, s.v. "Spirit of the Dead אוב": "This designation is analogous in form and content to the Sumero-Akkadian name for necromancers, the *lú gidim.ma* 'man/master of the spirit of the dead' and *ša eṭemmi* '(master) of the spirit of the dead.'"

"a man or a woman whom in them there is an ʾov or yideʿoni shall be put to death" (my translation). That the spirits are said to be "in them" (בָּהֶם/ bāhem) suggests a possession state typical of mediumship.[26]

The Septuagint translates the woman's occupation as a γυναῖκα ἐγγαστρίμυθον/gynaika engastrimython—that is, a "female belly speaker" or "ventriloquist."[27] This translation appears to reflect the belief that some necromancers engaged in a practice known as *gastromancy* (divination through the stomach), which may have involved interpreting the sounds of stomach noises or using ventriloquism techniques to speak on behalf of the spirit that inhabited them.[28] Indeed, Carlson argues that the way Samuel appeared to Saul was not in the form of a visible apparition, but through the necromancer "hosting the spirit of Samuel within her body and speaking all of Samuel's words as his host."[29] In a somewhat humorous passage from the Mishnah we are told that Lev 20:27's prohibitions against necromancy refer to the "one who has a Python which speaks from his armpits" and the "one whose [spirit] speaks through his mouth."[30] Similarly, the Tosefta interprets the same passage as referring to those who have "a python which speaks from between his joints or from between his elbows" and "one who has the bone of a familiar spirit in his mouth."[31]

---

26. Langton, *Good and Evil Spirits*, 184–87; Pedersen, *Israel*, 4:482.

27. LSJ, s.v. "ἐγγαστρίμυθος." According to Plutarch, *Def. orac.* 9 (ca. 46 CE–ca. 119 CE): "When Ammonius had said this and I remained silent, Cleombrotus, addressing himself to me, said, 'Already you have conceded this point, that the god both creates and abolishes these prophetic shrines.' 'No indeed,' said I, 'my contention is that no prophetic shrine or oracle is ever abolished by the instrumentality of the god. He creates and provides many other things for us, and upon some of these Nature brings destruction and disintegration; or rather, the matter composing them, being itself a force for disintegration, often reverts rapidly to its earlier state and causes the dissolution of what was created by the more potent instrumentality; and it is in this way, I think, that in the next period there are dimmings and abolitions of the prophetic agencies; for while the god gives many fair things to mankind, he gives nothing imperishable, so that, as Sophocles puts it, "the works of gods may die, but not the gods." Their presence and power wise men are ever telling us we must look for in Nature and in Matter, where it is manifested, the originating influence being reserved for the Deity, as is right. Certainly it is foolish and childish in the extreme to imagine that the god himself after the manner of ventriloquists (who used to be called "Eurycleis," but now "Pythones") enters into the bodies of his prophets and prompts their utterances, employing their mouths and voices as instruments. For if he allows himself to become entangled in mens needs, he is prodigal with his majesty and he does not observe the dignity and greatness of his preeminence.'"

28. Salverte, *Occult Sciences*.

29. Carlson, *Unfamiliar Selves*, 55–56.

30. m. Sanh. 7:7.

31. t. Sanh. 10:6. According to b. Sanh. 65b, the bone speaks of its own accord.

The rabbis go on to say the necromancer makes use of a skull so that the spirit "comes up in the normal way" with the added bonus that such activity will succeed even on the Sabbath.³²

Occultic Objects

The practice of scrying, as we saw in the instance of Joseph's divination cup, is another method of entering an ASC. Obviously, false prophets, sorcerers, and the general populace made use of shiny surfaces and objects too. In one example, the king of Babylon uses a series of polished arrows seemingly in order to scry (Ezek 21:21).³³ Similarly, either through actual optical illusion or the construction of images in their mind's eyes, diviners are said to "see lies" (Zech 10:2). Likewise, those who consult "teraphim" (תְּרָפִים/*tərāpîm*) only hear "nonsense" (אָוֶן/*ʾāwen*). The exact method of how these cultic objects were used is unclear, though it perhaps involved some kind of necromantic ritual.³⁴

Other Means

Hypnotism and magical rites may also induce motor automatisms. According to the *Greek Magical Papyri*, a love spell involving complex incantations and ingredients culminates in speaking a magical formula into the ear of a young boy or man seven times with the result that "right away he will fall down."³⁵ In another case, if one does not wear the prescribed protective amulet, a goddess will "hurl them from aloft down to the ground."³⁶ A spell for an "evil sleep," perhaps a form of catalepsy, to come upon someone is elsewhere recorded with added instructions to continue if you want the person to die.³⁷ Similarly, we read of a "charm of Solomon that produces a trance" though the title of this spell literally translates to "Solomon's Collapse," which is interpreted by some as a kind of "ecstatic seizure."³⁸

---

32. t. Sanh. 10:7.
33. See Haupt, "Crystal-Gazing."
34. See Boda, *Zechariah*, 466–67.
35. *PGM* IV. 850–929; cf. *PDM* XIV. 1188–89.
36. *PGM* IV. 2505–09.
37. *PDM* XIV. 675–94; See Betz, *Greek Magical Papyri*, 232n473.
38. *PGM* IV. 850–929.

Scriptural Allegations

Elsewhere in this book I have addressed the criticism that spiritual intoxication must not be of God because it seemingly lacks self-control. I have attempted to demonstrate that this is not the correct understanding of the Greek term Paul uses in his writings and so does not speak to the issue of automatisms generally nor the topic of spiritual intoxication more specifically. There are, however, additional criticisms that must be addressed. A number of passages from both the Hebrew Bible and New Testament have been used by critics to suggest that, even if spiritual intoxication is real, its origins are strictly demonic or fleshly.

Several passages from Isaiah use imagery of drunkenness in relation to God's judgment and the activity of false religious leaders. The first of these is as follows:

> The LORD has mingled within her a spirit of confusion, and they will make Egypt stagger in all its deeds, as a drunken man staggers in his vomit. (Isa 19:14)

Isaiah 9:1–15 consists of an oracle spoken against Egypt's leaders and wise men with the result that the prophetic figures of Egypt are shamed by their lack of knowledge.

God's pouring out of a "spirit of confusion" is not to be understood in a pneumatological sense—that is, it is not that God is literally sending deceptive spiritual entities to cause the Egyptians to act drunk. Rather, "spirit" here refers to their mental or emotional dispositions. They are confused like drunk men in a metaphorical sense.[39]

This ought not to be interpreted as God literally making them outwardly appear drunk through automatisms or spiritual intoxication in the sense that we have been discussing throughout this book. The second oracle under consideration also follows this theme:

> These also reel with wine and stagger with strong drink; the priest and the prophet reel with strong drink, they are swallowed by wine, they stagger with strong drink, they reel in vision, they stumble in giving judgment. (Isa 28:7)

This oracle begins in Isa 28:1 with an address to the "proud crown of the drunkards of Ephraim." Levitical prohibitions against priests drinking strong drink (Lev 10:8–10) and the perpetual mention of alcohol throughout this oracle suggest that literal alcohol, not spiritual intoxication was the issue with the priests and prophets being judged here. The prophets were

---

39. Smith, *Isaiah 1–39*, 358.

possibly using alcohol to initiate ASCs and thus delivering false prophetic visions as a result.[40] Moreover, the rest of Isa 28 seems to assume that the main issue at hand is false teaching and the inadequacy of those doing the teaching: "To whom will he teach knowledge, and to whom will he explain the message? Those who are weaned from the milk, those taken from the breast?" (Isa 28:9). These rhetorical questions are meant to emphasize the ineptitude of the prophets, priests, and teachers in Israel during this time.[41]

Another passage from the minor prophet Micah discusses drunkenness in relation to false prophets:

> If a man should go about and utter wind and lies, saying, "I will preach to you of wine and strong drink," he would be the preacher for this people! (Mic 2:11)[42]

This passage is situated within a criticism of those who do not wish to hear the truth from the legitimate prophets of God concerning the need of repentance and coming judgment of oppressors. Micah's oracle is thus a condemnation that such oppressors would only listen to a prophet that speaks about prosperity and drunkenness. It is not, therefore, a descriptor of modern charismatics who preach about spiritual intoxication, nor a critique of automatisms relevant to that experience.

An oracle delivered against Babylon by Jeremiah includes "drunkenness" as well:

> Babylon was a golden cup in the Lord's hand, making all the earth drunken; the nations drank of her wine, and so the nations went mad. While they are inflamed I will prepare them a feast and make them drunk, that they may become merry, then sleep a perpetual sleep and not wake, declares the LORD. (Jer 51:7, 39)

Once again, drunkenness here is used metaphorically of those who taste of Babylon's wealth and wrath. The "sleep" that is mentioned here is meant to

---

40. Smith, *Isaiah 1–39*, 479–80. See also Van der Toorn, "Echoes of Judean Necromancy."

41. Childs, *Isaiah*, 206–7.

42. Hillers, *Micah*, 34, translates this passage as follows: "If a man possessed of a deceiving spirit lied thus: 'I will prophesy to you of wine and beer,' He would be just the prophet for this people." Barker and Bailey, *Micah, Nahum, Habakkuk, Zephaniah*, 68n74, however, states that "רוּחַ characterizes the lies of the liar and deceiver as 'windy' or 'empty,'" and this seems more likely. The NET humorously translates it as "a lying windbag," though the KJV seems to render it most accurately as "a man walking in the spirit and falsehood," whereby "spirit" refers to their disposition, not an actual pneumatic entity.

be understood as death, not as a way of speaking about the outward signs of a trance state.[43]

The following oracle from Isaiah is often used by opponents of ASCs to suggest that any drunk-like behavior among modern Pentecostals and charismatics is inherently a judgment from God:

> Astonish yourselves and be astonished; blind yourselves and be blind! Be drunk, but not with wine; stagger, but not with strong drink! For the LORD has poured out upon you a spirit of [*tardēmâ*], and has closed your eyes (the prophets), and covered your heads (the seers). (Isa 29:10)

That this drunkenness is explicitly connected with not drinking wine or strong drink suggests that some form of spiritual drunkenness is envisioned. This view is strengthened by the presence of the Hebrew term *tardēmâ*. Yet, the result of this spirit of *tardēmâ* being poured out is the absence of visionary and prophetic activity![44] Once again, the presence of "spirit" in the line may suggest that it is their disposition that is affected, not their literal physical actions. Indeed, this passage is quoted by Paul in Romans:

> What then? Israel failed to obtain what it was seeking. The elect obtained it, but the rest were hardened, as it is written, "God gave them a spirit of stupor, eyes that would not see and ears that would not hear, down to this very day." (Rom 11:7-8).

Paul thus interprets this oracle as having to do with a disposition of stubbornness rather than literal spiritual intoxication.

Conclusion

Critics of ASCs sometimes deduce that because similar experiences take place in non-Christian contexts, the origins of contemporary Christian ASCs must be of a dubious source. Automatism, for example, has often been associated with the occult practice of "automatic writing" (psychography), a technique whereby spirits control the hand of the medium to write messages. Additionally, many people point to the strange jerking motions found in Kundalini Hinduism.[45] These two examples highlight a common trend among critics of automatisms and other spiritual manifestations. The argument essentially boils down to looking at parallels within both movements

---

43. Huey, *Jeremiah, Lamentations*, 426-27; Lundbom, *Jeremiah 37-52*, 477.
44. Roberts, *First Isaiah*, 367-70; Childs, *Isaiah*, 218; Smith, *Isaiah 1-39*, 498-500.
45. On Kundalini and ASCs, see Greyson, "Physio-Kundalini Syndrome."

and drawing the conclusion that they must be derived from the same source (usually an evil spirit).[46] Setting aside the issue that this is not how comparative religious studies ought to operate as a discipline (and so its usefulness in discernment is very limited), there is also the more obviously problematic issue that adherents of other religions pray, sing, engage in ritual meals, etc., and no Christian defers these to the demonic within their own traditions. Such parallels obviously oversimplify cross-cultural religious expressions and contain logically deficient methods for discerning authentic manifestations of the Spirit.

A further argument sometimes proposed is that involving oneself in repetitive or monotonous worship settings or other contemplative practices either opens one up to demonic activity or that it produces a false ASC of some kind. It is a confusing argument that somehow listening to lengthy worship music would somehow draw in or make one susceptible to demonic forces. Indeed, music was often one of the chief methods of warding away evil spirits in Second Temple Judaism (and possibly based on David's success with Saul).

Additionally, the biblical evidence seems to suggest that musical accompaniment and lengthy rituals could induce an ASC that resulted in divine visions and prophecies. Hanegraaff, for example, argues that "biblical trance states like that experienced by Peter are sovereignly initiated, not self-induced or induced through human agency. In contrast, unbiblical trance states can be self-induced, induced through sociopsychological manipulation, or initiated by the touch of a shaman/sorcerer."[47] Hanegraaff seems to confuse trance and revelation as if they were synonymous. Yet, a trance state does not always result in a prophetic revelation, nor does every revelation necessary involve a trance state.

One of the major takeaways from the analysis of this book is that there are two ways of experiencing an ASC in the Bible. The first way involves a series of ritual actions that can be cultivated through practice or activated through these rituals. Music (1 Sam 10:5; 2 Kgs 3:15; 1 Chr 25:1), dance (1 Kgs 18:26), and other activities such as scrying (Gen 44:5, 15) or fasting (Acts 10:10) could be utilized to enter ASCs that facilitated the reception of

---

46. Nyske, "Is the Holy Spirit," 148–63, concludes that "it may be assumed that those who want to enter into contact with the supernatural entity, may choose from two different spiritual paths and probably, regardless of their choices, there is increased likelihood of experiencing the presence of the same spirit." Obviously, similarities between other religions and Christianity is helpful, but Nyske's conclusion about what is happening at the metaphysical level is quite the leap. Additionally, Nyske concludes that Christians are dependant on Hindu gurus for their practices but offers no citation for such a connection.

47. Hanegraaff, *Counterfeit Revival*, 204.

oracles. Additionally, group ASCs seem to be common in the ancient world. This is not surprising.

In the same way that people can get caught up in group celebrations, concerts, etc., ASCs are also contagious. This comes with the risk that some ASCs are faked or the product of hysteria, but does not preclude legitimate mass ASCs during worship or other venues. Cultivating an ASC does not somehow compel God to speak to the individual, nor does every ASC result in prophetic inspiration. Rather, the ASC postures the individual so that they are more likely to receive revelation. Such practice makes sense in light of God's word to Miriam and Aaron in Num 12:6–8:

> And he said, "Hear my words: If there is a prophet among you, I the Lord make myself known to him in a vision; I speak with him in a dream. Not so with my servant Moses. He is faithful in all my house. With him I speak mouth to mouth, clearly, and not in riddles, and he beholds the form of the Lord. Why then were you not afraid to speak against my servant Moses?"

Because God speaks in riddles, the ASC of the prophet allows them to bypass natural distractions and focus on God's revelation of the meaning of the riddle. In other instances, the motor automatisms resulting from the ASC itself is evidence of God's Spirit. This appears to be the case with the elders of Israel, Saul, and the itinerant prophets of 1 Samuel.

The second (more common) way in the Bible that one experiences an ASC is directly by God. I refer to these as "uninduced" because they are initiated without any ritual actions on the part of the recipient, despite being "induced" by God. This reality is evident at a grammatical level. God is said to "have caused" a trance to fall on Adam in Gen 2:21.[48] Likewise, Abraham does not "fall into a trance," rather a trance "falls on" Abraham. It is unfortunate that English translations in some passages obscure the connection between the verb and its subject. While the ESV translates Acts 10:10 as "he [Peter] fell into a trance," for example, the actual Greek text states that it is the trance that fell on Peter! ASCs were also brought on by God either through a form of Spirit possession or through God's hand touching the individual (which is likely a metaphorical way of speaking *about* Spirit possession). While the prophets in 1 Sam 10 and 19 may have used instruments to induce their ASC, Saul is "rushed upon" by the Spirit of God and later the

---

48. The Hebrew word "to fall" in this passage is from the root נָפַל/*naphal*. It occurs in the *hiphil* conjugation, meaning that it is communicating that the subject of the sentence is "causing" something to occur. The LXX renders it likewise: ἔκστασιν ἐπὶ τὸν Αδαμ/*ekstasin epì tòn Adam*.

Spirit "comes upon" him.[49] The elders of Israel are also imputed a portion of the Spirit that invokes their ASC, as is the frenzied call to arms of the Israelite army in 1 Sam 11.

The induced ASC and the uninduced ASC do not seem to differ in their quality. Physical and verbal automatisms, visions, and other prophetic features appear to be part of both. Nor do there seem to be prohibitions put in place for induced ASCs anywhere in the Scriptures, aside from those that are induced through occultic or illegitimate means.

The use of repetitious worship music in contemporary church culture, while monotonous to some (and this is a personal preference), does not seem to be a disqualified means of inducing an ASC. While meaningless emotionalism is always a concern for modern worshipers, there is nothing inherently wrong with using music to become more susceptible to God's voice and to avoid outward distraction.

A colleague of mine recently told me about his experience growing up in a charismatic church where religious ecstasy and trance were commonplace. People were often slain in the Spirit or spoke in tongues, and he was witness to other manifestations. In an effort to see how serious the church was, he decided to fake these manifestations to see whether anyone could discern it as counterfeit. According to him, no one was able to see a difference between his fake manifestation and that of those who claimed to be experiencing genuine spiritual phenomena.

People in the ancient world also knew that an ASC could be the product of fakery. According to Josephus, a number of citizens gathered around the temple during a time of political turmoil and "indulged in transports of frenzy [ἐδαιμονία / edaimonia: "possessed by a god"] and fabricated oracular utterances."[50] Likewise, the false prophet who speaks *en pneumati* and asks for food or money in the Didache may be someone who is pretending to be in an ASC to con onlookers.[51]

This is why instructions are given in the New Testament and early Christian literature to discern between true and false prophets (1 Thess 5:20–21; 1 John 4:1–6; cf. Phil 1:9–10; Heb 4:10; 5:15) and in some instances this might require unique spiritual giftings (1 Cor 12:10).[52]

---

49. 1 Sam 10:6 uses the Hebrew word צָלַח/*ṣlḥ* and can also have the meaning of "penetrate" or "advance" or even "be successful." The LXX translates the word *ṣlḥ* with the Greek term ἐφαλεῖται/*ephaleitai* which means to "leap upon." In the similar account of 1 Sam 19:23, the Spirit of God is simply said to "come upon him" (עָלָיו/'*ālāyw*).

50. Josephus, *J.W.* 1.347. Whiston's edition of this text is problematic. See Aune, *Prophecy in Early Christianity*, 137.

51. Did. 11:7–12.

52. Fitzmyer, *First Corinthians*, 468.

Should this cause us to discount all experiences of this nature? Of course not. In the same way that people can fake emotions or mislead people about the intentions of their actions, people can also fake certain manifestations. We do not think that happiness or sadness are not real just because people feign them in certain instances. Likewise, we cannot use our experience as a litmus test for discerning ASCs.[53]

Like other spiritual practices such as prayer and fasting, ASCs can be found in other religious traditions. This does not mean that they are inherently illegitimate because they might share outward similarities with other faiths.

Similarly, occult activity that utilizes ASCs such as fortune telling should not cast doubt and suspicion on Christian prophetic expression that includes ASCs. Interpreting spiritual intoxication as a form of judgment from God seems to be based on a lack of contextual considerations and exegetical work of the passages just considered. While some ASCs may be from demons, drugs, or the flesh, the discernment process between such counterfeit trances and ecstasies should not be based solely on outward observations such as automatisms. Rather, one needs to discern the content of such manifestations, both the substance of what is being spoken and whether any meaningful long-term life change can be demonstrated from the experience.

---

53. Witherington, *Jesus the Seer*, 6: "Ecstasy certainly cannot by itself help to distinguish true from false prophecy."

9

Eliminating and Illuminating Ecstasy in the Church

> Gifts are free, but maturity is expensive.
> —Bill Johnson, *Spiritual Java*

GIVEN THE VARIOUS EXAMPLES of ASCs in the Bible, many of which are brought on by the Spirit of God, why is it that modern Christians consider them as something taboo or inherently demonic? Are such criticisms of ASCs a manifestation of modernism, intellectualism, and antisupernaturalism? Are people trying to suppress ASCs in their churches? The current chapter seeks to answer such questions.

While an entire analysis of church history is not within the scope of this book, I will highlight some of the most prominent reasons why ASCs were viewed with great suspicion and how this might inform current Christian praxis.

First, it should be noted that there is some evidence in the biblical text of historical and religious developments in the attitude toward ASCs. While in early Israelite religion various rituals may have been used to cultivate prophetic ASCs, such as music and ritual singing or through materials like Joseph's use of a divination cup for the purposes of lecanomancy, the trajectory of the Hebrew Bible is away from such technical arts and toward prophetic centrality within the temple priesthood and court prophets using prescribed methods of deciding God's will (e.g., lots, Urim and Thummim), and visionary/auditory prophetic experiences initiated by God through dreams and ASCs.

This can be seen most clearly in the prophets where ASCs seem to be induced by divine intervention and not human action and even in the postexilic writings of Chronicles where verbal automatisms become more normative in the literature. Thus, at least in *some* way we can see that attitudes toward ASCs may have shifted over time within the Hebrew Bible.

In the New Testament era, possession by the Spirit of God must have been normative enough for Paul's instructions in 1 Cor 12–14 to make sense, and instances throughout Acts support the idea that ASCs were a byproduct of the Spirit. While early Christians appear to have accepted and practiced ecstatic prophecy and automatism, by the end of the second century onward, this form of prophetic activity was viewed with suspicion by some Christian writers.[1] This shift in perspective was due to a general decline of regular ecstasy in church gatherings and the rise of the Montanists. The Montanists were a group of ecstatic prophets lead by a man named Montanus and two prophetesses, Priscilla and Maximilla. They considered themselves "The New Prophets" of the postapostolic age. Disputes about the legitimacy of the Montanist movement were heavily centered around whether prophetic ecstasy was a genuine expression of God's revelation to Israel and the church.[2] Some writers had difficulty accepting the Montanists' form of ecstasy since it seemed to displace the human mind while the agent was under Spirit possession.[3] The African apologist Tertullian, for example, while defending the Montanist prophetic practice, states:

> And therefore, because it was "in the spirit" that he had now spoken, and not in his natural senses, he could not know what he had said.[4]

Epiphanius (ca. fourth–fifth century CE), bishop of Salamis, Cyprus, on the other hand, condemns the practice:

> He does not know what he is saying and doing, for he has fallen into the ecstasy of folly.[5]

---

1. Epiphanius, *Pan.* 48.3.11–4.3. Trevett, *Montanism*, 88 states: "While Justin and Athenagoras had allowed that the prophets of old had spoken in ecstasy, anti-Prophecy writers seem not to have agreed. It was clear wits, said Epiphanius, and not derangement, which characterized the true prophet (*Panarion* xlviii. 7,8)."

2. Origen, *Princ.* 3.3.4 and *Cels.* 7.

3. On other reasons why Montanism was rejected, see Vokes, "Opposition to Montanism"; Ash, "Decline of Ecstatic Prophecy"; and Frend, "Montanism."

4. Tertullian, *Marc.* 4.22.5.

5. Epiphanius, *Pan.* 48.5.8.

According to some early Christian authors, the ecstasy of a prophet could signal either divine or demonic possession, requiring some practical criteria and spiritual discernment to differentiate the two.[6] Thus, Eugene C. Tibbs explains the rise of criticism concerning prophetic ecstasy this way:

> Early Christians faced two formidable realities that complicated discerning automatisms: 1) true and false spirits manifested identical ecstatic symptoms in a prophet; and 2) deceptive spirits were believed, at times, to behave and speak like true ones. As Christian communities grew more diverse and widespread throughout the ancient Mediterranean basin, these phenomena dwindled as prophets became scarcer and a clerical bishopric matured with an authoritative voice. . . . Thus, prophecy was spotty and many Christian congregations may have gone without experiencing prophets. The increasingly tenuous presence of prophecy throughout the second century made automatism—as true prophecy—unrecognizable to some church leaders, a situation that guided their judgment concerning its impropriety in the church when it resurfaced in Montanism. Discerning the ethics of prophetic agency in early Christian culture stood on the shifting sands of competing views on the nature of true and false prophecy.[7]

We saw in the Didache that prophets who were in an ecstasy and asked for money, lodging, or food were viewed as false prophets. Early Christians who were concerned about discerning between the spirit of truth and error often interpreted the command in 1 John 4 as dealing with prophecies, and thus the utterances, lifestyle, and doctrine of the prophets were scrutinized. Clint Tibbs thus concludes that:

> The coexistence of divine and demonic possession in early Christian culture accounted for the problem of deceptive spirits masquerading as holy ones through prophets. The headwaters of ambiguous spirit identity then originated in the belief that good and evil spirits may speak familiarly about Jesus and the Gospel through a prophet (2 Cor 11:4). This was the actual setting of early Christian prophecy.[8]

---

6. Herm. Mand. 11.3; Clement, *Strom.* 1.17, 6.8, 14.14; Tertullian, *1 Apol.* 47. On the general nature of discerning spirits and its relationship to prophecy, see Moberly, "Test the Spirits"; Aune, *Prophecy in Early Christianity*, 224–25; Brown, *Spirit*, 235–59; and Burge, "Spirit-Inspired Theology."

7. Tibbs, "Do Not Believe Every Spirit," 50.

8. Tibbs, "Possession Amnesia," 36.

Aside from the Montanists, ecstatic Christian movements throughout church history include the so-called Desert Fathers, later church mystics, Quakers, Shakers, and Pentecostals. Not all of these movements, naturally, are without their problems, such as those involved in the "Münster Rebellion," a millenarian sect of the Anabaptists that took over the city of Münster in Germany in order to usher in the kingdom of God, accompanied by ecstatic prophets running through the streets naked. ASCs can certainly be used to justify terrible beliefs and practices. But it does not take charismatic extremes to cause abuse. Leaders and lay people alike from all denominations and theological proclivities can use extremes to systematically abuse people.

Legalism, authoritarianism, and other systems of control can be used whether one is involved in a church that experiences ASCs or not. In some instances, ASCs are not used as the rationale for abuse at all. Instead, appeal to unbiblical interpretations is used to enforce hostile and toxic church environments. One would scarcely suggest that, therefore, we ought to remove Bible reading and interpretation from our church gatherings.

In terms of pragmatism, however, it is no wonder why Christian authorities may have wanted to quell ASCs in church gatherings. When one no longer had to deal with the (sometimes subjective) discernment process of determining which ASCs were of divine origin and those that were devious counterfeits, it likely made for a smoother ecclesiology. Moreover, it was probably easy for Christian authorities to point to aberrant sectarian movements and their strange behaviors and conflate their teachings and ASCs with the demonic, thus drawing a further, albeit unwarranted, connection between ASCs and the demonic more generally.

Despite criticisms, other church authorities seemingly were okay with ASCs. Such diverse views on ASCs in the early church should give us pause in modern times when discussing the issue. I suspect that just as Christians will continue to divide over topics of miniscule importance, topics that relate to God's manifestations will cause even further debate regardless of the scriptural evidence. Sectarianism and the elevation of particular theologians or systems of doctrine will often deter the skeptical from broaching a topic as difficult and uncomfortable as ASCs and those who are trying to convince others of their legitimacy must do so with great patience and grace.

Discernment certainly involves a process of biblical study and that is what this book has attempted to accomplish. But it is also true that discernment is rooted in relationship. When it comes to discerning strange manifestations of the Spirit, we do not have a long list of which physical symptoms are from God or not. Nor are we given insight into the exact mechanics of how one should experience an ASC.

When one looks at the strange events of the Bible, however, one is struck by the trust in God's character. Sacrificing your son, splitting seas, speaking to rocks for water, being spoken to in opaque riddles, filling jars with water at parties that are lacking wine, and catching fish to pay your taxes all involve a level of intimacy with the one asking you to do such things. One is only able to discern the true from the false based on an intimate relationship. If this is true of mundane day-to-day things, how much more is it necessary for spiritual things.

Examples of ASCs in Church History

At the beginning of this book, I listed a number of examples of people experiencing ASCs in modern church contexts. While this book does not attempt to be an exhaustive list of examples of ASCs throughout church history, I will mention a few such instances here. I also want to highlight some examples where physiological features of ASCs are mentioned, especially when they resemble drunkenness.

Many of the desert fathers experienced ASCs that include some level of descriptive physiological features. The Armenian monk John the Sabaite (sixth century CE) recalls a story about leaving his desert monastery to visit a fellow Christian. While visiting, John asked the man about another Christian who had a bad reputation and, upon hearing the report that his behavior had not changed, is said to have vocalized a short "ah!" before being "carried away by sleep as though in an ecstasy" where he had a vision of Golgotha.[9] This seems to be a case of verbal automatism brought on through a spontaneous ASC. In one instance, a certain Zachariah, a disciple of an abbot named Silvanus, entered a building and found the abbot "in a trance, his hand stretched out to heaven." Closing the door, Zachariah later returned asking the abbot what was going on. When the abbot attempted to dissuade him that anything had happened, Zachariah grabbed onto the abbot's feet and demanded to tell him or he wouldn't let go. Silvanus eventually acquiesced and told him that he had been "snatched away" to heaven and saw the glory of God.[10] Another story involving Silvanus is reported where he "went into a trance and fell on his face" (a motor automatism?) and after a long time got up weeping. When asked why he was crying, he stated that

---

9. *Sayings of the Holy Elders* N.761bis. Translations from Wortley, *Anonymous Sayings of the Desert Fathers.*

10. *Book of the Elders* Silvanus 3. Translations from Wortley, *Book of the Elders.*

"I was snatched away to the judgment, and I saw many wearing our habit going off to punishment and many worldlings going off into the kingdom."[11]

Trance-induced visions of the afterlife or judgment scenes seem to be common among the desert fathers. An anonymous Christian, who had previously been impeded by his own mother from pursuing an ascetic lifestyle, left home and squandered his time and eventually became ill. After his mother died, this Christian is said to have fallen into a trance and was "whisked away to the judgement," where he saw his ill-fated mother.[12] One elder falls into a trance and sees a "glorious place" where crowns are hanging above a throne.[13]

Likewise, John Colobos recalls that "I saw one of the elders in a trance, and here there were three elders standing on the other shore of the sea. A voice came to them from the other shore, saying, 'Take wings of fire and come to me.' Two of them took [wings] and flew to the other shore, but the other remained [there], weeping and crying out. Wings were eventually given to him, not of fire but feeble and weak. He got to the other side, being thrown into the sea as he toiled and getting up out of it with great difficulty. So it is with this generation: if it receives wings, they will still not be of fire; it will scarcely receive feeble and weak ones" (brackets original to source).[14]

Others experience an ASC in order to lead them to repentance. In one such instance, a man who had been told negative things about a local priest no longer wanted to receive the "holy mysteries" from him and slammed the door in the priest's face. Afterward, the man fell into a trance and saw "a golden well and a golden cord with a golden bucket," which was interpreted to be a sign for him to reinvite the priest back into his house.[15]

Saint Isaac the Syrian (seventh century CE) regularly discusses ecstasy in his works. He states, for example, that "constant solitude, with recitation and moderate food, easily arouse in the spirit a state of ecstasy, if perpetual solitude be not broken."[16] Isaac sometimes remarks on the physiological features of ecstasy as well. In one instance he describes ecstasy as "intoxication" or "drunkenness": "To think about Him and to dare foster such thoughts for the sake of delight and to get drunk at all times by ecstatic impulses as in the life after resurrection, are things greatly promoted by solitude, because

---

11. *Book of the Elders* Silvanus 2.
12. *Sayings of the Holy Elders* N.135/3.38 BHG 1444nb.
13. *Sayings of the Holy Elders* N.211/7.52.
14. *Book of the Elders* John Colobos 14.
15. *Sayings of the Holy Elders* N.254/9.16.
16. Isaac the Syrian, *On the Short Paths Towards God* 139. Translations from Wensinck, *Mystic Treatises by Isaac of Nineveh*.

the intellect has the opportunity of being with itself, in the peace that has its origin in solitude."[17] Elsewhere, he states "he to whom this contemplation happens becomes as a corpse without soul, in ecstasy."[18]

Along these same lines, Isaac believed that the biblical prophets "did not perceive any of the usual things nor could they use their thoughts at will nor had they any sensual apperceptions, because they were in ecstasy."[19] Evidently, the idea that ecstasy involved abnormal physical gestures as well as psychological disruption of the senses was not foreign to Christians during this period, despite being centuries removed from the Montanists.

The famous stigmatic, Saint Francis of Assisi (thirteenth century CE) is claimed to have had a number of miracles attributed to him, ecstasy being among them. Bonaventure's hagiography of Francis, for example, states that upon hearing the voice of God "Francis trembled, being alone in the church, and was astonished at the sound of such a wondrous Voice, and, perceiving in his heart the might of the divine speech, was carried out of himself in ecstasy."[20] Francis's ecstasies were often so intense that he was unable to perceive the world around him: "Ofttimes he was rapt in such ecstasies of contemplation as that he was carried out of himself, and, while perceiving things beyond mortal sense, knew naught of what was happening in the outer world around him."[21] In one case, Francis's ecstasy is likened to drunkenness. According to Bonaventure, while fasting and contemplating God, Francis "became like one inebriated in spirit, and rapt out of himself in ecstasy."[22]

The prolific author and mystic Teresa of Avila (sixteenth century CE) often speaks of ecstasy or "rapture," and discusses some of the psychological and physiological features of the experience. She states that after one endures a "deep rapture," they may experience a kind of "frenzy" and lack the full range of their mental faculties for a short time.[23] She also likens ecstasy to drunkenness in her autobiography: "With all this happening, the time spent in prayer may last, and does last, for some hours; for, once the two faculties have begun to grow inebriated with the taste of this Divine wine,

17. Isaac the Syrian, *Treatise in Questions and Answers* 254.
18. Isaac the Syrian, *On Various Experiences During Prayer* 164.
19. Isaac the Syrian, *On the Revelations and Powers* 155.
20. Bonaventure, *Life of Saint Francis of Assisi* 2.1.
21. Bonaventure, *Life of Saint Francis of Assisi* 10.2.
22. Bonaventure, *Life of Saint Francis of Assisi* 9.2. Compare the story of the Christian martyr Perpetua (ca. 180–203 CE) who was said to be "roused from what seemed like sleep, so completely had she been in the Spirit and in ecstasy." *Passion of Saints Perpetua and Felicity* 6.3 (ANF 3:705).
23. Peers, *Complete Works of Saint Teresa*, 1:293.

they are very ready to lose themselves in order to gain the more, and so they keep company with the will and all three rejoice together."[24]

In her work *Interior Castle*, Teresa makes a point to differentiate between ecstasy and emotionalism, stating that "it must be understood that I am referring to genuine raptures, and not to women's weaknesses, which we all have in this life, so that we are apt to think everything is rapture and ecstasy."[25] Despite her self-deprecation of women generally, Teresa's point is that, even though ecstasy does often involve an elation of the emotions, emotions themselves are not ecstasy. Her words ought to be taken to heart by some modern Christian movements who often conflate the two.

During the first Great Awakening in the early 1700s, Jonathan Edwards writes of the revival meetings that "it was a very frequent thing to see a house full of outcries, faintings, convulsions, and such like, both with distress, and also with admiration and joy."[26] Using our system of categorization, such outcries, faintings, and convulsions are best understood as verbal and motor automatisms. In another case, one of Edwards's critics records that at one meeting two women "fell down unable to walk ... (and) continued in a Sort of Extasie [sic], either lying as though in a Sleep, or uttering extatic Expressions of Joy, of the Love of Christ, and of Love to Him; of Concern for the Souls of Sinners, and the like."[27]

In some instances, Edwards sensed that certain people were taking advantage of the phenomenon for fleshly gratification and elevation and were being deceived by the devil.[28] Evidently, however, Edwards did not always discourage such manifestations, as he also writes, "If such things are enthusiasm, and the fruits of a distempered brain, let my brain be evermore possessed of that happy distemper! If this be distraction, I pray God that the world of mankind may be all seized with this benign, meek, beneficent, beatifical, glorious distraction!"[29]

One of the most influential historical characters for early Pentecostalism's ASCs is Maria Woodworth-Etter (1844–1924), whose evangelistic

24. Peers, *Complete Works of Saint Teresa*, 1:110.
25. Peers, *Complete Works of Saint Teresa*, 2:287.
26. Edwards, "Distinguishing Marks," 91.
27. Chauncy, *Seasonable Thoughts*, 126–29.
28. Edwards, "To the Reverend," 120: "There were some instances of persons lying in a sort of trance, remaining for perhaps a whole twenty-four hours motionless ... but in the meantime under strong imaginations, as though they went to Heaven, and had there a vision of glorious and delightful objects. But when the people were raised to this height, Satan took the advantage ... a great deal of caution and pains were found necessary to keep the people, many of them, from running wild."
29. Edwards, *Thoughts on the Revival*, 378.

ministry was accompanied by healing and mass trances. Woodworth-Etter, who was given a number of nicknames including the "trance evangelist," received plenty of criticism from Christians and skeptics alike. One report states:

> Thursday night five more were in a trance, and a man operating a restaurant was in a like condition for several hours at his place of business. Many went to see him. He had one hand uplifted and eyes wide open, and seemed to be muttering a prayer. When he came from under its influence he praised the Lord for an hour or more.... Saloons closed doors early in the evening to attend the meetings, and the different "poker dens" shut up shops, and the inmates wended their way to church.[30]

In the 1990s, American evangelist Rodney Howard-Browne became known as "God's Bartender."[31] This title reflects a common feature of Howard-Browne's ministry in which attendants commonly appear drunk, laugh

---

30. "Trance Evangelism." Other reports are worth sharing as well. The *Gazette* reports in "Sister Woodworth Names Her Date": "The announcement yesterday afternoon that Mrs. Woodworth, the evangelist, was in a trance caused hundreds of people to make a break for the place of meeting. She lay on the platform from 2:30 in the afternoon until 8:30 at night before recovering her senses. The daughter of John Malone soon after was similarly affected, and so death-like was her appearance that some of the members thought that she was dying, and her father was summoned. As he was known to be a man of violent temper, trouble was looked for. He was aroused from sleep, and at once commenced vowing all kinds of vengeance on Mrs. Woodworth and her assistants, keeping it up until he was inside the church. He soon weakened, however, and in ten minutes he was the noisiest convert in town, praising the Lord and shouting that he was glad he had found Christ."

The *New York Times* reports in "Said to Be Religion.": "Mrs. Woodworth, a lady evangelist, still continues with the most unusual manifestations.... Scores have been stricken down at these meetings, and whatever form the limbs or body chance to assume in that position, immovable as a statue, they remained—sometimes the hands were uplifted far above the head, the eyes open wide, and not a muscle of the entire body moved; they were as immovable as in death. Many have gone to these meetings in a spirit of jest, and were the first to be under the influence pervading the assembly. The people are wonderfully excited, and neighbor asks neighbor, 'What is it?' It is what is known as catalepsy, or is it a form of ecstasy where the mind absorbs an idea until every faculty of the soul is under its control, and the body becomes stilled as though dead—naught by circulation and the act of respiration remain to signify life. The features are as pale as marble, the pulse weak and feeble. This morning a young lady was found in a trance or ecstasy in bed and could not be aroused for hours. The eyes were lifted to the ceiling and the hand pointed to heaven. When she was restored to consciousness she shouted, clapped her hands, and sang 'hallelujah' for an hour, and said she was perfectly oblivious and totally unconscious to all about her. Is it contagious or infectious, epidemic or endemic, good or evil?"

31. Carnes, "Howard-Browne Takes New York."

uncontrollably, shake, and fall to the floor during services. Howard-Browne's ministry in America began in 1987, and he has conducted revival meetings in over 350 cities around the world with an estimated seventy-five thousand conversions recorded as of 1995.[32] Howard-Browne's revivalism is what set the spark of the Toronto Blessing through Randy Clark and John Arnot in 1993.

The nonprofit ministry Iris Global (formerly Iris Ministries) was founded by Heidi and Rolland Baker in 1980 and is best known for its poverty relief, evangelism, and signs and wonders.[33] In 1995 the Bakers moved to Mozambique where reports of healings now abound.[34] Heidi holds a doctorate in systematic theology from King's College London and Rolland holds a doctorate in ministry from United Theological Seminary. Of the two, Heidi has received the most attention, especially because of her preaching style in America in which she commonly exhibits ecstatic phenomena. Many videos show Heidi on stage attempting to preach while continually falling down, spontaneously jerking, and speaking into a microphone face down on the floor.[35] Heidi states that the extreme motor automatisms she experiences while preaching in America do not occur while she ministers in Africa. When she asked God why this is the case, she reports that God is using her body as a sign and a wonder against American sensibilities of individualistic autonomy and control. Despite this, ecstatic phenomena still frequently take place among those the Bakers themselves minister to in Africa.

The "Joy Apostles," Georgian and Winnie Banov also commonly experience religious ecstasy. After escaping the communist regime in Eastern Europe, Georgian encountered the Jesus People of the 1960s and "the heavens opened and there he was at the edge of the Throne Room. Balls of fire started falling on his chest burning through him, one after another with God's passionate love as Georgian was being baptized in the Holy Spirit and fire."[36] Using music as an avenue for reaching the lost, they served in North America, Europe, Africa, Australia, and New Zealand, speaking to over two hundred thousand at meetings in Bulgaria alone. In addition to hosting conferences and ministry training, their ministry Global Celebration is involved in "rescuing and caring for trafficked and at-risk children, helping

---

32. Riss, "Howard-Browne, Rodney M," 774.
33. Baker, "Iris Story."
34. Brown et al., "Study of Therapeutic Effects."
35. See, for example, Proverbs1:7Truth, "Drunken Delusion of Heidi Baker."
36. Global Celebration, "History," para. 3.

marginalized impoverished communities" in Nicaragua, India, Burma, Thailand, Mexico, Cambodia, and the Philippines.[37]

John Crowder is the dean of Cana New Wine Seminary, author, and editor of a biannual theological journal titled *The Ecstatic Magazine*, who reports that he experienced salvation after meeting Jesus through an acid trip.[38] Crowder's emphasis at Cana is on a mystical brand of Christianity and spiritual drunkenness as "a unique marriage of life-transforming, happy theology woven seamlessly with the intoxicating practice of the presence of God."[39] Crowder hosted an event called "Sloshfest" where he can be viewed dressed in monk robes preaching quite soberly.[40] His YouTube channel consists mostly of coherent theological teachings against what he considers aberrant inner-healing ministries and charismatic extremes. Additionally, he preaches globally in countries such as India, Ethiopia, and Thailand, among the most marginalized of society, including lepers, transgender people, and the poor.[41]

Conclusion

Naturally, I am not affirming all of these individuals' theology. From a missiological standpoint, however, there is no denying that gospel expansion has taken place through these odd manifestations. This is not to mention the countless others who were impacted by these individuals and subsequently have brought the gospel to unreached people groups as a result. Whatever one makes of the theological proclivities of groups like Bethel, Hillsong, Pensacola, and the Toronto Blessing movements, one must distinguish between what the Bible says about such manifestations, their modern expressions, and the groups impacted. Poisoning the well and using guilt by association to anathematize such practices is neither exegesis nor discernment.

---

37. Global Celebration, "Bio."
38. Crowder, "About Us," para. 2; and "High on Jesus," para. 17.
39. Crowder, "About Cana," para. 2.
40. Blisscoco, "Sloshfest."
41. Crowder, "Glory in Ethiopia"; "Miracles, Exorcisms & Fun in India"; and "Thailand Transvestite Mission."

Conclusion

The Supernatural Love of God

> An emphasis on ecstasy without an emphasis on comprehension is a distortion of the experience of the early church . . . an emphasis on comprehension without an equal emphasis on ecstasy is a distortion of the experience of the early church.
>
> —Jack Levison, *Inspired*

THE GREAT AWAKENINGS IN America, Azusa Street, the Welsh Revival, the Brownsville Revival, and the Toronto Blessing represent some of the most shocking displays of ASCs in recorded church history.[1] While in earlier cases we only have written evidence, in modern times we have videographic documentation that continues to amaze and offend those investigating these phenomena. Theological considerations about the place of ASCs and church growth are worth considering. Luke's account of the birth of the church and subsequent missionary expansion in Acts are both jump-started through ASCs. For Peter, the mission to the gentiles finds its premise in the promises given to Abraham which was confirmed via a trance state. If missionary expansion is still happening in modern times, we should not be surprised that God would use ecstatic experiences to jump-start such ministries and movements.

---

1. For more details on these manifestations in recent church history, I suggest Taves, *Fits, Trances, and Visions*.

While we are not always given clear physiological descriptions of the ASCs experienced in the Scriptures, God often uses trances and ecstasies as a vehicle for communicating. It is worth noting that in most circumstances the result of the ASC is often a form of embarrassment or uncomfortableness. Paul is struck blind for three days, Peter must come to grips with eating with unclean gentiles, and Abraham is struck with "terrible darkness" and told his descendants will be placed in slavery in Egypt. Yet, the theme of ASCs in the biblical text also reflects a concern for global missions which can be traced throughout Acts and is rooted in the Abrahamic trance. We should not be surprised, therefore, that contemporary Pentecostal-charismatic advancements in world missions are initiated or bolstered through ASCs as well. We are not given a list of outward signs to determine whether a manifestation is from God or not, rather we should look to the fruit of those experiences to validate their genuineness.

Those within the Pentecostal-charismatic movement understand these experiences as a means to transcend typical sense-perceptive models for understanding the world and missions. That is to say that these ASCs facilitate a suspension of what one considers logical procedures for ministry and instead rely on the outwardly absurd as a means to transcend what is typically possible. While such an approach may invite mockery from the uninitiated, it appears that ecstatic experiences promote deep emotional impact on the recipient, often initiating ministry endeavors that everyday Christians might not even consider attempting.

In the introduction I noted that ASCs are often accompanied by feelings of euphoria, and modern testimonies of their value range from repentance from sin and dead works to healing from depression and anxiety. From a purely utilitarian perspective, their positive value is relatively obvious. Condensing the role of ASCs into one uniform purpose does an injustice to why God uses such means to accomplish his will. Taking the biblical data as a guideline we can see that ASCs accomplish a number of God's objectives and roles within the human experience. God empowers his people through ASCs to accomplish the tasks put before them, whether leading his people (such as with the elders of Israel), confirming his promises (such as with Abraham), turning the heart of the wicked (such as with Balaam), identifying those who speak on his behalf (such as with the prophets), and promoting gospel expansion (such as with Paul and Peter), among other things.

Whether a sense of euphoria is always present is irrelevant, though one can hardly deny that a sense of peace and rejuvenation can come from God's presence.

ASCs are a product of God's loving embrace. When God's Spirit moves among his people they are changed. This can happen at a cognitive level where we become aware of our sins or are instructed or guided to do his will. This can also happen at an emotional level where we experience joyful bliss or deep repentance. In either case, we are altered by love. How this manifests may look different for each Christian. We serve a personal God and he chooses to embrace each of us uniquely. We do well not to become jealous of those whom the Father loves differently. He loves perfectly, which means he knows how best to embrace each of us. With some he calms their hearts with tranquil words of wisdom and with others he roughhouses and shakes us out of our funk. Just as natural fathers know how to play with their children, our heavenly Father does what he sees fit.

Christians often do not appreciate the Father-son relationship we have with God. This relationship with God is made clear by Paul: "God has sent the Spirit of his Son into our hearts, crying, 'Abba! Father!'" (Gal 4:6) and according to Jesus "whoever does not receive the kingdom of God like a child shall not enter it" (Mark 10:15). Good fathers play with their children.[2] They wrestle and tickle and tease.[3] You can see when someone has the joy of the Lord. Those who have been touched by God know what it means to not take themselves too seriously and to enjoy God even when it seems odd. In a spontaneous moment of worship, the American singer-songwriter Steffany Gretzinger sings out: "there's a line and we've crossed it / some would say that we've lost it / but who cares what the world thinks / I have found my joy."[4] Imagine if every Christian took these words to heart. Why is it that Western Christians often seem so disconnected from a supernatural brand of Christianity and the presence of ASCs?

Could it be that we have become so self-conscious, so burdened with appearances, and so "respectable" that we dare not let the world see the overflow of love? When you see a father playing with his child, blowing raspberries on their belly and hearing them laugh uncontrollably from

---

2. Vondey, *Beyond Pentecostalism*, 102: "The notion of play sheds particular light on the formulation of the doctrine of God. The Father, Son, and Holy Spirit, in engagement with the world, reveal a God who is 'at play' rather than 'at work.' Jean-Jacques Suurmond's Pentecostal proposal of the church as the play of Word and Spirit places the play element in the charismatic encounter *between* God and humanity. God is not synonymous with play but 'at play' with the world. The Father, in an ecstatic movement, literally, standing outside (*exstasis*) of himself, interacts through the Spirit by manifesting his identity as the Word in the economy of salvation. In this *perichoresis*, Christ becomes 'paraclete' through the Spirit, while the Holy Spirit also becomes 'paraclete' through Christ, both engaging and liberating each other and the world for dance with God as 'one of the most perfect forms of play.'"

3. Isaiah 66:12 pictures God like a mother with her baby including being "bounced upon her knees."

4. Bethel Music, "I Have Found My Joy (Spontaneous)."

excitement, do we not see that as natural? We ourselves might start giggling just from observing. But when Christians are overcome by God's presence, we scorn them for their "immaturity." Some Christians may even choose to quote Paul that we ought to give up "childish things" (1 Cor 13:11).

While it may be tempting to relegate ASCs to an early period of religious expression that no longer affects Western Christianity and should be quelled out of fear of ridicule by outsiders, this would be a mistake. Additionally, while those within the Pentecostal-charismatic movement may too highly laud outward manifestations, those outside are equally too quick to scoff and demonize manifestations they do not understand as meaningless emotionalism.

Judging the authenticity of manifestations based on outward observations—the "criterion of weirdness"—is not a biblical precedent.[5]

Data shows that the Pentecostal-charismatic movement is the fastest growing Christian movement globally, especially in terms of evangelism and missions.[6] Naturally, numbers do not equal "correctness," but it should cause us to pause and ask why this might be the case.

Allan Anderson notes that the expansion of Pentecostalism is rooted in several trends including what he refers to as "infectious enthusiasm."[7] Indeed, charismatic Christianity in general offers something that humans inherently crave: experience. The charismatic movement expands, in large part, through signs and wonders and experiences of God's love. Additionally, the liturgical structure of charismatic Christianity lends itself to a more experience-driven gathering. In summarizing Bobby Alexander's understanding of Pentecostal "liturgy," for example, Wolfgang Vondey states:

> Pentecostal liturgy consists not of rites that induce liminal activities but of a liminal, antistructural environment in which the participants redress established behavioral norms that otherwise suppress the operation of liminality. In this suspended structural environment, the liturgy is open to the playful invention of new behavior, freedom of expression, spontaneity, and enthusiasm that characterize Christian behavior as play.[8]

In other words, Pentecostals and charismatics do not always follow a rigid liturgy every Sunday, but create space for the Spirit's movement within broadly defined liturgical boarders. This lack of restriction facilitates expectation for spiritual creativity, especially for forms of ASCs. This does

---

5. See my book *The Weirdness of God*.
6. Burgess, *Pentecostal and Charismatic Movements*, 284–89.
7. Anderson, "Fruits of Pentecostal Globalization," 63.
8. Vondey, *Beyond Pentecostalism*, 135.

not mean that ASCs are not present in highly liturgical settings. In fact, Eastern Orthodox and Roman Catholic traditions often have charismatic expressions among their mystics and laity. Yet, one cannot help but notice the statistical difference between Pentecostals and charismatics and other denominations when it comes to experiencing ASCs.

When Jesus asks people to fill up large jars of water only to turn it into wine, or when he hides his identity on the road to Emmaus, or when he gets Peter to catch a fish only to find a coin inside, it is difficult not to see the humor and playfulness in these acts. In the age to come we are told that "the streets of the city shall be full of *boys and girls playing in its streets*" (Zech 8:5; emphasis added) and in the present age those who experience God are often said to leap for joy (Ps 87:7; 114:4; Isa 35:6; Jer 31:4, 13; Mal 4:2; Luke 1:44; 6:23; Acts 3:8). Acts of worship might offend others' sensibilities (e.g., Luke 7:36–50), but they please God.

We do not need to have a negative understanding of play. Play can look messy. Play can be costly. But play is also enjoyable. We can look goofy when we play with God. There is a difference between righteous play and carnal folly. You can be a holy fool or a hopeless fool. It all depends on your motives. Those who dance with all their might before the Lord please him. Those who dance to be praised by others like some kind of spiritual stripper lose their reward. The same is true of those who fake ASCs. The man or woman who falls in church every Sunday right on schedule but gets up unchanged is certainly "playing," but in what manner? Such people are acting rather than truly playing with God.

ASCs vary among those who experience them. In some instances, it is manifested as falling and stumbling, others with fits of laughter and joy, and still others with more overt "drunk-like" behaviors such as slurring of speech and motor automatisms. Additionally, many charismatics and Pentecostals avoid labels like "drunk in the Spirit" to describe their experience, instead using language such as "slain," "overwhelmed," "overcome," or "filled" by the Spirit. Thus, even within these movements the explanation and language used for such instances of intimacy with God vary.

While many mainline charismatics and Pentecostals likely have no problem with the idea of God overpowering someone and the consequent physical manifestations involved, others within the body of Christ are not so welcoming. This book will likely not have convinced those who are set on being against the charismatic movement due to theological tribalism, nor those who simply wish to engage in bad-faith polemical conversation. Yet, I hope that for those earnestly seeking answers to what the Bible has to say about modern manifestations, they have wrestled through the various passages explored in this book. Whether or not you have come to the same conclusions I have about these texts, hopefully it has at least broadened your understanding of the biblical world and the character of God.

Are ASCs something we should seek today? What role, if any, do ASCs have in a church service? How should a pastor deal with manifestations of the Spirit that seem wild, unruly, or out of the ordinary? These questions are important and may be what the reader has been hoping to find out throughout this book. Before addressing these questions, an important (and perhaps obvious) statement must be made: ASCs *are* biblical. Individuals throughout the Bible experienced genuine, God-given ASCs, and so while there is still the need to discern which ones are genuine, we must conclude that, at the very least, ASCs are something God has and can use to speak to individuals. Obviously, those who believe that certain gifts of the Holy Spirit have ceased will be less likely to embrace ASCs as a normative experience for Christians today, but since ASCs are not strictly a "gift" (at least not recorded for us by Paul), they should not be deemed as an impossibility even by the most ardent cessationist.

While all of the information in this book may be useful for meting out an understanding of ASCs in the biblical text, without some kind of practical theological instruction this topic will remain at the fringes of conversation and life. Ultimately, it is not my goal just to have entertaining "God talk." Rather, I want readers to come away with a sense of awe and curious expectation for experiencing God. The very idea of experiential theology or subjective theological speculation likely raises red flags to some readers.

Yet, I am not speaking about my own experience, nor the experience of others as a means of understanding Scripture. Rather, I am interested in what the Bible tells us about how we experience God's supernatural love in our lives and what this might look like. It should be recognized that much of the legwork has been accomplished in the previous chapters and as such I will be making some generalizations based on that material. As a result, I do not claim to be writing an exhaustive systematic theology of ASCs, but rather conducting a survey of the most salient features of ASCs as they relate to Christian praxis today.

Twice in 1 Corinthians Paul implores believers to seek spiritual gifts (12:31, 14:1) with an additional mention for them to earnestly desire the gift of prophecy (1 Cor 14:39).[9] Naturally, Paul does not list ASCs as a spiritual gift and while lumping it into the general heading of "deeds of power" (1 Cor 12:10) may be tempting, nowhere can we substantiate that Paul expected Christians to seek ecstasy in and of itself. Yet, in what we have discussed

---

9. For a discussion on whether 1 Cor 12:31 should be interpreted as an indicative or an imperative, see Thiselton, *Corinthians*, 1024–26.

prior, tongues may have included an ecstatic element and, as this outward manifestation was especially desirous to puff oneself up, was something Paul was attempting to obfuscate by contextualizing the more overt gifts. If this is correct, this would mean that seeking ASCs themselves is misguided if it lacks content useful for edifying the body of Christ.

Having said this, if in the process of seeking spiritual gifts the resultant prayer is answered and includes ASCs, we should not conflate the ASC as being the gift itself, even if it is an outward manifestation of the gift being exercised.

To give a specific example, one who receives a prophecy may enter an ASC while receiving or delivering the prophecy. The ASC is a byproduct of the gift, not the purpose of the gift itself. While the ASC may encourage both the prophet and the recipient, it is the substance of the prophecy that seems to constitute the gift. Indeed, since prophecy can be received without the need for an ASC, we must be careful not to conflate the two. Additionally, the nature of ASCs seems to invite false manifestations from people seeking attention or dominance in a religious context. This makes sense as to why many Christian groups both ancient and modern eventually dismissed such experiences as being nothing more than hysteria or self-indulgence.

If ASCs are not the "point" of spiritual gifts, why would God involve them when they seemingly cause so much confusion? We often forget that humans are both spiritual *and* physical beings. Biological reality should inform how we think about the way God communicates with us.[10] The audible voices or other sense-receptive experiences people had with God in the Scriptures were experienced through their physical bodies. ASCs as such are never condemned in the Hebrew Bible, perhaps because these are basic human experiences that are of neutral moral weight. It is the source and focus of these rituals and resultant ASCs that matter, not the mechanisms. However, there is some evidence in the text that certain practices used for inducing ASCs *are* prohibited, especially the use of illicit pharmaceuticals and self-mortification.

If you are a pastor, reading the contents in this book might have been helpful from an exegetical standpoint in understanding what the Bible says about this topic, but what should a pastor *do* in circumstances when people begin manifesting this way? This is especially important for pastors who have perhaps never had any exposure to charismatic expressions like this or who have a congregation primarily consisting of cessationists or skeptics.

---

10. On the issue of neuroscience and religious experiences, see Beauregard and O'Leary, *Spiritual Brain*; D'Aquili and Newberg, *Mystical Mind*; Giovannoli, *Biology of Belief*; Newberg and Waldman, *How God Changes Your Brain*; Newberg and Waldman, *Why We Believe*; and Verghese, "Spirituality and Mental Health."

Or, perhaps you are a worship leader in the church and want to know what the line is between using music to elevate God and bring people into the presence of God as opposed to manipulating people on a Sunday morning. Or, perhaps you have just become the pastor of a Pentecostal-charismatic church where people manifest abruptly and often and have become a distraction.

One thing I often recommend to people who are caught off guard by anything out of the ordinary in a church gathering is to breathe. God can handle people misinterpreting a situation and a congregation will not collapse in on itself for taking time to work through something God is doing. While God desires order in the church, one must come to grips with the fact that what one person finds distracting may not apply to another. For example, those in fundamentalist circles may be distracted seeing someone wearing a hat or for having tattoos in a congregation while others may not care at all. Yet, in some circles of Christianity, dancing, clapping, yelling, whistling, and people falling to the ground are so common that it does not distract anyone. Obviously, minimizing distractions is ideal, but we cannot go around policing every situation and indeed in some instances we may find ourselves guilty of quenching the Spirit and people's connection with God when we demand they cease expressing a form of worship we are unfamiliar with personally.

To give a specific example, while attending one charismatic church, a woman in the congregation perpetually hollered during the preaching time. The pastor told her to quiet down from the pulpit. I believe this was appropriate. It was not only distracting but had no edifying content. While one could claim this was a verbal automatism of some kind, it is important to note that other contributing factors were relevant in discerning that this was not such a case. For one, this individual had a habit of boasting and drawing attention for her own glory. Additionally, reports from other congregants seemed to suggest that false manifestations and false prophetic words had been communicated by this woman. Such discernment processes need to be taken seriously when addressing automatisms in the church. In another case, however, while attending a charismatic conference, verbal automatisms were common throughout the congregation but, because of the sound system and other factors (including the speaker's personal disposition), these manifestations were *not* a distraction and actually elevated the teaching and worship times. Still in another scenario, one church I attended for many years would sometimes create instrumental lulls in the worship time so that people could express the gift of tongues and interpretation. Again, this was not distracting or chaotic because it was structured within the broad liturgical lines of the church. There are no cookie-cutter ways of dealing with verbal automatisms and each must be taken on a case-by-case scenario.

When dealing with physical manifestations, sending a deacon, elder, or trusted church member to independently inspect the person experiencing the manifestation may be a healthy first step in the moment. Depending on the situation, that person may need to be guided to another area and prayed with (John 7:24). Resist the urge to rebuke someone for a manifestation simply because it looks strange. The process of weighing and discerning a manifestation may take time (Col 4:6; 1 Thess 5:14). If someone is intentionally (and chronically) disruptive, that person should be removed from the area and scripturally guided. Should they continue in such a way, leaders may want to discuss the possibility of church discipline (Prov 12:1; 1 Cor 14:40; Gal 6:1; 2 Thess 3:13-15; Titus 3:9-11; 2 John 9-10). Letting your congregation understand what is going on will likely help dispel anxiety in churches where such things are uncommon. This is especially true in cases where a congregant is abusing their alleged experiences.

Paul was not above mentioning people by name (1 Tim 1:19-20; 2 Tim 2:16-18). Depending on one's denomination, a leader tasked with discerning and evaluating spiritual manifestations may already exist. If not, your church may consider appointing leaders to this position. Many churches may wish to hold private meetings with the individual and leaders and perhaps refresh their congregation on what the New Testament teaches about spiritual gifts, miracles, and church order (Matt 18:15-20). Pray that God distributes the gift of discerning spirits to someone in the congregation, especially those in leadership positions (Ps 119:34; John 16:13; 1 Cor 2:12; 12:10; Heb 5:14; Jas 1:5; 1 John 4:1). Hear all sides of what Scripture says about the topic (Prov 17:27; 18:2, 17-20; 20:5). Do not discourage seeking spiritual gifts and manifestations but emphasize the need for order and evaluation (1 Cor 14:1, 39-40; 1 Thess 5:20-21). Churches may need to find appropriate outlets for certain manifestations in smaller groups or different times where accountability can still be managed.

These Manifestations Are "Too Weird" to Be Beneficial

This objection is unfortunate, as it seems to ignore the many bizarre stories found in the Bible. Are we to think that preaching a sermon on a talking donkey, catching fish with coins in their mouths, or turning water into wine isn't beneficial? Certainly, telling someone to dip themselves in a river seven times to cure them of leprosy seems a bit silly! Yet, whether or not someone likes God's methods, or a particular manifestation of the Spirit, is irrelevant to its value.

If we are being frank, it is not hard to imagine how such absurd looking manifestations could lead some to leave a church. Shouldn't this be proof that these things cannot be from God? Yet, Scripture clearly communicates the opposite. In many instances when Jesus teaches difficult things, his followers abandon him. Jesus's teachings on divorce, the need to eat his flesh and blood, and other radical sayings cause people to scoff and abruptly turn course. We should expect the same with manifestations that irk the flesh. Intellectualism and pride can easily cause people to abandon a church without properly searching the Scriptures or working through face-to-face with clergy or congregants.

For others it may just be a preference of style. Many people leave churches for the worship leader suddenly switching to contemporary Christian music instead of traditional hymns. Others may not be happy with the pastor's preaching style, regardless of its inherent content. While these may appear to be petty issues to leave a church over, we should at least consider having grace for those who find it exceedingly difficult to worship to a style that they internally hate. Relational discipleship is necessary to work with such people and it may be necessary to think about your church's liturgical structure and how it may need to change or not. But we cannot bend to the will of every critic either. And if God wants to work in a church through ASCs, we should be careful in how we posture ourselves in dealing with them.

This book has attempted to be a working out of Paul's instruction: "Do not quench the Spirit. Do not despise prophecies, but test everything; hold fast what is good" (1 Thess 5:19–21). Among charismatics and Pentecostals, it may be that the testing is what needs to take priority, while among cessationists or theological liberals it is the quenching of the Spirit that must be addressed. In both cases, one ought to make room for the bizarre while also keeping a level-headed footing in Scripture. I am not ignorant to the fact that many will find some of my arguments less persuasive than others. I am also too firmly aware that many within orthodox Christianity will struggle with some of the findings in this book. I have done my best to adopt a respectful hermeneutical process that conservative Christians can appreciate, even if much of this data seems foreign and strange. To quote the late biblical scholar Michael S. Heiser, however, "If something in the Bible is weird, it's probably important."

Bibliography

Achtemeier, Paul J. *1 Peter: A Commentary on First Peter*. Edited by Eldon Jay Epp. Hermeneia. Minneapolis: Fortress, 1996.
Ackerman, Susan. *Warrior, Dancer, Seductress, Queen: Women in Judges and Biblical Israel*. ABRL. New York: Doubleday, 1998.
Ackroyd, Peter R. *The First Book of Samuel*. CBC. Cambridge: Cambridge University Press, 1971.
Adam, Klaus-Peter. "'And He Behaved Like a Prophet Among Them.' (1 Sam 10:11b): The Depreciative Use of נבא Hitpael and the Comparative Evidence of Ecstatic Prophecy." *WO* (2009) 3–57.
Ahlberg, Nora. "Some Psycho-Physiological Aspects of Ecstasy in Recent Research." In *Religious Ecstasy: Based on Papers Read at the Symposium on Religious Ecstasy Held at Åbo, Finland, on the 26th–28th of August 1981*, edited by Nils G. Holm, 63–73. Stockholm: Almqvist & Wiksell, 1982.
Ahlström, Gösta W. "1 Samuel 1.15." *Bib* 60 (1979) 254.
Albright, W. F. "Are the Ephod and the Teraphim Mentioned in Ugaritic Literature?" *BASOR* 83 (1941) 39–42. https://doi.org/10.2307/3218744.
Alexander, P. H. "Slain in the Spirit." In *The New International Dictionary of Pentecostal and Charismatic Movements*, edited by Stanley M. Burgess, 1072–74. Rev. ed. Grand Rapids: Zondervan, 2007.
Allegro, John M. *The Sacred Mushroom and the Cross: A Study of the Nature and Origins of Christianity Within the Fertility Cults of the Ancient Near East*. London: Hodder and Stoughton, 1970.
Alvarsson, Jan-Åke. "Shamanism and Armed Conflict—A Case Study of the Interface Between Religion and War in Aboriginal South America." *Revista del CESLA* 1 (2010) 233–56. https://www.revistadelcesla.com/index.php/revistadelcesla/article/view/158/482.
Amaya, Ioanna A., et al. "Effect of Frequency and Rhythmicity on Flicker Light-Induced Hallucinatory Phenomena." *PLOS One* 18 (2023) 1–18. https://doi.org/10.1371/journal.pone.0284271.
Anderson, Allan. "The Fruits of Pentecostal Globalization: Current Trends and Challenges." In *Pentecostalism and Globalization: The Impact of Globalization on Pentecostal Theology and Ministry*, edited by Steven M. Studebaker, 50–69. McMaster Theological Studies. Eugene, OR: Pickwick, 2010.
———. *An Introduction to Pentecostalism: Global Charismatic Christianity*. Cambridge: Cambridge University Press, 2004.

Anderson, Arnold A. *2 Samuel*. WBC 11. Grand Rapids: Zondervan, 2000.

Anderson, Paul, dir. *Event Horizon*. Los Angeles: Paramount, 1997.

André, Gunnel. "Ecstatic Prophecy in the Old Testament." *Scripta Instituti Donneriani Aboensis* 11 (1982) 187–200. https://doi.org/10.30674/scripta.67139.

Andrews, E. A., ed. *Harper's Latin Dictionary: A New Latin Dictionary Founded on the Translation of Freund's Latin-German Lexicon*. New York: Harper, 1879.

Angel, Joseph L. "Maskil, Community, and Religious Experience in the 'Songs of the Sage' (4Q510–511)." *DSD* 19 (2012) 1–27.

Arie, Eran, et al. "Cannabis and Frankincense at the Judahite Shrine of Arad." *TA* 47 (2020) 5–28. https://doi.org/10.1080/03344355.2020.1732046.

Arnold, Bill T., and Bryan E. Beyer, eds. *Readings from the Ancient Near East: Primary Sources for Old Testament Study*. Encountering Biblical Studies. Grand Rapids: Baker Academic, 2002.

Ash, James L., Jr. "The Decline of Ecstatic Prophecy in the Early Church." *TS* 37 (1976) 227–52. https://doi.org/10.1177/004056397603700202.

Ashley, Timothy R. *The Book of Numbers*. NICOT. Grand Rapids: Eerdmans, 1993.

Auld, A. Graeme. *I & II Samuel: A Commentary*. OTL. Louisville: Westminster John Knox, 2011.

Aune, David E. *Prophecy in Early Christianity and the Ancient Mediterranean World*. Eugene, OR: Wipf and Stock, 2003.

———. *Revelation 1–5*. WBC 52A. Dallas: Word, 1997.

Baker, Heidi. "The Primacy of Love." *Renewal Journal* 13 (2012). https://renewaljournal.com/2012/07/19/primacy-of-love-in-missions-with-power-byheidi-baker/.

Baker, Rolland. "The Iris Story." Iris Global. https://www.irisglobal.org/about/the-iris-story.

Bangs, Nathan. *A History of the Methodist Episcopal Church*. 3rd rev. ed. 4 vols. New York: Mason and Lane, 1839–1842.

Barker, Kenneth L., and Waylon Bailey. *Micah, Nahum, Habakkuk, Zephaniah*. NAC 20. Nashville: B&H, 1998.

Barth, Markus. *Ephesians: Introduction, Translation, and Commentary on Chapters 4–6*. AYBC 34A. New Haven: Yale University Press, 2008.

Bartossek, Marie T., et al. "Altered States Phenomena Induced by Visual Flicker Light Stimulation." *PLOS One* 16 (2021) 1–23. https://doi.org/10.1371/journal.pone.0253779.

Bauckham, Richard J. *Jude, 2 Peter*. WBC 50. Waco: Word, 1983.

Bauckham, Richard J., et al., eds. *Old Testament Pseudepigrapha: More Noncanonical Scriptures*. Grand Rapids: Eerdmans, 2013.

Bazzana, Giovanni B. *Having the Spirit of Christ: Spirit Possession and Exorcism in the Early Christian Groups*. Synkrisis. New Haven: Yale University Press, 2020.

Beale, Gregory K. *The Book of Revelation: A Commentary on the Greek Text*. NIGTC. Grand Rapids: Eerdmans, 1999.

Beasley-Murray, George R. *John*. WBC 36. Waco: Word, 1987.

Beauregard, Mario, and Denyse O'Leary. *The Spiritual Brain: A Neuroscientist's Case for the Existence of the Soul*. New York: HarperOne, 2007.

Bechthold, Henry. *Pentecostal Fanaticism: False Prophets, False Apostles, Fake Healers, Unknown Tongues, Holy Laughter, Holy Rollers, Runners, Slain in the Spirit, Drunk in the Spirit*. Self-published, 2021.

Behrend, Heike. "Power to Heal, Power to Kill: Spirit Possession & War in Northern Uganda (1986-1994)." in *Spirit Possession, Modernity, and Power in Africa*, edited by Heike Behrend and Ute Luig, 20-34. Madison: University of Wisconsin Press, 1999.
Bellavance, Éric. "'C'est devant YHWH que j'ai dansé': Quelques réflexions sur la danse du roi David en 2S 6." *Théologiques* 25 (2017) 87-102. https://doi.org/10.7202/1055241ar.
Benet, Sula. "Early Diffusion and Folk Uses of Hemp." In *Cannabis and Culture*, edited by Vera Rubin, 39-50. World Anthropology. The Hague: Mouton, 1975.
Bethel Music. "Bethel Music Moments: I Have Found My Joy (Spontaneous)—Steffany Frizzell Gretzinger." YouTube, Mar. 13, 2014. https://www.youtube.com/watch?v=v1cYUmfWdt8.
Betz, Hans Dieter. *Galatians: A Commentary on Paul's Letter to the Churches in Galatia*. Hermeneia. Philadelphia: Fortress, 1979.
Björkvist, Kaj. "Ecstasy from a Physiological Point of View." In *Religious Ecstasy: Based on Papers Read at the Symposium on Religious Ecstasy Held at Åbo, Finland, on the 26th-28th of August 1981*, edited by Nils G. Holm, 74-86. Stockholm: Almqvist & Wiksell, 1982.
Blenkinsopp, Joseph. *Ezekiel*. Interpretation. Louisville: Westminster John Knox, 2012.
———. *Isaiah 1-39: A New Translation with Introduction and Commentary*. AYBC 19. New Haven: Yale University Press, 2000.
Blisscoco. "Sloshfest John Crowder Day 1." YouTube, Dec. 8, 2012. https://www.youtube.com/watch?v=MCNICVaorYI.
Block, Daniel I. *The Book of Ezekiel: Chapters 1-24*. NICOT. Grand Rapids: Eerdmans, 1997.
———. *Judges, Ruth*. NAC 6. Nashville: B&H, 1999.
Bloomfield, Michael. "Pentecostalism and the Adaptive Significance of Trance." PhD diss., University of East London, 2001. https://repository.uel.ac.uk/item/869vw.
Blount, Brian K. *Revelation: A Commentary*. NTL. Louisville: Westminster John Knox, 2009.
Böck, Barbara. "Mind-Altering Plants in Babylonian Medical Sources." In *The Routledge Companion to Ecstatic Experience in the Ancient World*, edited by Diana Stein et al., 121-37. London: Routledge, 2022.
Bock, Darrell L. *Acts*. BECNT. Grand Rapids: Baker Academic, 2007.
Boda, Mark J. *The Book of Zechariah*. NICOT. Grand Rapids: Eerdmans, 2016.
Boddy, Janice "Spirit Possession Revisited: Beyond Instrumentality." *Annual Review of Anthropology* 23 (1994) 407-34. https://doi.org/10.1146/annurev.an.23.100194.002203.
Bodner, Keith. *1 Samuel: A Narrative Commentary*. Hebrew Bible Monographs 19. Sheffield: Sheffield Phoenix, 2009.
Bonaventure. *The Life of Saint Francis of Assisi*. Translated by E. Gurney Salter. London: Dent & Sons, 1904.
Borchert, Gerald L. *John 1-11*. NAC 25A. Nashville: B&H, 1996.
Boring, M. Eugene. *Mark: A Commentary*. NTL. Louisville: Westminster John Knox, 2014.
Bourguignon, Erika, ed. *Possession*. Chandler & Sharp Series in Cross-Cultural Themes. San Francisco: Chandler & Sharp, 1976.

———, ed. *Religion, Altered States of Consciousness, and Social Change.* Columbus: Ohio State University Press, 1973.

———. "World Distribution and Patterns of Possession States." In *Trance and Possession States*, edited by Raymond Prince, 3–34. Montreal: R. M. Bucke Memorial Society, 1968.

Bovon, François. *Luke 1: A Commentary on the Gospel of Luke 1:1—9:50.* Edited by Helmut Koester, translated by Christine M. Thomas. Hermeneia. Minneapolis: Fortress, 2002.

———. *Luke 2: A Commentary on the Gospel of Luke 9:51—19:27.* Edited by Helmut Koester, translated by Donald S. Deer. Hermeneia. Minneapolis: Fortress, 2013.

Bowman, John, trans. and ed. *Samaritan Documents: Relating to their History, Religion and Life.* Pittsburgh Original Texts and Translations. Eugene, OR: Pickwick, 1977.

Bremmer, Jan N. *The Early Greek Concept of the Soul.* Mythos: The Princeton/Bollingen Series in World Mythology. Princeton: Princeton University Press, 1983.

Breneman, Mervin. *Ezra, Nehemiah, Esther.* NAC 10. Nashville: B&H, 1993.

Broome, Edwin C., Jr. "Ezekiel's Abnormal Personality." *JBL* 65 (1946) 277–92. https://doi.org/10.2307/3262666.

Brown, Candy Gunther, et al. "Study of the Therapeutic Effects of Proximal Intercessory Prayer (STEPP) on Auditory and Visual Impairments in Rural Mozambique." *Southern Medical Journal* 103 (2010) 864–69. https://pubmed.ncbi.nlm.nih.gov/20686441/.

Brown, Derek R., and Matthew M. Whitehead. *Ephesians.* Edited by Douglas Mangum. Lexham Research Commentaries. Bellingham, WA: Lexham, 2013. Logos.

Brown, Tricia Gates. *Spirit in the Writings of John: Johannine Pneumatology in Social-Scientific Perspective.* JSNTSup 253. LNTS. London: T&T Clark, 2003.

Brueggemann, Walter. *1 & 2 Kings.* SHBC. Macon, GA: Smyth & Helwys, 2000.

Bultmann, Rudolf. *Die Geschichte der synoptischen Tradition.* Göttingen: Vandenhoeck & Ruprecht, 1958.

———. *The Gospel of John: A Commentary.* Translated by G. R. Beasley-Murray, edited by R. W. N. Hoare and J. K. Riches. Philadelphia: Westminster, 1971.

Burge, Gary M. "Spirit-Inspired Theology and Ecclesial Correction: Charting One Shift in the Development of Johannine Ecclesiology and Pneumatology." In *Communities in Dispute: Current Scholarship on the Johannine Epistles*, edited by R. Alan Culpepper and Paul N. Anderson, 179–86. Atlanta: SBL, 2014.

Burgess, Stanley M., ed. *The New International Dictionary of Pentecostal and Charismatic Movements.* Rev. ed. Grand Rapids: Zondervan, 2007.

Burton, Ernest De Witt. *A Critical and Exegetical Commentary on the Epistle to the Galatians.* ICC. Edinburgh: T&T Clark, 1921.

Caird, George Bradford. *The Apostolic Age.* London: Duckworth, 1993.

Campbell, Stacey, and Wesley Campbell. *Ecstatic Prophecy.* Grand Rapids: Chosen, 2008.

Campbell, Wesley. *Welcoming a Visitation of the Holy Spirit.* Lake Mary, FL: Charisma House, 1996.

Cantalamessa, Raniero. *Sober Intoxication of the Spirit: Filled with the Fullness of God.* Translated by Marsha Daigle-Williamson. 2 volumes. Cincinnati: Servant, 2005.

Carlson, Reed. "Hannah at Pentecost: On Recognizing Spirit Phenomena in Early Jewish Literature." *Journal of Pentecostal Theology* 27 (2018) 245–58. https://doi.org/10.1163/17455251-02702005.

———. *Unfamiliar Selves in the Hebrew Bible: Possession and Other Spirit Phenomena*. Ekstasis 9. Berlin: De Gruyter, 2022.
Carman. "The Well." Track 1 on *Sunday's on the Way*. Priority, 1983.
Carnes, Tony. "Howard-Browne Takes New York." *Christianity Today*, Aug. 9, 1999.
Carroll R., M. Daniel. *The Book of Amos*. NICOT. Grand Rapids: Eerdmans, 2020.
Carson, D. A. *Exegetical Fallacies*. 2nd ed. Grand Rapids: Baker Academic, 1996.
———. *The Gospel According to John*. Leicester: Inter-Varsity, 1991.
Cely, Julian Ernesto, and William Mauricio Beltrán. "Towards a Typification of Motivations in Pentecostal Ecstasy." *PentecoStudies* 18 (2019) 178–99. https://doi.org/10.1558/pent.37166.
Chadwick, John, and J. T. Killen. "Linear B Tablets from Knossos." *Annual of the British School of Athens* 58 (1963) 68–88. https://doi.org/10.1017/S0068245400013794.
Chalmers, Aaron. *Exploring the Religion of Ancient Israel: Prophet, Priest, Sage & People*. Downers Grove, IL: IVP Academic, 2012.
Charlesworth, James H., with Brandon L. Allen. *Has Psalm 156 Been Found? With Images of MS RNL Antonin 798*. Eugene, OR: Cascade, 2018.
Chauncy, Charles. *Seasonable Thoughts on the State of Religion in New England*. 1743. Repr., Hicksville, NY: Regina, 1975.
Chepey, Stuart. *Nazirites in Late Second Temple Judaism: A Survey of Ancient Jewish Writings, the New Testament, Archaeological Evidence, and Other Writings from Late Antiquity*. AGJU 60. Leiden: Brill, 2005.
Chester, Stephen J. "Divine Madness? Speaking in Tongues in 1 Corinthians 14.23." *JSNT* 27 (2005) 417–46. https://doi.org/10.1177/0142064X05055747.
Childs, Brevard S. *Isaiah: A Commentary*. OTL. Louisville: Westminster John Knox, 2000.
Clark, David J., and Howard Hatton. *A Handbook on Haggai, Zechariah, and Malachi*. UBS Handbook. New York: United Bible Societies, 2002.
Cogan, Mordechai. *I Kings: A New Translation with Introduction and Commentary*. AYBC 10. New Haven: Yale University Press, 2001.
Cogan, Mordechai, and Hayim Tadmor. *II Kings: A New Translation with Introduction and Commentary*. AYBC 11. New Haven: Yale University Press, 2021.
Cole, R. Dennis. *Numbers*. NAC 3B. Nashville: B&H, 2000.
Collins, Adela Yarbro. *Mark: A Commentary*. Edited by Harold W. Attridge. Hermeneia. Minneapolis: Fortress, 2007.
Colpe, Carsten. "Ecstasy." *EC* 2:29–30.
Craffert, Pieter F. "Heavenly Journeys as Neurocultural Experiences: Social-Scientific Interpretation as a Challenge for Traditional Scholarship?" *Neot* 48 (2014) 387–403. https://hdl.handle.net/10520/EJC167284.
———. *The Life of a Galilean Shaman: Jesus of Nazareth in Anthropological-Historical Perspective*. Matrix: The Bible in Mediterranean Context 3. Eugene, OR: Cascade, 2008.
———. "Towards a Post-Colonial Reflection on *Shaman* and *Shamanism* as Conceptual Tools in Biblical Studies." *R&T* 26 (2019) 173–215. https://doi.org/10.1163/15743012-02603004.
Craghan, John F. "Mari and Its Prophets: The Contributions of Mari to the Understanding of Biblical Prophecy." *BTB* 5 (1975) 32–55. https://doi.org/10.1177/014610797500500102.
Creed, John Martin. *The Gospel According to St. Luke*. London: MacMillan, 1930.

Crosson, J. Brent. "What Possessed You? Spirits, Property, and Political Sovereignty at the Limits of 'Possession.'" *Ethnos* 84 (2019) 546–56. https://doi.org/10.1080/001 41844.2017.1401704.

Crowder, John. "About Cana." The New Mystics. https://www.johncrowder.net/products/cana-new-wine-seminary-online.

———. "About Us." The New Mystics. https://www.johncrowder.net/pages/about-us.

———. *The Ecstasy of Loving God: Trances, Raptures, and the Supernatural Pleasures of Jesus Christ*. Shippensburg, PA: Destiny Image, 2008.

———. "Glory in Ethiopia—The Jesus Trip." YouTube, Oct. 30, 2013. https://www.youtube.com/watch?v=mUMaYoDNPnk.

———. "High on Jesus." Faithfullydrunk, Tumblr, Feb. 25, 2013. https://www.tumblr.com/faithfullydrunk/43992247402/high-on-jesus-by-john-crowder.

———. "Miracles, Exorcisms & Fun in India." YouTube, Dec. 31, 2007. https://www.youtube.com/watch?v=O3qrCUw_yqE.

———. "Thailand Transvestite Mission—The Jesus Trip." YouTube, Nov. 23, 2014. https://www.youtube.com/watch?v=XOooEP1tIIM.

Cryer, Frederick H. *Divination in Ancient Israel and Its Near Eastern Environment: A Socio-Historical Investigation*. JSOTSup 142. Sheffield: Sheffield Academic, 1994.

Curtis, Maranda. "Open Heaven." Tracks 6–8 on *The Maranda Experience*, written by Maranda Curtis and Dana Sorey. Butterfly Works/C Bazz Pub/Fair Trade, 2018.

Cushman, Jeremy T., and Douglas J. Floccare. "Flicker Illness: An Underrecognized but Preventable Complication of Helicopter Transport." *Prehospital Emergency Care* 11 (2007) 85–88. https://doi.org/10.1080/10903120601021457.

Cutten, George Barton. *The Psychological Phenomena of Christianity*. New York: Scribner's Sons, 1908.

Dahl, Roald. *The Wonderful Story of Henry Sugar and Six More*. New York: Knopf, 1977.

Dahood, Mitchell. "Hebrew-Ugaritic Lexicography XII." *Bib* 55 (1974) 381–93. https://www.jstor.org/stable/42609912.

———. *Proverbs and Northwest Semitic Philology*. Rome: Pontificium Institutum Biblicum, 1963.

Dannaway, Frederick R. "Strange Fires, Weird Smokes and Psychoactive Combustibles: Entheogens and Incense in Ancient Traditions." *Journal of Psychoactive Drugs* 42 (2010) 485–97. https://www.tandfonline.com/doi/abs/10.1080/02791072.2010.10 400711.

D'Aquili, Eugene G., and Andrew B. Newberg. *The Mystical Mind: Probing the Biology of Religious Experience*. Theology and the Sciences. Minneapolis: Fortress, 1999.

David-Néel, Alexandra. *Magic and Mystery in Tibet*. New York: Dover, 1971.

Davies, J. G. "Pentecost and Glossolalia." *JTS* 3 (1952) 228–31. https://www.jstor.org/stable/23952857.

Davis, David. "Divination in the Bible." *JBQ* 30 (2002) 121–26. https://jbqnew.jewishbible.org/assets/Uploads/302/302_DIVINAT1.pdf.

Delitzsch, Franz. *A New Commentary on Genesis*. Translated by Sophia Taylor. 2 vols. Edinburgh: T&T Clark, 1888–1889.

Delling, Gerhard. *Worship in the New Testament*. Translated by Percy Scott. Philadelphia: Westminster, 1962.

DeMaris, Richard E. "Possession, Good and Bad—Ritual, Effects and Side-Effects: The Baptism of Jesus and Mark 1.9–11 from a Cross-Cultural Perspective." *JSNT* 23 (2001) 3–29. https://doi.org/10.1177/0142064X0102308001.

DeVries, Simon J. *1 Kings*. 2nd ed. WBC 12. Grand Rapids: Zondervan, 2004.
Dibelius, Martin. *Studies in the Acts of the Apostles*. Edited by Heinrich Greeven. London: SCM, 1956.
Dick, Michael B. "The Mesopotamian Cult Statue: A Sacramental Encounter with Divinity." In *Cult Image and Divine Representation in the Ancient Near East*, edited by Neal H. Walls, 43–68. ASOR 10. Boston: ASOR, 2005.
Dillistone, Frederick William. "Prospeinos (Acts x.10)." *ExpTim* 46 (1934–35) 380.
Dines, Jennifer M. *The Septuagint*. Edited by Michael A. Knibb. Understanding the Bible and Its World. London: T&T Clark, 2004.
Dirksen, Peter B. "Prophecy and Temple Music: 1 Chron. 25:1–17." *Henoch* 19 (1997) 259–65.
Duchesne, Véronique. "A Children's Game or a Ritual of Spirit Possession?" CNRS Images, Nov. 2004. Video, 9:14. https://images.cnrs.fr/en/video/1204.
Dunbar, Robin. *How Religion Evolved: And Why It Endures*. Oxford: Oxford University Press, 2022.
Dunkle, Brian P. *Enchantment and Creed in the Hymns of Ambrose of Milan*. OECS. Oxford: Oxford University Press, 2016.
Dunn, James D. G. *Jesus and the Spirit: A Study of the Religious and Charismatic Experience of Jesus and the First Christians as Reflected in the New Testament*. Grand Rapids: Eerdmans, 1997.
Duvall, Scott J., and J. Daniel Hays. *Grasping God's Word: A Hands-On Approach to Reading, Interpreting, and Applying the Bible*. 4th ed. Grand Rapids: Zondervan, 2020.
Dwyer, Timothy. *The Motif of Wonder in the Gospel of Mark*. JSNTSup 128. Sheffield: Sheffield Academic, 1996.
Edwards, Jonathan. "The Distinguishing Marks of a Work of the Spirit of God." In *Jonathan Edwards on Revival*, 75–147. Edinburgh: Banner of Truth Trust, 1984.
———. "To the Reverend Thomas Prince, December 12, 1743." In *Jonathan Edwards: Letters and Personal Writings*, edited by George S. Claghorn, 115–27. Works of Jonathan Edwards 16. New Haven: Yale, 1998.
———. *Thoughts on the Revival of Religion in New England, 1740, to Which Is Prefixed a Narrative of the Surprising Work of God in Northampton, Mass., 1735*. New York: American Tract Society, 1800.
Ehrenreich, Barbara. *Blood Rites: Origins and History of the Passions of War*. New York: Hachette, 1997.
Ehrlich, Arnold B. *Randglossen zur Hebräischen Bibel: Textkritisches, sprachliches und sachliches*. Leipzig: Hinrichs'sche, 1908.
Eichrodt, Walther. *Theology of the Old Testament*. Translated by J. A. Baker. 5th rev. ed. 2 vols. OTL. Philadelphia: Westminster, 1961–67.
Eidevall, Göran. *Amos: A New Translation with Introduction and Commentary*. AYBC 24G. New Haven: Yale University Press, 2017.
Eissfeldt, Otto. "The Prophetic Literature." In *The Old Testament and Modern Study: A Generation of Discovery and Research*, edited by H. H. Rowley, 115–61. 1951. Repr., Oxford: Clarendon, 1952.
Eitrem, Samson. *Orakel und Mysterien am Ausgang der Antike*. Zurich: Rhein, 1947.
Elkins, Dov Peretz, and Abigail Treu. *The Bible's Top 50 Ideas: The Essential Concepts Everyone Should Know*. Eugene, OR: Wipf & Stock, 2013.

Ervin, Frank R., et al. "The Psychobiology of Trance: II: Physiological and Endocrine Correlates." *Transcultural Psychiatry* 25 (1988) 267–84. https://doi.org/10.1177/136346158802500402.

Evans, Craig A. "Ephesians 5:18–19 and Religious Intoxication in the World of Paul." In *Paul's World*, edited by Stanley E. Porter, 181–200. Pauline Studies 4. Leiden: Brill, 2008.

Eve, Eric. *The Jewish Context of Jesus' Miracles*. JSNTSup 231. London: Sheffield Academic, 2002.

Farrer, D. S. "Cross-Cultural Articulations of War Magic and Warrior Religion." *Social Analysis* 58 (2014) 1–24. https://doi.org/10.3167/sa.2014.580101.

Fasullo, Lisa, et al. "The Innate Human Potential of Elevated and Ecstatic States of Consciousness: Examining Freeform Dance as a Means of Access." *Dance, Movement & Spiritualities* 6 (2020) 87–117. https://doi.org/10.1386/dmas_00005_1.

Faw, Calmer E. *Acts*. Believers Church Bible Commentary. Scottdale, PA: Herald, 1993.

Fee, Gordon D. *God's Empowering Presence: The Holy Spirit in the Letters of Paul*. Peabody, MA: Hendrickson, 1994.

Fenwick, Peter. "Automatism, Medicine and the Law." *Psychological Medicine Monograph Supplement* 17 (1990) 1–27. https://doi.org/10.1017/S0264180100000758.

Firth, David G. *1 & 2 Samuel*. ApOTC 8. Nottingham: Apollos, 2009.

———. "Is Saul Also Among the Prophets? Saul's Prophecy in 1 Samuel 19:23." In *Presence, Power, and Promise: The Role of the Spirit of God in the Old Testament*, edited by David G. Firth and Paul D. Wegner, 294–305. Downers Grove, IL: IVP Academic, 2011.

Fitzmyer, Joseph A. *First Corinthians: A New Translation with Introduction and Commentary*. AYBC 32. New Haven: Yale University Press, 2021.

———. *The Gospel According to Luke I–IX: Introduction, Translation, and Notes*. AYBC 28. New Haven: Yale University Press, 1970.

———. *The Letter to Philemon: A New Translation with Introduction and Commentary*. AYBC 34. New Haven: Yale University Press, 2021.

Fleming, Daniel E. "The Etymological Origins of the Hebrew nābî: The One Who Invokes God." *CBQ* 55 (1993) 217–24. https://www.academia.edu/31595404/Fleming_Daniel_E_The_Etymological_Origins_of_the_Hebrew_n%C4%81b%C3%AE_One_Who_Invokes_God_Catholic_Biblical_Quarterly_CBQ_55_1993_217_24.

Foster, Bejamin R. "Ecstatic Speech in Ancient Mesopotamia." In *The Routledge Companion to Ecstatic Experience in the Ancient World*, edited by Diana Stein et al., 430–40. London: Routledge, 2022.

Fowler, Harold N., et al., trans. *Plato*. 12 vols. LCL. Cambridge: Harvard University Press, 1914–1937.

Fox, Michael V. *Proverbs 10–31: A New Translation with Introduction and Commentary*. AYBC 18B. New Haven: Yale University Press, 2009.

France, Richard T. *The Gospel of Mark: A Commentary on the Greek Text*. NIGTC. Grand Rapids: Eerdmans, 2002.

Francia, Rita. "Plant-Based Potions and Ecstatic States in Hittite Rituals." In *The Routledge Companion to Ecstatic Experience in the Ancient World*, edited by Diana Stein et al., 138–51. London: Routledge, 2022.

Frend, William H. C. "Montanism: A Movement of Prophecy and Regional Identity in the Early Church." *Bulletin of the John Rylands Library* 70 (1988) 25–34. https://doi.org/10.7227/BJRL.70.3.3.
Galling, Kurt. "Königliche und nichtkönigliche Stifter beim Tempel von Jerusalem." *Beiträge zur Biblischen Landes- und Altertumskunde* 68 (1950) 134–42. https://www.jstor.org/stable/27930422.
Garcia-Romeu, Albert P., and Charles T. Tart. "Altered States of Consciousness and Transpersonal Psychology." In *The Wiley-Blackwell Handbook of Transpersonal Psychology*, edited by Harris L. Friedman and Glenn Hartelius, 121–40. Malden, MA: Wiley & Sons, 2013.
Garland, David E. *1 Corinthians*. BECNT. Grand Rapids: Baker Academic, 2003.
———. *2 Corinthians*. NAC 29. Nashville: B&H, 1999.
Garrett, Clarke. *Origins of the Shakers: From the Old World to the New World*. Baltimore: Johns Hopkins University Press, 1987.
———. *Spirit Possession and Popular Religion: From the Camisards to the Shakers*. Baltimore: Johns Hopkins University Press, 1987.
Garrett, Duane A. *Proverbs, Ecclesiastes, Song of Songs*. NAC 14. Nashville: B&H, 1993.
Garrett, Susan R. *The Demise of the Devil: Magic and the Demonic in Luke's Writings*. Minneapolis: Fortress, 1989.
George, Timothy. *Galatians*. NAC 30. Nashville: B&H, 1994.
Giovannoli, Joseph. *The Biology of Belief: How Our Biology Biases Our Beliefs and Perceptions*. Brooklyn: Rosetta, 2000.
Gladd, Benjamin J. *From Adam and Israel to the Church: A Biblical Theology of the People of God*. Essential Studies in Biblical Theology. Downers Grove, IL: IVP Academic, 2019.
Global Celebration. "Bio." https://www.globalcelebration.com/bio.
———. "History." https://www.globalcelebration.com/history.
Goldingay, John. *Genesis*. Baker Commentary on the Old Testament Pentateuch. Grand Rapids: Baker Academic, 2020.
Goldman, Mark S. "Expectancy Operation: Cognitive-Neural Models and Architectures." In *How Expectancies Shape Experience*, edited by Irving Kirsch, 41–63. Washington, DC: American Psychological Association, 1999.
Goll, James W. "3 Keys to Open Heavens, Minds and Doors." *Charisma*, Sep. 5, 2022. https://mycharisma.com/blogs/a-voice-calling-out/3-keys-to-open-heavens-minds-and-doors/.
Goodman, Felicitas D. *Ecstasy, Ritual, and Alternate Reality: Religion in a Pluralistic World*. Bloomington: Indiana University Press, 1988.
Goppelt, Leonhard, trans. *Der erste Petrusbrief*. Edited by Ferdinand Hahn. KEK 12.1. Göttingen: Vandenhoeck & Ruprecht, 1978.
Gorman, Michael J. *Elements of Biblical Exegesis: A Basic Guide for Students and Ministers*. 3rd ed. Grand Rapids: Baker Academic, 2020.
Graham, Hilary. "The Social Image of Pregnancy: Pregnancy as Spirit Possession." *Sociological Review* 24 (1976) 291–308. https://doi.org/10.1111/j.1467-954X.1976.tb00114.x.
Green, Gene L. *Jude & 2 Peter*. BECNT. Grand Rapids: Baker Academic, 2008.
Greenbaum, Lenora. "Societal Correlates of Possession Trance in Sub-Saharan Africa." In *Religion, Altered States of Consciousness, and Social Change*, edited by Erika Bourguignon, 39–57. Columbus: Ohio State University Press, 1973.

Greene, Merrill G. *The Weirdness of God: What the Bible Says About God's Character, How to Discern Manifestations, and Why the Church Has Attempted to Squash the Holy Spirit's Creativity.* Weird God, 2022.

Greyson, Bruce. "The Physio-Kundalini Syndrome and Mental Illness." *Journal of Transpersonal Psychology* 25 (1993) 43–58. https://www.researchgate.net/publication/284553384_The_physio-kundalini_syndrome_and_mental_illness.

Grudem, Wayne A. *The Gift of Prophecy in 1 Corinthians.* Eugene, OR: Wipf & Stock, 1999.

Grundmann, Walter. *Das Evangelium nach Lukas.* THKNT 3. Berlin: Evangelisch, 1981.

Gunkel, Hermann. *Die Propheten.* Göttingen: Vandenhoeck & Ruprecht, 1917.

———. "The Secret Experiences of the Prophets." *Expositor,* 9th ser., 1 (1924) 356–66, 427–35.

Hadidi, Hager el. *Zar: Spirit Possession, Music, and Healing Rituals in Egypt.* Cairo: American University in Cairo Press, 2016.

Haenchen, Ernst. *The Acts of the Apostles: A Commentary.* Translated by Bernard Noble and Gerald Shinn. Oxford: Blackwell, 1971.

———. *John 2: A Commentary on the Gospel of John Chapters 7–21.* Edited by Robert W. Funk and Ulrich Busse, translated by Robert W. Funk. Hermeneia. Philadelphia: Fortress, 1984.

Haldar, Alfred. *Associations of Cult Prophets Among the Ancient Semites.* Uppsala: Almqvist & Wiksell, 1945.

Hamori, Esther J. *Women's Divination in Biblical Literature: Prophecy, Necromancy, and Other Arts of Knowledge.* AYBRL. New Haven: Yale University Press, 2015.

Hanegraaff, Hank. *Counterfeit Revival Looking for God in All the Wrong Places.* 2nd ed. Nashville: Word, 2001.

Hannah, John D. "Jonathan Edwards, the Toronto Blessing, and the Spiritual Gifts: Are the Extraordinary Ones Actually the Ordinary Ones?" *TJ* 17 (1996) 167–90.

Harding, James E. "A Spirit of Deception in John 4:15? Interpretive Indeterminacy and Eliphaz's Vision." *BibInt* 13 (2005) 137–66. https://doi.org/10.1163/1568515053683103.

Harner, Michael. *The Way of the Shaman: A Guide to Power and Healing.* San Francisco: Harper & Row, 1980.

Harris, Murray J. *The Second Epistle to the Corinthians: A Commentary on the Greek Text.* NIGTC. Grand Rapids: Eerdmans, 2005.

Hartley, John E. *The Book of Job.* NICOT. Grand Rapids: Eerdmans, 1988.

The Harvest Sarasota. "Rolland Baker—Wednesday March 3, 2013." YouTube, Mar. 16, 2013. https://www.youtube.com/watch?v=44XqH4E4fig.

Haupt, Paul. "Crystal-Gazing in the Old Testament." *JBL* 36 (1917) 84–92. https://scholarlypublishingcollective.org/sblpress/jbl/article-abstract/36/1-2/84/194954/Crystal-Gazing-in-the-Old-Testament?redirectedFrom=fulltext.

Hauser, William. *The Hesperian Harp: A Collection of Psalm and Hymn Tunes, Odes and Anthems.* Philadelphia: Collins, 1874. https://shapenote.net/berkley/HesperianHarp.htm.

Heard, Christopher. "Biblical Composition and Biblical Inspiration." In *Revelation and Leadership in the Kingdom of God: Studies in Honor of Ian Arthur Fair,* edited by Andrei Orlov, 117–44. Gorgias Biblical Studies 72. Piscataway, NJ: Gorgias, 2020.

Heger, Paul. *The Development of the Incense Cult in Ancient Israel.* BZAW 245. Berlin: De Gruyter, 1997.

Heintz, Florent. "Trois études préliminaires: Actes 13:6–12; 16:16–19; 19:11–20; Pour servir à l'élucidation des rapports entre pratiques magiques et monde démoniaque dans le Christianisme primitif." Honor's thesis, Université de Genève, Faculté autonome de théologie protestante, 1991.

Henderson, Robert. *Prayers & Declarations That Open the Courts of Heaven*. Shippensburg, PA: Destiny Image, 2018.

Hess, Richard S. "The Name Game: Dating the Book of Judges." *BAR* 30 (2004) 38–41. https://library.biblicalarchaeology.org/article/the-name-game/.

Hiebert, D. Edmond. "Living in the Light of Christ's Return: An Exposition of 1 Peter 4:7–11." *BSac* 139 (1982) 243–54. https://www.galaxie.com/article/bsac139-555-05.

Hilgard, Ernest R. *Divided Consciousness: Multiple Controls in Human Thought and Action*. New York: Wiley & Sons, 1977.

Hiller, Harry H. "The Sleeping Preachers: An Historical Study of the Role of Charisma in Amish Society." *Pennsylvania Folklife* 18 (1968/69) 19–31. https://digitalcommons.ursinus.edu/cgi/viewcontent.cgi?params=/context/pafolklifemag/article/1034/&path_info=Pennsylvania_Folklife__Winter_1968_69.pdf.

Hillers, Delbert R. *Micah*. Edited by Paul D. Hanson and Loren Fisher. Hermeneia. Philadelphia: Fortress, 1984.

Hillier, Richard. *Arator on the Acts of the Apostles: A Baptismal Commentary*. OECS. Oxford: Oxford University Press, 1993.

Hillsong. "Open Heaven (River Wild)." Track 4 on *Open Heaven/River Wild*, written by Matt Crocker Sampson. Hillsong/Sparrow/Capitol, 2015.

Hillyer, Norman. *1 and 2 Peter, Jude*. New International Biblical Commentary. Peabody, MA: Hendrickson, 1992.

Hobbs, T. R. *2 Kings*. WBC 13. Waco: Word, 1985.

Holland, Drew S. "The Meaning of Ἔξέστη in Mark 3:21." *Journal of Inductive Biblical Studies* 4 (2017) 6–31. https://place.asburyseminary.edu/cgi/viewcontent.cgi?article=1076&context=jibs.

Holloway, Paul A. *Philippians: A Commentary*. Edited by Adela Yarbro Collins. Hermeneia. Minneapolis: Fortress, 2017.

Holtzmann, D. Oscar. *War Jesus Ekstatiker? Eine Untersuchung zum Leben Jesu* [Was Jesus an ecstatic? A study of Jesus's sanity]. Tübingen, Ger.: Mohr Siebeck, 1903.

Honeycutt, Roy L., and M. Pierce Matheney Jr. "1–2 Kings." In *1 Samuel–1 Nehemiah*, edited by Clifton J. Allen, 146–56. Vol. 3 of *The Broadman Bible Commentary*. Nashville: Broadman, 1970.

Hough, Walter. *Fire as an Agent in Human Culture*. United States National Museum Bulletin 139. Washington: Government Printing Office, 1926.

House, Paul R. *1, 2 Kings*. NAC 8. Nashville: B&H, 1995.

Howell, Alan. "Swapping Drinking Songs for Spiritual Songs: Skolia and Possession in Ephesians 5 and Mozambique." *International Journal of Frontier Missiology* 37 (2020) 161–69. https://scholarworks.harding.edu/bible-facpub/25/.

Huey, F. B., Jr. *Jeremiah, Lamentations*. NAC 16. Nashville: B&H, 1993.

Hultgård, Anders. "Ecstasy and Vision." In *Religious Ecstasy: Based on Papers Read at the Symposium on Religious Ecstasy Held at Åbo, Finland, on the 26th-28th of August 1981*, edited by Nils G. Holm, 218–25. Stockholm: Almqvist & Wiksell, 1982.

Hultkrantz, Åke. "A Definition of Shamanism." *Temenos* 9 (1973) 25–37.

Hüwelmeier, Gertrud. "Spirit Writing in Vietnam: Political Lessons from the Beyond." *Asia Pacific Journal of Anthropology* 20 (2019) 278–93. https://doi.org/10.1080/14442213.2019.1603250.

Isaacs, T. Craig. *In Bondage to Evil: A Psycho-Spiritual Understanding of Possession.* Eugene, OR: Pickwick, 2018.

Isbell, Charles D. "The Origins of Prophetic Frenzy and Ecstatic Utterance in the Old Testament World." *Wesleyan Theological Journal* 11 (1976) 62–80. https://wesley.nnu.edu/fileadmin/imported_site/wesleyjournal/1976-wtj-11.pdf.

Jenkins, Philip. *Hidden Gospels: How the Search for Jesus Lost Its Way.* Oxford: Oxford University Press, 2002.

Jennings, Mark. "Imagining Jesus Doing a Whole Lotta Shakin': Pentecostal Worship, Popular Music and the Politics of Experience." *Culture and Religion* 15 (2014) 211–26. https://doi.org/10.1080/14755610.2014.911195.

Jewett, Robert, and Roy D. Kotansky. *Romans: A Commentary.* Edited by Eldon J. Epp. Hermeneia. Minneapolis: Fortress, 2006.

Jobes, Karen H., and Moisés Silva. *Invitation to the Septuagint.* Grand Rapids: Baker Academic, 2000.

Johnson, Bill. *Open Heavens: Position Yourself to Encounter the God of Revival.* Shippensburg, PA: Destiny Image, 2021.

Johnson, Charles A. *The Frontier Camp Meeting: Religion's Harvest Time.* Dallas: Southern Methodist University Press, 1985.

Johnstone, William. *1 Chronicles 1–2 Chronicles 9: Israel's Place Among the Nations.* Vol. 1 of *1 & 2 Chronicles.* LHBOTS 253. Sheffield: Sheffield Academic, 1997.

Jones, Gwilym H. *1 and 2 Kings.* 2 vols. NCB. Grand Rapids: Eerdmans, 1984.

Jones-Hunt, Jackie. *Moses and Jesus: The Shamans.* Winchester, UK: O-Books, 2011.

Jordania, Joseph. *Why Do People Sing? Music in Human Evolution.* Tblisi, Georgia: Logos, 2011.

Joutard, Phillipe. *La légende des Camisards: Une sensibilité au passé.* Paris: Gallimard, 1977.

Kákosy, László. "Divination and Prophecy." In *Religions of the Ancient World: A Guide*, edited by Sarah I. Johnston, 370–91. Harvard University Press Reference Library. Cambridge: Harvard University Press, 2004.

Kashow, Robert C. "Lappidoth." *EBR* 15:827–28.

Keener, Craig S. *Acts: An Exegetical Commentary.* 4 vols. Grand Rapids: Baker Academic, 2012.

Keener, Craig S., and John H. Walton, eds. *NKJV Cultural Backgrounds Study Bible: Bringing to Life the Ancient World of Scripture.* Grand Rapids: Zondervan Academic, 2017.

Kennedy, Robinette. "Embodying Visions: Crete's Prehistoric Shamanic Trance Postures." *Sacred Hoop* 72 (2011) 20–21.

Kim, Koowon. *1 Samuel: A Pastoral and Contextual Commentary.* Asia Bible Commentary. Carlisle, UK: Langham, 2018.

Klein, Ralph W. *1 Chronicles: A Commentary.* Edited by Thomas Krüger. Hermeneia. Minneapolis: Fortress, 2006.

———. *1 Samuel.* 2nd ed. WBC 10. Grand Rapids: Zondervan, 2000.

Kleinig, John W., ed. *Lord's Song: The Basis, Function and Significance of Choral Music in Chronicles.* JSOTSup 156. Sheffield: Sheffield Academic, 1993.

Kleinman, Arthur. *Patients and Healers in the Context of Culture: An Exploration of the Borderland Between Anthropology, Medicine, and Psychiatry*. Comparative Studies of Health Systems and Medical Care 3. Berkeley: University of California Press, 1980.
Knoppers, Gary N. *1 Chronicles 10–29: A New Translation with Introduction and Commentary*. AYBC 12A. New Haven: Yale University Press, 2004.
Knox, Wilfred L. *The Acts of the Apostles*. Cambridge: Cambridge University Press, 1948.
Koester, Craig R. *Revelation: A New Translation with Introduction and Commentary*. AYBC 38A. New Haven: Yale University Press, 2014.
Köstenberger, Andreas J., and Richard D. Patterson. *Invitation to Biblical Interpretation: Exploring the Hermeneutical Triad of History, Literature, and Theology*. 2nd ed. Invitation to Theological Studies. Grand Rapids: Kregel Academic, 2021.
Krippner, Stanley. "Altered States of Consciousness." In *The Highest State of Consciousness*, edited by John White, 1–5. New York: Doubleday, 1972.
Kühn, Karl Gottlob. *Medicorum Graecorum opera quae extant*. 26 vols. Leipzig: Cnoblochii, 1821–33.
Kupitz, Yaakov S., and Katell Berthelot. "Deborah and the Delphic Pythia: A New Interpretation of Judges 4:4–5." In *Images and Prophecy in the Ancient Eastern Mediterranean*, edited by Martti Nissinen and Charles E. Carter, 95–124. FRLANT 233. Göttingen: Vandenhoeck & Ruprecht, 2010.
Lamb, William R. S., ed. and trans. *The Catena in Marcum: A Byzantine Anthology of Early Commentary on Mark*. TENTS 6. Leiden: Brill, 2012.
Landy, Francis. "Shamanic Poetics: Isaiah and the Strangeness of Language." *R&T* 27 (2020) 1–14. https://doi.org/10.1163/15743012-bja10002.
Langton, Edward. *Good and Evil Spirits: A Study of the Jewish and Christian Doctrine, Its Origin and Development*. London: Society for Promoting Christian Knowledge, 1942.
Lea, Thomas D., and Hayne P. Griffin Jr. *1, 2 Timothy, Titus*. NAC 34. Nashville: B&H, 1992.
Lecrae. "I'm Turnt." Single from *Church Clothes, Vol. 2*, lyrics by Kevin Erondu and Lecrae Moore, produced by Kevin Erondu. Reach Records, 2013.
Lentz, John C., Jr. *Luke's Portrait of Paul*. SNTSMS 77. Cambridge: Cambridge University Press, 1993.
Levack, Brian P. *The Devil Within: Possession & Exorcism in the Christian West*. New Haven: Yale University Press, 2013.
Levin, Yigal. *The Chronicles of the Kings of Judah: 2 Chronicles 10–36; A New Translation and Commentary*. London: T&T Clark, 2017.
Levine, Baruch A. *Numbers 1–20: A New Translation with Introduction and Commentary*. AYBC 4A. New Haven: Yale University Press, 1993.
Levison, Jack. *Inspired: The Holy Spirit and the Mind of Faith*. Grand Rapids: Eerdmans, 2013.
Levison, John R. "Inspiration and the Divine Spirit in the Writings of Philo Judaeus." *JSJ* 26 (1995) 271–323. https://doi.org/10.1163/157006395X00329.
———. "Prophecy in Ancient Israel: The Case of the Ecstatic Elders." *CBQ* 65 (2003) 503–21. https://www.jstor.org/stable/43725066.

———. "The Spirit, Simeon, and the Songs of the Servant." In *The Spirit and Christ in the New Testament and Christian Theology: Essays in Honor of Max Turner*, edited by I. Howard Marshall et al., 18–34. Grand Rapids: Eerdmans, 2012.

Lewis, Ioan M. *Ecstatic Religion: A Study of Shamanism and Spirit Possession*. 3rd ed. London: Routledge, 2003.

Lincoln, Andrew T. *Ephesians*. WBC 42. Grand Rapids: Zondervan, 1990.

Lindars, Barnabas, ed. *The Gospel of John*. NCB. Grand Rapids: Eerdmans, 1972.

Lindblom, Johannes. *Prophecy in Ancient Israel*. Philadelphia: Fortress, 1980.

———. "Theophanies in Holy Places in Hebrew Religion." *HUCA* 32 (1961) 91–106. https://www.jstor.org/stable/23524611.

Lloyd-Jones, David Martyn. *God the Father, God the Son*. Great Doctrines of the Bible 1. Wheaton, IL: Crossway, 1996.

Lloyd Weber, Andrew, and Tim Rice. *Joseph and the Amazing Technicolor Dreamcoat*. London: 1974.

Long, Burke O. "Social Dimensions of Prophetic Conflict." *Semeia* 21 (1981) 31–53.

Long, Fredrick J. *Kairos: A Beginning Greek Grammar*. Mishawaka, IN: self-published, 2005.

Long, Jesse C., Jr., and Mark Sneed. "'Yahweh Has Given These Three Kings Into the Hands of Moab': A Socio-Literary Reading of 2 Kings 3." In *Inspired Speech: Prophecy in the Ancient Near East; Essays in Honour of Herbert B. Huffmon*, edited by John Kaltner and Louis Stulman, 253–75. JSOTSup 378. New York: T&T Clark, 2004.

Longman, Tremper, III. *Proverbs*. BCOTWP. Grand Rapids: Baker Academic, 2006.

Luck, Georg, trans. *Arcana Mundi: Magic and the Occult in the Greek and Roman Worlds; A Collection of Ancient Texts*. 2nd ed. Baltimore: Johns Hopkins University Press, 2006.

Ludwig, Arnold M. "Altered States of Consciousness." *Archives of General Psychiatry* 15 (1966) 225–34. https://sites.duke.edu/haitilab/files/2014/11/1966-Ludwid-ALtered-States-of-Consciousness-Haiti.pdf.

———. "An Historical Survey of the Early Roots of Mesmerism." *International Journal of Clinical and Experimental Hypnosis* 12 (1964) 205–17. https://doi.org/10.1080/00207146408409107.

Lundbom, Jack R. *Jeremiah 37–52: A New Translation with Introduction and Commentary*. AYBC 21C. New Haven: Yale University Press, 2004.

Luz, Ulrich. *Matthew 21–28*. Edited by Helmut Koester, translated by James E. Crouch. Hermeneia. Minneapolis: Fortress, 2005.

MacArthur, John. *Charismatic Chaos*. Grand Rapids: Zondervan, 1992.

———. *Strange Fire: The Danger of Offending the Holy Spirit with Counterfeit Worship*. Nashville: Thomas Nelson, 2013.

Malina, Bruce J., and John J. Pilch. *Social-Science Commentary on the Book of Revelation*. Minneapolis: Fortress, 2000.

Marcos, Natalio Fernández. *The Septuagint in Context: Introduction to the Greek Version of the Bible*. Translated by Wilfred G. E. Watson. Leiden: Brill, 2000.

Marcus, Joel. *Mark 1–8: A New Translation with Introduction and Commentary*. AYBC 27. New Haven: Yale University Press, 2000.

Marshall, I. Howard. *The Gospel of Luke: A Commentary on the Greek Text*. NIGTC. Exeter, UK: Paternoster, 1978.

Martin, Ira Jay, III. "Glossolalia in the Apostolic Church." *JBL* 63 (1944) 123–30. https://doi.org/10.2307/3262649.
Mathews, Kenneth A. *Genesis 11:27—50:26*. NAC 1B. Nashville: B&H, 2005.
McCarter, P. Kyle, Jr. *I Samuel: A New Translation with Introduction, Notes and Commentary*. AYBC 8. New Haven: Yale University Press, 1980.
McGowan, Erin Ruth. "Experiencing and Experimenting with Embodied Archaeology: Re-Embodying the Sacred Gestures of Neopalatial Minoan Crete." *Archaeological Review from Cambridge* 21 (2006) 32–57.
McKechnie, Paul. "Montanism Part 1: The Origins of the New Prophecy." In *Christianizing Asia Minor: Conversion, Communities, and Social Change in the Pre-Constantinian Era*, 96–122. Cambridge: Cambridge University Press, 2019.
McNeill, William H. *Keeping Together in Time: Dance and Drill in Human History*. Cambridge: Harvard University Press, 1995.
Merkur, Daniel. "The Visionary Practices of Jewish Apocalyptists." In *From Genesis to Apocalyptic Vision*, 317–47. Vol. 2 of *Psychology and the Bible: A New Way to Read the Scriptures*, edited by J. Harold Ellens and Wayne G. Rollins. Psychology, Religion, and Spirituality. Westport, CT: Praeger, 2004.
Metzger, Bruce M. *A Textual Commentary on the Greek New Testament: A Companion Volume to the United Bible Societies' Greek New Testament (Fourth Revised Edition)*. 2nd ed. Stuttgart: Deutsche Bibelgesellschaft, 1994.
Meyers, Carol L., and Eric M. Meyers. *Zechariah 9–14: A New Translation with Introduction and Commentary*. AYBC 25C. New Haven: Yale University Press, 1993.
Milgrom, Jacob. *Numbers*. JPS Torah Commentary. Philadelphia: Jewish Publication Society, 1990.
Miura, Kentaro. *Berserk*. 42 vols. Milwaukie, OR: Dark Horse Comics, 1989–.
Moberly, R. W. L. "'Test the Spirits': God, Love, and Critical Discernment in 1 John 4." In *The Holy Spirit and Christian Origins: Essays in Honor of James D. G. Dunn*, edited by Graham N. Stanton et al., 296–307. Grand Rapids: Eerdmans, 2004.
Moritz, Thorsten. *A Profound Mystery: The Use of the Old Testament in Ephesians*. NovTSup 85. Leiden: Brill, 1996.
Mounce, William D. *Pastoral Epistles*. WBC 46. Nashville: Thomas Nelson, 2000.
Mount, Christopher. "1 Corinthians 11:3–16: Spirit Possession and Authority in a Non-Pauline Interpolation." *JBL* 124 (2005) 313–40. https://doi.org/10.2307/30041015.
Moussaieff, Arieh, et al. "Incensole Acetate, an Incense Component, Elicits Psychoactivity by Activating TRPV3 Channels in the Brain." *FASEB Journal* 22 (2008) 3024–34. https://doi.org/10.1096/fj.07-101865.
Müller-Kessler, Christa, et al. "An Inscribed Silver Amulet from Samaria." *PEQ* 139 (2007) 5–19.
Murphy, Francesca Aran. *1 Samuel*. Brazos Theological Commentary on the Bible. Grand Rapids: Brazos, 2010.
Murphy-O'Connor, Jerome. "What Really Happened at the Transfiguration?" *BRev* 3 (1987) 8–21.
Myers, Jacob M. *I & II Esdras: A New Translation, Introduction and Commentary*. AYBC 42. New York: Doubleday, 1974.
Nasrallah, Laura S. *An Ecstasy of Folly: Prophecy and Authority in Early Christianity*. HTS 52. Cambridge: Harvard University Press, 2003.
Neil, William. *The Acts of the Apostles*. NCB. Grand Rapids: Eerdmans, 1973.

Neufeld, Dietmar. "Eating, Ecstasy, and Exorcism (Mark 3:21)." *BTB* 26 (1996) 152–62. https://doi.org/10.1177/014610799602600403.

Neufeld, Thomas R. Yoder. *Ephesians*. Believers Church Bible Commentary. Scottdale, PA: Herald, 2001.

Newberg, Andrew, and Mark Robert Waldman. *How God Changes Your Brain: Breakthrough Findings from a Leading Neuroscientist*. New York: Ballantine, 2010.

———. *Why We Believe What We Believe: Uncovering Our Biological Need for Meaning, Spirituality, and Truth*. New York: Free Press, 2006.

Newsom, Carol A., and Sharon H. Ringe, eds. *Women's Bible Commentary: Expanded Edition with Apocrypha*. Louisville: Westminster John Knox, 1998.

Neyrey, Jerome H. *2 Peter, Jude: A New Translation with Introduction and Commentary*. AYBC 37C. New Haven: Yale University Press, 2004.

Nickelsburg, George W. E. *1 Enoch 1: A Commentary on the Book of 1 Enoch, Chapters 1–36, 81–108*. Edited by Klaus Baltzer. Hermeneia. Minneapolis: Fortress, 2001.

Niederwimmer, Kurt. *The Didache: A Commentary*. Edited by Harold W. Attridge, translated by Linda M. Maloney. Hermeneia. Minneapolis: Fortress, 1998.

Nielsen, Kjeld. "Ancient Aromas: Good and Bad." *BRev* 7 (1991) 26–33.

———. *Incense in Ancient Israel*. VTSup 38. Leiden: Brill, 1986.

Nigosian, Solomon A. "Anti-Divinatory Statements in Biblical Codes." *Theological Review* 18 (1997) 24–28.

Nilsson, Martin P. *Greek Piety*. Translated by H. J. Rose. Oxford: Clarendon, 1948.

Ní Riain, Íde M., trans. *Commentary of Saint Ambrose on Twelve Psalms*. Dublin: Halcyon, 2000.

Nissinen, Martti. *Ancient Prophecy: Near Eastern, Biblical, and Greek Perspectives*. Oxford: Oxford University Press, 2017.

———. "Prophetic Madness: Prophecy and Ecstasy in the Ancient Near East and in Greece." In *Raising Up a Faithful Exegete: Essays in Honor of Richard D. Nelson*, edited by K. L. Noll and Brooks Schramm, 3–30. Winona Lake, IN: Eisenbrauns, 2010.

Nolland, John. *The Gospel of Matthew: A Commentary on the Greek Text*. NIGTC. Grand Rapids: Eerdmans, 2005.

———. *Luke 1—9:20*. WBC 35A. Dallas: Word, 1989.

Noth, Martin. *Numbers: A Commentary*. OTL. Philadelphia: Westminster, 1968.

Nougayrol, Jean, et al., eds. *Ugaritica V: Nouveaux textes Accadiens, Hourrites et Ugaritiques des archives et biliothèques privées d'Ugarit; Commentaires des textes historiques (première partie)*. MRS 16. Bibliothèque archéologique et historique 80. Paris: Imprimerie Nationale et Librairie Orientaliste, 1968.

Nyske, Ewelina. "Is the Holy Spirit Confused with Kundalini Shakti During Many Healing Ministries? The Comparative Study of Spiritual Manifestations Among Christian Charismatics and the Followers of Hinduism." *Przegląd Religioznawczy* 276 (2020) 147–63. https://journal.ptr.edu.pl/index.php/ptr/article/view/157.

Oldridge, Darren, ed. *The Witchcraft Reader*. 3rd ed. Routledge Readers in History. New York: Routledge, 2020.

Olley, John. *Ezekiel: A Commentary Based on Iezekiēl in Codex Vaticanus*. Septuagint Commentary Series. Leiden: Brill, 2009.

Osborne, Grant R. *The Hermeneutical Spiral: A Comprehensive Introduction to Biblical Interpretation*. Downers Grove, IL: IVP Academic, 2006.

Osborne, William R. "A Biblical Reconstruction of the Prophetess Deborah in Judges 4." *Journal for the Evangelical Study of the Old Testament* 2 (2013) 199–214.
Oshima, Takayoshi. *Babylonian Poems of Pious Sufferers: Ludlul Bēl Nēmeqi and the Babylonian Theodicy*. Orientalische Religionen in der Antike 14. Tübingen: Mohr Siebeck, 2014.
Painter, John. *Mark's Gospel: Worlds in Conflict*. New Testament Readings. London: Routledge, 1997.
Papadimitropoulos, Panagiotis. "Psychedelic Trance: Ritual, Belief and Transcendental Experience in Modern Raves." *Durham Anthropology Journal* 16 (2009) 67–74. https://citeseerx.ist.psu.edu/document?repid=rep1&type=pdf&doi=0eac74aff21cd87fd21e609d11dc8847c4a1df23.
Park, Song-Mi Suzie. *2 Kings*. Edited by Ahida Calderón Pilarski. Wisdom Commentary 12. Collegeville, MN: Liturgical, 2019.
Parker, Simon B. "Possession Trance and Prophecy in Pre-Exilic Israel." *VT* 28 (1978) 271–85. https://doi.org/10.1163/156853378X00518.
Parsons, Mikeal C. *Acts*. Paideia Commentaries on the New Testament. Grand Rapids: Baker Academic, 2008.
Patterson, Richard D., and Hermann J. Austel. "1, 2 Kings." In *1 Samuel–2 Kings*, 615–954. Vol. 3 of *The Expositor's Bible Commentary: Revised Edition*. Grand Rapids: Zondervan, 2009.
Payne, David F. *I & II Samuel*. Daily Study Bible (Old Testament). Louisville: Westminster John Knox, 1982.
Peatfield, Alan A. D., and Christine Morris. "Dynamic Spirituality on Minoan Peak Sanctuaries." In *Archaeology of Spiritualities*, edited by Kathryn Rountree et al., 227–45. One World Archeology. New York: Springer, 2012.
Pedersen, Johannes. *Israel: Its Life and Culture*. Vols. 3–4. London: Oxford University Press, 1940.
Peers, E. Allison, ed. and trans. *The Complete Works of Saint Teresa of Jesus*. 3 vols. New York: Sheed & Ward, 1946–1947.
Pervo, Richard I. *Acts: A Commentary*. Edited by Harold W. Attridge. Hermeneia. Minneapolis: Fortress, 2009.
Pesch, Rudolf. *Das Markus-Evangelium*. Wege der Forschung 411. 2 vols. Darmstadt: Wissenschaftlich, 1979.
Petersen, David L. "Defining Prophecy and Prophetic Literature." *JBL* 119 (2000) 33–44.
Picard, F., and A. D. Craig. "Ecstatic Epileptic Seizures: A Potential Window on the Neural Basis for Human Self-Awareness." *Epilepsy & Behavior* 16 (2009) 539–46. https://doi.org/10.1016/j.yebeh.2009.09.013.
Piccardi, Luigi, et al. "Scent of a Myth: Tectonics, Geochemistry and Geomythology at Delphi (Greece)." *Journal of the Geological Society* 165 (2008) 5–18. https://doi.org/10.1144/0016-76492007-055.
Pieslak, Jonathan. *Sound Targets: American Soldiers and Music in the Iraq War*. Indiana: Indiana University Press, 2009.
Pike, Kenneth L. "Etic and Emic Standpoints For the Description of Behavior." In *Language in Relation to a Unified Theory of the Structure of Human Behavior: Part 1*, 8–28. Glendale, CA: Summer Institute of Linguistics, 1954.
Pilch, John J. *Flights of the Soul: Visions, Heavenly Journeys, and Peak Experiences in the Biblical World*. Grand Rapids: Eerdmans, 2011.

———. *Visions and Healing in the Acts of the Apostles: How the Early Believers Experienced God.* Collegeville, MN: Liturgical, 2004.

Polhill, John B. *Acts.* NAC 26. Nashville: B&H, 1992.

Poloma, Margaret M. "Divine Healing, Religious Revivals, and Contemporary Pentecostalism: A North American Perspective." In *The Spirit in the World: Emerging Pentecostal Theologies in Global Contexts*, edited by Veli-Matti Kärkkäinen, 21–39. Grand Rapids: Eerdmans, 2009.

———. *Main Street Mystics: The Toronto Blessing and Reviving Pentecostalism.* Walnut Creek, CA: AltaMira, 2003.

Pope, Marvin H. *Job: Translated with an Introduction and Notes.* AYBC 15. New Haven: Yale University Press, 1975.

Porter, Stanley E. "Ephesians 5:18–19 and Its Dionysian Background." In *Testimony and Interpretation: Early Christology in Its Judeo-Hellenistic Milieu; Studies in Honor of Petr Pokorný*, edited by Jiří Mrázek and Jan Roskovec, 68–80. JSNTSup 272. LNTS. New York: T&T Clark, 2004.

———. *Idioms of the Greek New Testament.* Biblical Languages: Greek 2. Sheffield: JSOT, 1992.

Propp, William H. C. *Exodus 1–18: A New Translation with Introduction and Commentary.* AYBC 2. New Haven: Yale University Press, 1999.

Prove All Things. "'Shaking Prophetess' Stacey Campbell." YouTube, Jan. 28, 2014. https://www.youtube.com/watch?v=UHjCa3Zw7g0.

Proverbs1:7Truth. "The Drunken Delusion of Heidi Baker." YouTube, Nov. 10, 2014. https://www.youtube.com/watch?v=983Sx7aZDRE&t=325s.

Rackham, Richard B. *The Acts of the Apostles: An Exposition.* WC. 1901. Repr., Grand Rapids: Baker, 1964.

Rad, Gerhard von. *Das geschichtsbild des chronistischen Werkes.* Stuttgart: Kohlhammer, 1930.

———. *Genesis: A Commentary.* OTL. Philadelphia: Westminster, 1972.

Ramirez, Robert, and Rob LaDuca, dirs. *Joseph: King of Dreams.* Glendale, CA: Dreamworks Animation, 2000.

Ramsey, Arthur Michael. *The Glory of God and the Transfiguration of Christ.* London: Longmans, Green, 1949.

Reid, Barbara E. *The Transfiguration: A Source—and Redaction—Critical Study of Luke 9:28–36.* CahRB 32. Paris: Gabalda, 1993.

Revkeithbarr. "Drunk in the Holy Ghost—Sometimes You Don't Know How to Act." YouTube, Apr. 27, 2015. https://www.youtube.com/watch?v=L88V4qAtUDU.

Riss, Richard M. "Howard-Browne, Rodney M." In *The New International Dictionary of Pentecostal and Charismatic Movements*, edited by Stanley M. Burgess, 774. Rev. ed. Grand Rapids: Zondervan, 2007.

Rizzo, John. "Marriage Wine." Track 3 on *Joy*. Forerunner Music, 2010.

Roberts, J. J. M. *First Isaiah: A Commentary.* Edited by Peter Machinist. Hermeneia. Minneapolis: Fortress, 2015.

———. "The Hand of Yahweh." *VT* 21 (1971) 244–51. https://doi.org/10.2307/1517290.

Robins, Gay. "Cult Statues in Ancient Egypt." In *Cult Image and Divine Representation in the Ancient Near East*, edited by Neal H. Walls, 1–12. ASOR 10. Boston: ASOR, 2005.

Rogers, Cleon L., Jr. "The Dionysian Background of Ephesians 5:18." *BSac* 136 (1979) 249–57. https://www.galaxie.com/article/bsac136-543-05.

Rothenberg, Celia E. *Spirits of Palestine: Gender, Society, and Stories of the Jinn*. Lanham: Lexington, 2004.
Rouget, Gilbert. *Music and Trance: A Theory of the Relations Between Music and Possession*. Translated by Brunhilde Biebuyck. Chicago: University of Chicago Press, 1985.
Rowley, H. H. "The Nature of Prophecy in the Light of Recent Study." *HTR* 38 (1945) 1–38. https://www.jstor.org/stable/pdf/1508365.pdf.
Rufinus. *Inquiry About the Monks in Egypt*. Translated by Andrew Cain. FC 139. Washington, DC: Catholic University of America Press, 2019.
Sabin, Marie Noonan. *The Gospel According to Mark*. New Collegeville Bible Commentary 2. Collegeville, MN: Liturgical, 2005.
"Said to Be Religion: Strange Scenes at 'Revival Meetings' Held in Indiana." *New York Times*, Jan. 24, 1885.
Salicrow. *The Path of Elemental Witchcraft: A Wyrd Woman's Book of Shadows*. Rochester, VT: Destiny, 2022.
Salverte, Eusèbe. *The Occult Sciences: The Philosophy of Magic, Prodigies and Apparent Miracles*. Translated by Anthony Todd Thomson. 2 vols. 1891. Repr., Secaucus, NJ: Princeton University Books, 1974.
Samorini, Giorgio. "Psychoactive Plants in the Ancient World: Observations of an Ethnobotanist." In *The Routledge Companion to Ecstatic Experience in the Ancient World*, edited by Diana Stein et al., 73–89. London: Routledge, 2022.
Sanders, E. P. *The Historical Figure of Jesus*. London: Penguin, 1993.
Sarna, Nahum M. *Genesis*. JPS Torah Commentary. Philadelphia: Jewish Publication Society, 1989.
———. *Understanding Genesis*. Heritage of Biblical Israel 1. New York: Schocken, 1966.
Sasson, Jack M. *Judges 1–12: A New Translation with Introduction and Commentary*. AYBC 6D. New Haven: Yale University Press, 2014.
Schaffler, Yvonne, et al. "Traumatic Experience and Somatoform Dissociation Among Spirit Possession Practitioners in the Dominican Republic." *Culture, Medicine, and Psychiatry* 40 (2016) 74–99. https://doi.org/10.1007/s11013-015-9472-5.
Schantz, Colleen. *Paul in Ecstasy: The Neurobiology of the Apostle's Life and Thought*. Cambridge: Cambridge University Press, 2009.
Scharbert, Josef. *Exodus*. NEchtB. Würzburg: Echt, 1989.
Schnackenburg, Rudolf. *The Epistle to the Ephesians: A Commentary*. Translated by Helen Heron. Edinburgh: T&T Clark, 1991.
Schniedewind, William M., ed. *The Word of God in Transition: From Prophet to Exegete in the Second Temple Period*. JSOTSup 197. Sheffield: Sheffield Academic, 1995.
Schreiner, Thomas R. *1, 2 Peter, Jude*. NAC 37. Nashville: B&H, 2003.
Screech, Michael A. "Good Madness in Christendom." In *People and Ideas*, 25–39. Vol. 1 of *The Anatomy of Madness: Essays in the History of Psychiatry*, edited by W. F. Bynum et al. London: Tavistock, 1985.
———. *Laughter at the Foot of the Cross*. London: Penguin, 1998.
Sekki, Arthur Everett. *The Meaning of Ruach at Qumran*. SBLDS 110. Atlanta: SBL, 1989.
Sellin, D. Ernst, trans. *Das Zwölfprophetenbuch*. 2 vols. 2nd–3rd ed. KAT 12. Leipzig: Deichertsch, 1930.

Sheils, Dean. "A Cross-Cultural Study of Beliefs in Out-of-the-Body Experiences, Waking, and Sleeping." *Journal of the Society for Psychical Research* 49 (1978) 697–741.

Siikala, Anna-Leena. "Siberian and Inner Asian Shamanism." *Finnish Anthropological Society* 17 (1992) 1–14.

Simons, Ronald C., et al. "The Psychobiology of Trance: I: Training for Thaipusam." *Transcultural Psychiatry* 25 (1988) 249–66. https://doi.org/10.1177/136346158802500401.

"Sister Woodworth Names Her Date for Fort Wayne—Remarkable Scenes at Pendleton." *Gazette* (Fort Wayne, IN), May 23, 1885.

Skaggs, Rebecca, and Priscilla Benham C. *Revelation*. Pentecostal Commentary. Blandford Forum, UK: Deo, 2009.

Skillet. "Better Than Drugs." Track 4 on *Comatose*, lyrics and production by John Cooper and Brian Howes. Atlantic Recording, 2006.

Slotki, Israel W. *Chronicles with Hebrew Text and English Translation*. Soncino Books of the Bible 14. London: Soncino, 1952.

Smith, Andra M., and Claude Messier. "Voluntary Out-of-Body Experience: An fMRI Study." *Frontiers in Human Neuroscience* 8 (2014) 1–10. https://doi.org/10.3389/fnhum.2014.00070.

Smith, Gary V. *Isaiah 1–39*. NAC 15A. Nashville: B&H, 2007.

Smith, James E. *1 & 2 Samuel*. College Press NIV Commentary. Joplin, MO: College, 2000.

Snaith, Norman Henry. "Pentecost, the Day of Power." *ExpTim* 43 (1932) 379–80.

Snoeberger, Mark A. "Old Testament Lot-Casting: Divination or Providence?" *Detroit Baptist Seminary Journal* 16 (2011) 3–18. https://www.galaxie.com/article/dbsj16-1-01.

Soanes, Catherine, and Angus Stevenson, eds. *Concise Oxford English Dictionary*. 11th ed. Oxford: Oxford University Press, 2004.

Sonik, Karen, and Ulrike Steinert, eds. *The Routledge Handbook of Emotions in the Ancient Near East*. Routledge Handbooks. London: Routledge, 2023.

Sorkin, Aaron, dir. *Molly's Game*. Toronto: STX Entertainment, 2017.

Sparks, Kenton L. *Ancient Texts for the Study of the Hebrew Bible: A Guide to the Background Literature*. Grand Rapids: Backer Academic, 2005.

Spronk, Klaas. "Deborah, a Prophetess: The Meaning and Background of Judges 4:4–5." Paper presented at the 11th joint meeting of Het Oudtestamentisch Werkgezelschap in Nederland en België and the Society for Old Testament Study, Soesterberg, Netherlands, Aug. 27–30, 2000.

Stanmanm059. "Mystic John Crowder Exposed—Part 1 of 2." YouTube, Dec. 17, 2008. https://www.youtube.com/watch?v=mNGPA6Idopg.

Staples, Jason A. "'Rise, Kill, and Eat': Animals as Nations in Early Jewish Visionary Literature and Acts 10." *JSNT* 42 (2019) 3–17. https://doi.org/10.1177/0142064X19855564.

Stein, David, et al., eds. *The Contemporary Torah: A Gender-Sensitive Adaptation of the JPS Translation*. Philadelphia: Jewish Publication Society, 2006.

Stein, Diana, et al., eds. *The Routledge Companion to Ecstatic Experience in the Ancient World*. London: Routledge, 2022.

Stein, Robert H. "Is the Transfiguration (Mark 9:2–8) a Misplaced Resurrection Account?" *JBL* 95 (1976) 79–95. https://doi.org/10.2307/3265474.

———. *Luke*. NAC 24. Nashville: B&H, 1992.
Steinert, Ulrike. "Ecstatic Experience and Possession Disorders in Ancient Mesopotamia." In *The Routledge Companion to Ecstatic Experience in the Ancient World*, edited by Diana Stein et al., 369–96. London: Routledge, 2022.
Steinmann, Andrew E. *1 Samuel*. Concordia Commentary. Saint Louis: Concordia, 2016.
Stiles, Andrew. "Making Sense of Chaos: Civil War, Dynasties, and Family Trees." In *Ancient Divination and Experience*, edited by Lindsay G. Driediger-Murphy and Esther Eidinow, 134–53. Oxford: Oxford University Press, 2019.
Stoebe, Hans Joachim. *Das erste Buch Samuelis*. KAT 8. Gütersloh: Mohn, 1973.
Stokes, Ryan E. "What Is a Demon, What Is an Evil Spirit, What Is a Satan?" In *Das Böse, der Teufel und Dämonen—Evil, the Devil, and Demons*, edited by Jan Dochhorn et al., 259–72. WUNT 412. Tübingen: Mohr Siebeck, 2016.
Stökl, Jonathan. "Female Prophets in the Ancient Near East." In *Prophecy and Prophets in Ancient Israel: Proceedings of the Oxford Old Testament Seminar*, edited by John Day, 47–61. LHBOTS 531. New York: T&T Clark, 2010.
———. *Prophecy in the Ancient Near East: A Philological and Sociological Comparison*. CHANE 56. Leiden: Brill, 2012.
Stoller, Paul. *Embodying Colonial Memories: Spirit Possession, Power, and the Hauka in West Africa*. New York: Routledge, 2013.
Stone, Michael Edward. *Fourth Ezra: A Commentary on the Books of Fourth Ezra*. Edited by Frank Moore Cross. Hermeneia. Minneapolis: Fortress, 1990.
Strauss, Mark L. *40 Questions About Bible Translation*. 40 Questions. Grand Rapids: Kregel Academic, 2023.
Strecker, Georg. *The Johannine Letters: A Commentary on 1, 2, and 3 John*. Edited by Harold W. Attridge, translated by Linda M. Maloney. Hermeneia. Minneapolis: Fortress, 1996.
Stronstad, Roger. *The Charismatic Theology of St. Luke: Trajectories from the Old Testament to Luke-Acts*. 2nd ed. Baker Academic, 2012.
Stuart, Douglas K. *Exodus*. NAC 2. Nashville: B&H, 2006.
———. *Hosea-Jonah*. WBC 31. Waco: Word, 1987.
Sweeney, Marvin A. *I & II Kings: A Commentary*. OTL. Louisville: Westminster John Knox, 2007.
Swete, Henry Barclay. *The Apocalypse of St. John: The Greek Text with Introduction and Notes and Indices*. Classic Commentaries on the Greek New Testament. New York: MacMillan, 1906. Logos.
———. *The Gospel According to St. Mark: The Greek Text with Introduction, Notes and Indices*. Classic Commentaries on the Greek New Testament. London: MacMillan, 1898. Logos.
Swincer, David A. *Confused by Ecstasy: A Careful Study of the Confusing Element of Ecstasy—A Cultural Study in Historical and Biblical Perspectives*. Vol. 1 of *Tongues*. Adelaide: Integrity, 2021.
Tabbernee, William. "Ecclesiastical Opponents of Montanism Ca. 324–550 C.E." In *Fake Prophecy and Polluted Sacraments: Ecclesiastical and Imperial Reactions to Montanism*, 261–306. Vigiliae Christianae Supplements 84. Leiden: Brill, 2007.
Tabor, D. "Babylonian Lecanomancy: An Ancient Text on the Spreading of Oil on Water." *Journal of Colloid and Interface Science* 75 (1980) 240–45. https://doi.org/10.1016/0021-9797(80)90366-5.

Taves, Ann. *Fits, Trances, and Visions: Experiencing Religion and Explaining Experience from Wesley to James.* Princeton: Princeton University Press, 1999.

Temkin, Owsei. *The Falling Sickness: A History of Epilepsy from the Greeks to the Beginnings of Modern Neurology.* Baltimore: Johns Hopkins University Press, 1971.

Tervanotko, Hanna K. *Denying Her Voice: The Figure of Miriam in Ancient Jewish Literature.* Journal of Ancient Judaism Supplements 23. Göttingen: Vandenhoeck & Ruprecht, 2016.

Thiessen, Matthew. "Paul, the Animal Apocalypse, and Abraham's Gentile Seed." In *The Ways That Often Parted: Essays in Honor of Joel Marcus,* edited by Lori Baron et al., 65–78. ECL 24. Atlanta: SBL, 2018.

Thiselton, Anthony C. *The First Epistle to the Corinthians: A Commentary on the Greek Text.* NIGTC. Grand Rapids: Eerdmans, 2000.

Thomson, James G. S. S. "Sleep: An Aspect of Jewish Anthropology." *VT* 5 (1955) 421–33. https://doi.org/10.2307/1516215.

Tibbs, Clint. "Mediumistic Divine Possession Among Early Christians: A Response to Craig S. Keener's 'Spirit Possession as a Cross-Cultural Experience.'" *BBR* 26 (2016) 173–94. https://doi.org/10.2307/26371648.

———. "Possession Amnesia: Patterns of Experience, Evidence for Spirits." *Pneuma* 44 (2022) 20–40. https://doi.org/10.1163/15700747-bja10032.

Tibbs, Eugene C. "'Do Not Believe Every Spirit': Discerning the Ethics of Prophetic Agency in Early Christian Culture." *HTR* 114 (2021) 27–50. https://doi.org/10.1017/S0017816021000043.

Tischendorf, Constantin von, ed. *Novum Testamentum Graece.* 3 vols. Lipsiae: Giesecke & Devrient, 1869–1894.

Towner, Philip H. *The Letters to Timothy and Titus.* NICNT. Grand Rapids: Eerdmans, 2006.

"Trance Evangelism: Continuance of Mrs. Woodworth's Meetings at Hartford, Ind." *Daily Democratic Times* (Lima, OH), Feb. 2, 1885.

Trevett, Christine. *Montanism: Gender, Authority and the New Prophecy.* Cambridge: Cambridge University Press, 1996.

Tsumura, David Toshio. *The First Book of Samuel.* NICOT. Grand Rapids: Eerdmans, 2007.

Tully, Caroline J. "Understanding the Language of Trees: Ecstatic Experience and Interspecies Communication in Late Bronze Age Crete." In *The Routledge Companion to Ecstatic Experience in the Ancient World,* edited by Diana Stein et al., 469–88. London: Routledge, 2022.

Uffenheimer, Benjamin. "Prophecy, Ecstasy, and Sympathy." In *Congress Volume Jerusalem 1986,* edited by J. A. Emerton, 257–69. VTSup 40. Leiden: Brill, 1988.

Van der Horst, Pieter W. "Hellenistic Parallels to the Acts of the Apostles (2.1–47)." *JSNT* 25 (1985) 49–60. https://doi.org/10.1177/0142064X8500802503.

Van der Toorn, K. "Echoes of Judean Necromancy in Isaiah 28:7–22." *ZAW* 100 (1988) 199–217.

Van Oort, Jessica. "The Spirit Moves: Christian Trance Dance in Late Medieval Europe and Early Nineteenth-Century America." In *Dance and the Quality of Life,* edited by Karen Bond, 135–51. Social Indicators Research 73. New York: Springer, 2019.

Verghese, Abraham. "Spirituality and Mental Health." *Indian Journal of Psychiatry* 50 (2008) 233–37. https://doi.org/10.4103/0019-5545.44742.

VICE. "Getting Drunk on God." YouTube, Dec. 18, 2013. https://www.youtube.com/watch?v=_Zj7OJjMcnM.
Vögeli, Alfred. "Lukas und Euripides." *TZ* 9 (1953) 415–38.
Voipio, Aarni. *Sleeping Preachers: A Study in Ecstatic Religiosity*. AASF B 75-1. Helsinki: Suomalaisen Tiedeakatemia, 1951.
Vokes, Frederick E. "The Opposition to Montanism from Church and State in the Christian Empire." StPatr 4 (1961) 518–28.
Vondey, Wolfgang. *Beyond Pentecostalism: The Crisis of Global Christianity and the Renewal of the Theological Agenda*. Grand Rapids: Eerdmans, 2010.
Wade, Jenny. "Going Berserk: Battle Trance and Ecstatic Holy Warriors in the European War Magic Tradition." *International Journal of Transpersonal Studies* 35 (2016) 21–38. https://doi.org/10.24972/ijts.2016.35.1.21.
Wafer, Jim. *The Taste of Blood: Spirit Possession in Brazilian Candomblé*. Contemporary Ethnography. Philadelphia: University of Pennsylvania Press, 1991.
Walton, John H. *The Lost World of Adam and Eve: Genesis 2–3 and the Human Origins Debate*. Downers Grove, IL: IVP Academic, 2015.
Wansbrough, Henry. "Mark III. 21—Was Jesus Out of His Mind?" *NTS* 18 (1972) 233–35. https://doi.org/10.1017/S0028688500012856.
Warf, Barney. "High Points: An Historical Geography of Cannabis." *Geographical Review* 104 (2014) 414–38. https://doi.org/10.1111/j.1931-0846.2014.12038.x.
Wegner, Daniel M. *The Illusion of Conscious Will: New Edition*. Cambridge: MIT Press, 2018.
Weidinger, Karl. *Die Haustafeln: Ein Stück urchristlicher Paränese*. UNT 14. Leipzig: Hinrichs'sch, 1928.
Wellhausen, Julius. *Prolegomena to the History of Israel*. Translated by J. Sutherland Black and Allan Menzies. Edinburgh: Adam & Charles Black, 1885.
Wenham, Gordon J. *Numbers: An Introduction & Commentary*. TOTC 4. Downers Grove, IL: InterVarsity, 1981.
Wensinck, A. J., trans. *Mystic Treatises by Isaac of Nineveh: Translated from Bedjan's Syriac Text with an Introduction and Registers*. Nieuwe Reeks 23.1. Amsterdam: Koninklijke Akademie van Wetenschappen, 1923.
The Wesleyan Church. "Articles of Religion." https://www.wesleyan.org/about/articles-of-religion.
Westcott, Brooke Foss. *The Gospel According to St. John: The Greek Text with Introduction and Notes*. Edited by Arthur Westcott. 2 vols. 1908. Repr., Ann Arbor, MI: Baker, 1980.
Wigglesworth, Smith. *Smith Wigglesworth on Spiritual Gifts*. New Kensington, PA: Whitaker House, 1998.
Williams, David J. *Acts*. New International Biblical Commentary. 1985. Repr., Peabody, MA: Hendrickson, 1990.
Williamson, Hugh G. M. "Prophetesses in the Hebrew Bible." In *Prophecy and Prophets in Ancient Israel: Proceedings of the Oxford Old Testament Seminar*, edited by John Day, 65–80. LHBOTS 531. New York: T&T Clark, 2010.
———. "'We Are Yours, O David.' The Setting and Purpose of 1 Chronicles xii 1–23." In *Remembering all the Way: A Collection of Old Testament Studies Published on the Occasion of the Fortieth Anniversary of the Oudtestamentisch Werkgezelschap in Nederland*, edited by Bertil Albrektson et al., 164–76. OtSt 21. Leiden: Brill, 1981.

Wilson, David C. *Depression and the Divine: Was Jesus Clinically Depressed?* Eugene, OR: Wipf & Stock, 2018.
Wilson, Robert R. "Prophecy and Ecstasy: A Reexamination." *JBL* 98 (1979) 321–37. https://doi.org/10.2307/3265758.
Winkelman, Michael. "Altered States of Consciousness and Religious Behavior." In *Anthropology of Religion: A Handbook*, edited by Stephen D. Glazier, 393–428. Westport, CT: Praeger, 1999.
Wiseman, Donald J. *1 & 2 Kings: An Introduction & Commentary*. TOTC 9. Downers Grove, IL: InterVarsity, 1993.
Witherington, Ben, III. *The Acts of the Apostles: A Socio-Rhetorical Commentary*. Grand Rapids: Eerdmans, 1998.
———. *Conflict and Community in Corinth: A Socio-Rhetorical Commentary on 1 and 2 Corinthians*. Grand Rapids: Eerdmans, 1995.
———. *The Gospel of Mark: A Socio-Rhetorical Commentary*. Grand Rapids: Eerdmans, 2001.
———. *Jesus the Seer: The Progress of Prophecy*. Minneapolis: Fortress, 2014.
Witmer, Amanda. *Jesus, the Galilean Exorcist: His Exorcisms in Social and Political Context*. Library of the Historical Jesus Studies 10. New York: Bloomsbury, 2013.
Wolff, Hans Walter. *Joel and Amos: A Commentary on the Books of the Prophets Joel and Amos*. Translated by Waldemar Janzen et al., edited by S. Dean McBride Jr. Hermeneia. Philadelphia: Fortress, 1977.
Wolters, Albert M. *Zechariah*. HCOT 19. Leuven, Belg.: Peeters, 2014.
Wood, Leon J. *The Prophets of Israel*. Grand Rapids: Baker, 1979.
Woolf, Alan. "Witchcraft of Mycotoxin? The Salem Witch Trials." *Journal of Toxicology: Clinical Toxicology* 38 (2000) 457–60. https://doi.org/10.1081/CLT-100100958.
Wortley, John, ed. and trans. *The Anonymous Sayings of the Desert Fathers: A Selection Edition and Complete English Translation*. Cambridge: University Press, 2013.
———, trans. *The Book of the Elders: Sayings of the Fathers; The Systematic Collection*. Collegeville, MN: Liturgical, 2012.
Wray Beal, Lissa M. *1 & 2 Kings*. ApOTC 9. Downers Grove, IL: InterVarsity, 2014.
Wright, Benjamin G. "'With a Spirit of Understanding' (Sir 39:6): Spirit and Inspiration in the Wisdom of Ben Sira." In *The Spirit Says: Inspiration and Interpretation in Israelite, Jewish, and Early Christian Texts*, edited by Ronald Herms et al., 149–65. Ekstasis 8. Berlin: De Gruyter, 2021.
Wulff, David M. *Psychology of Religion: Classic and Contemporary Views*. New York: Wiley & Sons, 1991.
Wyatt, Nicholas. *Religious Texts from Ugarit*. 2nd ed. BibSem 53. London: Sheffield Academic Press, 2002.
———. *Word of Tree and Whisper of Stone, and Other Papers on Ugaritian Thought*. Gorgias Ugaritic Studies 1. Piscataway, NJ: Gorgias, 2007.
Yoder, John C. *Power and Politics in the Book of Judges: Men and Women of Valor*. Minneapolis: Fortress, 2015.
Yohanan, Aharoni. *The Land of the Bible: A Historical Geography*. Translated and edited by A. F. Rainey. Rev. ed. Philadelphia: Westminster, 1979.
Young, Brad H. "The Ascension Motif of 2 Corinthians 12 in Jewish, Christian and Gnostic Texts." *Grace Theological Journal* 9 (1988) 73–103. https://biblicalelearning.org/wp-content/uploads/2022/01/Young-2CorAscension-GTJ.pdf.
Zemeckis, Robert, dir. *Contact*. Novato, CA: South Side Amusement, 1997.

Zimmerli, Walther. *Ezekiel 1: A Commentary on the Book of the Prophet Ezekiel, Chapters 1–24*. Translated by Ronald E. Clements, edited by Frank Moore Cross and Klaus Baltzer. Hermeneia. Philadelphia: Fortress, 1979.

Zöckler, Otto. *Die Tugendlehre des Christentums: Geschichtlich dargestellt in der Entwicklung ihrer Lehrformen, mit besonderer Rücksicht auf deren zahlensymbolische Einkleidung*. Gütersloh: Bertelsmann, 1904.

www.ingramcontent.com/pod-product-compliance
Lightning Source LLC
Chambersburg PA
CBHW071239230426
43668CB00011B/1505